Critical Praise for Th

'This remarkable book is a much welcome contribution to our understanding of the nature and dilemmas posed by recent capitalist development in rural areas of Asia, Africa and Latin America. The essays collected in this volume combine in-depth analyses of the political dynamics unleashed in the countryside by a host of very powerful social movements with a careful survey of the cleavages and ruptures produced by the harsh introduction of neoliberal policies. The reader will gain access to a wider and deeper understanding of all the complexities of the agrarian question under the impact of neoliberal globalization from an analytical perspective in which sound social science research fruitfully combines with the impassioned visions of rural activism.'

ATILIO A. BORON, Executive Secretary,
CLACSO, Buenos Aires

'This is a very important book which rows against the current. According to the dominant liberal paradigm, capitalist expansion has already abrogated (or is abrogating) the agrarian question, organizing the transfer of labour to urban activities and modernizing the rural sector, such that land reform programmes have become obsolete. The cases precisely studied in the book, covering Africa, Asia and Latin America, show that actually it is not so. On the contrary, imperialism appears thoroughly unable to resolve the agrarian question and to respond to the challenge of growing rural and urban dislocation. That structural failure is one of the major sources of growing poverty, as well as of progressive political mobilization, in the countryside.'

SAMIR AMIN, Director,
Third World Forum, Dakar

Reclaiming the Land

The Resurgence of Rural Movements in Africa, Asia and Latin America

**Edited by Sam Moyo
and Paris Yeros**

ZED BOOKS
London & New York

DAVID PHILIP
Cape Town

Reclaiming the Land was first published in 2005
by Zed Books Ltd, 7 Cynthia Street, London N1 9JF, UK,
and Room 400, 175 Fifth Avenue, New York, NY 10010, USA
www.zedbooks.co.uk

in association with
The African Institute for Agrarian Studies,
PO Box 3396, Causeway, Harare, Zimbabwe

Published in Southern Africa by David Philip
(an imprint of New Africa Books),
99 Garfield Road, Claremont 7700, South Africa

Designed and typeset in Monotype Bembo by Illuminati, Grosmont
Cover designed by Andrew Corbett
Printed and bound in Malta by the Gutenberg Press

Distributed in the USA exclusively by Palgrave Macmillan,
a division of St Martin's Press, LLC, 175 Fifth Avenue, New York, NY 10010

A catalogue record for this book is available from the British Library
Library of Congress Cataloging-in-Publication Data available

ISBN 1 84277 424 7 (Hb)
ISBN 1 84277 425 5 (Pb)

Contents

Introduction

Sam Moyo and Paris Yeros

In the last quarter-century, profound socio-economic and political changes have been under way in the countrysides of the periphery. Under the weight of structural adjustment programmes, peasants and workers have seen their conditions of social reproduction deteriorate, giving way to a desperate search for economic and political alternatives. As the most recent period of globalization draws to a close, marked by the crisis of neoliberalism in both centre and periphery, we intend here to reassess the status of the agrarian question and reflect upon its future.

Such a project has been under way in various academic and political circles. Certainly, the rise of new and militant rural movements from Brazil and Mexico to Zimbabwe and the Philippines have compelled such a reassessment. But also less directly, the numerous human catastrophies, which have largely been rural affairs, have also demanded answers – from chronic malnutrition and famine (most gravely in Africa where half the continent is on emergency food aid), to endless wars (Colombia, Indonesia, Central Africa), and even genocide (Rwanda). Suffice it to recall that, at its inception, structural adjustment claimed to be acting in the interest of the 'rural poor'.

Thus, over the course of the last quarter-century diverse interests and approaches have addressed themselves to agrarian issues. One tangent of inquiry, among development theorists especially, has departed from the classical terms of the agrarian question and turned towards the study of 'conflict resolution' and 'failed states'. Aside from a few exceptions concerned with the political economy of these conflicts, this inquiry has largely been managerial in purpose. A second tangent has remained closer to convention, focusing on such issues as land reform, food security, environmental management, and indigenous technology. But deriving largely from managerial and populist impulses as well, this too has shunned political-economic questions.

A third tangent has been exploring the long-term changes in the agro-food system on a global level. Generally informed by the concerns and methods of political economy, this tangent has been furnishing important empirical work and insight on the related processes of concentration of capital and stratification of the agro-food system, including the specific course of such issues as biotechnology and commodity chains. Nevertheless, the renewed search for a global theory of agrarian change has tended to fall short of holistic analysis of global capitalism (imperialism). The few exceptions that have engaged with larger historical questions have tended to overestimate 'globalization' and undermine the national question. As a consequence, contemporary global theory has not engaged squarely with the challenges that rural movements face under imperialism, namely the concentration of agrarian capital and political power at national levels, its alliance with financial and industrial capital, the subsumption of national capital as a whole under international capital, and the perverse pattern of national development that this continues to generate.

A fourth tangent of inquiry, well within the terms of the agrarian question, has been concerned with the dynamics of socio-economic change in the countryside, including proletarianization, semi-proletarianization, and re-peasantization, rural–urban linkages, and gender relations. While this has not sought to articulate global theory as such, focusing instead on more 'local' dynamics, it has also provided rigorous empirical research and robust debate. As we will soon see, this debate has lately focused on one question in particular: can we still speak of a 'peasantry' after a quarter-century of structural adjustment? A related political question has also been posed, which until now has been less prominent: how can we reconcile the posited 'disappearance' of the peasantry with the fact that the most progressive and militant movements in the world today are based in the countryside?

The aim of the present volume is to contribute to the above analysis of socio-economic change in the countryside, but even more so to bring to the forefront the politics of rural movements.

Together, these concerns constitute two of the three components of the classical agrarian question, the third being the question of accumulation in the process of national development (Byres 1991). While we do not seek to debate the latter question here, the contributors are generally agreed that land reform is a necessary but not sufficient condition for an alternative pattern of accumulation and development in the periphery, by virtue of its potential to widen the home market and break the political grip of extroverted capital with interests in land.

The contributors to this volume are researchers and activists based largely, but not exclusively, in the South, who have been vocal exponents of agrarian reform in their own countries and regions. Collectively we attempt a comparison of rural economic and political change across Africa, Asia and Latin America, with a specific interest in the social base, political strategies and ideologies of rural movements, and a further interest in their operational tactics, the most common being land occupation.

The more immediate stimulus for our book has been the radical shift in agrarian property rights in Zimbabwe, which followed on the heels of a militant land occupation movement. This has constituted the first radical shift in agrarian property rights in the post-Cold War world. While a controversial event for its own intrinsic reasons, it has nonetheless catalysed and internationalized the land reform debate in a unique way, even leading to pronounced confrontations at the level of international forums. This event has marked the culmination of the crisis of neoliberalism in Africa, and has numerous parallels in Latin America and Asia.

It is true that neoliberalism persists in full force. There is no doubt, however, that it has suffered ideological defeat. Its perseverance owes, in fact, to the weakness and disarray of the social forces in opposition. As the Brazilian sociologist Francisco de Oliveira (2003) has observed – in a country that persists on the neoliberal path despite rejection of neoliberalism at the polls – such crises of hegemony as the present have historically been riveted by revolutionary upheavals; neoliberalism today perseveres by default. With this in mind, we seek to understand better the nature and potential of rural movements and to contribute constructively to their ideological consolidation.

The principal issue that has guided our thought, as editors, has been the relationship between the classical agrarian question and the national question. From the closing decades of the nineteenth century until the crisis of the 1970s, the relationship between these two questions occupied a central framework of analytical reference for the understanding of imperialism, development and underdevelopment. But with the onset of 'globalization', the relationship between the two questions has come under sustained ideological assault, to that point of being swept away by claims that globalization has either resolved the two questions in practice and/or displaced them as an analytical points of reference. Specifically, the 'globalization' claim has assumed two discernible varieties: the first is that the periphery has entered a new trajectory of industrial transition and hence realization of sovereign statehood, based on foreign direct investment and export orientation; the second is that industrial transition is unnecessary in the periphery, that clinching 'comparative advantage' in a global market is sufficient for national development. For both, more demanding claims on national sovereignty are 'ideological'.

Accompanying these claims have been a series of related assessments concerning the nation-state and world politics. Liberals, of diverse shades, have concluded that, by virtue of the emergence of a global market civilization, the state had 'retreated' (Strange 1996) and the world had become 'borderless' (Ohmae 1990). Other observers, both of liberal and more 'critical' provenance, have concluded that the global market is now operating on the basis of discreet international rules and procedures – or 'regimes', from money and trade to 'food' – above and beyond the state (Keohane 1984; McMichael 1997). Marxism, for its part, has absorbed and reproduced many of these assessments, affirming either that the periphery has indeed embarked on a trajectory of industrial transition under imperialism (Warren 1980), or that, with the deepening of global communication and global protest, the principle of national self-determination has run its course – that is, imperialism has been superseded by a borderless 'empire' (Hardt and Negri 2000). Importantly, the latter assessments have sought to vindicate a perennial 'internationalist' impulse within Western Marxism, intent to overcome the nationalist 'curse', not by affirming the principle of national self-determination but by demoting it, by obscuring both unequal development and the states–system and by denying the material sources of nationalism under imperialism, in both centre and periphery.

To be sure, neither the agrarian nor the national question is subject to facile analysis, or resolution. But abandoning the two as analytical and political points of reference is to succumb to the ideological force of imperialism itself. Any reconstitution of anti-capitalist opposition in the twenty-first century, not least in the countrysides and shantytowns of the periphery, where imperialism is experienced most brutally, must retrieve and clearly reflect upon the meaning and future of both questions.

Chapter 1 of this volume offers a more extensive editorial overview, whose purpose is to assess the contemporary status of the agrarian question in the international political economy. It offers a theoretical statement on the relationship between the agrarian and national questions, with special reference to the neoliberal period, before proceeding with a comparative analysis, first, of rural socio-economic change in Africa, Asia and Latin America, and, second, of the politics of contemporary rural movements. Among the issues addressed are those concerning the 'disappearance of the peasantry' and the emergence of 'new rural movements'. Changes and continuities are identified in relation to both issues: regarding the former, it is argued that underdevelopment has persisted and expanded under neoliberalism, through the contradictory forces of proletarianization, urbanization, and re-peasantization, yielding a 'semi-proleratiat' which in turn constitutes the core social base of rural movements; regarding the latter, a critical-constructive assessment is offered in relation to their strategies, tactics and ideologies, including their relations with the larger 'anti-globalization' movement.

The book is separated into three parts – Africa, Asia and Latin America – each of which begins with a continental overview chapter, provided by Henry Bernstein, Filomeno V. Aguilar and Henry Veltmeyer, respectively. These chapters offer a comparative analysis of rural socio-economic and political transformations within each continent and serve also to situate the national case studies that follow within each section. The Africa section includes the national case studies of Ghana (by Kojo Sebastian Amanor), Malawi (Fidelis Edge Kanyongolo), South Africa (Mfaniseni Fana Sihlongoyane) and Zimbabwe (Sam Moyo and Paris Yeros); the Asia section comprises the cases of India (Minar Pimple and Manpreet Sethi) and the Philippines (Salvador H. Feranil); and the Latin America section has two chapters on different aspects of the Brazilian case, one on the experience of agrarian reform in the 1990s (Lauro Mattei) and one on the mobilizational tactics of the MST (Bernardo Mançano Fernandes), plus the cases of Colombia (Igor Ampuero and James J. Brittain) and Mexico (Armando Bartra and Gerardo Otero).

Together, the case studies address a variety of rural movements, ranging from the more organized, such as the MST in Brazil, the Zapatistas in Mexico, the FARC in Colombia, and UNORKA in the Philippines; to the more recent movements in Africa subject to varying modes of mobilization, such the LPM in South Africa and the Zimbabwe land occupation movement led by the National Liberation War Veterans Association; to the more embryonic, diffuse and spontaneous land occupation movements of Ghana, Malawi and India. The strategies and tactics of the movements are also diverse, most commonly seeking land redistribution by means of land oc-cupations, but also opting for armed struggle either for constitutional reform and regional autonomy (e.g. the Zapatistas), or for larger-scale national democratic transformation at the level of the state (e.g. the FARC). Relatedly, the movements demonstrate significant ideological diversity, ranging from human rights and developmentalist discourses to those of indigenous rights and national liberation; these are ac-companied by a growing emphasis on women's rights, generally weak emphasis or articulation of a project for socialist transformation, and most often, but not always, within an 'anti-state' and 'anti-politics' strategic framework. Finally, relations with others sectors of society are examined, including political parties, trade unions, farmers' unions, NGOs and donor agencies, as well as regional organizations and inter-national forums, such as the World Social Forum. We conclude that, despite ongoing problems of mobilization and political articulation, and under the most oppressive of circumstances, rural movements today constitute the core nucleus of opposition to neoliberalism and the most important sources of democratic transformation in national and international politics.

References

Byres, T.J. (1991), 'The Agrarian Question and Differing Forms of Capitalist Agrarian Transition: An Essay with Reference to Asia', in *Rural Transformation in Asia*, ed. Jan Breman and Sudipto Mundle, Oxford, Delhi and New York: Oxford University Press.

De Oliveira, Francisco (2003), 'O Enigma de Lula: Ruptura ou Continuidade?', *Margem Esquerda* 1: 37–41.

Hardt, Michael, and Antonio Negri (2000), *Empire*, Cambridge, MA: Harvard University Press.

Keohane, Robert O. (1984), *After Hegemony: Cooperation and Discord in the World Political Economy*, Princeton, NJ: Princeton University Press.

McMichael, Philip (1997), 'Rethinking Globalization: The Agrarian Question Revisited', *Review of International Political Economy* 4(4): 630–62.

Ohmae, Kenichi (1990), *The Borderless World: Power and Strategy in the Interlinked Economy*, London: Collins.

Strange, Susan (1996), *The Retreat of the State: The Diffusion of Power in the World Economy*, Cambridge: Cambridge University Press.

Warren, Bill (1980), *Imperialism: Pioneer of Capitalism*, ed. John Sender, London: Verso.

I

The Resurgence of Rural Movements under Neoliberalism

Sam Moyo and Paris Yeros

A central feature of the development of capitalism in the twentieth century has been the rapid expansion of the world's labour force.[1] Beginning with the national development projects of the postwar period, most notably the green revolution, and continuing with the structural adjustment programmes of the neoliberal period, this expansion has been accompanied by the creation of an international reserve army of labour of an unprecedented scale. By and large, this labour force is located in the periphery of the system and, moreover, it remains in a state of semi-proletarianization, straddling town and country, and reproducing itself, in part, outside the circuit of capital – the process known as underdevelopment.

While the process of proletarianization has been the natural consequence of the transition to capitalism worldwide, its truncated nature has been the result of a historically specific type of transition to capitalism, characterized by the absence, or incompleteness, of industrial transformation in the periphery – that is, resolution of the agrarian question. The further consequence has been the failure of peripheral states to fulfil national sovereignty, the principle established as a universal right upon the abolition of race as a principle of world order (formal imperialism).

The prevailing wisdom in the last quarter-century has claimed otherwise: in conceptual terms, it has claimed that the agrarian and national questions have been resolved and/or become irrelevant; in concrete terms, that the development and diversification of national productive forces has in fact proceeded apace satisfactorily by means of foreign direct investment, or that they need not proceed apace, that finding 'comparative advantage' in agriculture suffices for development. Such claims are in fact highly ideological, and indeed essential to the conduct of imperialism in the neoliberal period. What is worse, the conceptual structure of these claims has infiltrated the forces of 'opposition' to neoliberalism, including international trade unionism and the anti-globalization movement.

The latter event is itself a continuation of the historical contradictions within 'labour internationalism', which, deriving from the centre–periphery relationship of the states-system, are marked by the persistent failure of the working class as a whole to commit to the fulfilment of national sovereignty in the periphery. To be sure, the burden of neoliberal restructuring has been carried by the working class in both centre and periphery – even eroding the democratic rights historically obtained in the centre. But the resulting 'human rights' and 'post-national' discourses of contemporary internationalism have conveniently submerged the agrarian and national questions. It is no coincidence that the bulk of the crisis of the 1970s has been displaced, by means of structural adjustment programmes, outside the borders of central states, such that the social reproduction of the working class as a whole has continued to rely on the development of underdevelopment in the periphery.

In this book, we inquire into the socio-economic and political dynamics of underdevelopment in the course of neoliberal restructuring. Socio-economically, we find that the peasantry has not entirely 'disappeared', but that semi-proletarianization has continued to absorb the costs of social reproduction, as these have been systematically 'expelled' by capital. Politically, we find a diversity of rural movements: these range from the more organized to the more spontaneous; they have different modes of mobilization; and they exhibit notable divergences in ideology, strategy and tactics. However, they share the same social basis in the semi-proletarianized peasantry, landless proletarians and urban unemployed; they are militant on land and agrarian reform, most often employing the land occupation tactic; and, in the most organized of cases, they have become the leading forces of opposition to neoliberalism and the neocolonial state, at the same time as trade unionism has suffered disorganization and co-optation. The conclusion at which we arrive is that the nucleus of anti-imperialist politics today – and hence of genuine labour internationalism – is to be found in the countrysides of the periphery.

The National and Agrarian Questions
under Neoliberalism

The period following the crisis of the 1970s has come to be known as that of 'globalization'. Originating in the profit squeeze of the late 1960s, it has been characterized by the restructuring of industrial capital and its financialization, the deregulation of the global monetary and financial systems, and ultimately the collapse of the welfare-state compromise at the centre and the national development project in the periphery. Globalization has certainly entailed a 'rupture' with the past. But precisely what kind of rupture? This remains a matter of dispute.

The national question under neoliberalism

On one side of the debate are those who have insisted that a 'convergence' has been taking place between North and South, by virtue of the restructuring and relocation of capital. Some have even concluded that the lifting of barriers to capital, or otherwise the deepening of transnational social and political networks, has led to the redundancy of the state. The general implication has been that capitalism has been fulfilling its historic destiny, that the centre–periphery inheritance has been superseded, and that the national question is itself redundant.[2] Such positions have not been the exclusive pet of liberal utopians (Ohmae 1990), but have been propagated by unorthodox liberals (Strange 1996), as well as influential Marxists (Warren 1980; Hardt and Negri 2000). Arrayed on the other side of the debate are those who have qualified the global restructuring in scope and substance and have pointed out its highly uneven and polarizing tendencies. Moreover, they have argued that the state, far from 'retreating', has been 'restructured' to the requirements of international capital. The state has been employed systematically to lift barriers, to deepen the commoditization of social life, and to enforce the new order by coercive means (Amin 1997; Petras and Veltmeyer 2000; Boron 2002). The general implication here has been that the centre–periphery structure has not been dismantled; that the state as a coercive apparatus remains firmly in place; and that national self-determination has not been made redundant but violated to an ever-greater degree. This is our founding position.

Looking back to the period preceding 'globalization', we observe that the two hegemonic projects across centre and periphery
– welfare-statism and nation-building – shared in one thing: their
vision of the state as principal agent of social progress. However,
the two were far from complementary, for the social relations that
underpinned the state in each case differed, as did the pattern of
accumulation – 'articulated' at the centre and 'disarticulated' in the
periphery – these being the legacies of imperialist nation-building
in the North and colonization in the South, respectively. More that
this, the two were in contradiction (Amin 1976; de Janvry 1981).
For the postwar dialectic inhered not in a capital–labour relation
understood in the abstract: concretely, the survival of the welfare-state
compromise at the centre demanded the security and productivity
of central-state capital in the periphery, and hence the persistence of
disarticulated accumulation in the latter. Thus, while the periphery
sought to emulate the centre (as a means of fulfilling its nationhood)
through a policy of industrialization, it did so against the objective
logic of the centre–periphery relation and the structural dominance
in which it consisted. As Alain de Janvry observed, this is a structural
dominance that 'molds the external necessities of the periphery into
possibilities for the centre to overcome its barriers of accumulation
and growth' (de Janvry 1981: 26).

The Cold War fully galvanized this process, such that socio-
political stability for the operation and accumulation of international
capital translated immanently into a 'national security' issue at the
centre. Despite proliferating social struggles, developmentalist class
alliances, generally controlled agrarian reforms, and many impressive but highly skewed and ultimately unsustainable growth experiences in the periphery – including in the few states that obtained
'semi-peripheral' status by succeeding, under import-substitution, in
endogenizing the capital goods sector – the multilateral order that
was born of World War II and decolonization did not redeem the
principle of national self-determination. Indeed, the single case in
which peripheral growth was sustained consistently under capitalism was in East Asia, where the internal and external constraints to
peripheral accumulation were lifted under the aegis of the United
States, for geostrategic reasons, in a Cold War context (So and Chiu
1995; Arrighi 2003). But even in this case of imperial patronage, the
Faustian exchange of sovereignty for development was to meet its
fate. The end of the Cold War brought with it the reimposition of

imperial discipline on export-dependent East Asian allies – including those in the wider region that experienced dynamic growth in the 1990s (the Philippines, Thailand, Indonesia, Malaysia) – most vividly in the course of the 1997–98 financial crisis (Bello 1998; Wade and Veneroso 1998; Gowan 1999). Experiences of sustained growth in the periphery are to be seen as cases in which the constraints of peripheral accumulation have either been relaxed 'from the outside', or overcome 'from the inside' by the agency of progressive social forces; but in no case are they to be seen as evidence that the constraints do not exist (Yeros 2002b).

What goes as 'globalization' consists in fact in the partial disarticulation of central state economies and their integration among themselves, along with a handful of industrial satellites, into what Paul Hirst and Graham Thompson (1999) have called a 'regionalized triadic bloc structure'.[3] This has given rise to only one notable and ongoing project of supersession of national sovereignty (bumpy and undemocratic, to be sure), namely the European Union, which itself is incomplete as well as undemocratic. Beyond that, it has sprung the G6/7/8, a coordinating forum between the United States and its junior partners, whose task has been to deliberate on global monetary and other affairs in circumvention of the multilateral form. And this has been complemented by a deepening web of global institutions, the IMF–IBRD–WTO, claiming multilateralism but remaining de facto under the control of the centre for the purpose of administering its affairs with the periphery. In this sense, post-World War II capitalism realized the ultra-imperial alliance envisioned prematurely by Karl Kautsky (1970) on the eve of World War I. Precisely to what extent this alliance is unravelling in the wake of the Iraq invasion – and of the Cold War more generally – it is too early to tell.

What is certain, however, is that the periphery has remained in a perverse, disarticulated pattern of accumulation, and this applies to the few semi-peripheral states that obtained rapid domestic agro-industrial integration, at the expense of social and financial articulation. Moreover, disarticulated accumulation has proceeded to become the prevailing principle of 'development'. If previously the proclaimed ideal of development had called for the integration of the national market on its own terms, the neoliberal reaction has demanded the integration of the national into the global, and prescribed the global as a panacea for every national ailment. Under the pretext of a 'crisis of development', a standard surgical operation

Imperialist organisations WB Imf.

has ensued: the deregulation of national currencies and prices; the commercialization and privatization of previously state-controlled industries and public services; the cutting of social services; the unilateral withdrawal of support for agriculture; the titling and commodification of peasant agricultural land; and the flexibilization of labour relations. The results have been the intensification of socioeconomic degradation, the reinforcement of the peripheral tendency to crisis, and an unprecedented degree of dependence since the end of formal imperialism.

Yet, as reactionary as this process has been, it is not to be equated with the supersession of national sovereignty. It is worth recalling that the principle of national sovereignty has been invoked by international finance in no uncertain terms, from the late 1970s to the present, to settle the question of adjustment to global payments imbalances and to justify the structural adjustment exercise itself. In the new monetary and financial order of flexible exchanges and deregulated capital, responsibility for adjustment is strictly *national*. This phenomenon is not to be equated with the supersession of national sovereignty, but more precisely with its *instrumentalization*. The further implication is that national adjustment is made subject to the full force of power politics among states, across centre and periphery, and between central states themselves; meanwhile, the only instances of sharing of adjustment responsibility have been *ad hoc* and among the ultra-imperial partners (Arrighi 2003).[4] It is thus no surprise that the international financial institutions have never proclaimed 'global government' but *governance*, a vaguism fully compatible with formal national sovereignty and structural dominance (Yeros 2002b). In fact, the first instance since decolonization in which the principle of national sovereignty has been formally suspended with the unanimous approval of the Security Council of the United Nations has been in relation to Iraq in the wake of the US-led invasion.

The principle of national self-determination is certainly in crisis. But it has not been superseded, and it should not be, whether in theory or in practice, so long as its *raison d'être* (imperialism) exists. Such a reaffirmation of nationalism is not a threat to internationalism − or to democratic regionalism or globalism − but its precondition. With these observations in mind, we turn to the agrarian question, whose resolution remains key to any democratic transformation.

The globalization of the agro-food system

A central preoccupation of the classic agrarian question was the problem of transition from feudal/agrarian to capitalist/industrial society, implying modern sovereign statehood, as a prelude to socialism. Among classical theorists, this historic transformation was generally seen as reducible (with various caveats) to the transition to capitalism in agriculture (Engels 195; Kautsky 1988; Lenin 1964). What we have seen in the twentieth century, however, is that the various processes have diverged: capitalism has subordinated agriculture to its logic worldwide, but without creating, by necessity, home markets capable of sustaining industrialization, or fulfilling the sovereignty of decolonized states. In this sense, the agrarian question remains unresolved, and in this sense also it remains intimately related to the national question.

What we may further observe is that the corollary of retarded industrialization and unfulfilled sovereignty in the periphery is the globalization of the agro-food system. Indeed, agriculture is the only market in the world today that is 'globalized', if by this we mean that every country in the world is producing for it. The origins of globalization in agriculture are to be found in the following (see Friedman and McMichael 1989; Friedmann 1993; McMichael 1997; Bernstein 2000): (a) the nineteenth-century rise of tropical agro-exports from the colonies to the metropoles for mass consumption (i.e. sugar, coffee, tea, vegetable oils) and industrial expansion (cotton, timber, rubber); (b) the concurrent rise of ex-colonial settler states, the USA, Australia, New Zealand, Canada, to constitute the agricultural core of the world economy, exporting cheap grain, fuelling industrialization, and developing agro-industrial linkages; and (c) the collapse of the free trade regime, most resolutely in the interwar period, with the consequent rise of protectionism in agriculture and industry at the centre, the concerted management of national agro-industrial linkages, and the reliance on imperial trade preferences with the colonies. Following World War II and decolonization, the above historical dispensation set the stage for a new contradiction: the attempt by peripheral states to emulate the national model of agro-industrial integration, at the same time as this was coming undone at the centre, by the incremental integration of the agro-industrial complex on a global scale under the leadership of US firms. By and large, this contradiction has been resolved in favour of transnational capital, which has gone on to construct a global agro-food system characterized by high corporate concentration and a highly stratified international division of labour in agriculture.

We will only outline the main contours of this history here, as they have been analysed in detail by others (Friedman and Mc-Michael 1989; Friedmann 1993; McMichael 1997; Bernstein 2000). The postwar order of managed capitalism across the Atlantic reserved a special role for agriculture. In the United States, the prewar New Deal model remained in place, implementing a price support system based on state purchases, generating chronic surpluses with a need for external outlets, and encouraging over time the deepening of the agro-industrial complex, most notably by means of 'hybrid' seed technology, under the aegis of large corporations. Meanwhile, the model was being exported to Europe together with the Marshall Plan, for the purpose of supporting rapid Cold War reconstruction. The objective was to reconstruct dynamic economies with integrated agricultures and industries, while also integrating all of them across the Atlantic in a compatible way. Hence the US-supported European protection of wheat and dairy products, while Europe exempted US maize and soy from the import controls of its CAP, and in fact purchased them with Marshall funds. As Harriet Friedmann has shown, 'Under the Marshall administration, dumping was secondary to recovery' (1993: 35). The project was successful, for a time. It integrated the Atlantic in a single agro-industrial complex, allowed the US to dispose of its surpluses, and enabled Europe to regain its own footing, even against the United States. Eventually, the same characteristics obtained on both sides of the Atlantic, namely industrialized agriculture, corporate concentration and over-production, which did not bode well for transatlantic partnership, or, for that matter, balanced development in the periphery. Notably, the only peripheral states at this time that were spared integration into the Atlantic agro-food complex and allowed for independent agro-industrial integration were the East Asian ones.

The rest of the periphery was to become the dumping ground for US and European surpluses, beginning with those of the United States, which by the 1950s was losing its European market due to the latter's own maturation. Thereafter, the US sought outlets in Japan and, above all else, in the Third World, for whom the imperial plan was not 'control through reconstruction' but through the fostering of dependency and underdevelopment, to the extent possible. Of the many instruments of imperial statecraft, 'food aid' was an important one.[5] Food aid was enabled by the constraints of peripheral accumulation in a nation-building context, taking advantage of both the industrialization project and the foreign exchange gap; it provided wheat to countries implementing industry-oriented cheap food policies and without making demands on their limited foreign exchange resources. While some resisted more than others, the effect was certain: 'Import policies created food dependence within two decades in countries which had been mostly self-sufficient in food at the end of the second world war' (Friedmann 1993: 38).

The process of integration into the Atlantic agro-industrial complex was deepened by the 'green revolution', which, on the one hand, sought to replicate the idealized national model, while, on the other, it served to further subordinate the periphery to US firms for high-technology seeds, chemical inputs and agricultural equipment (Friedmann 1993; Petras 2000). Notably, the green revolution itself was inserted through the levers of the centre–periphery structure, promising higher agricultural productivity, national food self-sufficiency and foreign exchange respite, against the constraints of peripheral accumulation. Moreover, it was propagated at the time in which the nation-building was failing to deliver its promises, and radical social mobilization was spreading across Latin America, Asia and Africa. Over time, a handful of 'new agricultural countries' (NACs), in the semi-periphery, developed competitive agro-industrial capacity of their own (e.g. India and Brazil), even to challenge US and European markets, but without obtaining food security or fully resolving the agrarian and national questions.[6] Finally, while these changes were under way, peripheral nation-building was being further undermined by the technical substitution of tropical export products (e.g. sugar cane and vegetable oil), which had hitherto been the key source of foreign exchange underpinning industrialization. 'By the early 1970s', Friedmann concludes, 'the food regime had caught the third world in a scissors. One blade was food import dependency. The other blade was declining revenues from traditional exports of tropical crops' (1993: 38).

The 1970s was a time of generalized crisis, characterized by overaccumulation and the crisis of hegemony, the two being mutually reinforcing (Cox 1987; Arrighi 2003). In industry, this led to the relocation of capital and its financialization, while in global money and finance it led to flexible exchange rates and deregulated capital.

In turn, in labour relations it led to a mutation in the Fordist structure of accumulation at the centre, marked by deconcentration and flexibilization of production, with similar trends in the industrializing periphery, together with the persistence of the dominant condition of semi-proletarianization in the periphery as a whole. Concomitantly, at the global-institutional level, the 'tripartite' model of industrial relations itself came under crisis (Cox 1977, 1987; Fröbel et al. 1980). The net result has been twofold: first, the postponement of a generalized deflationary spiral within the alliance, entailing the partial displacement of the crisis onto the more vulnerable workers in the centre and the bulk of it onto the semi-proletarianized masses of the periphery; second, the re-establishment of global hegemony by the US and its junior partners, founded in a series of reconstituted state–society relations under the dominance of financial capital, and exercised in the first instance by means of the 'Dollar–Wall Street regime' (Gowan 1999).

In agriculture, the same postwar process of overaccumulation was in progress, as members of the transatlantic alliance matured under subsidy and protection, and were now being challenged by a small number of new agricultural competitors in the south. Thus, the stage was set for crisis in global agriculture as well. As Friedmann documents in detail, the combination of détente between East and West and oil shocks transformed the political economy of food: the Soviet Union entered the market, Japan diversified its import sources to include NACs, and the US and EU increased subsidies and overproduction as they fought for market shares. The new agrofood situation was no longer easily amenable to imperial statecraft, however, as transnational firms now had power and agendas of their own. In the event, the direction of change was led by transnationals, culminating in the Uruguay Round of GATT negotiations, which brought about the re-alignment of imperial states behind corporate agendas, namely liberalization and expansion into services and intellectual property rights, while also remaining subject to the postwar demands for managed agriculture – that is, protection. Yet such demands have been on the defensive, especially after the end of the Cold War (Friedmann 1993).

By far the burden of structural adjustment has fallen on the periphery, reinforcing the postwar trends of commoditization and integration into the centrally based corporate agro-industrial complex. Moreover, the periphery has been caught in a second scissor: on the one hand, the export imperative deriving from debt-service; on the other, northern protection. The result has been a new division of labour in agriculture (see McMichael and Myhre 1991; Moyo 2000; Raikes and Gibbon 2000; Petras 2000): the centre has specialized in capital-intensive production of grains and dumped them in the periphery, while peripheral states have battled for saturated markets for traditional exports,[7] or have discovered 'comparative advantage' in various 'non-traditional' goods and land uses, namely 'exotic' fruits, cut flowers and vegetables, as well as ostrich husbandry and 'wildlife' management (ecotourism). In turn, all of these have been biased towards large-scale landholding, controlled by corporate capital, and destined for luxury peripheral and metropolitan consumption. A less noted result has been the intensification of competition for control over high-value goods and minerals, from timber and oil to coca and diamonds, which are fuelling criminality and war (Moyo forthcoming, a).

The most cynical claim of all has been that the purpose of structural adjustment has been 'development'; in other words, that the abandonment of industrialization as a project, and its replacement by export agriculture in saturated and luxury markets, would deliver African, Asians and Latin Americans from underdevelopment. Structural adjustment has reinforced and deepened the postwar trend of incorporation of the peasantry into the sphere of commodity production at the same time as it has marginalized it. To be sure, postwar nation-building was always dependent on agriculture and export markets; and this in turn was always biased in favour of large-scale farming, whether state or private, due to the use of resource-biased technology and other privileges in the realm of infrastructure, credits, subsidies and land. Moreover, it was postwar nation-building that 'locked in' petty commodity production, first by state agencies and the World Bank, then together with agribusiness, which specialized peasant production, standardized the production process, and integrated it with upstream and downstream national and international markets (de Janvry 1981; Harriss 1987; Bernstein 1990). Yet the aggressive liberalization of the last quarter-century should be seen as a turning point: it has gone far in removing state support for peasants in the sphere of both production and reproduction; it has unleashed suffocating market forces, especially by devaluating currencies and raising the costs of production; it has transferred wholesale the organization of production to agribusiness, which in the new export domains has marginalized peasants entirely; and it has set out to establish private property rights in land, which has taken the brakes off land alienation. Combined with experiences of declining real incomes in off-farm employment, trends in deindustrialization, and all-round deterioration of living standards, what structural adjustment has successfully done is deepen dependence and underdevelopment.

Whether we can still speak of a 'peasantry' is something to which we will return. Suffice it here to round off the discussion by noting that the globalization of agriculture is not to be compartmentalized into a 'regime' theory, which would have its regime counterparts in money, trade, labour, security or oil (e.g. Keohane 1984).[8] Imperial power does not operate in separable domains, and the evolution of agriculture has never operated through discrete sets of rules, principles and procedures. The 'system' has always been the centre–periphery structure through the prism of the Cold War and its evolving aftermath. Accordingly, separating the agrarian question from the national question, such as by suggesting that the state has lost relevance in the course of 'globalization' (McMichael 1997), is not only to misinterpret the state but also to lose one's bearing in international relations.

The geopolitics of agrarian reform

Late nineteenth-century theorists of the agrarian question, namely Kautsky (1988) and Lenin (1964), observed a particular phenomenon in Europe which did not conform to Marx's deterministic formulations regarding the transition to capitalism in agriculture. This was that primitive accumulation did not render petty commodity production obsolete but that small peasant plots continued to coexist alongside large capitalist farming, and that, in fact, they served the interests of capital by subsidizing the social reproduction of labour and, hence, lowering wages. Kautsky thus called peasant plots 'production sites for new labour-power'. This condition of semi-proletarianization was not seen as permanent, however; it was bound to disappear with the further development of the home market.

A century later, semi-proletarianization persists as the dominant condition in the countrysides of the periphery. In the postwar period, the sources of this condition were grasped by the underdevelopment school, in particular Samir Amin (1976) and Alain de Janvry (1981), who saw semi-proletarianization as inhering in the disarticulated pattern of accumulation. This both inhibited the development of the home market and continued to subsidize capital in its export capacity. This fundamental problem remains to this day. So long as capital does not need to realise its profits nationally, semi-proletarianization and poverty are 'functional' to its reproduction. It is notable that this 'functional dualism' between the capitalist and (apparently) non-capitalist sectors is not necessarily a rural affair, but operates in the urban areas as well – whether by self-employment in activities of low capitalization and/or self-housing in slums.

It is in this context that agrarian reform, with its land reform component, has historically gained its economic and political significance. Whether propounded by radical nationalists or socialists, agrarian reform has constituted a direct challenge to the prevailing pattern of peripheral accumulation, and imperialism itself. In the postwar period, therefore, its fate was to be determined largely by Cold War geopolitics. While the demand for agrarian reform has always been local, springing from local class tensions and conflicts, and while generally a 'redistributive' model of reform guided thinking until the 1970s, reform was not reducible to either of these, and was typically suppressed or streamlined by extroverted national capital and imperial allies. Contrary to recent interpretations (Kay 1998; Bernstein 2002), agrarian reform in the course of nation-building did not derive from a redistributive model in the first instance, but from the balance of class forces in the Cold War. It follows that agrarian reform did not reach its 'historical end' with the onset of the new 'market-based' model of reform, but remains subject to class struggles in a context characterized by the ongoing reorganization of progressive forces after the Cold War.

Two events in particular can be said to have influenced the course of agrarian reform worldwide: the Chinese and Cuban revolutions – both instances in which imperial control was lost to radical forces. The first set of agrarian reforms after World War II took place under the auspices of the United States in East Asia. In fact, they were radical by any measure, and served as a laboratory for subsequent US policy on agrarian reform (Olson 1974). Under the threat of proliferating revolutionism in the region, led by Chinese communists, US officials rapidly reached the conclusion that unless feudal relations were abolished, influence in the region would be ceded to the Soviet

Union. Thus, in the five years after the war, Japan, South Korea and Taiwan underwent large-scale land redistributions, combined with armed suppression of radical forces until the reforms (some of which had already been under way in liberated zones) were under control. In all cases, reform was instituted *without* the political marginalization of the landed oligarchies; these were compensated, induced towards industrial development, and tranformed into a political class with allegiance to the United States.

The same type of agrarian reform acitivism was not necessitated in the nearby Philippines, or in Guatemala soon after, where radical forces in each case were defeated by military means, and existing land reforms, where in progress, were reversed (Olson 1974). The case of Bolivia in this same period is of further interest, in so far as a popular revolt brought a radical nationalist government to power which set out on an extensive redistributive agenda. But, in this case, the political oligarchy was not effectively displaced and the direction of internal change was successfully streamlined in the medium term, not by military means but through instruments of foreign aid. Reforms were also carried out by a nationalist gover-ment in Egypt, ultimately to neocolonial effect, and in Iran under the Shah, to disarm social unrest. In non-US spheres of influence, namely the colonial territories of Britain and France, reform ex-periences fit the general pattern: in Kenya and Algeria, imperial armies were mobilized to crush rural-based anti-colonial revolts and eventually to negotiate neocolonial transitions. In general then, the agrarian reforms under imperial auspices from 1946 to 1959 were controlled, limited (even reversed) in all cases except East Asia; they were typically combined with repression; and they aimed to secure and stabilize the reproduction of peripheral capitalism in a Cold War context. Fitting these into a 'redistributive' category is either flawed or tangential to the reality.

The next impetus for agrarian reform came with the Cuban Revolution. This fuelled a new wave of militancy in Latin America, and compelled the US government to act against feudal remnants on this continent as well. Under the banner of the Alliance for Progress, launched in 1961, a series of redistributive land reforms were implemented, generally against the wishes of local ruling classes. Once again, however, the object was a controlled land reform strategy of co-optation, entailing the creation of a conservative agrarian petty bourgeoisie, and repression against the excluded (de Janvry

1981; Petras and Veltmeyer 2000a). Yet, by the mid-1960s, the new reformism was running aground, against proliferating militancy in the countryside and the closing of ranks between modernisist and reactionary bourgeoisies. Under these circumstances, the US shifted agrarian policy away from land redistribution and towards social and technological modernization of *latifúndios*, combined with support for military dictatorships, as necessary. Thus, a series of *coups d'état*, from Brazil in 1964 to Chile in 1973, provided the political framework for the reorganization of Latin American agricultures, to modernize them with limited redistribution and without displacement of national ruling classes, to integrate them to varying degrees into the US agro-industrial complex, and to maintain extroverted accumulation. In South Asia, the same 'passive' reorganization of agriculure was being launched at the same time, by means of the green revolution, especially in North India. Meanwhile, further east, in Vietnam, the US was escalating aggression against a potent national liberation movement, while in Africa a series of national liberation movements were launching armed struggles of their own against colonial rule and white supremacism – in Guinea-Bissau, Angola, Mozambique, Namibia, Zimbabwe and South Africa (all except the latter being rural-based).

To reiterate, the period before liberalization was as much the period of 'redistribution' as it was of 'nation-building'; while these were the prevailing developmental models, the determinant of change was class struggle within the centre–periphery structure under Cold War conditions. Some further comments can be made at this point. First, rural-based social struggles have compelled the transition of agriculture to capitalism worldwide, characterized in the main by the transformation of large landownership into capitalist farming along with several other tendencies (which we will specify in the next section). Second, the whole experience of postwar reformism, rounded off in the 1970s by 'integrated rural development' programmes administered by global agencies, served as a minimum subsidy to the social reproduction of the rural proletariat and semi-proletariat on a global scale. Such policies put a break on more rapid proletarianization, as well as more radical alternatives (de Janvry 1981; Harriss 1987). Third, reformist measures that have safeguarded the political and economic status of ruling classes, and allowed them to steer the direction of reform back to extroverted accumulation, have failed outright. As Atilio Boron has put it, 'History teaches that, in Latin

America, to make reforms you need revolutions' (2003: 205), and this can certainly be generalized. While revolutions may not be on the cards under the circumstances, the point to stress is that economistic approaches to agrarian reform (Bernstein 2003) will continue to suffer unless the political dimensions of reform are taken seriously, and the *political* grip of large capital broken.[9]

The ensuing period of market-based development, roughly from the 1970s to the present, altered the model of agrarian reform away from redistribution. This period began with the *coup d'état* in Chile and reached its symbolic height in Latin America in 1992 with the amendment of Article 27 of the Mexican constitution, which had been protecting communal/reformed land since 1917 (consequent upon the Revolution of 1910–20). The onset of reactionary thinking expressed itself through neoclassical economic doctrine, and it called for both the restitution of land in reformed sectors to previous landowners and the establishment of individual title within the sectors that were communal/indigenous, collectivized or state-owned. This policy framework spread throughout Latin America, Asia and Africa under structural adjustment, and then on to Eastern Europe after the collapse of the Soviet bloc (Szelényi 1998). Although actual implementation has been uneven – more significant in tenure systems in Latin America and Eastern Europe than in Africa – the impact has been momentous. This policy framework was modified in the 1990s when land reform was brought back to the agenda, along with 'poverty', under the auspices of the World Bank (Binswanger et al. 1993), now combining neoclassical economic doctrine with a renewed small-farm populism (see the critique in Bernstein 2002). As we will see in more detail below, the new agenda has sought to redistribute land by market means or otherwise provide 'access to land' in some other form (e.g. rental markets). This latest turn of events has wrongly been dignified as the 'third phase' of land reform in Latin America (de Janvry, Sadoulet, and Wolford 2001), for it does not constitute a break with the period that began with Pinochet.

Once again, however, it has not been the 'model' of agrarian reform that has driven the course of events, but class struggles in the closing years of the Cold War and in its wake. Thus, at the same time as Latin America was about to embark on structural adjustment, the Nicaraguan Sandinistas launched the last Cold War revolution in Latin America, with a radical agrarian agenda. This was fought bitterly by CIA-organized counter-revolutionary forces and ultimately undermined. A decade later, after the end of the Cold War, the Zapatistas launched armed struggle in southern Mexico to coincide with NAFTA, demanding land, indigenous autonomy and national democracy; they received a combination of military repression and unfulfilled promises by the Mexican state. Then, in Africa, Zimbabwe closed the century with a militant land occupation movement, led by veterans of the national liberation war, to bring about a radical redistribution of land. Certainly, the relative geopolitical insignificance of Zimbabwe in a post–Cold War context has provided some room for manoeuvre.[10] Yet, the point is *not* that Southern Africa, or Zimbabwe in particular, is 'exceptional' (Bernstein 2002 and Chapter 2 in this volume), but that the social basis for land reform exists everywhere and it is explosive. Claims therefore regarding 'the end of land reform' appear odd; a generalized defeat of progressive forces has occurred, but larger historical conclusions need not follow. Moreover, as we will see below, progressive forces are undergoing a significant reorganization whose social base is located primarily in the countryside.

A final comment is necessary regarding the conceptual connections between the land and agrarian questions. Whereas the resolution of the agrarian question is tied up with industrial transformation, the land question is directed more immediately to the issue of land redistribution and the related issues of land tenure and land use (Moyo forthcoming a). In regions with histories of large-scale farming/landlordism, namely Latin America, Asia, and Southern Africa, the land and agrarian questions are often treated synonymously, and often they are compounded with indigenous rights issues (e.g. Zimbabwe, Mexico). While the differences between the two questions should be kept in mind, it is also true that agrarian reform without land reform is unrealistic, for the political and economic reasons related to structural transformation and broad-based development of the home market. In the specific case of tropical Africa, it is often said that there is no land question, only an agrarian question (Mafeje 1987).[11] Yet, while tropical Africa may not share the Southern African history of settler colonial capitalism, it has fully undergone colonial and postcolonial integration into generalized commodity production and experienced the typical pressures and trends of land alienation and concentration of capital, both within the communal areas and without, where state and freehold tenure hold (Moyo forthcoming, a). These trends have been deepening with liberalization, privatization and demographic pressure to render a situation where the land question can be just as explosive (witness Rwanda). While within communal areas questions of race and landlordism may not pertain, the issues that do pertain are potent: insecurity of tenure, land sub-division and informal land markets; land alienation and concentration, combined with externally determined land use changes; and undemocratic, patriarchal systems of local government to adjudicate and administer land disputes.

Socio-economic Change in the Countryside

Disappearing peasantries?

The contemporary debate over the fate of the peasantry has revived the familiar historical questions over the socio-economic character and political significance of the peasantry under capitalism. The positions are roughly arrayed among those who see the peasantry as disappearing economically and/or politically and those who argue otherwise.[12] The debate has been given impetus by a recent collection of essays entitled *Disappearing Peasantries?* (Bryceson et al. 2000). Focusing mainly on the socio-economics of agrarian change, this collection has concluded that, generally, 'the implementation of structural adjustment policies and market liberalization worldwide have had a dissolving effect on peasant livelihoods' (Bryceson 2000a: 29). The conclusion is qualified in variable ways by the contributors, as well as contested in some cases. This is partly attributable to the use of differing definitions of the 'peasantry'.

Our point of departure is that the peasantry — the small-scale/family agriculturalists operating within the generalized system of commodity production — does not constitute a class in itself but inherent in it are the antagonistic tendencies of proletarian and proprietor (Kautsky 1988; Lenin 1964; de Janvry 1981; Gibbon and Neocosmos 1985; Bernstein 1988, 2000). In other words, the ideal-type 'peasant household' reproduces itself as both capital and labour simultaneously and in internal contradiction. In reality, however, the combination of capital and labour is not spread evenly within the peasantry, for two reasons. First, the peasantry is differentiated between the rich, middle and poor petty-commodity producers, a spectrum that ranges from the capitalist that employs labour-power, beyond the family, to the semi-proletarian that sells it; as such, only the middle peasantry embodies the ideal-type of petty-bourgeois production, managing neither to hire nor sell labour-power – and which in turn is rare. Second, the combination of capital and labour is not spread evenly within a single household either; differentiated by gender and generation, patriarchs will control the means of production, women and children will provide unwaged labour. While this may appear on the surface as a 'different' mode of production, it has been argued convincingly that petty-commodity production is firmly embedded in the capitalist system and in fact is a normal feature of capitalist society, even if subordinate and unstable (de Janvry 1981; Gibbon and Neocosmos 1985).

Capitalism maintains the peasantry in a state of flux; its historical fate in the North Atlantic birthplace of capitalism has been that of proletarianization. Yet, more generally, the direction of change has not admitted of historical determinism, whether of the absolute type (Marx) or of the more cautious (Kautsky, Lenin), for within the centre–periphery structure spawned by colonialism, proletarianization has coexisted with enduring semi-proletarianization as well as re-peasantization. For our purposes, discerning the present reality – that is, whether a peasantry still exists – remains both an empirical and an interpretive problem. Empirically, two indicators are useful: the decomposition of household income by source, to include also analysis of non-exchangeable sources of sustenance; and analysis of household residential patterns, as between town and country.

Between peasants and workers

In Zimbabwe in the early 1990s, it was estimated through an organizational survey conducted by the national trade-union centre that 75 per cent of households maintained dual homes in town and country (Peta et al. 1991). Such data strongly suggested that the dominant phenomenon was neither the middle peasant ideal type, nor full proletarianization, but *semi-proletarianization*, whereby petty commodity production and wage labour together sustained the household. To these we may add the non-exchangeable sources of sustenance, the use-values derived from the land and its natural resources, such as food, water and fuelwood, as well as the security that the rural residence provides against economic fluctuations, sickness and old age (Moyo 1995a and forthcoming, a). The condition of semi-proletarianization is dynamic, as semi-proletarianized peasants struggle for a living against richer peasants, large-scale commercial farmers, and other employers who hire semi-proletarians at wages below the cost of social reproduction.

In *Disappearing Peasantries?* it has been argued that under structural adjustment peasants have become 'problematic', in so far as they are 'multi-occupational, straddling urban and rural residences, [and] flooding labour markets' (Bryceson 2000a: 30). But, with some give and take, the peasantry has been problematic in this way for much of the twentieth century; semi-proletarianization has a longer, pre-SAP history that is not well acknowledged, and is indeed generalizable to Africa (First 1983; Cohen 1991; Mamdani 1996), and the rest of the periphery, as we will see. The case of Zimbabwe above demonstrated a high degree of semi-proletarianization just at the inception of structural adjustment, and this, in what was the second most industrialized country in sub-Saharan Africa. It is more appropriate, therefore, to seek changes *within* this diachronic phenomenon of semi-proletarianization. We will revisit some of these, but suffice it here to preface our argument that structural adjustment, rather than fulfilling a secular process of 'primitive accumulation', as Bryceson (2000b: 55) seems to suggest *vis-à-vis* Africa specifically, has on the one hand intensified the process of land alienation but on the other *increased* the demand for land and its natural resources, as a consequence of the generalized decline in sources of income (farm, off-farm and non-farm). Thus, within a context characterized by 'the enforced extension of peasant survival strategies under pressure of impoverishment' (Raikes 2000: 68) – to such activities as petty-trading, craft-making, and gold-panning – there has also been an intensified struggle to access land illegally ('squatting') in both rural and urban areas, as well as an intensified political struggle to reclaim land. The most important case of re-peasantization in Africa under neoliberalism has been that of Zimbabwe at the millennium (see Moyo and Yeros, Chapter 6 in this volume).

Structural adjustment has been accompanied by intensified migration. Africa now has notched up the fastest rate of urbanization in the world (3.5 per cent annually), and nearly 40 per cent of the population is now urbanized. This fact is often used as proof that the land/agrarian question is losing its relevance. Yet facts remain to be interpreted. Migration should not be taken to mean full proletarianization, or permanent urbanization, but the spreading of risk in highly adverse circumstances. Had this urbanization been accompanied with industrialization and job creation, the conclusion could well have been otherwise. But the reality is different: urbanization together with deindustrialization and retrenchments. Urbanization takes the predominant form of illegal and unplanned settlement, such that half the urban population of Kenya and South Africa lives in slums (Moyo forthcoming, a). It is notable in this connection that migration is not merely one-way, as workers retrenched from mines and farms are also known to pursue peasantization, as recorded in a case study of rural 'squatting' in Zimbabwe (Yeros 2002b), or as urbanites enter the land reform process (Moyo and Yeros, Chapter 6 in this volume).

The situation in Latin America appears, to some observers, to be substantially different, given that the population is nearly twice as urbanized, at between 60 and 80 per cent. However, for the same reasons given above, such figures do not tell the whole story. In the late 1980s, de Janvry and Sadoulet (1989) estimated, on the basis of eleven case studies, that households on 'subfamily farms' do not derive, on average, more than 40 per cent of their income from their own farms, while the rest derive primarily from wages in rural and urban areas. This category of agricultural producers was large in absolute numbers, accounting for 50 per cent of the total number of farms but occupying less than 2 per cent of the total area farmed.

The specific case of Brazil, the most industrialized country on the continent, provides some valuable insights. To begin, there are those (de Oliveira 2003) who argue that 'primitive accumulation' has run its course in Brazil, by virtue of the expansion of the service sector and the absorption of the industrial reserve army of labour into flexibilized employment. But rigorous analysis of data continues to suggest differently. For example, a careful study of census data form 1985 showed that while semi-proletarianization was indeed under stress, 57 per cent of farms continued to consist of semi-proletarian families in the rural areas, living on 3.6 per cent of the total area farmed; in absolute numbers, this was nearly equal to those declared as fully proletarianized in the rural areas. More recent data from the 1990s has shown (Graziano da Silva 1999) that, in fact, production for own consumption as well as self-housing have expanded, and also that, as in Africa, peasant producers have sought precarious refuge in the proliferation of rural non-agricultural employment, largely of low qualification (domestic service, leisure industry, construction, etc.), serving elite consumption needs. The principal differences with past realities of underdevelopment is that subfamily farmers are now increasingly complementing their incomes with rural *non-agricultural* employment (termed 'multi-occupationalism' and entailing the 'urbanization' of rural areas), while competing more aggressively for rural employment and rural residential space with unemployed urban workers ('ruralization' of urban areas). We may add here that this process includes 're-peasantization', both independently and by means of current land reform programmes. Lauro Mattei (Chapter 12 in this volume), for example, shows that in the 1990s, 450,000 peasant properties disappeared while 270,000 families were being settled by land reform – in other words, for every three peasant families dispossessed of land, two gained land through land reform. Finally, we may expect that underdevelopment in the less industrialized countries of Latin America persists on an even greater scale. Cristóbal Kay has affirmed this more recently, arguing that 'most of Latin America's peasantry appears to be stuck in a state of permanent semi-proletarianisation' (2000: 131–2).

The Asian continent is much harder to generalise about, given that it includes the highly industrialized countries (Japan, East Asian 'tigers') and the underdeveloped, as well as China, which is industrializing at a rapid rate. Yet, among the underdeveloped, the same general pattern of semi-proletarianization continues to prevail. Asia as a whole has a relatively low level of urbanization – nearly three-quarters of the population inhabit rural areas. Moreover, as much as two-thirds of the population (with variation among countries) is employed in agriculture (Mooij 2000: 213). Rural differentiation in Asia has a pre-capitalist history, as Breman (2000) shows, but was enhanced by insertion into the capitalist market and accelerated by the green revolution (Mooij 2000: 219). The effect has been the rise of a richer class of peasants against the rest, who have either been semi-proletarianized or rendered landless. It has been argued, however, that full proletarianization has generally been forestalled, not least by state action, and that rural households, by and large, have held on to a plot of land and maintained the dual income strategy of petty-commodity production and wage labour (Harriss 1992, Breman 2000). It has also been the case that rural *non*-agricultural activities and markets have proliferated, such that between 30 and 40 per cent of household incomes now derive from off-farm sources (see overview in Mooij 2000: 222). Moreover, the dual trend of ruralization of the city and urbanization of the country is also observed in Asia, and with similar qualifications: 'The informal sector [in the urban economy] is not a stepping stone towards a better and settled urban life, but a temporary abode for labour which can be pushed back to its place of origin when no longer needed' (Breman 2000: 241). Meanwhile, it is noted that 'there is no New World in which to settle, as there had been for the proletarianized mass from Europe a century earlier' (Breman 2000: 240) – a point which serves to relocate contemporary agrarian change in its proper centre–periphery context.

Dynamics of rural change in the periphery

The transition to capitalism in the periphery has taken place under disarticulated accumulation, subordinate not only to the accumulation needs of domestic bourgeoisies but also to (and in alliance with) the accumulation needs of central-state capital. In consequence, it has been characterized *not* by an 'American path', as identified by Lenin – that is, a broad-based accumulation by petty-commodity producers 'from below' – but by the following five paths, which have combined in various ways (see *inter alia* de Janvry 1981; Byres 1991; and Moyo forthcoming, a):

- A dominant *junker path* of landlords-turned-capitalists in Latin America and Asia (outside East Asia), with its variant in the white-settler societies of Southern Africa. This path matured in the course of the twentieth century and culminated in the green revolution. In economic and political terms, this path of large-scale commercial farming now operates in tandem with transnational capital (whether landowing or not). More recently, large agrarian capital has also expanded/converted land away from farming and on to wildlife management, or 'ecotourism' ventures.
- A *merchant path* of non-rural capital, including merchant capital, petty-bourgeois elements, bureaucrats, military personnel, and professionals, who have gained access to land, whether leasehold or freehold, via the state, the market or land reform. They farm on a smaller scale than the above, but they are properly integrated into export markets and global agro-industry. This path is present across the periphery.
- A *state path* involving land appropriated by states in the course of nation-building, present throughout the periphery. This path is now in reversal by way of privatizations, concessions to national

and internation capital, or conversion to eco-tourism, and feeding directly into the above two paths.

- A limited *middle-to-rich peasant path* of petty-commodity producers created by a combination of generic tendencies to rural differentiation and active state policies in the postwar period. During nation-building, this stratum was subject to contradictory policies of low producer prices, subsidy and land reform. Under neoliberalism it has been augmented by parcelization and decollectivization, but also forced to sink or swim on its own. It operates in a variety of tenurial arrangements, including freehold and communal; under liberalization it has also diversified investments to off-farm activities, such as transport, trading and small-scale hospitality services. This stratum may also include 'contract farming', whereby transnational capitals contract petty-commodity producers directly, controlling their conditions of production (providing inputs, standards and output markets) but without taking title of the land or becoming embroiled in labour issues.

- Finally, a *rural poor path*, including the masses of fully proletarianized and semi-proletarianized peasants. This path is characterized by the contradictory tendencies of full proletarianization and retention/acquisition of a family plot for petty-commodity production and social security (consistent with functional dualism). The rural proletariat and semi-proletariat migrates within rural areas, from rural areas to urban centres, and across international boundaries; it enters the informal economic sector, both rural and urban, through such activities as petty trading, craft-making and flexibilized employment; and it struggles for re-peasantization, sometimes successfully. Under liberalization, this path has been joined by retrenched workers from mines, farms and urban industries. It is notable that this large underclass of displaced, insecurely employed and unemployed is also known to provide the foot soldiers to the many economic/non-emancipatory wars over control of the production and trade of high-value resources, including oil, timber, diamonds and coca.

We have already noted that liberalization lifted some of the impediments to full proletarianization that were operating in the postwar decades. The final and most notable of such measures had been the 'poverty agenda' led by the World Bank in the 1970s and encapsulated in the 'integrated rural development programme', which sought to bolster functional dualism in its moment of crisis. With the neoliberal departure of the 1980s and the abandonment of the poverty agenda, the tendency to proletarianization accelerated. Nonetheless, direct and indirect political action and a series of social catastrophies have compelled its return – as announced by the *World Development Report 1990* (World Bank 1990) – and have even brought back land reform in its market-based form. The new agenda has been much less ambitious than its predecessor and virtually ineffective in bolstering functional dualism. In one of the most highly publicized exercises of social development, that of Cardoso's Brazil, land alienation has been rapid and only partially stemmed by land reform, and this on account of rural political activism, not a concerted agrarian reform policy (Fernandes, Chapter 11 in this volume). Meanwhile, in another case where the neoliberal social agenda failed spectacularly, in Zimbabwe, large-scale re-peasantization has taken place outside the control of the World Bank; in this case, heavy imperial penalties have been imposed and a new pattern of 'accumulation from below' has not yet emerged (see Moyo and Yeros, Chapter 6 in this volume). These two cases, as the many others, are to be seen as 'normal' cases of agrarian change in the periphery under neoliberalism, where rural populations have been subjected to unfettered market forces, where they have struggled for re-peasantization among other political and economic ends, and have in effect struggled to reproduce functional dualism *on their own*, with variable success, and involving different and contingent levels of support from state and non-state agencies.

Alongside semi-proletarization there is a flourishing of social hierarchies which derive from gender, generation, race, caste and ethnicity, even to such an intensified degree as to produce forms of 'personal dependence' that may properly be called 'human bondage' under capitalism. Such 'non-capitalist' phenomena did not go unnoticed by classical theorists: Marx (1976: ch. 13), for example, saw the trafficking of children in England as a function of industrialization; and Lenin (1964: 204–6), the persistence of a quasi-feudal labour service in Russia as compatible with the accumulation needs of capital. Both underestimated, however, the propensity of capitalism to re-create such phenomena in the longer term. In the contemporary world, disarticulated accumulation and its corollary of semi-proletarianization provide the structural economic basis for the flourishing of these phenomena. Thus, in the absence of an objective relation between the rewarding of labour and the development of the productive forces, the 'dull compulsion' of market forces is capable of driving wage labourers into relations of 'personal dependence', often mediated through powerful social hierarchies that either fuse with class (e.g. race, caste), or cut across it (gender). To be sure, they may appear as 'non-capitalist' on the surface, but they are fully contingent upon the operation of the capitalist market. Moreover, they continue to produce forms of 'landlordism' despite the historical culmination of the 'junker path'.

In this volume, the synergy between class and race is noted with reference to Mexico and Zimbabwe (Bartra and Otero, Chapter 14, and Moyo and Yeros, Chapter 6), and between class and caste with reference to India (Pimple and Sethi, Chapter 8). In these cases, both historical domination and the process of resistance have fused class and race/caste languages. Consequently, demands for agrarian reform have struck at the heart of the dominant national/cultural identities though which the conditions of super-exploitation are reproduced. The case of Africa is similar, with the difference that here issues of race and class have been stongly politicized for a longer period (Fanon 2001; Cabral 1979).[13] Armed national liberation struggles against colonialism were launched as early as the 1950s (starting with Algeria and Kenya) and spread to West Africa (Guinea-Bissau) and Southern Africa. The result has been the attainment of majority rule across the continent, but within the neocolonial framework, characterized by the nurturing of small indigenous ex-troverted bourgeoisies to defend nationally the disarticulated pattern of accumulation. In Southern Africa specifically, neocolonialism has largely coincided with structural adjustment. In these cases, national politics have been galvanized by rural and urban class struggles but also by growing class differentiation among blacks. The latter has given impetus to a new period of inter-capitalist conflict between emergent black bourgeoisies and established white capital, both extroverted and both bidding over the land question. The result has been a stark bifurcation of the national question: on the one hand, black capital has confronted white capital, transforming the meaning of 'national liberation' in its own terms and hijacking land reform; while on the other hand, the historical realities of class and race persist, characterized by functional dualism within a white supre-macist framework, including the racialized landlordisms to which it gives rise (Moyo 2001; Rutherford 2001; Yeros 2002b).

Gender hierarchy has been as intrinsic to functional dualism as race. In Africa's late-colonial period, for example, the process of securing male labour for mines and farms rested on a policy of confining women to communal areas by institutionalized means, under despotic chieftaincies (Channok 1985; Schmidt 1990; Mamdani 1996). Functional dualism thus had two discrete pillars, one male and one female. While chieftaincy has gone on to be transformed in various ways, and women have entered the labour market in large numbers, they have continued to be a pillar of functional dualism, in both rural and urban areas. This situation is generalizable in the periphery. In fact, under structural adjustment gender hierarchy has been thoroughly instrumentalized, as SAPs have curtailed social services and relied on female reproductive labour, which in turn has intensified. At the same time, women have also been compelled to diversify the sources of household income. However, the traditional obstacles to access to land have persisted and remained subject to patriarchal kinship relations, while the illegal use of land has in many cases proliferated (Moyo 1995b; Agarwal 1994; Deere and León 2001). In the labour market, they have typically entered on the lowest rung, where they have routinely been denied 'worker' status (Sylvester 2000), even to the point where their labour has been bonded via the debt of male kin (Kapadia 2000). Women have further resorted to petty trade, across rural and urban areas and international boundaries, with various implications for family organization (Gwaunza 1998).

Finally, child labour has intensified under crisis and has compelled children to work under highly precarious and exloitative conditions. Children have themselves become a basic pillar of functional dualism. The phenomenon is all too common: withdrawing children from school and putting them to work, or putting children in the care of other children while parents go to work or succumb to HIV/AIDS. It is estimated that 180 million children are engaged in the worst forms of child labour, mainly in agriculture, but also in manufacturing, domestic service and 'sex tourism' (ILO 2002a). Many are subject to trafficking and bonded labour, as well as to recruitment in armed conflicts (ILO 2002b). It is also estimated that there are now 13 million AIDS orphans, many of whom become heads of households, with the highest incidence being in Africa where the pandemic has cut aggregate life expectancy to 48 years. Meanwhile, among the 'developing' countries as a whole, the average annual rate of reduction of the mortality rate of children under five years has *halved* in the period 1990–2001 as compared to 1960–1990 (UNICEF 2002). It is no exageration to say that, from 'lost decade' to 'lost decade', the rural and urban poor are confronting systemic genocide.

Politics in the Countryside

If peasants have not 'disappeared', in the sense that the rural poor continue to be partly peasantized or seek to re-peasantize, then what is their political significance and potential? Leading analysts of agrarian change, including Cristóbal Kay, Henry Bernstein and Alain de Janvry, have played down the political potential of the countryside, either by discounting progressive rural agency (Kay), or peculiarizing it after 'the end of land reform' (Bernstein), or fitting it into the welfarist 'access to land' and 'poverty alleviation' framework of the World Bank (de Janvry). Other authors, including ourselves, have differed markedly (Petras 1997; Petras and Veltmeyer 2001; Moyo 2001; Yeros 2002a). Our counterpoint has been that, despite the immense economic and political forces arrayed against them, the rural poor have been striking back in a progressive way, in a significant number of cases, and across the three continents. We point out that rural movements today rely most commonly, though not exclusively, on the mass land-occupation tactic, and most immediately to secure their livelihood; but more than this, they confront land-based political power head-on, pry open oppressive national debates, and challenge neoliberalism outright. Indeed, we claim that the countryside of the periphery today has become the most significant location of anti-imperialist politics worldwide.

This is a position that requires qualification in many ways, and, importantly, it demands *critical* engagement with rural movements, in the way that Petras (1997) and Boron (2003) have undertaken. In what follows, we will begin with some conceptual issues pertaining to rural politics before moving on to a comparative and critical analysis.

The peasant and the polis

The question over the political significance of the peasant has its origins in late-nineteenth-century Europe. This was a most turbulent time: economically, industrialization was proceeding apace and agrarian transitions among late starters (Germany and France) were facing severe competition from the ex-colonial settler states; politically, universal male suffrage was spreading. The question thus became how to manage the countryside in the course of transition, or otherwise gain its support for socialist transformation (Engels 1953a). For the socialists, the question imposed itself most poignantly during the isolation and defeat of the Paris Commune. Meanwhile, inter-capitalist conflict was fuelling competition among states and setting imperialism on a new footing, marked by the partition of Africa. Thus the concern with the countryside transplanted itself to the colonies as well, but here it took the form of 'the native question' – that is, how to organize the labour process while maintaining geographic, political and moral control over the 'natives'. Since then, peasants have gone on to play important roles in progressive social transformations, from the socialist revolutions of the century – notably Russia, China, Cuba and Vietnam – to republican and national liberation struggles – from Mexico in the 1910s, to India in the 1940s and Africa as late as the 1990s. In this sense, the subjective conditions of the peasantry today are much more advanced than the development of the productive forces. Consequently, the political theory of the peasant has also undergone transformations, among both bourgeois and Marxist theorists.

In the neoliberal period, as we have seen, the countryside has played the key role in absorbing the global adjustment process. While the economic theory of structural adjustment was conducted in the terms of 'urban bias' – whereby 'urban workers' were set apart from 'rural peasants', and the former blamed for the poverty of the latter (Bates 1981; World Bank 1981) – its political theory developed more or less as a sideshow. It was nurtured in the course of the 1980s among 'neo-institutionalists' and others (North 1981, 1990; Bates 1989a, 1989b; Diamond 1987), but its democratic pretensions were laid bare by the open calls for the repression of popular forces (Bates 1981: 131; Lal 1997: 33). But then the lull gave way to a storm of political theorizing. The proliferation of social protest worldwide combined with a collapsing Soviet bloc and the developmentalist challenge in Asia to 'bring the state back in' and, in the event, to shift the emphasis of SAPs from 'getting the prices right' to 'getting the *politics* right' (Yeros 2002b).

The new political debate engaged with social protest by unearthing the notion of 'civil society' and extolling its virtues, but also stripping it of its transformative potential. For 'civil society' – the domain designated by the 'proper' content and form of politics under capitalism – came to be opposed conceptually to 'the state' in a formalistic manner, such that, in practice, political opposition to the state, and in particular its meddling in the market, became the sine qua non of civilized political expression. Thereafter, the 'right' politics would be 'market friendly' politics. The first and obvious consequence was the depoliticization of the class basis of civil society – in Marx's words, the equation of the 'real human being' with the 'private human being' (1975: 148) – and the relegation of fundamental class issues to 'uncivilized' terrain. A second consequence at this juncture was the *urbanization* of democratic theory – that is, the focusing of inquiry on the geographic area where formal, organized and civilized political activism prevailed, as among the bulk of trade unions and mushrooming NGOs. A third consequence, following from the above, was the reaffirmation of *Eurocentrism*: (a) the depoliticizing of centre–periphery relations, by positing a generic, undiversified 'state', devoid of context, history, or international relations; and (b) denying the semi-proletarianized specificity of the periphery, by assuming an industrialized conception of 'the worker', one who is urbanized, settled, unionizable and ultimately insertable into formal (or 'tripartite') channels of political expression – at the same time, we add, as this was mutating in industrialized societies themselves. We elaborate on these below.

These issues have raised once again the historical controversy over the relationship between democracy and capitalism. At the turn of the nineteenth century in Europe, it was generally believed that the national democratic revolution was an important stage for both the expansion of industrial capital and the strengthening of the working class – Engels (1953b), for example, famously eulogized universal suffrage for the great political gains that it had afforded to the working class, especially in Germany. More recently, it has been argued by Ellen Meiksins Wood (1995) and Boron (2001) that there is an inherent 'contradiction' or 'incompatibility' between capitalism and democracy; that the social and political gains of the last century have derived from popular struggles themselves and not from the operation of capitalist logic, which is constantly poised to limit and dismantle social gains. In response, Petras and Veltmeyer (2000c) have qualified this position, theorizing the relationship in 'instrumental' terms; that is, capitalism may tolerate democracy but only to the extent that democracy is compatible with the reproduction of the profit system. Two points emerge on our part. The first is that we cannot properly theorise national democracy at a level of abstraction that does not clearly identify the centre–periphery relationship, given that within the hierarchically structured states-system peripheral political economies relate to those of the centre subordinately. While capitalism exhibits an organic tendency to economic crisis globally, crisis in the periphery is more frequent − even when the centre is booming, as in the 1950s/60s − and accompanied by frequent lapses into authoritarianism and repression. Central states need not resort to similarly drastic measures as long as, and to the measure in which, they can displace crisis outside their borders. In this sense, democracy at the centre is more 'stable' and in the periphery more 'unstable'.

Second, in the periphery, in which industrial expansion has been generally stunted and national self-determination denied, we cannot properly speak of full national democratic revolutions as having taken place. They have been partial and tentative throughout, even in the states which have undergone significant industrial transformation. While all peripheral states may have gained juridical independence, and most of them universal suffrage, all have continued to operate within a fundamentally disarticulated pattern of accumulation that has diachronically constricted electoral possibilities and failed to fulfil even the minimum of modern social demands, namely the guarantee of the costs of social reproduction. State violence against popular forces is therefore endemic, the suspension of democratic procedures recurrent, and 'non-capitalist' social relations of production free to germinate. It is no accident that the political science branch of development theory has had such a perennial interest in 'democratization' (from the early modernization theorists to the present), for which the problematic has been precisely how to obtain that missing condition, the stable bourgeois democracy of the centre, without recourse to the centre–periphery contradiction.

In this light, we argue that it is more rewarding to investigate not only the domestic social relations of citizenship (against merely procedural notions of democracy) but also its international relations, such that the significance of external sovereignty is properly theorized. The modern principle of popular sovereignty is a coin of two sides, with an internal and an external face, whereby the negation of external sovereignty is at the same time a negation of internal sovereignty. What this also means is that while the *polis* in its most elementary unit remains the nation-state, the nation-state is only understandable within the community of nation-states – the *polis* of *poleis*. The fact that the international political system does not assume the bureaucratic features that obtain in the nation-state is not an argument for its relegation to the status of 'non-community'.[14] Neither does the fact that it is hierarchically structured negate its ethical substance, this being the demand for equality among nation-states.

The above framework enables us to identify the global determinants of 'civilization' in which citizenship resides. It also enables us to specify the falsity of 'democratic transitions' in the neoliberal period and to emphasise the continuing significance of the national democratic revolution. And in this regard, there is a fundamental continuity in the political-economic and ideological structure of world order that has survived the period of formal imperialism: although race as a principle of political order has been abolished, its Eurocentrism persists in practice, in a de-biologized, culturalized form (Amin 1989). Postwar imperialism lays exclusive claim to universal values ('civilization') as a matter of course; routinely arrogates the right to determine the affairs of the international community; and renders the process of development and underdevelopment in terms of successful 'imitation' or a stubborn 'failure to imitate' – the latter typically attributed to national social and political 'traits'. Under imperialism, the meaning of 'development' may undergo changes over time, but its Eurocentrism does not; it continues 'to consort with its damned soul: ineradicable racism' (Amin 1989: 77).

Looking at the postwar era, across the periods of nation-building and neoliberalism, we observe that 'development' has consistently conformed to the requirements of extroverted accumulation. However, we also observe that, from one period to the next, there has been a shrinking of 'civilized' political space: while the enemies of civilization used to be the 'property unfriendly' forces, the radical nationalists and socialists seeking to endogenize the economy, the enemies of today are the 'market-unfriendly', a much wider band of barbarians. In both cases, the barbarians have been routinely subjected to co-optation tactics and outright repression, by the agencies of neocolonial and imperial states, and the aid of international trade unionism (Yeros 2002b). Where full-blown military dictatorships have emerged – to suspend formal democratic procedures – this has been the culmination of an otherwise uncontrollable class struggle.

We observe, finally, that at the turn of the twenty-first century, civilization has gained some new features. With the Cold War well behind us and a deepening global crisis ahead, progressive politics have found themselves treading on the militarized coordinates of a 'war on terror'. This now holds in both centre and periphery. We thus also observe the erosion of democratic rights in the centre and the militarization of its foreign policy, and a new phase of instability in the periphery. We also observe the emergence of a worldwide 'anti-globalization' movement with a new *modus operandi*, but without, as yet, a clear political direction, class understanding of itself, or resolution of Eurocentrism.

Where does this leave rural movements? First, we must recognize that the nineteenth-century classical assessment of the peasantry as isolate, conservative and reactionary, while justifiable at the time, is no longer accurate. The countryside has been thoroughly rolled over in the twentieth century and fully integrated not only into the capitalist economy but also into the humanist dialectic of consciousness, through the nationalist and socialist mobilizations, to the feminist and environmentalist ones of the present. Contrary to 'localist' approaches to rural politics (Scott 1985), whether populist or relativist, the above modern moral languages are global in reach, they infuse local notions of 'dignity' and 'reason', and are the moral basis of social protest worldwide. Second, we must recognize that, contrary to much postwar theorizing about the political 'behaviour' of peasants, the countryside does not exhibit 'essential' behavioural tendencies of any kind – as, for example, the preoccupation with 'everyday forms of resistance' implies. The rural poor engage in a variety of politics, both simultaneously and over time. They vote in local and national elections, engage in covert and unorganized acts of defiance (trespassing, squatting, poaching, stealing), participate in overt and organized land occupation movements, and also enter trade unions. They fight in rebellions and revolutions, as well as non-emancipatory wars. Their politics may be progressive or regressive; they may conform to the demands of civil society or they may confront them outright.

Third, we must recognize the ambiguities of peasant-worker consciousness and the problems of political organization that pertain to them. Recent commentaries by leading analysts of 'global social movements', 'new internationalisms' or 'the multitude' (Munck and Waterman 1999; Cox 1999; O'Brien et al. 2000; Hardt and Negri 2000), leave much to be desired. Semi-proletarianization yields a workforce in motion, within the rural areas, across the rural–urban divide, and beyond international boundaries. This workforce is also poor and abundant, relatively unhealthy and illiterate, and devoid of bargaining power. Neither full peasants nor settled proletarians, semi-proletarians have grievances that arise from both the family farm (land shortage, insecurity of tenure) and the workplace (wages and conditions of employment). Their political languages are often 'ethnic' or 'national', and while these may contain democratic elements, and may be powerful sources of mobilization, they are not in themselves adequate to the task of articulating wider class interests and defending them on a sustained basis.

Meanwhile, a plethora of organizations seek to 'speak' for the rural poor, enlist them in their ranks, or otherwise secure their support, from NGOs and church organizations, to political parties, trade unions, farmers' unions, and landless peoples' movements. If the neoliberal theory of 'civil society' naturally gravitated to urban areas in the early 1990s, in practice development agencies and NGOs had long penetrated rural areas through the funding of 'projects'. This activity expanded under structural adjustment, as the social responsibilities of states were renounced and global development agencies found new and willing partners in NGOs to take over from states. As has been well demonstrated (Petras et al. 1997; Moyo and Romadhane 2002), NGOs have served to depoliticize and co-opt rural grievances into welfarist projects, maintain their own selves in business by means of external funding, and indeed serve as the new vehicles of 'indirect rule' (Moyo 2001).

Trade unions have not fared much better. Throughout the Cold War period, peripheral trade unions struggled to maintain independence, but the hard facts of chronic economic insolvency (deriving from the poverty of their membership) and political repression imposed two alternatives: to accept the patronage of either states (often through political parties and nationalist movements) or international trade union centres, mainly of the Western-based ICFTU, and to a lesser extent of the Soviet-backed WFTU. An important consequence was the failure of trade unions to enter into independent class alliances with rural movements or to enlist the semi-proletariat as a whole and articulate its dual rural–urban grievances. With the onset of structural adjustment and economic deterioration, trade unions lost membership, their chronically weak financial bases weakened further, and the sources of their dependence on patrons intensified. And with the collapse of the Soviet bloc and the withering away of the WFTU, trade unions have either succumbed to liberalizing states or flocked to the 'market friendly' agenda of the ICFTU. Consequently, they have been systematically 'civilized', have retreated further from the peasant-worker project, and thereby enlarged the political vacuum in the countryside.

Farmers' unions (particularly the small-farmers' unions with which we are concerned here) have not been spared 'civilization', except that they have generally been civilized by states and not international movements. Two features have been prevalent here. The first is that states have routinely incorporated farmers' unions into their structures and used them as branches of the state in pursuit of agrarian or industrial policy. Notably, this practice has been characterized by divide-and-rule tactics vis-à-vis peasant-workers, whereby 'peasant interests' have been treated separately from 'worker interests', and farmers' unions separately from trade unions. The second and related feature is that small-farmers' unions have generally fallen hostage to bourgeois elements within them, which have eschewed advocacy of land issues and development policies aimed at smallholder accumulation. This again has been evident generally (see the chapters on Mexico and Zimbabwe in this volume), while it is particularly notable in contemporary India (Banaji 1995; Brass 1995), where, despite enormous land problems, farmers' unions do not espouse the land cause and land occupation movements are relegated to the margin of political life (see Pimple and Sethi, Chapter 8 in this volume). The result again is a deepening political vacuum in the countryside at a time of economic deterioration.

Political parties of the left have had ambiguous relations with the countryside, although by and large they have succumbed to the logic of capital, either to obtain state power or after obtaining it. Examples in the twentieth century abound, and include cases of immediate concern to us here, such as the PT in Brazil, ZANU–PF in Zimbabwe, and the ANC in South Africa. The statist phenomenon has been common enough to have given rise in the 1990s to an 'anti-statist' and 'anti-political' strategy; this has been proclaimed most famously by the Zapatistas and gone on to receive theoretical justification by John Holloway in his book entitled *Change the World without Taking*

Power (2002). Yet the strategy has had problematic origins of its own, while the summary dismissal of political party and state power has failed to solve the historical conundrums of the left. We will elaborate on this point below, but suffice it to note here that while the strategy correctly identifies the powerful conditioning dynamics of the *raison d'état*, it falls short of identifying with similar sharpness the *raison* of civil society and the obstacles to its transformation (Boron 2003). Indeed, the proposed alternative of 'demanding change without taking power', if understood as a form of praxis in the strict sense, appears as a mere recipe for reformism. We argue that the lesson to be learned is not that the political party and state power should be eschewed doctrinally, but that the task, as always, is to build self-sufficient peasant-worker movements that can withstand imperialism at the levels of both civil society and the state.

The present conjuncture is a most inauspicious one, in which civil society has been transformed into a tool of neoliberalism – whether through the 'development aid' network or international trade unionism. Civil society, including conformist trade unions, farmers' unions, and NGOs, has been patently incapable of expressing the dual rural–urban grievances of the semi-proletariat. In this context, the countryside has been left to its own devices, largely to low-profile ('everyday') politics, which have often been explosive; the cases of India, Ghana and pre-1998 Zimbabwe, in this volume, demonstrate this point. Together with many more, these have contained both regressive and progressive potential. It will be argued in the next section that the progressive potential is now being cultivated by rural movements, whose emphasis has been on direct action rather than electoral politics. However, it will be shown that in one important case, that of Zimbabwe, a 'loosely organized' rural movement obtained radical land reform directly through the ruling party and the state, this appearing as the only viable alternative to the suffocating closures of civil society. In another case, that of the Philippines, direct action on the land combined with the positioning of reformist elements within the state – the dual '*bibingka* strategy' – to push through a significant round of land reforms in the 1990s (Borras 1998; Feranil, Chapter 9 in this volume). More generally, it will be argued that the objective of state power should remain in clear sight but not pursued at the expense of grassroots organizational work, while the contemporary lack of a clearly articulated plan for the seizure of power is a weakness of rural movements, not a strength.

Before proceeding to taking a closer look at contemporary rural movements, we note that by the mid-1990s the urban bias of liberal democratic theory was being overcome. The World Bank at this time relaunched its land reform agenda, and central to this has been an attempt to co-opt rural grievances into the 'community-initiated market-assisted' (CIMA) land acquisition and redistribution programme (to which we will return). We note also that since the 1990s an extensive body of rural research and analysis has been produced by Marxist theorists who have been seeking to give coherence to the political dimensions of the research agenda, including Banaji (1995), Brass (1995), Mamdani (1996), Petras (1997), Borras (1998), Bernstein (2000), Petras and Veltmeyer (2001), Moyo and Romadhane (2001), Deere and León (2001), Deere (2003), Moyo (forthcoming, a), Yeros (2002b) and Boron (2003).

New rural movements?

The question arises of how to label contemporary rural movements. Here we will be concerned with movements that are *organized* – to various degrees, including those in the process of organizing – and have a *progressive* agrarian reform agenda. Such movements have proliferated over the last two decades, becoming important sources – in many cases, the nuclei – of oppositional politics within their respective states.

In a seminal article, James Petras (1997) argued that there is a 'third' wave of left politics in Latin America, comprising movements that have been filling the neoliberal political vacuum of the 1990s and whose stronghold has been the countryside (see also Petras and Veltmeyer 2001). Petras characterizes these as a 'new peasantry', whose features we surmise as follows:

- their *social base* is a rural–urban mix of small cultivators and proletarians, including urban retrenched and unemployed;
- their *leadership* is composed of 'peasant intellectuals', as opposed to university intellectuals, eschews personality cults and operates on the principle of 'every member an organizer', rather than on the hierarchical formulas of the past;
- their *tactics* are characterized by direct action, mainly on the land but also in other private and public spaces;
- their *strategy* is 'anti-political', characterized by autonomy from political parties and state, but also by the pursuit of strategic

alliances with political parties, trade unions and other social movements;

- their *ideologies* tend to fuse Marxian and ethnic/racial political languages, and are increasingly gender and ecologically sensitive;
- they are *cosmopolitan*, cultivating an internationalist vision and engaging in international debates and alliances on their own behalf.

This would certainly amount to a substantively 'new' rural politics. However, it is fair to say that most Latin American rural movements would subscribe to this model as an *ideal*, rather than embodying it, while some would not subscribe to much of it, and others have adopted aspects of it against their will. We add here that the model is not specific to Latin America, but has counterparts in Asia and Africa. We proceed by addressing each feature separately.

Social base This is similar throughout the periphery and comprises semi-proletarians and unemployed rural and urban proletarians, both men and women, straddling the rural–urban divide. Contemporary rural movements worldwide are becoming an organizing centre for the masses of rural poor discarded by neoliberalism.

Leadership We observe the phenomenon of 'peasant intellectuals' mainly among movements that have proclaimed autonomy from political parties and their associated intellectuals. Such rural movements have proceeded to cultivate durable local and wider national structures on their own, setting in motion an independent process of conscientization. This is most evident in Latin America, but is also evident in the Philippines, where rural movements in the 1990s have parted ways with the Communist Party, as well as in South Africa where the Landless Peoples' Movement was formed in 2001. By contrast, in Zimbabwe, where mobilization occurred largely within the ruling party, leadership has been provided by the National Liberation War Veterans Association, its local branches, and its cadres within the state; while many war vets themselves have been among the rural poor, and hence 'peasant intellectuals', the idea of generalizing this, to create durable, democratic structures, with systematic political education, has not been the case. We ought to note, however, that even among the 'anti-state' movements, 'peasant intellectuals' are not the exclusive phenomenon. Maintaining a commitment to the spirit of the 'peasant intellectual' is to be seen as an ongoing challenge.

Tactics The predominance of direct action on the land is a very significant and widespread development. It is partly associated with the rift with political parties, but not entirely, as is shown in the case of Zimbabwe, and indeed in the longer history of land occupations around the world, including both the unstructured and low-profile and the more organized and high-profile. What is new is that under neoliberalism many organized rural movements have consciously placed land occupation at the centre of their arsenal of political tactics, and, more specifically, through occupations they have confronted market-based land reforms head-on, either compelling them to work more effectively or displacing them entirely. We have seen the organized use of land occupations in Brazil, the Philippines, Indonesia, Thailand, India, South Africa and Zimbabwe, among other countries. (We elaborate on the land occupation tactic in the next section.) There are important exceptions to this, as among the rural movements that have opted for armed struggle, namely the Zapatistas in Mexico (see Bartra and Otero, Chapter 14 in this volume) and the FARC in Colombia (Ampuero and Brittain, Chapter 13 in this volume).

Strategy The 'anti-political' phenomenon is also a very significant development, and has an impact on the two preceding features. Autonomy from political parties and the state is mainly observed in Latin America, but also in Asia and Africa. However, the issue of 'autonomy' in its more holistic sense, which would include the 'non-state' sites of imperial power, namely 'oppositional politics', is not conceptualized adequately. Thus, in so far as the new strategy has been concerned with gaining 'autonomy', the record has been more problematic. For breaking with the state has meant that rural movements have had to enter the realm of NGOs, trade unions and churches, where no less intense and systematic forces of co-optation operate. Among those that have pursued a strategy of autonomy from political parties and the state are the rural movements in the Philippines, India, the newly founded movement in South Africa, the Zapatistas in Mexico, and the MST in Brazil. By contrast, the movement that has eschewed civil society and pursued direct action through the ruling party and the state is that of Zimbabwe. A closer look at the particular cases of Mexico, Zimbabwe, Brazil and the Philippines may be instructive with regard to the problem of autonomy in its holistic sense.

The Zapatistas launched an armed struggle against the state in 1994, and at that time proclaimed a vision for socialist transformation (Petras 1997; Otero 1999; Bartra and Otero, Chapter 14 in this volume). However, very soon military confrontation and encirclement took their toll, and the movement was compelled incrementally to narrow its political vision. It began to shift emphasis from class language to that of indigenous rights; it focused on democratic reform, courted civil society, and even offered a qualified renunciation of armed struggle. The results of the combined uprising and civil transition have been mixed: on the one hand, the Zapatistas have inspired and invigorated oppositional politics in Mexico – indeed throughout Latin America; on the other hand, the hard reality of not having 'taken power' has translated into mere promises for reform, which have not yet been delivered, and are no longer likely to be. In this case, it appears that the Zapatistas have had to reconcile themselves to an 'anti-statist' strategy, rather than vice versa.

The case of the Philippines is somewhat similar (see Feranil, Chapter 9 in this volume). The radical rural movements of the 1980s, which had close links to the Communist Party and its armed wing, were defeated and dispersed by the 'total war' campaign of the Aquino government. The succeeding period of the 1990s saw the reconfiguration of rural movements, the renunciation of armed struggle, and the pursuit of alliance-building within the constitutional framework, although on its 'edges'. The difference here has been the qualified success of the '*bibingka* strategy', a dual approach of implanting reformist elements within the state while persisting with land occupations and campaigns. The *bibingka* strategy obtained a significant round of land reforms in the 1990s. Yet the correlation of forces has again been changing, reformers have been displaced, and the strategy of the 1990s has been rendered obsolete. In turn, rural movements have been searching for a new strategy, while this is increasingly inclining to the use of 'human rights' language, rather than that of social transformation.

Zimbabwe provides the contrast. This is the case of a militant movement that broke with civil society, acted directly through the state, achieved radical land reform, but failed to sustain itself and defend its interests systematically (see Moyo and Yeros, Chapter 6 in this volume). The postcolonial period of Zimbabwe has been characterized by closure to rural demands at the levels of both the state and oppositional politics. It has also been characterized by un-structured and low-profile land occupations, which have expanded under structural adjustment. The trade-union movement (ZCTU) was the only source of hope for a short period in the late 1980s and early 1990s, as it took a militant stance against neoliberalism and proclaimed the unification of peasant-workers as an organizational task. However, by mid-decade the ZCTU had been co-opted into the civil domain by a combination of neoliberal economic deterioration, state repression, and the patronage of international trade unionism. By the decade's end, trade unions were operating within the inter-nationally respectable framework of 'good governance', which in turn was impervious to the increasingly militant rural demands. It was at this time that the National Liberation War Veterans Association began to agitate within the framework of the ruling party to the effect of re-radicalizing nationalism and land reform. However, the movement has significantly been streamlined by the ruling party, the indigenous bourgeoisie has been allowed to gain a sizeable foothold on the land, and the rural poor are now facing a new challenge without a tangible organizational structure of their own.

Brazil, finally, is a case in which the question of autonomy is now at a critical juncture. In the 're-democratization' period following military rule, the MST cultivated close links with the Workers' Party (PT), while maintaining its independence from it, and while also entering into a strategic alliance with the trade-union centre (CUT). However, throughout the 1990s, both the CUT and the PT suffered co-optation and accommodation, to the point of accepting the dictates of neoliberalism upon obtaining state power. In turn, since the electoral victory of PT, the MST has been in a process of incorporation into the state structures, while the Lula government has failed to formulate an agrarian reform agenda that is different from its predecessor. Thus the relationship of the MST to both the state and its traditional allies is now in question, as is the identity of the MST itself. The process, however, is strewn with contradictions and is far from resolved, for the MST has also been intensifying its land occupation campaign during Lula's government, ushering in a new period of rural confrontation. The question of who will give what orders to the police and what will be done with the hired militias of the landowners – which are both fundamentally 'state' questions – will undoubtedly impact on the direction of change.

We may conclude here that most rural movements have, in one way or another, adopted the 'anti-politics' strategy, but that this has by no means realized their coveted 'autonomy' of political action. The objectives remain to obtain that rare freedom, the genuine autonomy from imperialism at the levels of both the state and oppositional politics, to cultivate a strong and politically conscious social base, and to articulate a clear strategy for the seizure of power. This strategy, by necessity, will have national specificities, and, contra Holloway, should neither submit to, nor proclaim, 'universal' application.

Ideology This remains a weak dimension of rural movements. This is partly due to the rightward drift of political parties and their associated intellectuals, and the resulting rift between rural movements and parties. Yet a positive development has been the emergence precisely of the 'peasant intellectual', which has resulted in the fusion of Marxian language with ethnic/racial language – in effect, the incipient indigenization of Marxism. This has been evident in Bolivia and Mexico, and in other countries as well. However, this indigenization of Marxism has been unstable, as the case of the Zapatistas demonstrates, and has not yet consolidated itself. In Africa, where indigenized Marxism has had a longer history, contemporary rural movements have lagged behind. The LPM in South Africa has broken with the nationalist party (ANC), which succumbed to the bourgeois forces within it, only to find itself struggling against the superficial 'multiracialism' of civil society, where white, middle-class intellectuals continue to exercise strong influence; meanwhile the war-veterans-led movement in Zimbabwe has broken with civil society and operated within the vacillating bourgeois/petty-bourgeois parameters of Zimbabwe's nationalist movement. Although nationalism has always contained potent mobilizational and emancipatory potential and nurtured the possibility of a national democratic revolution, it has not, in itself, sufficed for the longer-term interests of the working class.

Other positive signs in Latin America are the new ecological sensitivity and recognition of patriarchy as a fundamental problem (Stephen 1996; Petras 1997; Deere and León 2001; Deere 2003). These perspectives are perhaps most evident in Brazil and Mexico. With regard to gender specifically, rural movements in the late 1990s have adopted a conscious policy of equity, which, in turn, has been bearing fruit in terms of mobilization and internal democratization, as well as in terms of lobbying effectively against the state for the inclusion of gender-specific legislation in the agrarian reform process. In Zimbabwe, by contrast, the land occupation movement has fallen far short of a gender-sensitive politics, despite the fact that women have participated in the occupations in large numbers. In this case, the strong patriarchal currents of the nationalist movement remain dominant.

Cosmopolitanism   The question of internationalism is central to the question of ideology. The development of international interaction between rural movements on their own behalf is the latest of the several rural political developments. This takes regional forms, as in the Congreso Latinoamericano de Organizaciones del Campo (CLOC), the Asociación de Organizanioces Campesinas Centroamericanas para la Cooperación y el Desarrollo (ASOCODE), and the Southern African Network on Land (SANL). It has also taken global forms, as in the Vía Campesina, a global association of farmers, and the World Social Forum (WSF), in which all of the above participate actively.

The historical context of these developments is the decade of the 1990s, and especially its closing years, the time in which the left began to regroup and reconstitute itself, without the Soviet Union and the Cold War. This is the context in which the 'anti-globalization' movement, embodied in the WSF, has emerged as a conference of global oppositional politics. The question of internationalism and ideology has reimposed itself at this juncture, and along with it a host of new and old debates and divergences. Despite the heterogeneity and pluralism of the WSF, there do exist dominant ideological currents, and this impacts on how the participants resolve the question of internationalism for themselves. Thus we observe that the 'anti-state' and 'anti-politics' strategy is a dominant current, and more recently it has been given conceptual rigour in the writing of Michael Hardt and Antonio Negri (2000) in the United States and Europe, and in that of John Holloway (2002) in Mexico. To be sure, there are other intellectuals in other parts of the world who have also been prominent, and who would not adhere to 'anti-politics', or at least in the strict sense, such as Walden Bello (1998) in the Philippines and Patrick Bond (2002a, 2002b, 2002c) in South Africa. While we recognize the diversity of the WSF, as well as its necessary function at the present time for the purpose of global conscientization and articulation (Monal 2003), we focus on three strong tendencies that do not bode well for internationalism.

First is the idea that we live in a 'post-national' world. The invasion of Iraq and the world reaction to it — not least through WSF channels — has shown just how important the idea of national sovereignty remains and just how perilous it is to speak of a 'non-state' world. We live in an imperialist world in which the postcolonial promise of national self-determination has been denied, and this cannot be wished away. The idea of post-nationalism, nonetheless, continues to infiltrate ways of thinking, obscuring imperialism and Eurocentrism, demoting the principle of national self-determination, and proclaiming internationalism (or 'multiracialism') on the cheap. Recognition of national difference and equality in *substance* is the precondition of internationalism, and this demands commitment to the resolution of the agrarian question in its classical sense, and thereby the logic and ideology of unequal development.

We argue, in this connection, that for all their differences in tactics, strategies and results, the Zapatista uprising and the Zimbabwe war-veterans-led movements have both been among currents that have laid claim to the most demanding of internationalisms. That the Zimbabwe war veterans movement did not capture the 'imagination' of the left worldwide has less to do with the violence that was associated with it (which is comparable to, and in fact far less than, other political convulsions in Africa, Asia and Latin America) and more to do with the civilized 'post-national' and 'anti-state' norms of the anti-globalization movement; only the LPM in South Africa defended the land occupations.

Second is the lack of rigorous class analysis. This applies as much to the Eurocentrists who propagate vacuous concepts like 'the multitude' (Hardt and Negri 2000), as to those who may not subscribe to this but also fail to identify precisely the class structure of civil society. This is especially the case in Africa at present, and particularly in relation to Zimbabwe's civil society (Bond 2002a, 2002c), where the 'working-class' proclamations of trade unions and civic organizations are taken at face value and the material basis of the movements (to include sources of funding, alliances, etc.) is not investigated.

Third is the lack of recognition of the semi-proletarianized specificity of peripheral capitalism. There are two notable tendencies, either to 'urbanize' social protest in the familiar way and efface the agrarian question (Bond 2002c), or to 'ruralize' protest, by lumping semi-proletarians into a 'farmer' category that applies universally, to France and the USA, to Zimbabwe, the Philippines and Brazil. This is the case of Vía Campesina (Desmarais 2002). For all the advocacy work that Vía Campesina has been undertaking worldwide, the idea of uniting organizations from centre and periphery into a 'Farmers' International', with the objective of defending 'the peasant way of life', has its obvious limits. Economic and political realities demand that organizational priority is given to the unification of peasant-workers across the rural–urban divide, with the objective of defending articulated accumulation.[15]

Land occupations and land reform

We arrive finally at the relationship between land occupations and land reform. We have noted that not all rural movements rely on land occupations, while some of those that do also cultivate a larger policy agenda. Nonetheless, the land occupation is the basic political tactic of many movements, and requires particular attention especially in its interaction with market-based reforms. Land reform returned to the development agenda in the mid-1990s under the auspices of the World Bank. At this time, 'access to land' was recognized as an important 'poverty alleviation' issue. It is undoubtedly true that access to land for the rural poor, and especially women, is a crucial means of improving the social reproduction of the household. But the significance of the new 'access to land' lies not in 'poverty alleviation' as such, but more fundamentally in its larger political economic objective, the reinforcement of functional dualism and the safer reproduction of capital in a period of economic, social and political crisis. By no coincidence, this latest World Bank land reform initiative has sought to obtain land redistribution *within* the given national political structures, the same structures that are not only hostile to reform but also naturally committed to 'accumulation from above', as much before as after reform. We reiterate that the importance of land reform, beyond the short-term reprieve that it offers to the rural poor, is its potential to break the political structures that foster underdevelopment.

Several observers have noted that that there are three different models of land reform in existence, and that in fact these interact in a politically dynamic way (de Janvry, Sadoulet and Wolford 2001; Moyo 2003; Veltmeyer, Chapter 10 in this volume). The models may be roughly identified as 'state', 'market' and 'popular'. In order to specify this process, we point to four elements of land reform: (a) the selection of land; (b) the method of acquisition of land; (c) the selection of beneficiaries; and (d) the method of land transfer to the beneficiaries. These elements may combine in different ways in historical circumstances, such that the state, market and popular models may not be easily distinguishable. We argued earlier that the agency of the landless and land-short has been the basic source of agrarian reform historically, through the Cold War and in the present. As such, land reforms have always been 'popular'. What is new in the present context is the more conscious attempt by the rural poor to influence the state and market through land occupations, and thereby lead the way through the various steps: they self-select as beneficiaries, they select the land, they acquire it de facto, and then await their legal formalization by the state. This may indeed follow, or it may not. More generally, the low-profile (illegal 'squatting') tactic is also known to exercise influence over the policy process, but in a much more diffuse and contingent manner.

The 'state' model is one in which the state plays a prominent role in the reform process, as it did throughout the 'developmentalist' period, but also in the present. The state may perform in one of two ways, inclining either to the 'popular' or to the 'market'. It may acquire land compulsorily, the radical scenario: the state selects the land, confiscates it without compensation (or token compensation), selects the beneficiaries (if they have not self-selected already), and transfers the land directly to them through collective or individual title. The state may also acquire the land through market means, the reformist 'willing-seller, willing-buyer' scenario: here, the market (i.e. the landlords) selects the land (if and when the landlords wish), the state purchases the land and compensates the landlords (often with external aid), the state selects beneficiaries (unless again they have acted pre-emptively), and the state transfers title to them. There exist other hybrids, such as when the state seeks to stimulate land transfers via land taxes, or stipulates a minimum productivity requirement on land, or values the price of the land administratively by taking the market into account. The 'state' variations may coexist in a country's constitution and, in fact, compete for prominence in the social and political process. This was the case in Zimbabwe in the 1990s, a process which was resolved in favour of compulsory acquisition. This is also the case currently in Brazil, where there are ongoing 'market experiments', but where the main method remains as follows: the state assesses whether or not the land is being utilized productively, which constitutionally justifies acquisition; then, if and when the state proceeds, it compensates landlords by the issue of bonds; the state then chooses the family to be settled, though by and large the family has self-selected; and the state transfers the title. Variations on the state model are in existence in many other places, such as Nicaragua, El Salvador, Namibia, South Africa and the Philippines.

The 'market' model, although present within the reformist state model throughout the postwar period, has sought to consolidate itself in the 1990s. The market model has sought to displace the state from the various steps of the land reform process, but it has not yet predominated (in its pure form). The model has come to be known as 'community-inititated, market-assisted' (CIMA), and has operated as follows: 'communities' (the rural poor) select themselves, enter into negotiations with landlords over the location and price of land, purchase the land, and receive the title from the landlord. This process is monitored at arm's length by the state, which also seeks to massage the process by taxes or incentives to landlords to dispose of land. Meanwhile, the ever-willing NGOs provide technical assistance to the communities for the purpose of identifying land and navigating the legal circuits; and states and development agencies, in 'joint ventures', provide a variable mix of loans and grants to the rural poor to buy the land, build infrastructure and set up viable farming. As research on this is now emerging, its contradictions are becoming abundantly clear, precisely because 'negotiation' over land and price between masters and servants makes for a seller's market: the land reform process inflates land prices and does not deliver productive land. Moreover, the funding provided to the rural poor is generally insufficient to set up viable farming. The model has been 'tested' in Brazil, Colombia, Guatemala, South Africa, Thailand and Zimbabwe (Barros et al. 2003).

In reality, where the market has been known to 'work', it has been on the heels of militant action. In Zimbabwe's early land re-form experience within the 'willing-buyer, willing-seller' framework, the only cases in which land with high agro-ecological value was redistributed to the poor was the land of white settlers who had been evicted from the liberated zones of the war. The experience of Brazil corroborates the significance of militant agency. Fernandes (Chapter 11 in this volume) shows that from 1995 to 1999, 85 per cent of all new settlements conducted by government had their immediate origin in direct land occupations; 2,800 land reform settlements were created with nearly 300,000 families in total, and these settlements followed 1,800 occupations with 256,000 families participating. Still, the quality of the land acquired has been inferior and post-redistribution rural development policy has been notoriously weak.

The case studies in this volume offer various insights into the process of land occupations and land reform. Among the issues considered are: the social composition of occupations; the problems of gender equity in land reform; the methods of mobilization and spacialization of land occupations; relations with other social movements and political parties; and the strategies of landowners and the state to undermine, divert, or obstruct land occupations.

Conclusion

We have sought in this chapter to provide a holistic interpretation of the agrarian question in the international political economy, with special reference to the neoliberal period. We have argued that the agrarian question, despite its globalization, remains intimately tied up with the national question. We have also argued that the challenges to the resolution of the agrarian question, and the national question itself, have become ever greater under neoliberalism.

Nonetheless, neoliberalism is clearly on a weaker footing now than it was a quarter-century ago, having failed to deliver 'development' and ultimately suffered ideological defeat. The new historical conjuncture thus provides a rare opportunity for progressive movements to bring about a post-liberal order; it also presents the immense challenge of building a world order that sustains peripheral accumulation. It is perhaps ironic that rural movements have become the 'natural' leaders of progressive change, not by virtue of being exploited by capital, but by being expelled from it. But under the circumstances of severe political co-optation among the exploited and the crisis of social reproduction among the expelled, it is no surprise that rural movements are coming of age and taking up militant positions. We hope that this volume will contribute positively to debate over, reflection on, and strengthening of rural movements, as well as their urban counterparts. We also hope that the wider anti-globalization movement will become the place where genuine international solidarity thrives.

Notes

1. We wish to thank Henry Bernstein, Claus Germer, Gerardo Otero and Nilson Maciel de Paula for their insightful comments and criticisms. Errors of fact and interpretation remain our own.

2. The argument has tended to obscure two differing notions of state, as a normative-juridical entity and as a bureaucratic–coercive apparatus.

3. The most overstated measure of globalization is that of foreign direct investment. As much as 50 per cent of 'global FDI' comprises cross-border mergers and acquisitions, associated with the wave of privatizations, which do not alter the asset structures of acquired enterprises. Moreover, over 90 per cent of it originates in the US–EU–Japan triad, and 75 per cent is destined for the triad, while the rest of it is largely accounted for by East Asia, including China. As much as 70 per cent of the world's population is 'virtually written off the map' (Hirst and Thompson 1999: 72–4).

4. To be sure, the Bretton Woods system was not substantially different. While it involved a commitment to exchange rate stability and called for regulated capital movements, it never subscribed to an adjustment mechanism that was free of power politics – as J.M. Keynes, for example, had proposed. The Bretton Woods adjustment 'system' was the Cold War (Strange 1985; Walter 1991).

5. Other more obvious ones include monopoly control of the international currency, grants and credits, technology, and military aid; direct intervention and covert operations; co-optation of international trade unionism.

6. These NACs gained food 'self-sufficiency' in the sense of no longer relying on imports, but not in the sense of food security, for self-sufficiency has been based on low effective national demand – that is, mass poverty and chronic malnutrition (Patnaik 1990). Moreover, the social costs of transforming domestic agriculture into globally competitive agro-industry have been immense: rapid land alienation and unemployment, rural conflict, mass migration and urban criminality.

7. Raikes and Gibbon (2000) indicate that between the mid-1980s and mid-1990s the terms of trade for the main traditional crops of Africa (cotton, coffee, cocoa, tea, tobacco, bananas, oranges) have dropped dramatically (over 35 per cent for most goods), due to market saturation; notably, Africa has lost market shares to Asia.

8. The (imperial) fallacies of regime theory in International Relations have long been noted, even by conservative theorists (Strange 1982).

9. The debate over the redivision of land spans over a century. At its inception, it pitted the orthodoxy of the Second International against petty-bourgeois

elements and 'populists', but also, in time, against other dissidents in the revolutionary left, most notably Lenin. After the failed revolution of 1905 in Russia, Lenin recognized the political and democratic significance of land redivision, especially the imperative of preventing the landed oligarchy from directing the course of political change. To this day, the argument against economism is not to be dismissed as 'populist', nor as incensitive to economic questions. The latter remain significant – including issues of tenure type, organization of production, and inter-sectoral relations – but economics cannot be allowed to take precedence over politics.

10. Indeed, the contrast with 1970s is striking. At that time, Henry Kissinger dealt with rural-based armed struggle in Southern Africa in no uncertain terms, by means of overt and clandestine military and economic support for white supremacism, to ensure neocolonial transitions.

11. There has even been a variant of this in Southern Africa in the post-apartheid context (Mamdani 1996, Neocosmos 1996), whereby the political-economic relations between white-settler farmers and petty-commodity producers have been obscured and the land question itself undermined (see critique in Yeros 2002b).

12. For an overview of the debate in Latin America, see Petras and Veltmeyer 2001, and for Southern Africa, with particular reference to Zimbabwe, see Yeros 2002a.

13. It is notable that the politicization of class/race in Latin America continues to be undermined by dominant European culture. It thus remains perfectly acceptable, even for leading intellectuals, to write a history of radical political thought in Latin America without an engagement with the pan-Africanism of Frantz Fanon, himself Caribbean-born (e.g. Löwy 1999).

14. In the discipline of International Relations, the dominant 'realist' tradition, as the academic mouthpiece of US imperialism, has consistently made such an argument (Waltz 1979), while more 'normative' bourgeois renditions of world order have been offered by 'English' realists, liberals and postmodernists (Bull 1995; Linklater 1998; Walker 1988) – but also neo-Gramscians (Cox 1987).

15. We may add that valuable insights into the principles, applications and problems of articulated accumulation in the periphery, as well as the lessons they provide for the future, are offered by Samir Amin (1981).

References

Agarwal, Bina (1994), *A Field of One's Own: Gender and Land Rights in South Asia*, Cambridge: Cambridge University Press.

Amin, Samir (1976), *Unequal Development*, trans. Brian Pearce, Brighton: Harvester.

Amin, Samir (1981), *The Future of Maoism*, trans. Norman Finkelstein, New York: Monthly Review Press.

Amin, Samir (1989), *Eurocentrism*, trans. R. Moore, London: Zed Books.

Amin, Samir (1997), *Capitalism in the Age of Globalization*, London: Zed Books.

Arrighi, Giovanni (2003), 'The Social and Political Economy of Turbulence', *New Left Review* II(20), March–April: 5–71.

Banaji, Jairus (1995), 'The Farmers' Movements: A Critique of Conservative Rural Coalitions', in *New Farmers' Movements in India*, ed. Tom Brass, London: Frank Cass.

Barros, Flávia, Sergio Sauer, and Stephan Schwartzman, eds (2003), *The Negative Impacts of World Bank Market Based Land Reform*, Brasília: Rede Brasil.

Bates, Robert (1981), *Markets and States in Tropical Africa: The Political Basis of Agricultural Policies*, Berkeley and Los Angeles, CA, and London: University of California Press.

Bates, Robert (1989a), *Beyond the Miracle of the Market: The Political Economy of Agrarian Development in Kenya*, Cambridge: Cambridge University Press.

Bates, Robert, ed. (1989b), *Toward a Political Economy of Development: A Rational Choice Perspective*, Berkeley, CA: University of California Press.

Bello, Walden (1998), 'East Asia: On the Eve of the Great Transformation?', *Review of International Political Economy* 5(3): 424–44.

Bernstein, Henry (1988), 'Capitalism and Petty-Bourgeois Production: Class Relations and Divisions of Labour', *Journal of Peasant Studies* 15(2).

Bernstein, Henry (1990), 'Agricultural "Modernisation" and the Era of Structural Adjustment: Observations on Sub-Saharan Africa', *Journal of Peasant Studies*, 18(1): 3–25.

Bernstein, Henry (2000), '"The Peasantry" in Global Capitalism: Who, Where, and Why?', in *Socialist Register 2001: Working Classes, Global Realities*, ed. Leo Panitch and Colin Leys, London: Merlin.

Bernstein, Henry (2002), 'Land Reform: Taking a Long(er) View', *Journal of Agrarian Change* 2(1): 433–63.

Bernstein, Henry (2003), 'Land Reform in Southern Africa in World-Historical Perspective', *Review of African Political Economy* 96: 21–46.

Binswanger, Hans P., Klaus Deininger and Gershon Feder (1993), 'Power, Distortions, Revolt, and Reform in Agricultural Land Relations', *Policy Research Working Paper Series*, Washington, DC: World Bank.

Bond, Patrick (2002a), *Zimbabwe's Plunge*, London: Merlin.

Bond, Patrick (2002b), *Against Global Apartheid*, Cape Town: University of Cape Town Press.

Bond, Patrick (2002c), 'Cultivating African Anti-Capitalism', mimeo.

Boron, Atilio A. (2001), *A Coruja de Minerva*, Buenos Aires and Petrópolis: CLACSO and Editora Vozes.

Boron, Atilio A. (2002), *Império e Imperialismo*, Buenos Aires: CLACSO.

Boron, Atilio A. (2003), 'A Selva e a Polis: Interrogações em Torno da Teoria Política do Zapatismo', in Atilio A. Boron, *Filosofia Política Marxista*, Buenos Aires and São Paulo: CLACSO and Cortez.

Borras, Saturnino M. (1998), 'The Bibingka Strategy to Land Reform and Implementation: Autonomous Peasant Mobilizations and State Reformists in the Philippines', Working Paper Series No. 274, The Hague: Institute of Social Studies.

Brass, Tom (1995), 'Introduction', in *New Farmers' Movements in India*, ed. Tom Brass, London: Frank Cass.

Breman, Jan (2000), 'Labour and Landlessness in South and South-east Asia', in *Disappearing Peasantries?*, ed. D. Bryceson et al., London: ITDG Publishing.

Bryceson, Deborah (2000a), 'Peasant Theories and Smallholder Policies: Past and Present', in *Disappearing Peasantries?*, ed. D. Bryceson et al., London: ITDG Publishing.

Bryceson, Deborah (2000b), 'African Peasants' Centrality and Marginality: Rural Labour Transformations', in *Disappearing Peasantries?*, ed. D. Bryceson et al., London: ITDG Publishing.

Bryceson, Deborah, Cristóbal Kay, and Jos Mooij, eds (2000), *Disappearing Peasantries? Rural Labour in Africa, Asia, and Latin America*, London: ITDG Publishing.

Bull, Hedley (1995), *The Anarchical Society: A Study of Order in World Politics*, London: Macmillan.

Byres, T.J. (1991), 'The Agrarian Question and Differing Forms of Capitalist Agrarian Transition: An Essay with Reference to Asia', in *Rural Transformation in Asia*, ed. Jan Breman and Sudipto Mundle, Oxford, Delhi and New York: Oxford University Press.

Cabral, Amilcar (1979), *Unity and Struggle*, New York: Monthly Review Press.

Channock, Martin (1985), *Law, Custom and Social Order: The Colonial Experience in Malawi and Zambia*, Cambridge: Cambridge University Press.

Cohen, Robin (1991), 'Peasants to Workers and Peasant-Workers in Africa', in *Contested Domains: Debates in International Labour Studies*, London: Zed Books, ch. 5.

Cox, Robert (1977), 'Labor and Hegemony', *International Organization* 31(3): 385–424.

Cox, Robert (1987), *Production, Power and World Order*, New York: Columbia University Press.

Cox, Robert (1999), 'Civil Society at the Turn of the Millennium: Prospects for an Alternative World Order', *Review of International Studies* 25(1): 3–28.

Deere, Carmen Diana (2003), 'Women's Land Rights and Rural Social Movements in the Brazilian Agrarian Reform', *Journal of Agrarian Change* 3(42): 257–88.

Deere, Carmen Diana, and Magdalena León (2001), 'Who Owns the Land? Gender and Land Titling Programmes in Latin America', *Journal of Agrarian Change* 1(3): 440–67.

de Janvry, Alain (1981), *The Agrarian Question and Reformism in Latin America*, Baltimore, MD, and London: Johns Hopkins University Press.

de Janvry, Alain, and Elisabeth Sadoulet (1989), 'A Study in Resistance to Institutional Change: The Lost Game of Latin American Land Reform', *World Development* 17(9): 1397–407.

de Janvry Alain, Elisabeth Sadoulet and Wendy Wolford (2001), 'The Changing Role of the State in Latin American Land Reforms', in *Access to Land, Rural Poverty, and Public Action*, ed. A. de Janvry et al., Oxford: Oxford University Press.

de Janvry, Alain, Gustavo Gordillo, Jean-Philippe Plateau and Elisabeth Sadoulet, eds (2001), *Access to Land, Rural Poverty, and Public Action*, Oxford: Oxford University Press, 2001.

de Oliveira, Francisco (2003), 'O Ornitorrinco', in *Crítica à Razão Dualista e Ornitorrinco*, São Paulo: Boitempo.

Desmarais, Annette-Aurélie (2002), 'The Vía Campesina: Consolidating an International Peasant and Farm Movement', *Journal of Peasant Studies* 29(2): 91–124.

Diamond, Larry (1987), 'Class Formation in the Swollen African State', *Journal of Modern African Studies* 25(4): 567–96.

Engels, Friedrich (1953a [1894]), 'O Problema Camponês na França e na Alemanha', in Karl Marx and Friedrich Engels, *Obras Escolhidas*, Volume III, São Paulo: Editora Alfa-Omega.

Engels, Friedrich (1953b [1895]), Introduction to Karl Marx, 'As Lutas de Classe na França de 1848 a 1950', in Karl Marx and Friedrich Engels, *Obras Escolhidas*, Volume I, São Paulo: Editora Alfa-Omega.

Fanon, Frantz (2001[1961]), *The Wretched of the Earth*, London: Penguin Books.

First, Ruth (1983), *Black Gold: The Mozambican Miner, Proletarian and Peasant*, Brighton: Harvester.

Friedmann, Harriet (1993), 'The Political Economy of Food: A Global Crisis', *New Left Review* 197, January–February: 29–57.

Friedmann, Harriet, and McMichael, Philip (1989), 'Agriculture and the State System: The Rise and Decline of National Agricultures', *Sociologia Ruralis* 29(2): 93–117.

Fröbel, Folker, Jürgen Heinrichs and Otto Kreye (1980), *The New International Division of Labour*, trans. P. Burgess, Cambridge: Cambridge University Press.

Germer, Claus (1994), 'Perspectivas das Lutas Sociais Agrárias nos Anos 90', in *A Questão Agrária Hoje*, ed. João Pedro Stédile, Porto Alegre: UFRGS and ANCA.

Gibbon, Peter, and Michael Neocosmos (1985), 'Some Problems in the Political Economy of "African Socialism"', in *Contradictions of Accumulation in Africa*, ed. Henry Bernstein and Bonnie Campbell, Beverly Hills, London and New Delhi: Sage.

Gowan, Peter (1999), *The Global Gamble*, London and New York: Verso.

Graziano da Silva, José (1999), *O Novo Rural Brasileiro*, Campinas: UNICAMP.

Gwaunza, Elizabeth (1998), 'The Impact of Labour Migration on Family Organisation in Zimbabwe', in *Labour Markets and Migration Policy in Southern Africa*, ed. Lloyd Sachikonye, Harare: SAPES Trust.

Hardt, Michael, and Antonio Negri (2000), *Empire*, Cambridge, MA: Harvard University Press.

Harriss, John (1987), 'Capitalism and Peasant Production: The Green Revolution in India', in *Peasants and Peasant Societies*, ed. Teodor Shanin, 2nd edn, Oxford and New York: Basil Blackwell.

Harriss, John (1992), 'Does the "Depressor" Still Work? Agrarian Structure and Development in India: A Review of Evidence and Argument', *Journal of Peasant Studies* 19(2): 189–227.

Hirst, Paul, and Grahame Thompson (1999), *Globalization in Question*, 2nd edn, Cambridge: Polity Press.

Holloway, John (2002), *Change the World without Taking Power*, London and Sterling, VA: Pluto Press.

ILO (2002a), *A Future Without Child Labour*, Geneva: ILO.

ILO (2002b), *Unbearable to the Human Heart: Child Trafficking and Action to Eliminate It*, Geneva: ILO.

Kapadia, Karin (2000), 'Responsibility without Rights: Women Workers in Bonder Labour in Rural Industry in South India', in *Disappearing Peasantries?*, ed. D. Bryceson et al., London: ITDG Publishing.

Kautsky, Karl (1988 [1899]), *The Agrarian Question*, trans. P. Burgess, London and Winchester, MA: Zwan.

Kautsky, Karl (1970), 'Ultra-Imperialism', *New Left Review* 59, January–February: 41–6.

Kay, Cristóbal (1998), *The Complex Legacy of Latin America's Agrarian Reform*, Working Paper Series No. 268, The Hague: Institute of Social Studies.

Kay, Cristóbal (2000), 'Latin America's Agrarian Transformation: Peasantization and Proletarianization', in *Disappearing Peasantries?*, ed. Bryceson et al., London: ITDG Publishing.

Keohane, Robert (1984), *After Hegemony: Cooperation and Discord in the World Political Economy*, Princeton, NJ: Princeton University Press.

Lal, Deepak (1997), *The Poverty of 'Development Economics'*, 2nd edn, London: Institute of Economic Affairs.

Lenin, V.I. (1964 [1899]), *The Development of Capitalism in Russia*, 2nd edn, Moscow: Progress Publishers.

Linklater, Andrew (1998), *The Transformation of Political Community: Ethical Foundations of a Post-Westphalian Era*, Cambridge: Polity Press.

Löwy, Michael, editor (1999), *O Marxismo na América Latina*, São Paulo: Fundação Perseu Abramo.

Mafeje, Archie (1997), 'The Agrarian Question in Southern Africa and Accumulation from Below', *SAPEM* 10(5): 33–9.

Mamdani, Mahmood (1996), *Citizen and Subject: Contemporary Africa and the Legacy of Late Colonialism*, Princeton, NJ: Princeton University Press.

Marx, Karl (1975), 'Critique of Hegel's Doctrine of the State', in *Early Writings*, introduced by Lucio Colletti, Harmondsworth: Penguin Books.

Marx, Karl (1976), *Capital*, Volume I, London: Penguin Books.

McMichael, Philip (1997), 'Rethinking Globalization: The Agrarian Question Revisited', *Review of International Political Economy* 4(4): 630–62.

McMichael, Philip, and David Myhre (1991), 'Global Regulation vs the Nation-State: Agro-Food Systems and the New Politics of Capital', *Capital and Class* 43: 83–105.

Monal, Isabel (2003), 'Porto Alegre en Lucha', *Crítica Marxista* 16: 122–6.

Mooij, Jos (2000), 'Changing Peasantries in Asia', in *Disappearing Peasantries?*, ed. D. Bryceson et al., London: ITDG Publishing.

Moyo, Sam (1995a), *The Land Question in Zimbabwe*, Harare: SAPES Books.

Moyo, Sam (1995b), 'A Gendered Perspective on the Land Question', *SAFERE* 1(1): 13–31.

Moyo, Sam (2000), *Land Reform under Structural Adjustment in Zimbabwe: Land Use Change in the Mashonaland Provinces*, Uppsala: Norkiska Afrika Institutet.

Moyo, Sam (2001), 'The Land Occupation Movement and Democratisation in Zimbabwe: Contradictions of Neoliberalism', *Millennium: Journal of International Studies* 30(2): 311–30.

Moyo, Sam (2002), 'Peasant Organisations and Rural Civil Society in Africa: An Introduction', in *Peasant Organisations and Democratisation in Africa*, ed. Sam Moyo and Ben Romadhane, Dakar: CODESRIA Book Series.

Moyo, Sam (2003), 'The Interaction of Market and Compulsory Land Acquisition Processes with Social Action in Zimbabwe's Land Reform', in *Pan Africanism and Integration in Africa*, ed. Ibbo Mandaza and Dani Nabudere, Harare: SAPES Books.

Moyo, Sam (forthcoming, a), *The Land Question in Africa: Research Perspectives and Questions*, Dakar: CODESRIA Green Book.

Moyo, Sam (forthcoming, b), 'Land Redistribution in Zimbabwe: Allocations and Beneficiaries'.

Moyo, Sam, and Ben Romadhane, eds (2002), *Peasant Organisations and Democratisation in Africa*, Dakar: CODESRIA.

Munck, Ronaldo, and Peter Waterman (1999), *Labour Worldwide in the Era of Globalization: Alternative Union Models in the New World Order*, London: Macmillan.

Neocosmos, Michael (1993), *The Agrarian Question in Southern Africa and 'Accumulation from Below'*, Uppsala: Nordiksa Afrikainstitutet.

North, Douglass C. (1981), *Structure and Change in Economic History*, New York: Norton.

North, Douglass C. (1990), *Institutions, Institutional Change, and Economic Performance*, Cambridge: Cambridge University Press.

O'Brien, Robert, Anne Marie Goetz, Jan Aart Scholte, and Marc Williams (2000), *Contesting Global Governance: Multilateral Economic Institutions and Global Social Movements*, Cambridge: Cambridge University Press.

Ohmae, Kenichi (1990), *The Borderless World: Power and Strategy in the Interlinked Economy*, London: Collins.

Olson, Gary (1974), *US Foreign Policy and the Third World Peasant: Land Reform in Asia and Latin America*, London and New York: Praeger.

Otero, Gerardo (1999), *Farewell to the Peasantry?*, Boulder, CO: Westview Press.

Patnaik, Utsa (1990), 'Some Economic and Political Consequences of the Green Revolution in India', in *The Food Question: Profits Versus People?*, ed. Henry Bernstein et al., London: Earthscan.

Peta, Gregory, Gift Chibatwa, Etwell Whanya, Trust Ngirandi and Douglas Phiri (1991), *An Organisational Survey of Five Trade Unions in Zimbabwe*, ed. Yash Tandon, Harare: Zimababwe Congress of Trade Unions.

Petras, James (1997), 'Latin America: The Resurgence of the Left', *New Left Review* 223, May–June: 17–47.

Petras, James (2000), 'Política Agrícola Estadunidense para a América Latina', in James Petras and Henry Veltmeyer, *Hegemonía dos Estados Unidos no Novo Milênio*, Petrópolis: Editora Vozes.

Petras, James, and Henry Veltmeyer (2000), *Hegemonía dos Estados Unidos no Novo Milênio*, Petrópolis: Editora Vozes.

Petras, James, and Henry Veltmeyer (2001), 'Are Latin American Peasant Movements Still a Force for Change? Some New Paradigms Revisited', *Journal of Peasant Studies* 28(2): 83–118.

Petras, James, Henry Veltmeyer and Steve Vieux (1997), *Neoliberalism and Class Conflict in Latin America*, London: Macmillan.

Raikes, Philip (2000), 'Modernization and Adjustment in African Peasant Agriculture', in *Disappearing Peasantries?*, ed. D. Bryceson et al., London: ITDG Publishing.

Raikes, Philip, and Peter Gibbon (2000), '"Globalisation" and African Export Crop Agriculture', *Journal of Peasant Studies* 27(2): 50–93.

Rutherford, Blair (2001), *Working on the Margins: Black Workers, White Farmers in Post-colonial Zimbabwe*, Harare, London and New York: Weaver Press and Zed Books.

Schmidt, Elizabeth (1990), 'Negotiated Spaces and Contested Terrain: Men, Women, and the Law in Colonial Zimbabwe, 1890–1939', *Journal of Southern African Studies* 16(4): 622–48.

Scott, James C. (1985), *Weapons of the Weak: Everyday Forms of Peasant Resistance*, New Haven, CT, and London: Yale University Press.

So, Alvin Y., and Stephen W.K. Chiu (1995), *East Asia and the World Economy*, Thousand Oaks, CA, London and New Delhi: Sage.

Stephen, Lynn (1996), 'Democracy for Whom? Women's Grassroots Political Activism in the 1990's, Mexico City and Chiapas', in *Neolibrealism Revisited: Economic Restructuring and Mexico's Political Future*, ed. Gerardo Otero, Boulder, CO and Oxford: Westview Press.

Strange, Susan (1982), '*Cave! Hic Dragones*: A Critique of Regime Analysis', *International Organization* 36(2): 337–54.

Strange, Susan (1988), *States and Markets*, 2nd edn, London: Pinter.

Strange, Susan (1996), *The Retreat of the State: The Diffusion of Power in the World Economy*, Cambridge: Cambridge University Press.

Sylvester, Christine (2000), *Producing Women and Progress in Zimbabwe: Narratives of Identity and Work from the 1980s*, Portsmouth, NH: Heinemann.

Szelényi, Iván (1998), 'Introduction', in *Privatising the Land: Rural Political Economy in Post-Communist Societies*, ed. Iván Szelényi, London and New York: Routledge.

UNICEF (2002), *The State of the World's Children 2003*, New York: UNICEF.

Wade, Robert, and Frank Veneroso (1998a), 'The Asian Crisis: The High Debt Model versus the Wall Street–Treasury–IMF Complex', *New Left Review* 228: 3–22.

Walker, R.B.J. (1988), *One World, Many Worlds: Struggles for a Just World Peace*, Boulder, CO, and London: Lynne Rienner and Zed Books.

Walter, Andrew (1991), *World Power and World Money: The Role of Hegemony and International Monetary Order*, Hemel Hempstead: Harvester Wheatsheaf.

Waltz, Kenneth N. (1979), *Theory of International Politics*, Reading, MA: Addison-Wesley.

Warren, Bill (1980), *Imperialism: Pioneer of Capitalism*, ed. John Sender, London: Verso.

Wood, Ellen Meiksins (1995), *Democracy against Capitalism*, Cambridge: Cambridge University Press.

World Bank (1981), *Accelerated Development in Sub-Saharan Africa*, Washington DC: World Bank.

World Bank (1990), *World Development Report 1990*, Oxford: Oxford University Press for the World Bank.

Yeros, Paris (2002a), 'Zimbabwe and the Dilemmas of the Left', *Historical Materialism* 10(2): 3–15.

Yeros, Paris (2002b), 'The Political Economy of Civilisation: Peasant-workers in Zimbabwe and the Neo-colonial World', Ph.D. thesis, University of London.

PART I

AFRICA

2

Rural Land and Land Conflicts in Sub-Saharan Africa

Henry Bernstein

This chapter sketches the place of land in the agrarian questions of modern sub-Saharan Africa. It proceeds via a periodization of its history, from the generalization of systematic colonization through the processes that subsequently integrated African farmers within the structures and circuits of commodity economy, both local and international. Although processes of commoditization have generated neither large-scale landed property nor generalized dispossession in most of Africa – by stark contrast with the formation and legacies of settler colonial capitalism in southern Africa – they necessarily have intrinsic class dynamics which underlie increasing tensions and conflicts over land today. That is, in conditions of widespread immiseration, associated with the structural adjustment lending and globalization of recent decades, pressures on the reproduction of labour, together with intensifying social inequality, enhance the significance as well as prevalence of struggles over land. That the social sources and political forms of those struggles are usually very different from equivalent struggles in Latin America and Asia is an effect of the specificities of sub-Saharan Africa, which the chapter also tries to illustrate and explain.

Colonial Establishment and Consolidation, 1880s–1930s[1]

A defining feature of the modern historical experience of Africa, marking one of its 'world-historical' specificities, is that comprehensive colonial rule was established in most of the continent relatively late in the long history of European overseas expansion.[2] As Julius Nyerere remarked (in a speech at the University of Dar es Salaam in the 1970s, which the author attended): 'for Lenin imperialism was the last stage of capitalism, but for us in Africa it was the first'. The 'scramble for Africa', along with European colonization of the other remaining imperial frontiers in southeast and western Asia, occurred within the formative period of modern (capitalist) imperialism as analysed by Lenin, and also within what is now often regarded as the first 'golden age' of globalization from the 1870s to 1914. Furthermore, by the late nineteenth century, the principal European powers that established vast colonial territories in Africa (Britain and France) not only were industrialized countries, but their 'second industrial revolution', from the 1870s (Hobsbawm 1987), generated a massive growth of demand for agricultural and mineral raw materials, including a number of tropical products which were to be supplied precisely by the colonial economies in an expanding (and shifting) international division of labour. This timing of systematic colonization, as well as its modalities and effects, indicates some of the specificities of the trajectories of Africa's modern history within the centre–periphery relations sketched more generally by Sam Moyo and Paris Yeros in Chapter 1 of this collection.

A second source or type of specificity is the immense range of social formations, habitats and modes of livelihood that colonial rule encountered and on which it attempted to impose its own structures, and notions of order and progress, first through 'pacification' and then through its various – and contradictory – forms of social engineering. Samir Amin (1976: 317–33) distinguished three 'macro-regions' of sub-Saharan Africa by a broad typology of their colonial formations. The *économie de traite* of West Africa was characterized by agricultural export production by peasant farmers, and in some cases by larger-scale indigenous producers, and typically organized by metropolitan trading houses through various intermediary layers of merchant capital.[3] The *économie de traite* did not therefore entail widespread dispossession. Its patterns of commoditization of rural economy proceeded without the institution of private property rights and markets in land, and in many cases were realized through movement into, and clearing of, new areas to farm cocoa and oil palm (in the forest belts), and cotton and groundnuts (in the savannah): the four classic export crops of West Africa.

The second, equally extensive, 'macro-region' is that of 'labour reserve' colonies stretching from east through parts of central to southern Africa, in which there was widespread alienation of land to colonial settlers. The rationale of dispossessing Africans and concentrating them in 'native reserves' was twofold: to provide land for white settlement and its capitalist farming; and to enforce regular supplies of labour to these large farms and plantations, as well as to the mining complexes of the Rhodesias, North and South (later Zambia and Zimbabwe) and of South Africa, which drew in massive numbers of migrant miners from southern Mozambique, Nyasaland (later Malawi) and Basutoland (later Lesotho).

Amin's third category is 'the Africa of the concessionary companies' in the region of the Congo river basin, of which Congo/Zaire is emblematic of an extremely brutal history of resource extraction/plunder to this day.[4] The concessionary companies were granted vast territories for exploitation, with serious consequences for both their inhabitants and natural resources. Generally, however, they were unable to establish the conditions of systematic and sustained capitalist agriculture (both settler and plantation) that came to prevail to the east (Kenya) and south (Southern Rhodesia/Zimbabwe and South Africa).

Amin's broad schema, and the geographical coordinates of its 'macro-regions', are a useful first approximation, but the trajectories of Africa's modern history are, inevitably, less clear-cut. In the colonies of the *économie de traite*, for example, land was often expropriated for extractive activities (mining and timber), as in Gold Coast/Ghana, if not for purposes of white settlement. Some countries combined elements of all three types of colonial economy, notably Mozambique (and to a lesser degree Angola). Kenya, at the northern boundary of its 'macro-region', provided the clearest – and somewhat atypical – example of a 'labour reserve' economy centred on the needs of settler agriculture, without any major mining or other extractive industry (although the political economy of settler agriculture there during the colonial period had many parallels with its counterparts further south). At the same time, peasant commodity production (and its associated class differentiation) was never completely extinguished in 'labour reserve'/settler colonies like Kenya and Southern Rhodesia, even within the severe constraints imposed by their 'native reserves'. Likewise (and surprisingly), Amin's sketch of the 'Africa of the concession companies' does not mention the crucial mining industry, and its labour needs, of Kinshasa in southern Congo/Zaire (sharing the same mineral rich geology as the adjacent Copper Belt of northern Zambia). More important perhaps is that the features, and combinations, of these types or elements of colonial economy shifted over time, and not uncommonly towards a greater weight of peasant commodity production, which was actively promoted in the later colonial period (see below).[5]

The key point is that in most of sub-Saharan Africa, with the exception of the territories of most extensive (white) settlement (Kenya, Southern Rhodesia, South Africa), 'peasant' farmers (including pastoralists) were not dispossessed but 'encouraged' by various means to enter the monetary (commodity) economy as producers of agricultural commodities and/or labour-power: in effect, the conditions of full proletarianization of the great majority of producers were not established, as Samir Amin and many others have emphasized. While the various means of 'encouragement' – taxation, obligations to cultivate certain crops, to provide labour service or enter (migrant) labour contracts – at first typically involved 'forced commercialization' (to use a term employed with reference to colonial India (Bharadwaj 1985)), some African farmers pioneered commodity production for export by mobilizing land and labour through customary means and without, or despite, the actions of colonial states – for example, the 'classic' case of cocoa production in Ghana presented in the seminal study by Hill (1963).

At the same time as African colonial economies were organized to produce tropical agricultural products (and minerals) for export to world markets, this activity was also expected to yield the revenues to pay for colonial administration. The formation and functioning of colonial states was marked by what Berry (1993) calls 'hegemony on a shoestring'. This is also a theme in the analysis of colonial state formation and its legacy by Mamdani (1996), who emphasizes the 'decentralized despotism' of indirect rule in Africa. Under indirect rule, the lower tiers of state administration in the countryside were allocated to the authority of chiefs and headmen governing by the ostensibly 'customary law' of particular 'tribes', to which rural people were subject on the basis of their 'tribal' identity as perceived and legislated by colonial rulers. While the powers of chiefs were thoroughly subordinated to those of colonial state authority – for example, in relation to duties of tax collection, labour recruitment for military and public works, and ultimately in terms of the deposition and replacement of chiefs – they were often greatly increased in relation to their subjects. Mamdani suggests that the colonial refashioning of chieftancy (with the active participation of many chiefs and their allies) in effect fused executive, legislative and judicial powers of 'customary' authority as the exercise of indirect rule in the countryside. One of the many merits of Mamdani's analysis is that it connects the politics of the 'native question' in South Africa with that of the colonies to its north, suggesting how indirect rule (in British colonies), 'association' (in French colonies) and segregation (later apartheid) in South Africa were similar responses to common issues of establishing and maintaining 'native' subjection.[6]

This had particular and potent effects for land tenure and use (as for other areas) that connect with issues of emergent forms of agricultural commoditization, in turn associated with integration in world markets and divisions of labour. There is widespread recognition that through the institution of indirect rule, the 'customary' in Africa − in relation to land as well as, or connected with, political status − was refashioned (or even 'invented') by colonial interventions (Colson 1971; Peters 1994, 2002; Berry 1993; Mamdani 1996), and that the commoditization of land, including development of land markets, was suppressed. The ways in which 'communal' or 'customary' land, on the one hand, and state land (in British colonies Crown land), on the other − and their tenures, jurisdictions, and claims on them − were defined (and contested) retain a powerful resonance in many parts of Africa today, and a resonance intensified by widespread immiseration and growing inequality (to which I return below).

The processes outlined were accompanied by various perceptions of, and concerns with, 'nature' in Africa, from idealized conceptions of a pre-(or non-)industrial 'Eden' (Anderson and Grove 1987) to the bracketing of a savage and dangerous 'nature' and 'culture' (Vaughan 1991), to more pragmatic concerns with the ostensibly destructive and 'wasteful' (mis)use by natives of the fragile resource endowments of their habitats − for example, through 'shifting cultivation' leading to deforestation, and pastoralism leading to overstocking and the degradation of rangelands, in the view of colonial officials (Leach and Mearns 1996; McCann 1999; Anderson 2002). These early currents, and links between scientific investigation of Africa's physical environments and conservation as an element of 'native policy', became more central to the colonial agenda with a more concentrated impetus to state intervention in the 1930s. In some respects, this reflected the impact of scientific and policy response to the problem of 'dust bowls' in the USA − a key moment in the

formation of applied environmental science as we know it today and
one that had many international repercussions, including in colonial
Africa (Anderson 1984). In other respects, this more intense concern
with conservation was one feature, among others, of a conjuncture
in which colonial rule was consolidated at a time when the great
Depression of the 1930s occurred, with its manifold – and charac-
teristically disturbing – effects for a range of economic, political and
social ideas and practices in capitalism, not least those of the colonial
project in Africa and how its inherent contradictions were perceived
and acted on by both colonial rulers and subjects.[7]

The central contradiction of that project for its architects and
engineers – as identified by Phillips (1989), Cowen and Shenton
(1991a, 1991b, 1996: ch. 6), Grischow (1998), among others – was
how to develop commodity production in the African colonies
without generating the social (especially class) divisions and tensions
of (industrial) capitalism in Europe, and moreover to do so within
the political constraints of 'hegemony on a shoestring'. Indirect
rule, together with its comprehensive discursive formations that
naturalized/essentialized African 'culture', 'community' and 'tribe'
within the responsibilities and demands of 'trusteeship' and 'respect'
for native 'custom' and 'tradition', exemplifies this contradiction
very clearly. It was, in vital respects, not only an attempt to exercise
political domination at low cost to imperial exchequers, but also to
prevent, limit or otherwise manage dynamics of class formation, for example
by returning migrant workers to their (ostensibly solidary) tribal
'communities' and the benign patriarchal authority of their chiefs,
and also by preventing chiefs and others (merchants, entrepreneurs,
those acquiring Western education) from emerging as a distinct class
of accumulators. 'Detribalization' was such a potent expression of this
contradiction of the colonial project because it was typically (if not
exclusively) a code word for the formation of a working class, and
above all an urban working class.

Cowen and Shenton (1991a) coined the suggestive term 'Fabian
colonialism' for that set of ideas and practices consolidated by the
1930s, in which the central motif of the colonial project was to 'protect' the natives from the costs of capitalism while gradually allowing
them to share in its benefits. The former required prevention (or
at least postponement *sine die*) of such mixed blessings of bourgeois
civilization as private property rights in land, and ease of access to
commercial credit for African entrepreneurs (Cowen and Shenton

1991b). As well as the responsibilities and demands of prophylactic regulation, the Fabian impulse also sanctioned more proactive interventions to 'advance' Africans as well as 'protect' them. In the 1930s, this was expressed in a number of areas of economic and social policy, including land use planning and environmental conservation, which were to move to centre stage in the postwar moment of 'colonial welfare and development'. Similarly, in this second period, the many expressions of contradictions between the colonial project and its subjects were also carried forward (and developed). These were manifested in the 1930s in the rising activism of African workers and peasant 'strikes' and other actions against the falling crop prices of the Depression decade, but also in a range of less dramatic and overt processes and contestations through which Africans – and different groups of Africans, from labour migrants to chiefly and other emergent accumulators – sought to evade, deflect or otherwise turn to their advantage the institutions, forms and practices of colonial rule with their many ambiguities and tensions.

Late Colonialism, 1940s–1950s

Ideas and practices of economic development, and of the role of government in promoting it, were changed profoundly by the effects of the Depression followed by the Second World War and postwar reconstruction – not just of Europe and Japan and its former colonies in East Asia, but also by the new 'Bretton Woods' institutions established to create and maintain stability in international monetary and trade relations. The central economic role of government in wartime and postwar reconstruction, coupled with booming primary commodity markets in the 1950s and adoption of Keynesian macroeconomic policies, resulted in state-provided or -sponsored investment in physical and social infrastructure and in increasing production. This was true of the metropolitan countries, as well as of the colonies under the rubric of 'colonial welfare and development' on a suitably more modest scale (in terms of imperial expenditure and concern) but still of considerable significance to colonial economies. The crop marketing boards of the Depression years now took on more 'developmental' (rather than simply fiscally extractive) functions, and other parastatals – various forms of development corporations and schemes – were established.

During the 1950s, at least some European colonies in Africa were being 'prepared' for independence through measures to implement reform of their governance. In many British colonies indirect rule through customary authority was partly replaced by belated efforts to institute representative local government in the form of municipal, township and rural councils with legislative powers to discharge specific functions, to raise part or much of their revenue, and to recruit and manage their own staff (Kasfir 1993). The partial and uneven, hence ambiguous, character of such reforms – and the activists they attracted into local (as well as national[ist]) politics (typically younger, better-educated, and/or entrepreneurial men) – often added additional layers of complexity and tension to those of indirect rule and the claims and counter-claims of chiefly authority (which was challenged rather than necessarily extinguished).

The combinations of new economic and political initiatives and discourses in the postwar period were especially marked in relation to agricultural and conservation policies, in ways that qualified but also reproduced aspects of the earlier versions of the colonial project and its antinomies. An important example of this dynamic was the new desire to establish a class of 'progressive' or 'yeoman' African farmers. These 'family' or petty capitalist farmers, typically specialized in the production of higher-value export crops using 'modern' inputs and techniques on government-managed schemes, were to serve as a vanguard of technical modernization and agricultural productivity growth, as exemplars of cultural modernity, and as a force for civic responsibility and social stability following independence. For example, the objective of the Tanganyika Agricultural Corporation, established in 1953, was to promote 'a healthy, prosperous yeoman farmer class, firmly established on the land, appreciative of its fruits, jealous of its inherent wealth, and dedicated to maintaining the family unit on it' (as cited in Cliffe and Cunningham 1973: 134).

This vision, and the means of realizing it, raised difficult issues about 'customary' or 'communal' land tenure: as one of the foundations of indirect rule and chiefly authority (and rural 'stability'), customary tenure was now seen as an obstacle to agricultural modernization/development that required a basis of private property right and incentive (albeit under state supervision). Significantly, perhaps the most important attempt at 'land reform' – land allocation combined with individual title – in the late colonial period was the Swynnerton Plan in Kenya's Central Province in the wake of the armed rebellion of Mau Mau (Kitching 1980; Leo 1984).

The other side of the coin of such agricultural modernization, and linked by growing investment in and attention to agricultural and environmental research, was the growing concern with soil conservation and land use planning. While efforts were made to promote the specialized and modernized production of higher value crops, fertilizer use and mechanization on 'progressive' farmer schemes, this was also the moment when notions of the 'carrying capacity' of particular environments for human and livestock populations were 'operationalized' (the military term 'operations' being a characteristic if not novel feature of the discourses of the time) in settlement and resettlement schemes. Implementing such schemes to establish 'model' small-scale mixed arable and livestock farming units typically involved greater or lesser coercion, such as, for example, in 'betterment' in South Africa (de Wet 1995), the Swynnerton Plan in Kenya (Sorrenson 1967), resettlement in Northern Rhodesia/Zambia (Allan 1965), and *encadrement* by CFDT cotton-growing schemes in francophone West Africa (Raynault et al. 1997). Coercion was particularly pronounced in the least 'developed' colonies where market incentives were lowest and where political compulsion to cash cropping, *corvée* labour, and labour migration continued into the 1950s in the Belgian Congo and the 1960s in Portugal's colonial territories.

Parastatal development corporations and (export) crop promotion, land use planning, and conservation regulations, rudimentary macroeconomic planning and project/scheme state investment and management – the apparatuses and practices of contemporary versions of 'modernization' – were all among the many legacies of late colonialism to the moment of independence. By that moment, generalized commodity production had been established throughout sub-Saharan Africa. That is to say, from initial conditions of 'forcible commercialization', the great majority of Africans now had to pursue their reproduction under the 'dull compulsion of economic forces', in Marx's term. The basic social relations and compulsions of capitalism were internalized in 'peasant' production, in the circuits of (rural) household and 'community', as in the growing urban centres.[8] Moreover, many regions were already characterized by multiple links between farming and other economic practices in the social divisions of labour constituted by commodity relations, such as wage employment and self-employment in non-agricultural commodity production. The demarcation of certain rural areas as 'labour reserves' for agricultural estates, plantations and mines, which they supplied through cyclical labour migration, was well established across quite different regions of sub-Saharan Africa – for example, migration from the Sahelian zones of West Africa to the dynamic petty capitalist export crop production of its forest belts as well as labour migration to the great mining complexes of southern Africa. Hence combinations of 'hoe and wage' (the title of Cordell et al. 1996)[9] were central to the reproduction of many African 'peasantries' by the moment of independence, in some cases from the early colonial period and in many cases beyond the most evident zones of 'labour reserves' like southern Mozambique and South Africa's bantustans.

Independence and Developmentalism, 1960s–1970s[10]

The late colonial model of state-led economic development was largely assimilated by newly independent African governments, albeit reinforced and reconfigured in some cases by aspirations to more comprehensive planning and accumulation and the commitment to 'nation-building' as a political and social project.[11] The outcome was to increase greatly the scale of state investment in both economic and social sectors, and in relation to the former to direct much of it to import-substituting industrialization and major infrastructural projects (in communications, power generation, water) as well as primary production (agriculture, mining, timber), typically through the formation of parastatal companies (in manufacturing, finance and public utilities, agricultural inputs and services). Much of this investment was funded by foreign aid, whose agencies, and not least the World Bank, were also heavily involved in the design – and even the management, through technical assistance – of many of these ambitious ventures of state developmentalism in the initial, and optimistic, period of independence.

The advent of political independence in most of sub-Saharan Africa came at a propitious moment in the world economy, then in its most sustained period ever of rapid growth (the 'golden age' of the postwar long boom).[12] The 1960s saw the largest rate of growth of agricultural exports since the 1920s, and for many African countries this, their first decade of independence, witnessed the strongest period of national economic growth they have experienced since the end of colonial rule (Arrighi 2002). During the 1970s, however, the African version of a fiscal crisis of the state was gathering, exposing the extreme vulnerability of African economies and their peoples within imperialism, which was experienced with increasing intensity as worldwide recession dealt a series of 'external shocks' to African economies (except initially oil exporters and a newly established diamond exporter in the case of Botswana).

As the above implies, independence witnessed a major growth of the state in terms of its economic and social ambitions, its expenditure and share of GDP and employment, and its political and administrative centralization. All these features were considered necessary to, or at least justified by, the demands of 'national development' and 'nation building' after the enforced underdevelopment of colonial rule and exploitation – as were the prevalence of one-party states, in de jure or de facto forms, and the increasingly frequent military coups and regimes, which similarly claimed their legitimacy in the failure of civilian governments to deliver on the promise of development. Where institutions of decentralized government had been promoted, notably in the later years of colonial rule, they were widely perceived after independence as inefficient and conducive to ethnic and regional rivalries subversive of development and nation-building. They were progressively abolished, or otherwise rendered gestural through loss of control of budgets and staff appointments, with the tasks of development now located so strongly in central government and its necessary concentration of resources and expertise (Kasfir 1993). Mamdani (1996) identifies two legacies/outcomes of the late colonial state: what he terms 'conservative' states (e.g. Kenya, Botswana, Nigeria) retained a key place for chiefs (and therefore 'tribal' identity) in the structures of local administration in the countryside, while 'radical' states (Tanzania, Mozambique after 1975, and, to a lesser extent, francophone West African states such as Guinea, Mali and Senegal) abolished customary authorities, but reproduced 'decentralized despotism' through the 'commandist' practices of local cadres, both political and administrative, towards rural subjects (of which the implementation of Tanzania's villagization 'campaigns' – another appropriately military metaphor – in the 1970s can be seen as emblematic).

State-led modernization policies in agriculture continued after independence. In many instances, the scale of intervention increased, particularly in the form of large irrigation projects, state farms, and joint ventures with foreign agribusiness capital. These and similar agricultural development interventions involved increasing appropriations of land, often within a wider constitutional assertion of state land ownership which took over or extended the provisions of colonial government (Francis 1984; Shivji 1994). Otherwise, land tenure remained largely unchanged from the late colonial period. Where colonial government had initiated land titling to establish free-hold tenure (e.g. Kenya), this tended to continue. Where customary tenure was recognized under colonial rule, explicitly or by default, this tended to continue albeit, as indicated above, often as a terrain that was contested due to the pressures on simple reproduction for most (and opportunities for accumulation for some) of deepening commodity relations and associated demographic change, including migration to new farming frontier zones.

In other ways there were significant shifts from colonial antecedents: for example, in a more central emphasis on overcoming rural poverty as a goal of development policies, by raising farm incomes through agricultural schemes and household welfare through social consumption of public/merit goods (clean water, education, health care). Marketing boards and other parastatal corporations, in both export crops and food staples, were often refashioned as proactive agencies of vertical integration along their respective commodity chains, providing everything from inputs, credit and extension services to marketing, storage and distribution of food staples. Modelled on the increasing integration of agriculture in the advanced capitalist countries by agribusiness and food industry capital upstream and downstream of farming (aided by US and EU farm, trade and foreign policies), such institutional expansions were part of a more general strategy of 'modernization' of 'peasant' or 'household' farming premissed on intensifying commoditization, especially in the production of export crops (Bernstein 1981; Raikes 1988). In the initial political conditions of independence, however, there was probably a reduction in interventions in land in the name of environmental regulation and conservation (at least in arable and mixed farming rather than pastoral areas), because they were subordinated to imperatives of agricultural production (and productivity) growth, and because their imposition and policing by colonial states had generated resistance in the countryside that made its own contribution to popular anti-colonialism and the legitimacy of the nationalist parties that demanded independence.

In the 1970s the optimism and aspirations – and indeed some of the achievements, patchy as these were – of the first decade of postcolonial state-led development became subject to increasing strains, partly due to its intrinsic contradictions (analysis of which was pioneered by African socialist intellectuals) and certainly compounded by adverse trends in world markets, and the global economic restructuring and political realignments that followed. This generated a flood of discourse centred on the pathology of African states, hence state-led development, in a moment when environmental themes (degradation, conservation, sustainability) were also reinserted at the centre of concerns, not least because the 1970s added dramatic images of drought and famine in Africa to the ensemble of manifestations of African 'crisis'.

The Era of Structural Adjustment, 1980s to the Present

The ambitious spending plans and commitments of state-led development after independence, combined with the rising costs of oil imports (and other strategic imports) after the OPEC price increases of the 1970s, led to escalating foreign borrowing by African governments (encouraged by European and American banks with vast quantities of petrodollars to lend). The debt that resulted was compounded by recession in industrialized economies with downward pressure on primary commodity prices, reducing the foreign-exchange earnings of many African countries and undermining their ability to service loans, especially as real interest rates increased. The incidence of major droughts in many parts of Africa exacerbated foreign-exchange shortages by increasing the need for food imports (Raikes 1988). In a growing number of countries (Ethiopia, Somalia, Sudan, Angola, Mozambique, Rwanda, Zaire/Congo, Liberia, Sierra Leone) these pressures were dramatically aggravated by warfare. Through combinations of these factors, virtually every country on the continent entered into negotiations with international financial institutions (the IMF and the World Bank) to seek debt rescheduling and other financial support in return for adopting and implementing 'structural adjustment' policies and pursuing their advantage in globalizing commodity and financial markets.[13]

The price for such support was the introduction of comprehensive (if unevenly implemented) 'structural adjustment' reforms in economic policy (macroeconomic and microeconomic), social policy and public institutions. The main lines of such reforms are well known. The first phase of structural adjustment lending (SAL) emphasized 'rolling back the state' in order to 'get the prices right' – that is, to allow 'the market' (or market mechanism) to do its job of achieving allocative efficiency by removing the myriad sources of price 'distortion' resulting from government intervention. At the macroeconomic level, this centred first and foremost on devaluation (overvalued exchange rates were held to be the principal bias favouring imports, and importers, against the producers of export goods, notably the agricultural sector), combined with internal and external trade liberalization, sharp reductions in public spending (and employment), the privatization of state-owned industries and services, and so on. A second phase of SAL, added to the first a concern with 'capacity building' of government/public institutions, when it was appreciated that restoring economic growth and welfare in Africa required states that were not only 'leaner' but more efficient. A more generalized discourse of 'good governance' is incorporated in what may or may not be a third phase of SAL, informed by what is claimed (and contested) as a 'post-Washington consensus', marking the demise (modification?) of earlier more virulent (and triumphalist) neoliberal ideas (see Fine et al. 2001).

The general thrust of SAL concerning agriculture is, of course, to encourage agricultural exports in line with the 'comparative advantage' of African economies (and their resource and factor endowments) in international trade, so as to revive the engine of economic growth and restore and maintain macroeconomic stability (Bernstein 1990, Gibbon 1992). This is to be achieved, as appropriate, by the rehabilitation of historic export crops (whose production had deteriorated in the 1970s and 1980s) and/or the promotion of (relatively) high-value 'non-traditional' exports aimed at global niche markets – typically horticultural products, including cut flowers and ornamental plants, usually grown through contract farming arrangements and requiring highly organized and efficient marketing (Little and Watts 1994; Raikes and Gibbon 2000; Daviron and Gibbon 2002).[14] Some of the conditions (and constraints) of this (intensified) agricultural export drive in contemporary globalization, as well as its modalities and effects, are sketched in Chapter 1 of this volume.

Juxtaposed (rather than integrated) with this 'export platform' strategy (Friedmann 1993) of agricultural revival and productivity and income growth, is the concern with environmental degrada-tion and conservation, which resumed a centrality from the 1980s comparable with that of the 1930s to 1950s, now also linked with discourses of food security, rural poverty and livelihoods. The on-set of prolonged drought in the Sahel in the 1970s and elsewhere (northeast Africa in the 1970s and 1980s, southern Africa in the early 1980s and again in the early 1990s) revived colonial perceptions of African land users as agents of environmental destruction. While alternative interpretations linked Sahelian destitution to patterns of commoditization which drove expansion of arable cultivation into more drought-prone areas (see, for example, Franke and Chasin 1980), these were largely overshadowed by the dominance of the neo-Malthusian narrative in much European and North American environmental thought: that increasing poverty and recurrent fam-ine crises in rural Africa are linked to declining productivity of the biophysical resource base (land, vegetation, water), a process of 'degradation' (of which 'desertification' is emblematic) generated by population pressure on fragile ecologies.

The environmental view of rural crisis – from the Sahelian droughts of the 1970s to subsequent crop failures in Ethiopia and southern Africa – as the consequence of overcultivation and degrada-tion of 'fragile ecosystems' by rapidly increasing and poverty-stricken rural populations, has returned as a central and potent element in the symptomatology of Africa's miseries. While variants of this narrative also attribute blame to incompetent or predatory African governments that exacerbate rural poverty through distorting agri-cultural markets, the essential neo-Malthusian paradigm persists in the rhetoric of international development agencies. Thus the World Bank (1996: 22–5) characterizes as 'shifting cultivation' farming in the Sudano-Sahelian region, where 'one of the most rapid annual population growth rates of the continent ... has resulted in a down-ward spiral of extensive land degradation and fuelwood shortage ... increased water scarcity, and loss of natural habitats.' Similarly, the International Fund for Agricultural Development (IFAD 1994: 10) refers to 'a vicious cycle of negative synergies' in which, 'Unable to increase yields, increasing numbers of poor people put pressure on the environment – mining soils, destroying forests, and depleting wildlife stocks.... And because the poor tend to have high fertility rates ... population growth rates remain elevated and the destructive cycle recommences.'[15]

The enduring and compound 'crisis' of sub-Saharan Africa today – of 'development', of poverty and social security, and of governance, punctuated by wars and the ravages of HIV/AIDS, and compounded by ecological 'disaster' – makes it virtually an ideological 'free fire' zone for a spectrum of diagnoses and prognoses which converge in explaining crisis by problems internal to Africa, whether the environmentally destructive practices of its rural poor (just cited), the rapacity of its 'neo-patrimonial states' (van der Walle 2001), or through the recycling of what may be called 'primordial' narratives of African 'exceptionalism' (of colonial provenance): that is, the root problem of Africa is its African-ness (e.g. Hyden 1983; Chabal and Daloz 1999). Having sketched these aspects of the broader context, the next step is to consider in closer focus (albeit still in general terms) aspects of farming and livelihoods/reproduction, and the place in them of access to land, in the current conjuncture of structural adjustment and globalization.

Labour and Land, Reproduction and Class

The late Phil Raikes observed (2000) that in an important sense there is no 'African agriculture' but a range of agricultures (far greater than in Europe) defined not only by the environmental conditions and technologies of farming but also by the social relations and forms of its organization, and its contributions to livelihoods: the reproduction of labour. The patterns and contradictions of change concerning labour, land and reproduction in modern African history, with all their specificities of time and place, defy any simple empirical generalization. To acknowledge this is not to surrender to the ethnographic particularism favoured by (some) anthropologists or historians but to avoid overly schematic notions of a common – and uniform – African syndrome.[16] The purpose, rather, should be to identify 'general themes' from which specific histories create 'complex variations' – to adapt a term formulated in another context by Gilsenan (1982: 51). The general themes of concern here are processes of commoditization, of deteriorating macroeconomic conditions including those of labour markets, and of mounting pressures on social reproduction combined with growing social inequality, in the current period of globalization and structural adjustment. Their complex variations include differences in how they are experienced and in the forms of social struggle that individual and collective responses to them generate.[17]

One generalization that can be made with confidence, however, is that poverty and insecurity have increased, and standards of well-being have declined, for the great majority of Africa's people in recent decades. This is the effect of deteriorating conditions of reproduction through both farming and wage labour, and the many ways they are combined, as well as widespread decline in the provision of such public goods as health care and education (however inadequate it was previously), especially in rural areas.[18] At least half of the countries of sub-Saharan Africa recorded lower volumes of agricultural exports in the late 1990s than they had in the 1970s (Sender 2002: 191). The pressures on export crop production include, in varying measure, aspects of change in world market conditions (including systemic overproduction of many tropical export crops); the reorganization of global commodity chains and a general, if not uniform, shift from 'seller-' to 'buyer-driven' chains in processes of globalization (from deregulated financial markets to new processing and transport technologies, from food standard regulation to the sourcing and branding strategies of increasingly concentrated food industry corporations); and the effects of structural adjustment, specifically privatization and liberalization, on the conditions of agricultural production (for example, the significant drop in fertilizer use by small farmers) and trade (deterioration of rural transport infrastructure), hence on the quantities and qualities of crops delivered for export – which are also affected, of course, by the adverse price and income effects of the globalizing (world market) tendencies noted.[19]

On the other hand, it is reasonable to conclude that (aggregate) food production has done much better. Although food production data for sub-Saharan Africa are notoriously unreliable, they are more likely to be under- than over-estimated for various reasons, both technical and political (Berry 1984; Raikes 1988; Wiggins 2000; Sender 2002), including their gender biases (Guyer 1983). Many rural areas close(r) to centres of (growing) urban demand have seen shifts from export crops – with their typically annual one-off payments after harvest, and declining returns – to food crop production, stimulated also by the attractions of what Ponte terms 'fast crops' that help meet 'the increasing need for larger amounts and more regular supplies of cash' (2002: 122). He also shows how shifts to 'fast crops' can lead to new forms of labour hiring contracts and arrangements (2002: ch. 7).

Deborah Bryceson (1998: 185) notes the 'fundamental problem' (exacerbated, if not solely caused, by structural adjustment) of 'African peasant agriculture's inability to compete in today's global market', as a component of her broader thesis of 'deagrarianization' (Bryceson 1996) or 'depeasantization' (Bryceson 1998), manifested in the growing proportion of rural incomes 'derived from non-farm sources' (Bryceson 1998: 172).[20] At the same time – and this is a second generalization, or at least a 'general theme' with its attendant variations – there is a kind of scissors effect at work for those in rural Africa whose reproduction is secured from combinations of own farming and off-farm wage and self-employment, including the many whose off-farm income has been essential, historically, to meeting the entry and reproduction costs of their farming enterprises. That is, 'the shrinkage of the peasant sector', as Bryceson calls it, occurs alongside the collapse of real wages (and employment opportunities) in the formal sector.[21] The latter, then, exerts additional pressure on the reproduction of farming (and through farming), and hence intensifies the pursuit of means of livelihood both on and off the land. Bryceson suggests that one manifestation of this generalized 'scramble for cash' (also noted by Ponte) is new localized markets for goods and services. Moreover, these new branches of rural economic activity entail changes in the gender, generational and (other) familial relations through which household farming was organized – for example, towards greater individualization of economic activity as well as towards class differentiation.

A third empirical generalization is that Africa's economic crisis is so encompassing that it includes many of the professional petty bourgeoisie that proliferated after independence, and especially those in state employment. This then links to an associated general theme (again with many complex variations in practice): that when commodity relations and dynamics are internalized in the social functioning of even the most remote countrysides, as in contemporary Africa, economic and social crisis generates opportunities (of expanded reproduction or accumulation) for some, as well as new pressures (on simple reproduction) for many. This points to the terrain of social (class and other) inequality, which, in the conditions of Africa today, requires attention (as always) to the dynamics and tendencies of class (and other) differentiation among 'peasants' (Bernstein 2000, 2004) but also among 'worker-peasants' (semi-proletarians; see Bernstein 2003, 2004) and large sections of the petty bourgeoisie indicated, including how their various individual and collective struggles for both 'survival' and advantage intersect in particular instances and with what effects. Concerning farming, a fairly mainstream agricultural economist observes:

> if access to markets were much or all of the story, then all farmers in any given locality should be able to benefit. But do they? Social differentiation among the peasantry is no longer a fashionable area of inquiry, so case studies published during the last decade tend to be weak on such differences. What is reported, though, confirms our worst fears: differences are substantial. When and where farm economies blossom, it seems that the great bulk of the marketed surplus comes from a small fraction of the farmers. (Wiggins 2000: 638)

In short, the 'crisis of African agriculture' – in terms of production (and productivity), income, contributions to reproduction, and any possibility of profit – is not distributed equally across the social groups that farm or otherwise have an interest in farming and access to land. Some of those with recognized claims on land are otherwise too poor to farm: they lack capital (to secure inputs), command over labour through the social relations of kinship (typically mediated by patriarchal relations of gender and generation) or market, and/or access to credit (that is affordable and timely). This registers an important qualification to persistent notions that 'most people in rural areas have access to land, and are therefore able to cultivate on their own account' (Berry 1993: 135). The second observation does *not* necessarily follow from the first, for the reason given, and is likely to lead to systematic underestimation of those who are unable to farm on their own account (or to do so to any significant extent) in many rural areas.[22] On the other hand, those able to reproduce relatively robust agricultural petty commodity enterprises, and *a fortiori* to expand the scale of their farming, typically do so with reproduction/investment funds derived from wage employment (and also from trade and transport), as Wiggins (2000) further notes. Indeed, sophisticated analyses of 'worker-peasant' trajectories in Southern Africa – by, among others, First (1983) on Mozambique; Bush and Cliffe (1984) and Cousins et al. (1992) on Zimbabwe; and Levin and Neocosomos (1989) on South Africa – suggest that differential labour market conditions and earnings from wage employment at different times can feed the differentiation of 'peasant' farming (petty commodity and petty capitalist production) in the rural areas to which labour migrants return.

And, indeed, even the first part of Berry's generalization is problematic, as there is growing evidence of shortages of arable land
(and often grazing land), especially in areas of better soils and/or
transport links to urban markets, due to a combination of population
pressure (see note 15 above) and patterns of commoditization. And,
perversely, commoditization – including the need for greater and
more continuous money income noted by Bryceson and Ponte – is
intensified by the sustained decline in macroeconomic conditions (the
combined effect of globalization and structural adjustment policies),
and the scissors effect of pressures on both farming and non-farm
employment and income opportunities, in short on reproduction.
A wide range of recent evidence concerning competition for land,
and the conflicts it generates, is presented by Pauline Peters (2004),
who concludes that such competition and conflict are permeated
by increasing social inequality and class formation:

> competition over land for different purposes intensifies due to growing
> populations and movements of people looking for better/more land
> or fleeing civil disturbances; rural groups seek to intensify commod-
> ity production and food production while retrenched members of a
> downsized salariat look for land to improve food and income options;
> states demarcate forestry and other reserves, and identify areas worthy of
> conservation (often under pressure from donors and international lob-
> bying groups); representatives of the state and political elites appropriate
> land through means ranging from the questionable to the illegal; and
> valuable resources both on and under the land (timber, oil, gold, other
> minerals) attract intensifying exploitation by agents from the most local
> (unemployed youth or erstwhile farmers seeking ways to obtain cash) to
> transnational networks (of multinational corporations, foreign governments
> and representatives of African states).... [There is] not only intensifying
> competition over land but deepening social differentiation and, though
> this differentiation takes many forms – including youth against elders, men
> against women, ethnic and religious confrontations – these also reveal
> new social divisions that, in sum, can be seen as class formation...The
> proliferating tensions and struggles between generations and genders, or
> between groups labelled by region, ethnicity or religion, are intimately
> tied up with the dynamics of division and exclusion, alliance and inclu-
> sion that constitute class formation. (Peters 2004: 279, 291, 305)

Politics of Land

The complex variations of the politics of land include differences in
how Africa's development crisis is experienced and in the forms of
social struggle that individual and collective responses to it gener-

ate, as noted above. The range of variation, as well as its complexity, extends from contestations of land in many rural areas around highly localized claims and counter-claims of 'community' (and 'ethnic') origins and rights, and their tensions of patriarchy and generation, to Zimbabwe's highly contradictory 'fast track resettlement' since early 2000 – the 'only case of sweeping, regime-sanctioned confiscatory land redistribution in the world today' (Bernstein 2003: 37). In Chapter 1, and from a Zimbabwean perspective, Moyo and Yeros write of Africa's zones of peasant farming that:

> While within communal areas questions of race and landlordism [as in South Africa and Zimbabwe] may not pertain, the issues that do pertain are potent: insecurity of tenure, land subdivision, and informal land markets; land alienation and concentration, combined with externally determined land use changes; and undemocratic systems of local government to adjudicate and administer land disputes.

The issues they highlight connect with those surveyed by Peters (as quoted above); at the same time, they are recognizable as the effects of the 'colonial and postcolonial integration into generalized commodity production' that Moyo and Yeros indicate, and that I have also argued (while emphasizing its many specific historical trajectories and forms in sub-Saharan Africa). This now needs some further elaboration. First, and to reiterate, generalized commodity production is now *internalized* in the social relations and circuits of farming and labour in Africa, hence necessarily generates the class dynamics Peters points to. The implication is that Africa's crisis can not be attributed exclusively to a (malign) 'exterior'.[23]

Second, however – as Peters also suggests – those class dynamics usually do not take the phenomenal form of self-evident class entities and practices. One reason for this is the absence in most of Africa of landed property on a scale, and of a historical and social depth, familiar from much Latin American and Asian history (and that of southern Africa), as Moyo and Yeros acknowledge, and, on the other hand, the continuing prevalence (if not universality) of some degree of farming to the reproduction of labour in the absence of generalized dispossession of land (a point also observed by Peters).

Another type of reason is that the dynamics of generalized commodity production, including their internalization in a wide range of forms of agricultural petty commodity production, generate tensions and struggles in African countrysides that are experienced and fought over, not as 'pure' class divisions but 'between generations

between groups labelled by region, ethnicity or
quoted above). This is part of the legacy of the
tion, and connection, of 'tribal' identity, 'customary'
(patriarchal) political authority, which serve as the
idioms through which class tensions may be played out as 'civil war
within the tribe' (Mamdani 1996), as well as in struggles between
(cross-class) corporate entities – ethnic group, clan, rural 'community' – over resources of arable and grazing land, water and forest.
Moreover, such struggles are typically articulated by those claiming
the political legitimacy of 'tradition' to represent the interests of their
clan or 'community', and who themselves may be drawn from, or
in alliance with, elements of the urban (based) petty bourgeoisie,
whose interest in rural land has been intensified by their own crises
of reproduction, as noted earlier.

Third, there is little experience in modern African history of
popular rural political *organization* on a broader scale centred on
agrarian and land issues, again by contrast with Latin America and
Asia with their histories (subject to their own 'complex variations')
of rural social movements, and peasant leagues, unions and other
forms of organization, *and* agricultural workers' associations and
struggles – both those that are (relatively) autonomous and those
allied with, or organized by, socialist and communist parties. It was
indicated above (in note 10) that armed struggle with a rural base
was an important feature of the politics of liberation in the territories
of Portugal (and its 'backward' colonialism) in the 1960s and 1970s,
and in (other) settler colonies, notably Kenya in the 1950s and later
Rhodesia/Zimbabwe. Today, and more generally, in 'peasant' Africa
(that of the *économie de traite*) – apart from full-scale 'ethnic wars',
in which land is often a significant issue[24] – the most overt, and
occasionally violent, confrontations over land manifest the resistance
of clan and 'community' to large-scale dispossession, typically by the
state and in the name of major (typically donor-funded) 'development' projects (irrigation schemes, state farms or joint ventures
with agribusiness, mining and/or forestry). As such, they are both
principally *defensive* actions and unlikely to have any unambiguous
class composition and orientation, let alone ideology and broader
social programme, which is not to deny their importance (or indeed
limits) as popular-democratic struggles.

In sum, tensions and conflicts over land driven by the kinds of
general processes outlined, involving a range of social actors and

individual and collective practices, and marked by often strongly local features – complex variations of time and place – are widespread in Africa's countrysides, and appear to be intensifying, as Peters convincingly argues. At the same time, the underlying class dynamics of these tensions and conflicts are not manifested in evident formations of class organization, ideology and political practice. Here, as elsewhere, this provides ample ideological space for populist advocacy of 'community' rights and of the struggles of that amorphous category, the 'rural poor'. To drive this (contentious) point further, let me finish by suggesting – in the form of some summary observations – that a number of the issues indicated are also key to understanding the dialectics of the unique *offensive* against (capitalist) landed property in Zimbabwe.[25]

First, many of the dynamics, contradictions and tensions of the emergence and reproduction of generalized commodity production in Africa's zones of 'peasant' farming, including its tendencies to class differentiation, are also found in the historic 'communal areas' of Zimbabwe. Discourses of 'squatting' on land subject to competing claims, and associated practices of eviction, are not confined to (white) landed property but are also widespread in (black) communal area lands (e.g. Hammar 2001; Nyambara 2001).

Second, the 'invasions' of (mostly) white-owned farms from late February 2000 (subsequently termed 'fast-track resettlement' in official parlance) were initially led by the peculiar political formation of the Zimbabwe National Liberation War Veterans' Association (ZNWLVA), in many cases in association (in some cases overlapping) with officials and activists of the ruling political party ZANU–PF and supported by elements of the police and army (Marongwe 2003). Following a history of more local politics of contestation and occupation of large landed property since independence (in some instances followed by state repression and eviction), and in the midst of an accelerating economic and political crisis, the ZANU–PF regime – after two decades of vacillation and inconsistency on the land question – finally sanctioned 'fast-track resttlement'. In an early review of the various instances, locations, timings and agents of land occupation during the upsurge of 2000, Moyo (2001) acknowledged its 'numerous localized and contradictory waves'; the great range of actors involved, with a focus on the actual or aspiring 'leadership' of party politicians, state officials, war veterans and chiefs, acting in concert with or independently of national directives from ZNLWA and ZANU–PF; and the heterogeneous social mix of participants, from rural 'communities' to members of the urban middle class, and – as many observed – the militias of unemployed youth, urban and rural, mobilized by ZANU–PF.

Third, there is no reason to doubt that popular political energies – those of what I have called elsewhere the agrarian question of labour (Bernstein 2004) – were mobilized in Zimbabwe's land invasions, but it should be just as clear that they constituted *only one element* of the class forces in this massive redistribution of land. The 'contradictory waves' (Moyo) of 'fast-track resettlement' also included further land grabbing by the state class and (black) bourgeois elements (which already possessed nearly 20 per cent of large landed properties) as well as many of the petty bourgeoisie, both urban and rural. Exactly who got what land, where, and with what kind of effective possession, remains to be clarified with any precision. Farm workers (on whom more below) and others who are members or supporters of the opposition Movement for Democratic Change, or were accused of being so, lost out on redistributed land (Sachikonye 2003; Marongwe 2003). Otherwise, one suspects that those rural (and urban) social groups that lack political clout and/or connections (for example, through local and wider relations of patronage) did relatively less well out of the redistribution, and not least (poorer) women farmers.

Fourth, the immediate effects of land redistribution have been fairly disastrous for production and for employment, albeit subject – as ever – to considerable local variation. At the end of the 1990s there were an estimated 320,000 to 350,000 wage workers on Zimbabwe's large capitalist farms. Together with 1.8 to 2 million other family members, they accounted for about 20 per cent of the country's population, proportionally by far the largest agricultural proletariat in sub-Saharan Africa, whose position and interests in the country's class structure have been almost completely ignored in critical scholarship and political analysis.[26] By the beginning of 2003, only about 100,000 farm workers were still employed (Sachikonye 2003: 5) and the vast majority of those who had lost their jobs had not gained land either, as noted above.

Fifth, land redistribution, especially in the mostly chaotic fashion in which it occurred in Zimbabwe, is not the same as the immediate (re)settlement of farmers, nor resettlement as the immediate commencement of farming, let alone at a level that first replaces and then expands production on land redistributed. This is the nub of land redistribution as a development strategy. In this respect, Zimbabwe is highly distinctive. On one hand, the dominant thrust of radical land reforms in the modern world has been to abolish predatory, pre-capitalist landed property as an essential aspect of transitions to capitalism (Bernstein 2002, 2004). In this case, the prospect − and much of the actuality, according to various reports − is the dismantling of large-scale production, including many well-established and successful capitalist farms, with the immediate effect of the losses of output and employment noted. On the other hand, significant examples of the confiscation of large-scale capitalist landed property in recent time have featured its nationalization or socialization in one form or another (for example, Cuba and Nicaragua) rather than its replacement by small-scale ('peasant') farming.

Yeros (2002: 12−13) puts the case for land redistribution qua development strategy in Zimbabwe as 'an historic opportunity to break the inherited structure of the home market'. However, he acknowledges that this is not sufficient: the widening of the home market also needs state support to build the infrastructure for 'dynamic accumulation ... in the smallholder sector'. He is right about this, and thereby returns us from the distinctive feature (uniqueness?) of Zimbabwe's land reform − the dismantling of large-scale capitalist farming − to issues already indicated in the discussion above of the dynamics and effects of generalized commodity production in Africa's countrysides.[27] That discussion suggests that it is difficult to imagine how 'dynamic accumulation', including by 'smallholders', can occur without rural labour markets, which means class differentiation. Moreover, in the absence of adequate state support to enable farmers to settle on land they have been allocated, and to establish viable farms there − the case so far in Zimbabwe − many will remain too poor to farm, thereby accentuating tendencies to differentiation. Only richer peasant or 'worker-peasant' households (as well as some of the urban and rural petty bourgeoisie) can command the resources (capital) to establish production on new and/or additional and/or better land acquired through redistribution.

Conclusion

The purpose of the above observations is not to deny the significance of land redistribution in Zimbabwe as an aspect of its national democratic revolution, but to draw attention to some of its deeply contradictory aspects – including those it shares with more typically localized land struggles elsewhere in Africa of similarly democratic potential, albeit in very different social conditions. Those latter struggles often remain hidden from the gaze of outside observers and analysts, and when recognized are often misunderstood for reasons noted: in the absence of entrenched landed property and generalized dispossession of small(er) producers, and lacking the forms of class expression more evident elsewhere, their underlying class dynamics are neglected or denied. Facilitating such neglect or denial is the stark contrast between Africa's 'peasant' zones and countries of settler colonial provenance, above all South Africa and Zimbabwe, in whose histories the establishment and formation of racialized landed property has been so definitive. This effect is also facilitated by the absence in 'peasant' Africa of wider political movements based on land conflicts, with the kinds of historical lineages, forms of organization, and programmatic ideologies found in Latin America and Asia.

Nonetheless, it is increasingly untenable to ignore the proliferating tensions and conflicts over land in sub-Saharan Africa today in the context of a generalized crisis of reproduction, however varied, complex and contradictory the social forces and forms of struggles over land may be. Extrapolating from my observations about land redistribution in Zimbabwe, I would say that the agrarian question of labour is usually one element of those social forces and struggles. To the extent that it may become – and be articulated as – a leading element, then the significance and effects of land struggles will make their own stronger and clearer contributions to a broader democratic politics.[28]

Notes

1. The following account utilizes, and in parts draws upon, the periodization proposed and sketched in Bernstein and Woodhouse 2001. Relatively more space is devoted here to this first phase of colonialism, when many of the processes of change, which are of continuing significance to this day, were established.

2. This is not to ignore the far longer history of involvement of many African societies and economies with international patterns of exchange and power, most notoriously the Atlantic and Indian Ocean slave trades. In this chapter, and for sake of convenience, 'Africa' and 'African' refer to sub-Saharan Africa only.

3. As Amin explained (1976: 329), 'The concept of the *économie de traite* has

often been used as a mere description of the exchange of agricultural products for imported manufactured goods: actually, it describes analytically the exchange of agricultural commodities provided by a peripheral society, shaped in this way, for the products of a central capitalist industry, either imported or produced on the spot by European enterprises.'

4. When its agents include the militaries of neighbouring countries (Rwanda, Uganda, Zimbabwe).

5. For example, Sukumaland in colonial Tanganyika (now Tanzania) ceased to be a major source of labour migration to the country's sisal plantations once cotton was established there as a viable peasant cash crop.

6. Mamdani's (1996) aspiration to a non-reductive account of political domination in colonial Africa resulted in a sharp distinction between the 'labour question' (exploitation by colonial capitalism) and the 'native question' (oppression by the colonial state). Some critics consider that the distinction was drawn too sharply: it is one thing to avoid a reductionist (economistic) account of the political, another to leave the economic and political forever separate (see O'Laughlin 2000).

7. By the 1930s, the capitalist world economy was in a phase of 'deglobalization', as Desai (2002) terms it; that is, through (political) barriers to the international mobility of commodities, money and people that had not existed in the 'golden age' that ended in 1914. Needless to say, the effects of the Depression intensified the efforts of the European powers to achieve higher levels of extraction of economic and fiscal benefit from their African colonies.

8. The theoretical rationale for this observation has never been better explained than in the seminal paper by Gibbon and Neocosmos (1985), who also make clear the critical misconceptions of investigations of capitalism in the imperialist periphery that fail to find it, or labels its forms of commodity relations less than 'fully' or 'properly' capitalist because they do not replicate those of an ideal-typified (or 'stereotypical', in Lenin's term) 'advanced' capitalism.

9. This provided the principal object of much of the theorization of the 'articulation of modes of production' in the African context, and was anticipated by a South African communist, D.I. Jones, in 1921: 'This, then, is the function of the native territories, to serve as cheap breeding grounds for black labour – the repositories of the reserve army of native labour – sucking it in or letting it out according to the demands of industry. By means of those territories capital is relieved of the obligation of paying wages to cover the cost to the labourer of reproducing his kind', as quoted by Legassick and Wolpe (1976: 87).

10. Most of sub-Saharan Africa achieved political independence in a short space of time from the late 1950s to the mid-1960s. It is striking that the principal exceptions were in Central and Southern Africa in countries with extensive landed property of (white) settler origin (dates of independence/liberation in parentheses): Angola and Mozambique (1975), Zimbabwe (1980), Namibia (1990), and finally South Africa itself (1994, following the transition from 1990). In all these cases (as in Portugal's other major colony, Guinea Bissau in West Africa), armed struggle played a role in liberation, unlike the earlier wave of decolonization in sub-Saharan Africa apart from the insurrection of Mau Mau (the Land and Freedom Army) in Kenya in the 1950s.

11. Cooper (2002, especially ch. 5) argues that the continuities of the (statist) 'developmental' project were more significant in certain respects than the political moment of rupture from colonial rule to independence.

12. This was also the 'golden age of *national* capitalism' (Desai 2002: ch. 14) – centred in the USA, western Europe, and increasingly Japan and East Asia more widely – before such 'national capitalism(s)' gave way to an accelerating (second) wave of globalization from the 1980s, catalysed by the profound international recession of the 1970s. On parallel lines, Friedmann (1993) provides a seminal analysis,of the 'international food regime' under the hegemony of a unique 'national agriculture', that of the USA, until the early 1970s: how that hegemony (and its relative stability) was undermined by the formation of rival 'national agricultures' that emulated the US model (of an agribusiness–state alliance), and how agribusiness corporations have since increasingly globalized their strategies and business practices.

13. Desai, who believes in the benefits as well as the inevitability of globalization, comments that the 'IMF's pretensions to omniscience would have been farcical if their consequences had not been so tragic' (2002: 286); similarly Stiglitz 2002.

14. Drugs may be among the most dynamic and important of Africa's current 'non-traditional' exports (marijuana/cannabis) and re-exports (heroin, cocaine) in the brave new world of contemporary 'globalization' (Bernstein 1999).

15. This is not to deny the importance of demographic change. On one hand, Malthusian views are pervasive, and typically reactionary in purpose and/or effect (Ross 1998); on the other hand, there is a strong counter-Malthusian narrative in studies of Africa, which contains rather mixed blessings. Boserup (1965) is a classic source of counter-Malthusian argument applied to the development of agriculture, in which a historically sparsely populated Africa is seen as the exemplar of 'female-centred' farming systems. Of a quite different ideological slant is Tiffen et al. (1994), which merges a kind of natalism with a belief in the virtues of markets, on which see the critical commentary of Murton (1999). The main point is that patterns of population growth – *and* distribution, given the marked mobility of African rural producers historically and today – and their effects, in conditions of specific social relations and dynamics (themselves key to demographic change), are central to any properly materialist analysis.

16. Including any such notions with a different (positive) ideological content and purpose to the (negative) examples given above; for example, Samir Amin's notion of 'the unity of Africa's personality' (1976: 318).

17. On 'complex variation', A. Sivanandan (1990: 8) describes how his experience of different places where he grew up, studied and worked in Ceylon/Sri Lanka later helped him 'see how it was that British and other colonialisms had impacted on our country at different historical periods, on different parts of the country, in many different ways, and thrown up such diverse social formations', and, he continues, 'left us underdeveloped in different ways and shored up the differences between the peoples of our country which then became defined in ethnic or racial terms'. Both his points – the diversity of social formations and the processes through which difference becomes defined in ethnic terms – are highly relevant to the consideration of land questions, as of other social questions, in contemporary Africa.

18. See van der Walle 2001: ch. 2 for a useful overview of patterns of public expenditure under structural adjustment.

19. Friis-Hansen 2000 is a useful overview and discussion of the effects of structural adjustment for agriculture in sub-Saharan Africa; Raikes and Gibbon (2000) provided an analytically and empirically nuanced account of global commodity chains and African export agriculture, aspects of which are further developed in Daviron and Gibbon (2002) with a particular focus on how structural adjustment has affected the marketing of export crops within producer countries.

20. For these non-farm sources, she gives a crude average (across regional and household variations) of about 40 per cent. The village surveys conducted by Ponte (2002: ch. 8) in Tanzania in 1994/5 gave results of over 52 per cent and 68 per cent of off-farm income in total rural household income in Songea and Morogoro Rural Districts, respectively. My hunch is that even Bryceson's crude average is likely to be an underestimate. As Francis (2000) and Peters (2004) rightly emphasize, 'diversification' of income sources for farmers in Africa is hardly novel, but has undoubtedly increased, taken new forms, and is pursued with intensifying desperation by many, in today's conditions. From the other direction, as it were, Cousins (1996), Ferguson (1999), Nyambara (2000), and O'Laughlin (1998), among others, illustrate some of the effects for rural economies of the quest for land and farming opportunities by workers retrenched from mining and manufacturing industry in South Africa, Zambia, Zimbabwe and Botswana, respectively.

21. Bryceson also refers to 'the meaninglessness of an informal sector without a formal sector contrast' (1998: 186). It is certainly the case that to the extent the 'informal sector' has a part to play in processes of accumulation and economic growth, this is through its symbiotic links with the development of large-scale industry via subcontracting, service and repair, reducing the cost of wage goods, and so on, which has featured much less in sub-Saharan Africa's economic history, even before the current crisis, than in Latin America, or much of Asia (Meagher 1995).

22. This is analogous to the Maasai notion that 'the poor are not us' – that is, those without cattle in a pastoralist society become by definition non-pastoralists; see Anderson and Broch-Due 1999, which contains useful studies that trace patterns of commoditization and differentiation affecting pastoral groups in East Africa.

23. Even while African economies and producers are especially vulnerable to the effects of globalization, such ideological inversion may be understandable in the light of the extremely negative images of African crisis and its attribution to deficiencies intrinsic to 'Africa', noted earlier, but distracts from, rather than contributes to, the demands of analysing the realities of that crisis. An example of a similar (and connected) 'mirror image' effect of ideological inversion was given in note 16 above.

24. Not least in the horrific example of the genocide in Rwanda. However – and it is a major 'however' – proper understanding of the events in Rwanda involves both the origins of tensions over land in pre-colonial processes of state building and its contestations (Pottier 2002) and a specifically political analysis of the state and its formation (Mamdani 2001). Massive pressures on land and

reproduction, exacerbated by declining world market prices for principal export commodities (coffee in the case of Rwanda) and World Bank structural adjustment policies – conditions that are widespread in Africa – are not sufficient to explain what happened in Rwanda. The 'translation' of such 'social facts' into (different kinds of) 'political facts' always requires another mode of analysis (Mamdani 1996).

25. I draw here on the fuller discussion of Zimbabwe in Bernstein 2004.

26. The exception in critical scholarship is the work of Blair Rutherford (e.g. 2001a, 2001b). Tandon 2001 is the only example I have found that addresses directly this manifest failure of political analysis and vision in consideration of the land question in Zimbabwe – a failure comparable in its seriousness to that in South Africa in the 1980s concerning the exclusion of, and hostility to, migrant workers (especially those from the then KwaZulu) whose hostels then became bases for systematic violence against adjacent townships organized by the ANC and UDF (United Democratic Front); see Mamdani 1996: ch. 7, also Morris and Hindson 1992.

27. As well as to the concerns of the 'classic' agrarian question, and (re-) interpretation of them in the conditions of 'disarticulated accumulation', 'functional dualism' etc., in peripheral social formations, as summarized in Chapter 1 of this collection.

28. Cousins (forthcoming) provides a systematic discussion of the land question in relation to democracy across the southern African region.

References

Allan, William (1965), *The African Husbandman*, London: Oliver & Boyd.

Amin, Samir (1976), *Unequal Development: An Essay on the Social Formations of Peripheral Capitalism*, Hassocks: Harvester.

Anderson, David M. (1984), 'Depression, Dust Bowl, Demography and Drought: The Colonial State and Soil Conservation in East Africa during the 1930s', *African Affairs* 83: 321–43.

Anderson, David M. (2002), *Eroding the Commons: The Politics of Ecology in Baringo, Kenya 1892–1963*, Oxford: James Currey.

Anderson, David M., and Richard Grove (1987), 'The Scramble for Eden: Past, Present and Future in African Conservation', in *Conservation in Africa: People, Policies and Practice*, ed. D.M. Anderson and R. Grove, Cambridge: Cambridge University Press.

Anderson, David M., and Vigdis Broch-Due, eds (1999), *The Poor Are Not Us: Poverty and Pastoralism in Eastern Africa*, Oxford: James Currey.

Arrighi, Giovanni (2002), 'The African Crisis: World Systemic and Regional Aspects', *New Left Review* II(15): 5–36.

Bernstein, Henry (1981), 'Notes on State and Peasantry', *Review of African Political Economy* 21: 44–62.

Bernstein, Henry (1990), 'Agricultural "Modernisation" and the Era of Structural Adjustment: Observations on Sub-Saharan Africa', *Journal of Peasant Studies* 18(1): 3–35.

Bernstein, Henry (1999), 'Ghana's Drug Economy: Some Preliminary Data', *Review of African Political Economy* 79: 13–32.

Bernstein, Henry. (2000), '"The Peasantry" in Global Capitalism: Who, Where and Why?', in *Socialist Register 2001*, ed. Leo Panitch and Colin Leys, London: Merlin Press.

Bernstein, Henry (2002), 'Land Reform: Taking a Long(er) View', *Journal of Agrarian Change* 2(4): 433–63.

Bernstein, Henry (2003), 'Land Reform in Southern Africa in World-Historical Perspective', *Review of African Political Economy* 96: 21–46.

Bernstein, Henry (2004), '"Changing Before Our Very Eyes": Agrarian Questions and the Politics of Land in Capitalism Today', *Journal of Agrarian Change* 4(1–2): 190–225.

Bernstein, Henry, and P. Woodhouse (2001), 'Telling Environmental Change Like It Is? Reflections on a Study in Sub-Saharan Africa', *Journal of Agrarian Change* 1(2): 283–324.

Berry, Sara (1984), 'The Food Crisis and Agrarian Change in Africa: A Review Essay', *African Studies Review* 27(2): 59–111.

Berry, Sara (1993), *No Condition is Permanent: Social Dynamics of Agrarian Change in Sub-Saharan Africa*, Madison: University of Wisconsin Press.

Bharadwaj, Krishna (1985), 'A View on Commercialisation in Indian Agriculture and the Development of Capitalism', *Journal of Peasant Studies* 12(4): 7–25.

Boserup, Ester (1965), *The Conditions of Agricultural Growth: The Economics of Agrarian Change under Population Pressure*, London: Allen & Unwin.

Bryceson, Deborah Fahy (1996), 'Deagrarianization and Rural Employment in Sub-Saharan Africa: A Sectoral Perspective', *World Development* 24(1): 97–111.

Bryceson, Deborah Fahy (1998), 'African Rural Labour, Income Diversification and Livelihood Approaches: A Long-term Development Perspective', *Review of African Political Economy* 80: 171–89.

Bush, Ray, and Lionel Cliffe (1984), 'Agrarian Policy in Labour Migrant Societies: Reform or Transformation in Zimbabwe?', *Review of African Political Economy* 29: 77–94.

Chabal, Patrick, and Jean-Pascal Daloz (1999), *Africa Works: Disorder as Political Instrument*, Oxford: James Currey.

Cliffe, Lionel, and G.L. Cunningham (1973), 'Ideology, Organization and the Settlement Experience in Tanzania', in *Socialism in Tanzania, Volume II, Policies*, ed. L. Cliffe and J. Saul, Dar es Salaam: East African Publishing House.

Colson, Elizabeth (1971), 'The Impact of the Colonial Period on the Definition of Land Rights', in *Colonialism in Africa, Volume III, 1870–1960*, ed. Victor Turner, Cambridge: Cambridge University Press.

Cooper, Frederick (2002), *Africa since 1940: The Past of the Present*, Cambridge: Cambridge University Press.

Cordell, Dennis D., John W. Gregory and Victor Piché (1996), *Hoe and Wage: A Social History of a Circular Migration System in West Africa*, Boulder, CO: Westview Press.

Cousins, Ben (1996), 'Livestock Production and Common Property Struggles in South Africa's Agrarian Reform', in *The Agrarian Question in South Africa*, ed.

Henry Bernstein, London: Frank Cass.

Cousins, Ben (forthcoming), 'The Zimbabwe Crisis in its Wider Context: The Politics of Land, Democracy and Development in Southern Africa', in *Zimbabwe's Unfinished Business: Rethinking Land, State and Nation in the Context of Crisis*, ed. Amanda Hammar, Brian Raftopoulos and Stig Jensen, Harare: Weaver Press.

Cousins, Ben, Dan Weiner and Nick Amin (1992), 'Social Differentiation in the Communal Lands of Zimbabwe', *Review of African Political Economy* 53: 5–24.

Cowen, Michael P., and Robert W. Shenton (1991a), 'The Origin and Course of Fabian Colonialism in Africa', *Journal of Historical Sociology* 4(2): 143–74.

Cowen, Michael P., and Robert W. Shenton (1991b), 'Bankers, Peasants and Land in British West Africa, 1905–1937', *Journal of Peasant Studies* 19(1): 26–58.

Cowen, Michael P., and Robert W. Shenton (1996), *Doctrines of Development*, London: Routledge.

Daviron, Benoit, and Peter Gibbon, eds (2002), *Global Commodity Chains and African Export Agriculture*, Special Issue of *Journal of Agrarian Change* 2(2).

Desai, Meghnad (2002), *Marx's Revenge: The Resurgence of Capitalism and the Death of Statist Socialism*, London: Verso.

De Wet, Christopher (1995), *Moving Together, Drifting Apart: Betterment Planning and Villagisation in a South African Homeland*, Johannesburg: Witwatersrand University Press.

Ferguson, James (1999), *Expectations of Modernity: Myths and Meanings of Urban Life on the Zambian Copperbelt*, Berkeley: University of California Press.

Fine, Ben, Costas Lapavitsas and Jonathan Pincus, eds (2001), *Development Policy in the Twenty-first Century: Beyond the Post-Washington Consensus*, London: Routledge.

First, Ruth (1983), *Black Gold: The Mozambican Miner, Proletarian and Peasant*, Brighton: Harvester.

Francis, Elizabeth (2000), *Making a Living: Changing Livelihoods in Rural Africa*, London: Routledge.

Francis, Paul (1984), '"For the Use and Common Benefit of All Nigerians": Consequences of the 1978 Land Nationalization', *Africa* 54: 5–28.

Franke, Richard W., and Barbara H. Chasin (1980), *Seeds of Famine: Ecological Destruction and the Development Dilemma in the West African Sahel*, Montclair and New York: Allanheld & Universe.

Friedmann, Harriet (1993), 'The Political Economy of Food: A Global Crisis', *New Left Review* 197: 29–57.

Friis-Hansen, E., ed. (2000), *Agricultural Policy in Africa after Adjustment*, CDR Policy Paper, Copenhagen: Centre for Development Research.

Gibbon, Peter (1992), 'A Failed Agenda? African Agriculture under Structural Adjustment with Special Reference to Kenya and Ghana', *Journal of Peasant Studies* 20(1): 50–96.

Gibbon, Peter, and Michael Neocosmos (1985), 'Some Problems in the Political Economy of "African Socialism"', in *Contradictions of Accumulation in Africa*, ed. Henry Bernstein and Bonnie K. Campbell, Beverly Hills, CA: Sage.

Gilsenan, Michael (1982), *Recognizing Islam*, Beckenham: Croom Helm.

Grischow, Jeff (1998), 'Corruptions of Development in the Countryside of the Northern Territories of the Gold Coast, 1927–57', *Journal of Peasant Studies* 26(1): 139–58.

Guyer, Jane I. (1983), 'Women's Work and Production Systems: A Review of Two Reports on the Agricultural Crisis', *Review of African Political Economy* 27: 186–91.

Hammar, Amanda (2001), '"The Day of Burning": Eviction and Reinvention in the Margins of Zimbabwe', in *The New Agrarian Politics in Zimbabwe*, ed. Eric Worby, Special Issue of *Journal of Agrarian Change* 1(4): 550–74.

Hill, Polly (1963), *The Migrant Cocoa Farmers of Southern Ghana*, Cambridge: Cambridge University Press.

Hobsbawm, Eric J. (1987), *The Age of Empire 1875–1914*, London: Weidenfeld & Nicolson.

Hyden, Goran (1983), *No Shortcuts to Progress: African Development Management in Perspective*, London: Heinemann.

IFAD (1994), *A Dialogue on Capitol Hill: Workshop on Land Degradation and Poverty in Sub-Saharan Africa – Challenges and Opportunities*, Rome: International Fund for Agricultural Development.

Kasfir, Nelson (1993), 'Designs and Dilemmas of African Decentralization', in *Local Government in the Third World: Experiences of Decentralization in Tropical Africa*, ed. Philip Mawhood, Pretoria: Africa Institute of South Africa.

Kitching, Gavin (1980), *Class and Economic Change in Kenya: The Making of an African Petite-Bourgeoisie, 1905–1970*, New Haven: Yale University Press.

Leach, Melissa, and Robin Mearns, eds (1996), *The Lie of the Land: Challenging Received Wisdom on the African Environment*, Oxford: James Currey.

Legassick, Martin, and Harold Wolpe (1976), 'The Bantustans and Capital Accumulation in South Africa', *Review of African Political Economy* 7: 87–107.

Leo, Christopher (1984), *Land and Class in Kenya*, Toronto: University of Toronto Press.

Levin, Richard, and Michael Neocosmos (1989), 'The Agrarian Question and Class Contradictions in South Africa: Some Theoretical Considerations', *Journal of Peasant Studies* 16(2): 230–59.

Little, Peter, and Michael Watts, eds (1994), *Living under Contract: Contract Farming and Agrarian Transformation in Sub-Saharan Africa*, Madison: University of Wisconsin Press.

Mamdani, Mahmood (1987), 'Extreme but not Exceptional: Towards an Analysis of the Agrarian Question in Uganda', *Journal of Peasant Studies* 14(2): 191–225.

Mamdani, Mahmood (1996), *Citizen and Subject: Contemporary Africa and the Legacy of Late Colonialism*, Cape Town: David Philip.

Mamdani, Mahmood (2001), *When Victims Become Killers: Colonialism, Nativism, and the Genocide in Rwanda*, Princeton: Princeton University Press.

Marongwe, Nelson (2003), 'Farm Occupations and Occupiers in the New Politics of Land in Zimbabwe', in *Zimbabwe's Unfinished Business: Rethinking Land, State and Nation in the Context of Crisis*, ed. Amanda Hammar, Brian Raftopoulos and Stig Jensen, Harare: Weaver Press.

McCann, James C. (1999), *Green Land, Brown Land, Black Land: An Environmental History of Africa, 1800–1990*, Oxford: James Currey.

Meagher, Kate (1995), 'Crisis, Informalization and the Urban Informal Sector in Sub-Saharan Africa', *Development and Change* 26: 259–84.

Morris, Mike, and Doug Hindson (1992), 'South Africa: Political Violence, Reform and Reconstruction', *Review of African Political Economy* 53: 43–59.

Moyo, Sam (2001), 'The Land Occupation Movement and Democratization in Zimbabwe: Contradictions of Neoliberalism', *Millennium: Journal of International Studies* 30(2): 311–30.

Murton, Andrew (1999), 'Population Growth and Poverty in Machakos District, Kenya', *Geographical Journal* 165(1): 37–46.

Nyambara, Pius S. (2001), 'The Closing Frontier: Agrarian Change, Immigrants and the "Squatter Menace" in Gokwe, 1980s–1990s', in *The New Agrarian Politics in Zimbabwe*, ed. Eric Worby, Special Issue of *Journal of Agrarian Change* 1(4): 534–49.

O'Laughlin, Bridget (1998), 'Missing Men? The Debate over Rural Poverty and Women-headed Households in Southern Africa', *Journal of Peasant Studies* 25(2): 1–48.

O'Laughlin, Bridget (2000), 'Class and the Customary: the Ambiguous Legacy of the *Indigenato* in Mozambique', *African Affairs* 99: 5–42.

Peters, Pauline E. (1994), *Dividing the Commons: Politics, Policy and Culture in Botswana*, Charlottesville: University Press of Virginia.

Peters, Pauline E. (2002), 'The Limits of Negotiability: Security, Equity and Class Formation in Africa's Land Systems', in *Negotiating Property in Africa*, ed. K. Juul and C. Lund, Portsmouth, NH: Heinemann.

Peters, Pauline E. (2004), 'Inequality and Social Conflict over Land in Africa', *Journal of Agrarian Change* 4(3): 269–314.

Phillips, Anne (1989), *The Enigma of Colonialism*, Oxford: James Currey

Ponte, Stefano (2002), *Farmers and Markets in Tanzania: How Policy Reforms Affect Rural Livelihoods in Africa*, Oxford: James Currey.

Pottier, Johann (2002), *Re-imagining Rwanda: Conflict, Survival and Disinformation in the Late Twentieth Century*, Cambridge: Cambridge University Press.

Raikes, Philip (1988), *Modernising Hunger: Famine, Food Surplus and Farm Policy in the EEC and Africa*, Oxford: James Currey.

Raikes, Philip (2000), 'Modernization and Adjustment in African Peasant Agriculture', in *Disappearing Peasantries: Rural Labour in Africa, Asia and Latin America*, ed. Deborah Bryceson, Cristóbal Kay and Jos Mooij, London: IT Publications.

Raikes, Philip, and Peter Gibbon (2000), '"Globalisation" and African Export Crop Agriculture', *Journal of Peasant Studies* 27(2): 50–93.

Raynault, Claude, Emmanuel Gregoire, Pierre Janin, Jean Koechlin and Philippe Lavigne Delville (1997), *Societies and Nature in the Sahel*, London: Routledge.

Ross, Eric B. (1998), *The Malthus Factor: Poverty, Politics and Population in Capitalist Development*, London: Zed Books.

Rutherford, Blair (2001a), *Working on the Margins: Black Workers, White Farmers in Postcolonial Zimbabwe*, Harare: Weaver Press.

Rutherford, Blair (2001b), 'Commercial Farm Workers and the Politics of (Dis)placement in Zimbabwe: Colonialism, Liberation and Democracy', *Journal of Agrarian Change* 1(4): 626–51.

Sachikonye, Lloyd M. (2003), *The Situation of Commercial Farm Workers after Land Reform in Zimbabwe: A Report Prepared for the Farm Community Trust of Zimbabwe*, London: CIIR.

Sender, John (2002), 'Reassessing the Role of the World Bank in Sub-Saharan Africa', in *Reinventing the World Bank*, ed. J. Pincus and J. Winters, Ithaca, NY, and London: Cornell University Press.

Shivji, Issa (1994), *Report of the Presidential Commission of Inquiry into Land Matters*, Volume I, *Land Policy and Land Tenure Structure*, Uppsala: Government of the United Republic of Tanzania and the Scandinavian Institute of African Studies.

Sivanandan, A. (1990), *Communities of Resistance: Writings on Black Struggles for Socialism*, London: Verso.

Sorrenson, M.P.K. (1967), *Land Reform in the Kikuyu Country*, Nairobi: Oxford University Press.

Stiglitz, Joseph (2002), *Globalization and Its Discontents*, London: Penguin Books.

Tandon, Yash (2001), 'Trade Unions and Labour in the Agricultural Sector in Zimbabwe', in *Striking Back: The Labour Movement and the Post-colonial State in Zimbabwe 1980–2000*, ed. B. Raftopoulos and L. Sachikonye, Harare: Weaver Press.

Tiffen, Mary, Michael Mortimore and Francis Gichuki (1994), *More People, Less Erosion: Environmental Recovery in Kenya*, Chichester: John Wiley.

Van der Walle, Nicolas (2001), *African Economies and the Politics of Permanent Crisis, 1979–1999*, Cambridge: Cambridge University Press.

Vaughan, Megan (1991), *Curing Their Ills: Colonial Power and African Illness*, Cambridge: Polity Press.

Wiggins, Steve (2000), 'Interpreting Changes from the 1970s to the 1990s in African Agriculture through Village Studies', *World Development* 28(4): 631–62.

World Bank (1996), *Toward Environmentally Sustainable Development in Sub-Saharan Africa: A World Bank Agenda*, Washington, DC: World Bank.

Yeros, Paris (2002), 'Zimbabwe and the Dilemmas of the Left', *Historical Materialism* 10(2): 3–15.

3

Night Harvesters, Forest Hoods and Saboteurs: Struggles over Land Expropriation in Ghana

Kojo Sebastian Amanor

Land in Ghana is owned not by the state but by chiefs. In turn, the expropriation of land is carried out not by the state but by an alliance between the state and chiefs. In turn, this situation complicates struggles for land. Not only do such struggles have dual local and national dimensions but they also have complex ideological ramifications about rights and identities, given that expropriations themselves are accompanied by various national or cultural justifications. The latter situation further complicates the struggle for land, as it limits the legal channels through which the peasantry can challenge the processes of expropriation.

The process of land expropriation and appropriation has involved three important movements: (a) the migration of export crop farmers since the late nineteenth century, who purchased lands from chiefs for oil palm and cocoa plantations; (b) the expropriation of land by the state for the creation of forest reserves since the 1920s, to the extent that today 20 per cent of the high forest zone in Ghana lies under forest reserves; and (c) the expropriation of land for agricultural modernization, which began in the postwar period with the creation of colonial agricultural resettlement schemes that were transformed in the 1970s and 1980s into agribusiness projects. In addition to expropriating land, the state also appropriates natural resources for use by concession holders.

This chapter examines the impact of the process of land alienation for the creation of forest reserves, concessions and agricultural schemes, as well as the process of resistance to alienation on the part of the peasantry.

Land Policy in Historical Perspective

The current framework for the administration of land in Ghana has been largely determined by colonialism. With the establishment of colonial rule in Ghana the colonial authority attempted to gain control over land. This occurred during a period of rapid expansion of land sales and concession grants in Ghana, in response to demands for land by cocoa farmers and gold speculators during the gold rush of the late nineteenth century. Land sales were important in Ghana, such that a significant class of property speculators and land lawyers emerged (Amanor 1999; Kimble 1963). In turn, the colonial authority sought to gain control over land sales through the 1910 Lands Bill, which attempted to vest 'waste land' in the Crown. This attempt was resisted by chiefs and the nascent Gold Coast merchant class, who organized the Aborigines Rights Protection Society and petitioned the Colonial Office in London. The Lands Bill was also opposed by British companies, which brought pressure to bear on the British government through the Manchester and London Houses of Commerce. In the face of public opposition the Lands Bill was rescinded.

However, the main result of this dispute was the subsequent development of the colonial framework for indirect rule, based on Native Administration. Under Native Administration, the colonial authority was to rule through an alliance with traditional rulers, who were empowered to enact by-laws. This also entailed a new framework of land administration. Trusteeship over land came to be vested in paramount chiefs, while farmers retained only user rights to land. Thereafter, transaction over land and concessionaires could only be negotiated by chiefs, thus preventing the development of internal land markets. However, various forms of land markets still continued to exist: chiefs alienated lands to migrant farmers, and many other land transactions took the form of long-term sharecrop leases which appropriated land from the pool available to local citizens. Native administration proved to be highly unpopular among the peasantry, and in many areas youth and commoners organized, frequently through the precolonial commoner associations (*asafos*), to oppose the arbitrary rule of chiefs, and frequently attempted to destool (dethrone) them.

Commenting on the *asafo* movement in Kwawu, Asiamah (2000: 73) writes:

Notably, the Asafo severely criticized the astronomical court fines imposed upon the commoners accused of breaking the chiefs' oath, laws and taboos. Other more serious charges were bribery and misappropriation of stool land revenues. For instance, money that accrued from land sales, tolls, special levies, timber concessions, mineral concessions, cocoa revenues, and others, were freely squandered, as if they were the personal incomes of the chiefs while the commoner who toiled to bring in the revenue did not benefit from his labour!

By the late 1940s, the *asafo* movement had become a strong rural force supporting the Convention People's Party (CPP) of Kwame Nkrumah, and opposing colonial rule and rule by chiefs. Following riots in 1948, a commission of enquiry was set up under Aitken Watson. Numerous representations to the commission by commoners in the rural areas complained of the autocratic impositions of chiefs under the Native Authority system. As chiefs had alienated significant areas to migrants for cocoa farming from the early twentieth century, creating land shortage problems for some commoners, the local peasantry blamed the chiefs directly, rather than entering into internecine conflict with migrants. In some situations migrants and local commoners united against the abuses of chiefs (Addo-Fenning 1997). In the postwar period, Native Administration was no longer tenable and the 1951 Local Government Ordinance set up a new structure of democratically elected local government. However, the administration of land was not brought under local government but retained under the office of the chief, effectively creating parallel structures for local government in which land administration remained outside the structures of democracy.

With attainment of independence this structure was maintained. The CPP had a large rural following opposed to chiefs and chiefly control over land, and in favour of land reform. But the CPP did little to put forward a programme of land reform. Instead, its espousal of African socialism adopted colonial ideological positions of African communal ownership of land, despite the overwhelming evidence of social differentiation and appropriation of land in Ghana during the colonial period. While the CPP engaged in a rhetorical attack on chiefs who supported the National Liberation Movement, the main opposition party, the legislation it introduced on land strengthened chiefly claim to ownership of land and natural resources. The Concession Ordinance, the Stool Lands Ordinance, and the State Lands Ordinance created a framework for land and natural resource administration in which land was recognized as the right of chiefs, but was vested in the state to manage on behalf of the chiefs. Chiefs could no longer negotiate concessions with the private sector. These were now negotiated by government agencies. But the chiefs still gained the royalties and rents that accrued from this process. Thus the chiefs had a vested interest in this process of appropriation of land from commoners, who would pay no royalties or land taxes, by the corporate sector which would purchase land and pay royalties and concession fees.

This alliance between the state and chiefs, which continues to the present, enables the state to expropriate land through the chiefs, with recourse to the ideological construct that land is owned by the chief and not the people. The implication of this is that land expropriation is not a violation of the rights of the people, and that compensation for the land only has to be paid to the chiefs. This recognition of chiefs as customary custodians of land also implies that chiefs are recognized as the institution that represents the rights of the community in land and the rights of the peasantry in land. This effectively parochializes land issues into individual community rights and prevents associations of peasants being recognized as representing peasants' interests in land. While the peasantry is also theoretically recognized via its elected representatives in the democratic process, this has limited impact on the land question, since land matters are recognized as the preserve of chiefs, not elected local councils.

Accountability in democratic decentralization is limited, and the government, in consultation with chiefs, has the right to appoint one-third of the local authority delegates. The district chief executive is appointed by government rather than elected. This limited democracy enables the government to impose its development objectives on the rural areas and to build up a united core of cadres within the structures of local government that ensures that elite political lines prevail. Since independence, 'every political regime has to a greater or lesser degree attempted to exploit what remains of these grassroots institutions in the furtherance of their interest' (Songsore and Denkabe 1995: 90). With the legitimation of the structure that expropriates land for private capital and the closing down of political spaces in which to represent their interests, the peasantry have found that attempts to defend their rights in land have been criminalized by the state. Thus, the main struggles for land have taken place outside of the legal framework and involve spontaneous local organization attempting to repossess land.

Forest Land: Alienation, Encroachment and Resistance

The alliance between state, chiefs and private capital can be seen very clearly within the forestry sector. During the 1920s, paramount chiefs were responsible for creating forest reserves in their Native Authorities through byelaws. The main rhetorical justification for creating forest reserves was to protect the environment and conserve forests and watersheds. The creation of forest reserves invariably involved expropriation of farmland. The paramount chiefs had an interest in this process, since the expropriation of land was carried out in their name. The gazetting of forest reserves created effective title to the land for the chief, prevented commoners from colonizing the land for agricultural purposes, and ensured the chiefs' revenues from future exploitation of timber. By the 1940s, more than 20 per cent of the high forest zone had been demarcated as forest reserves.

Halting Operation Halt

Timber exploitation did not become significant until the postwar period. In the early colonial period, export timber production was largely limited to coastal forest areas in the Western Region and the immediate hinterland of the large rivers through which logs could be floated down to the coast. With large demands for timber for European postwar reconstruction, the development of a network of roads in the interior and the invention of the timber truck, timber exports grew rapidly in the late colonial and early independence period. This coincided with a period of rapid expansion of cocoa production into the Western and Brong Ahafo region, in response to favourable world commodity prices. The conversion of large areas of forests to cocoa was of concern to the timber industry, which viewed this as a loss of valuable timber.

To gain hold of these timber resources, the timber industry pressurized government to introduce new legislation to control expansion of the cocoa sector. In 1959, the CPP government introduced the Protected Timber Lands Act, which aimed to regulate farm expansion in heavily forested areas. These areas could be declared protected areas, and farmers were prohibited from farming in these areas. These areas were then released to timber concessionaires to log. The farmer could only return to the land when the concessionaire had finished logging. The logging process could take twenty years and more. The main area affected by this legislation was the new cocoa frontier in Sefwhi Wiawso in the Western Region. Most of the land in this area had been sold by chiefs to migrant cocoa farmers.

The Forestry Department was responsible for managing these areas and set about prosecuting offending land encroachers. Cocoa farmers had spent considerable capital in purchasing land in these areas, and they continued to encroach within the protected lands, establishing cocoa plantations on what they considered to be their land. During the years of economic recession in 1970s, an increasingly poorly equipped Forestry Department was unable to manage the reserves effectively. Cocoa farmers returned to their lands and began to establish farms in the protected areas. However, forestry was one of the sectors to benefit immediately from the structural adjustment programme in the 1980s, and large donor funds were used to rehabilitate the private sector and support export-oriented growth. The Forestry Department was a beneficiary of this funding and was supported to monitor the timber sector. In 1992, the Forestry Department launched Operation Halt, a campaign to cut out illegal cocoa farms in the Western Region and plant them with timber trees. Infuriated farmers responded by destroying the timber saplings and replanting cocoa. Violent conflicts emerged between groups of farmers and the Forestry Department, and the Forestry Department turned to the police and military to back up its campaign against farmers. With an increasingly violent situation, the Forestry Department was forced to halt Operation Halt (Kotey et al. 1998).

Forest hoods and biodiversity protection parks

The Atewa Forest Reserve is a Special Biodiversity Protection Reserve (SBPR). It is considered to consist of a rare type of upland evergreen forest. However, the Atewa range is bordered by densely settled towns and villages, and in the precolonial period was an important agricultural centre, comprising the heartlands of the Akwamu empire in the eighteenth century. The Atewa reserve has also been heavily logged in the 1960s and 1970s, and much of this protected reserve no longer consists of thick forest with an unopen canopy. Many farmers were farming inside the area that was to become the reserve, and lost their land. The reserve has resulted in serious land shortage in settlements bordering the reserve, since the expropriation of land did not take into account the future needs of the people. The existence of the forest reserve in the vicinity of large settlements has also resulted in the development of livelihoods based on forest resources. This has included rattan cane weaving and timber.

The area is also rich in minerals, with small-scale diamond-winning and gold-mining activities being widespread. Gold is an old industry in the area, and was an important source of livelihood in precolonial times. During the colonial period, small-scale gold-mining was discouraged by the colonial authority, but in the postcolonial period it has re-emerged. It continued to be an important livelihood activity among youth around Atewa, who have difficulty in getting access to sufficient farmland. However, with the expansion of mining concessions in the 1990s, the area in which small-scale miners can operate has been curtailed, as concessions have encroached into areas in which small-scale mining has predominated, while many youth have found their livelihood activities criminalized.

During the early 1980s, chainsaw activities expanded in the area. With serious economic crisis in the late 1970s, most timber companies had ground to a halt and lacked capital to renovate obsolete equipment and timber trucks. Chainsaw operators occupied the void, supplying timber for the domestic market. With the rehabilitation of the timber sector in the 1980s, large donor loans were made available for private-sector investment in timber, and the private sector rapidly grew and developed a capacity that exceeded the available timber resources. With bad publicity for management of timber from environmental NGOs, such as Friends of the Earth – who published a major exposé, *Plunder in Ghana's Rainforest for Illegal Profit* (1992), detailing corruption in the forestry sector following implementation of the structural adjustment programme – the Forestry Department and donors were forced to introduce a policy on sustainable harvesting to maintain their credibility. An annual allowable cut was introduced in the forestry reserves. Timber concessionaires moved into farmland, and during the late 1980s and early 1990s over 80 per cent of timber exports were sourced from farmland. The expansion of concessionaires into farmland brought them into conflict with farmers, who had no recognized legal rights to the timber they nurtured on their farmlands, and informal sector chainsaw operators, who mainly worked in farming areas and remunerated farmers for timber they accessed from their land. During the 1990s, struggles developed between farmers, chainsaw operators, and concessionaires for rights to timber on farmland.

Recognizing that some order had to be brought into the off-reserve situation, the Forestry Department introduced a policy of collaborative forest management which sought to solicit the participation of farming communities in forest management. A series of 'consultative stakeholder workshops' were initiated over the need to reform timber legislation and create incentives for farmers to participate in forest management. However, the process of reform was resisted by vested interests who declared any change in rights over timber to be unconstitutional. Instead, vague Interim Measures for the Control of Illegal Felling in Off-Reserve Areas were introduced. These gave farmers rights to individually negotiate compensation for damage to their farms with timber contractors. However, this was followed by legislation which banned chainsaw lumber processing and criminalized the processing of timber by farmers from trees they have nurtured on their land.

The chainsaw industry still remains important and continues to be the main source of domestic timber supply, since concessionaires largely produce for the export markets, and usually only release the most inferior timber for the domestic market. Lumber sawing and carrying timber boards to lorry parks have been important livelihoods for rural poor youth in the vicinity of forest reserves, since they are frequently the most affected by the scarcity of land. The criminalization of informal timber activities has not dissolved informal timber activities, but has forced them to go underground. Emboldened by their criminalization, youth are not only processing timber on farmlands but moving into forest reserves. The criminalization of informal sector timber activities has resulted in increasing domestic prices for timber, and large urban interests have moved into chainsaw timber, commissioning youth to fell timber in the forests and paying off all the security taskforces on the roads that police timber. Frequently violent conflicts have occurred between forest guards and youth over illegal timber, while the Forestry Department has brought in military support to help manage the forest reserves.

While some sections of youth are involved in harvesting timber in the forest reserves, others also create farms within the forest reserves. This is a risky activity, since their farms would be destroyed if discovered by forestry guards. However, with little land available within the forest-edge communities, the youth do not have many choices available. Up in the forest reserve on the forested slopes around the towns which form the forest reserve, large numbers of trees are being felled, and as the chainsaws whirr some youth are staking claims to land. All around the houses in the towns that dot the Atewa range, one can find stacks of timber boards, which the townspeople invest in, use for building, and sell to timber merchants coming into town with lorries. Many of the farmers are welcoming the felling of the forest reserve by chainsaw gangs. They are convinced that when all the trees are felled they will be able to claim back their lands: 'After all, when there are no trees there what will the Forestry Department have to defend?' Some farmers also recognize that the illegal felling of timber has brought new wealth into town. In research carried out at the village of Apapam (Amanor 1999), one elderly farmer commented:

> Although the youth are cutting down trees, it is better for us now. There used to be a lot of disease here but now most people are able to attend hospital and fewer people are dying. After all, if they are not cutting trees from my plot but the government plot and people are healthy because they eat well, what is the problem?

By pandering to narrow elite interests and the export trade in timber, the Forestry Service has alienated rural people from forestry policy and lost its moral authority to manage timber resources for posterity and the 'national interest'. The destruction of timber trees within the forest becomes an act of defiance against the export trade in timber which has come to plague the lives of forest-edge communities and is a symbolic assertion of rights to land.

Agricultural Land: Alienation and Resistance

During the 1970s, major expropriation of land began to take place for agricultural schemes, private estate agriculture, and agribusiness. The expropriation followed a familiar pattern of agreement between state and chiefs, compensation for chiefs for the land, and compensation for farmers for any crops of the land. Farmers usually resisted this process through a number of legal and illegal channels, resulting in forceful expropriation and counter-responses.

Sabotage in state plantations

Konings (1986) provides interesting case studies of the range of responses by farmers to land expropriation. At Mim, in the Brong Ahafo area, land was expropriated by the state for the creation of a state cocoa plantation. In September 1977, the Mimhene, the chief of Mim, informed farmers that 1,075 acres of land had been released by him to the Cocoa Production Division for the establishment of a cocoa plantation. Between a hundred and two hundred families would have their land expropriated. Farmers were given two months to quit their land. When a delegation of farmers approached the chief to rescind his decision, he informed them that he was upholding the 'national interest'. The following week, employees of the Cocoa Production Division entered the land and began working on the plantation site. Angry farmers armed themselves and marched into the area. The police intervened. The actions of the farmers stalled the work, and the Cocoa Production Division did not resume work in the area for another four months.

Farmers within the area began to organize the Mim Farmers' Association. Among the farmers were many retired civil servants and educated young men who had taken up farming in the face of recession and lack of employment opportunities. Several of these farmers had invested considerable capital in farming and had been able to get bank loans. These educated farmers became articulate in organizing the farmers and developing a concerted plan of legal action. This included petitioning political authorities and the para-mount chiefs. However, this tactic merely solicited the reply that the farmers only had rights to the crops and not the land, and that the expropriation of land was in the 'national interest'. The farmers' association also hired a lawyer and took legal action, questioning the validity of the expropriation since the formal procedures for government compulsory acquisition of land had not been followed. However, the legal case moved slowly and the Cocoa Production Division resumed work in developing the plantation.

The farmers then began to sabotage work on the plantation, destroying the hybrid cocoa seedlings in the plantation nursery. A spokesman for the association explained that 'the cutting off of the cocoa seedlings by the unknown persons possibly reflects the reaction of a section of the inhabitants of Mim against what they term the "illegal seizure" of their lands and farms for the plantation project' (Konings 1984: 136). Similar acts of sabotage have occurred in other areas. For instance, when peasant farmers were unable to prevent the alienation of land to large-scale commercial rice farmers in the 1970s, they then responded by deliberately setting fire to the commercial rice farms (Goody 1980). However, in many cases initial attempts by farmers to resist expropriation are followed by acquiescence, when they realize they are up against the full might of state security services.

Night harvesters in palm plantations

One of the most significant alienations of land in southern Ghana has been for the establishment of oil palm plantations. This includes the Ghana Oil Palm Development Corporation (GOPDC), a joint project between the government of Ghana and the World Bank, which was established in the early 1970s and has now been privatized; and the Benso Oil Palm Plantations and Twifo Oil Palm Plantations, both now owned by Lever Brothers.

The GOPDC project was set up in the Kwae area of Akyem Abuakwa as an agribusiness scheme, with a nucleus estate, a processing mill and contract farmers. The land was acquired under the Stool Lands Act of 1962. The government approached the Okyenehene, the paramount chief of Akyem Abuakwa, for land and he identified the Kwae area as a suitable concession. The concession involved the expropriation of 9,000 hectares of land and 7,000 farmers. Compensation for the land was paid only to the chiefs, who were recognized as the legitimate owners of the land. The state was only prepared to pay compensation to farmers who could establish proof of ownership through land title deeds. Since land titling was uncommon in the area, this in effect meant that farmers did not get compensation for the land but only for the crops on their land. Food crop farmers, including a large proportion of women, only received compensation for their food crops (Gyasi 1992). No provisions were made for the farmers to gain alternative sources of land, or to establish alternative livelihoods. The project made provisions for some of the land acquired on the project to be redistributed to 200 smallholder contract farmers. These were to be provided with 20 acres of land (8 hectares), of which they had to cultivate 7 hectares under oil palm following prescriptions of the Ghana Oil Palm Development Corporation (GOPDC) and to sell their fruits to the company at dictated prices. Failure to comply with these prescriptions would lead to eviction from the land.

The government justified its expropriation of land on the basis that it was in the 'national interest'. It attempted to placate angry farmers by promising them the fruits of modernization, jobs and modern infrastructure, including roads, electricity, water and modern houses. However, there were no concrete provisions for these developments in the project plans. The GOPDC employs about 600 people (mostly drawn from out of the locality) and had redistributed land to 200 contract farmers who are incorporated into the project. There has been no development of roads within the area, and no social provisions for surrounding settlements. The town chiefs supported the project and represented their own individual demands, including provision of new palaces for the five town chiefs, the granting of 20 acres (8 hectares) of GOPDC smallholder land to the five chiefs, annual presentation of gifts (sheep, bottles of schnapps, cash donations and oil palm fruits) to each of the chiefs at the annual festivals, annual royalty payments to each of the stools, the erection of a 2-metre wall around the royal cemetery at Kwae, and the creation of a health post for the Minta royal family (Amanor 1999; Daddieh and Jonah 1987).

Most of the farmers were concerned about the expropriation of their land without proper compensation or provision of alternative land. Some of the farmers petitioned the Lands Department for compensation for their land and took up legal proceedings (which in turn have become protracted). Some communities have also refused to allow the Kwae authorities to enter their lands, such as migrant farmers at Atobriso and Okaikrom. Other farmers have taken to squatting on undeveloped parts of the plantation, which they refuse to vacate, such as at Kwae. As a result of these actions, the GOPDC has not been able to use 4,400 hectares of their concession (Daddieh and Jonah 1987; Gyasi 1992; Amanor 1999).

The GOPDC plantation has created a major crisis for the livelihoods of many people in the area and a large class of landless farmers now exists, who have to gain land on a sharecrop basis for farming or search for alternative livelihoods. Those most affected by this expropriation have been the peasant youth, who have few opportunities beyond working as casual farm labour. Most of them have taken to illegal harvesting of palm oil bunches from the estate during the night. Harvested bunches are taken to hiding places outside the plantation and then conveyed by lorries and trucks out of Kwae to buyers. Some of the fruits are also processed by women in the towns around the plantation, who have also lost their farm lands. Small-scale artisan processing mills are springing up around the plantations. While some of their supplies come from independent farmers who have moved into oil palm production and from disgruntled outgrowers who feel that GOPDC pays them too low a price for their production, other supplies come from night harvesting in the plantation. The youth in Kwae justify their nocturnal activities with the comment 'we have to eat too'. They argue that the land belongs to them and was taken away unfairly, so they have a moral right to harvest the fruits. Theft of palm bunches has become a major problem in the GOPDC plantation and the company has to maintain a large security force, constantly policing the plantation.

Small-scale mining gangs

Similar developments can also be found in the small-scale mining sector. Adoption of adjustment policies and emphasis on export-led growth resulted in a rapid expansion of small-scale gold and diamond mining by youth, who suffer from land shortage and few viable opportunities for employment outside of casual farm labour. However, as a mining boom developed, many foreign companies moved into mining in Ghana and signed concession agreements with the government. In turn, the small-scale miners found dwindling opportunities for mining. This particularly affected youth in Akyem towns, who were essentially panning for gold in streams around their settlements and diamond winning in fallow lands. With the crimi-nalization of these activities, youth have been forced to move into other sectors or engage in clandestine mining. The criminalization of their livelihoods and the possibility of making large amounts of money have emboldened some sections of the youth to organize and arm themselves to go into major concessions in an aggressive defence of their rights to a livelihood. The *Daily Graphic* of 30 July 1994 vividly depicts such an incident:

> Twenty security personnel of the Ghana Consolidated Diamonds Limited (GCD) received bullet wounds when they were attacked by an armed group suspected to be illegal diamond miners last Wednesday at Nsukosua Mining Area, near Kakoase, popularly known as 'Anoma Kwadwo'....

A spokesman for GCD security told the *Ghana News Agency* that following a tip-off on Saturday July 23 that some people were prospecting for diamonds on a GCD concession at Nsukosua near Kakoase, a security gang was sent in to the area.... On Wednesday July 27, 52 security personnel and armed police went to the site and found more than 300 workers were prospecting for diamonds and that Mr Dartey [the leader of the illegal miners] and his security were therefore arrested.

It was then that unknown to the security personnel, some of the illegal miners who were arrested opened fire on them. Even though one policemen fired a warning shot, the attack of the group was such that both the armed police and the security had to run for their lives.

Problems of Political Articulation

These developments in small-scale mining mirror the timber sector, where violent confrontations between state military organs and rural youth have become common, and where informal-sector activities have moved beyond small groups of youth processing timber to shady organizations sponsoring local youth to work timber and organizing the transportation to urban areas. This type of organization, of youth prepared to defend their livelihood with arms, also carries ramifications of the tragic conflicts in Sierra Leone and Liberia, where groups organized around control of the diamond trade were able to transform themselves into political movements playing on the existence of dissatisfied youth who could not envisage any future within the existing system. In recent years, an unprecedented wave of armed robberies has occurred in both urban and rural areas in Ghana, casting doubt over the ability of the state to provide security for its citizens. This is also a telling indictment of the failure of the state to provide any form of economic security and well-being to the vast majority of its citizens, who are condemned to abject poverty and no vision of a future, while the state confines a number of valuable resources for the exclusive rich and the export trade.

During the years of structural adjustment, youth have increasingly been regarded as a problem by policymakers and caricatured as lazy, greedy, irresponsible and prone to 'social vices'. Those who bad-mouth the young argue that they migrate to the city in search of cheap thrills, rather than staying in the rural areas to help their parents. They follow quick money and engage in environmentally unfriendly and illegal activities, such as chainsaw timber, mining and charcoal burning, instead of helping their parents on their farms. They no longer respect their elders, they smoke marijuana, and teenage pregnancy is rife. This maligning of youth seeks to divide the rural people and to deflect from the major causes of crisis in rural areas in recent years, which results from the expropriation of land and natural resources in the service of capital and world markets. This has created a crisis both in rural agriculture, which struggles to be productive in a hostile market environment, and in alternative livelihoods where the rural people find increasing numbers of natural resources appropriated by the state for its patrons. Perhaps struggles are more acute in the natural resource sectors outside of agriculture, since, in the present climate of depressed agriculture and increasing risk in agricultural production, other resources become more valuable. Small-scale farming provides meagre incomes, and successful farming requires large capital to invest in labour, inputs or farm expansion.

The major struggles for land have been in resistance to compulsory acquisition of land by the state, either for itself or for the private sector. The struggles have been largely spontaneous and parochial. The peasantry is weakly organized and unable to articulate its demands. This is partly a product of its history and its containment in parochial settlements by policies of Native Administration under colonial rule and by concepts of 'community development' which have predominated in the postwar period. Within the present structures of decentralization, the peasantry can elect its representatives to district assemblies; however, their assembly members represent the parochial interests of the settlement in its competition with other settlements for infrastructural development, not the economic and class interests of the constituents. Farmers' mass organizations are government bodies that organize farmers for implementation of government agricultural policy. They are dominated by large farmers who are appointed as leaders by government.

Conclusion

In the colonial period the main struggles over land took the form of a political movement for the removal of the Native Authority system based on chiefs and for ending the colonialism which supported this system. However, the system of local government that obtained in the terminal phase of colonialism did not reform the land situation. Land administration was maintained under chiefs. Since then, subsequent governments have strengthened their alliance with chiefs and used chiefs to expropriate land. They have also co-opted popular movements, transforming them into wings of local government that represent government policy to the people. Since chiefs are recognized as the legitimate owners of land and the representatives of the rural people, the ability of the peasantry to represent its interests in land and defend its rights and interests are extremely limited, while any act of self-defence can easily be interpreted as a criminal act that goes against the 'national interest'. However, this delegitimizes the state in the eyes of rural people, and the spontaneous movement is forced to take up arms, to sabotage state enterprises, to occupy 'state land', and to engage in criminal activities to defend its interests and to maintain vestiges of livelihoods.

References

Addo-Fenning, Robert (1997), *Akyem Abuakwa 1700–1943: From Ofori Panin to Sir Ofori Atta*, Trondheim: Department of History, Norwegian University of Science and Technology.

Amanor, Kojo S. (1999), *Global Restructuring and Land Rights in Ghana: Forest Food Chains, Timber and Rural Livelihoods*, Research Report No. 108, Uppsala: Nordisk Afrikainstitutet.

Asiamah, Alfred Effah A. (2000), *The Mass Factor in Rural Politics: The Case of the Asafo Revolution in Kwahu Political History*, Accra: Ghana University Press.

Daddieh, D.K., and Jonah Kwesi (1987), 'Contract Farming in the Oil Palm Industry: A Ghana Case Study', mimeo, Legon: University of Ghana.

Friends of the Earth (1992), *Plunder in Ghana's Rainforest for Illegal Profit: An Exposé of Corruption, Fraud and Other Malpractices in the International Timber Trade*, London: Friends of the Earth.

Goody, Jack (1980), 'Rice-burning and the Green Revolution in Northern Ghana', *Journal of Development Studies* 16(2): 136–55.

Gyasi, Edwin A. (1992), 'State Expropriation of Land for a Plantation and its Impact on Peasants in Ghana', in *Indigenous Land Rights in Commonwealth Countries*, Proceedings of a Commonwealth Geographical Bureau Workshop, ed. C. Cant and E. Pawson, Christchurch: Commonwealth Geographical Bureau.

Kimble, David (1963), *A Political History of Ghana, 1850–1928*, Oxford: Clarendon Press.

Konings, Piet (1986), *The State and Rural Class Formation in Ghana: A Comparative Analysis*, London: Routledge & Kegan Paul.

Kotey, E., N. Ashey, J. Francois, J.G.K. Owusu, R. Yeboah, K.S. Amanor, and L. Antwi (1998), *Falling into Place: Ghana*, Policy that Works for People and Forest Series, No. 4, London: IIED.

Songsore, Jacob, and Aloysius Denkabe (1995), *Challenging Rural Poverty in Northern Ghana: The Case of the Upper-West Region,* Trondheim: University of Trondheim, Centre for Environment and Development.

4

Land Occupations in Malawi: Challenging the Neoliberal Legal Order

Fidelis Edge Kanyongolo

Land occupations in Malawi have attracted very little academic attention. In the vast literature on the land and agrarian questions in Malawi, land occupations are generally mentioned in a cursory manner and largely conceptualized as a social pathological phenomenon. From the perspective of the law, land occupations are viewed as illegal activities, and land occupiers as criminals guilty of trespass. Meanwhile, neoliberal economists view occupations as a disincentive to investment because they undermine 'the rule of law'. Even to the extent that the state and other critics of land occupations acknowledge that land occupations are the direct result of landlessness and land hunger, they argue that the solution lies in gradualist land reforms by modifications in state laws and policies.

Despite their invisibility from academic and policy debates in Malawi, land occupations are one of the strategies that both rural and urban poor have increasingly used to engage in direct action against private landowners and the state. Since the late 1890s, when European settlers subordinated the existing population and the British government declared the territory to be its protectorate, the state has played a critical role in shaping class struggle. Even in terms of contemporary land occupations, the state has a decisive role to play, particularly in determining whether land occupations are to be recognized as a legitimate democratic strategy for redressing injustice or alternatively as an activity that undermines the democratic order.

Land occupations are especially worthy of study in the context of Malawi because of their potential impact on agrarian development, which is central to the national political economy. This point is best appreciated by considering some basic characteristics of the Malawian economy and society. At the time of the last national census in 1998, the population of Malawi was estimated at 11 million people, with a growth rate of 3.2 per cent per annum. The population is characterized by significant inequalities. It is estimated that 65.3 per cent of the population is 'poor', with 28.2 per cent of the total population living in 'dire poverty'. In terms of income distribution, the richest 20 per cent of the population consumes 46.3 per cent of the resources, while the poorest 20 per cent consumes only 6.3 per cent. Literacy rates are low, estimated at 51 per cent for women and 64 per cent for men. Poverty in Malawi has a spatial dimension as well, with the Southern Region having the highest proportion of poor. This is partly due to the small size of cropland holdings per capita, estimated at 0.178 hectares in the south, compared to 0.257 hectares and 0.256 hectares for Central and Northern regions, respectively (Malawi Government 1998, 2002b).

The dominant economic activity is agriculture, which employs 85 per cent of the economically active population (Malawi Government 1987: 2–3). Almost 80 per cent of the economically active population of Malawi were smallholder farmers who periodically supplemented their farming activities with other economic activities, including wage labour, trading, and fishing (BDPA 1998: 29). Smallholder agriculture accounts for nearly 64 per cent of income for the rural poor in Malawi (Malawi Government 2002b: xv). For its part, commercial farming, mainly of tobacco, tea and cotton, contributes about 90 per cent of the country's export earnings (Reserve Bank of Malawi 2002: 73).

National economic policy conforms to the neoliberal model, placing emphasis on private-sector initiative for economic growth, with the government and non-governmental organizations acting only in a facilitative role. The dominance of this approach since 1981 has been largely due to the adoption of a series of structural adjustment programmes (SAPs) under the auspices of the International Monetary Fund and the World Bank, which have made liberalization a key condition of assistance. Such assistance has been critical to the sustenance of Malawi's economy, which had experienced a severe decline in the late 1970s due to various factors ranging from drought in the 1980–81 season, a rise in interest rates on the international financial markets, and the closure of the Beira–Nacala trade corridor, which had provided a cost-effective outlet to the sea for landlocked Malawi (Chinsinga 2002: 29).

The neoliberal economic thrust found normative expression in a liberal constitution of 1994, which guaranteed the right to private property and placed limitations on the powers of the state. Despite the new constitution and neoliberal economics, economic growth has remained unsustainable, which, according to government, has been largely due to external shocks, inconsistent implementation of reforms, fiscal policy slippages and the narrow base of production capacity (Malawi Government 2002b: 12). In addition to the lack of economic growth, economic conditions of Malawians have not changed significantly, with poverty and inequalities still persisting (Chinsinga 2002; Chilowa et al. 2000; Chipeta 1993).

This chapter inquires into the dynamics of land occupations. It begins with a historical background to land alienation and land reform, before proceeding to analyse the social basis of land occupations and the strategies and alliances of the movement. A central argument is that, although the demand for land is strong and widespread in the political economy of Malawi, the landless movement remains largely unorganized, due to the structure of civil society. Civil society is understood here as a realm of social life that is neither autonomous from the state – having only limited or no independence from it – nor inherently democratic (Sachikonye 1995, 1998; Bangura 1992). At present, civil society in Malawi is struggling to define itself, in the minimal sense of the existence of free associations outside state control; moreover, it continues to embody various class and gender cleavages which render it incapable of being a progressive force in various struggles over land and property rights.

The conceptual framework of this chapter derives from legal theory, and specifically critical legal theory. In contrast to liberal legal theory, which naturalizes and objectifies legal norms and institutions (Rhode 1990), critical theory seeks to historicize the law and reveal normative tensions within it (Munzer 1990; Kelman 1984, 1987). In particular, critical theory identifies competing claims for rights with the purpose of unmasking the class and gender basis of the law (Unger 1976; Tushnet 1991; Cotterrell 1992; McLellan 1995; Olsen 1995). This approach is essential to our understanding of the struggle over land and property rights in Malawi (as well as other African countries), whose legal structure is characterized by pluralism, meaning the coexistence of civil and customary law. In such a context, land occupations generate not only material conflict but also normative conflict over the dual legal structure. This conflict is one which liberal jurisprudence has so far been incapable of resolving.

The History of Land Alienation and Reform

Colonial land policy

The most pronounced phase of class struggles in Malawi commenced with the emigration of British settlers to the territory and the establishment of the colonial state in the late nineteenth century. Typically, the state facilitated and entrenched the acquisition of large tracts of land by the colonial settlers, particularly in the southern part of the country. There they proceeded to engage in the growing of tea, coffee and cotton, almost exclusively for export. From the colonial era to the present, the Malawian state has implemented various land acquisition and reform policies whose aim has been the creation and maintenance of a capitalist economy based on large-scale export-oriented agriculture, at the expense of peasants (Mhone 1992). The colonial and postcolonial land policies, undertaken in 1920, 1946, 1967 and 2001, can be distinguished in so far as the colonial policies defined land ownership and occupation on the basis of race, while postcolonial policies deracialized ownership in the freehold agricultural sector.

Contemporary state-driven reforms have their genesis in colonial policies. As was the case in the other colonial territories, the main aim of colonial land policy in Malawi was the facilitation of white economic enterprise (Krishnamurty 1972: 385). Unlike the other territories in the region, however, Malawi was relatively unattractive to colonial settlement because it lacked mineral resources, good communications and a conducive climate (Rotberg 1965; Macdonald 1975). As late as 1921, therefore, Malawi had fewer than two thousand settlers, most of them engaged in farming. Most settlers acquired land as a result of agreements with local chiefs who purported to transfer ownership on behalf of their communities. In reality, such transfers were mostly frauds of dubious legal validity, although subsequently the colonial administration issued the settlers with titles of ownership. The acquisition of the land by colonial settlers generated new forms of property relations, which, in turn, led to a reconfiguration of local economies. The most immediate impact of this development,

particularly in the Southern Region where most settlers were located, was that it converted subsistence farmers, whose land had
been transferred to private owners, into labour tenants (paying rent
in the form of labour). A related consequence was an increase in
labour migration, as previously communal farmers resorted to wage
labour, albeit subject to legal restrictions on their mobility.[1]

Based on the recommendations of the 1920 land commission appointed by the government, policies and laws were put into place
aiming to assure settlers of the security of their holdings and also
to attract new settlers (Nyasaland Government 1920: iii). The 1920
land laws appear to have achieved their aim of expanding white
settlement, as the total area under settler ownership between 1919
and 1921 increased from 13,757 acres to 118,506 acres (Gray 1960:
73). Needless to say, the 1920 reform process did not have any significant input from the black peasantry, the process having involved
the interview by the commission of only eight 'natives', compared
to twenty-five whites and five Asians. In addition, the Commission
also received nine memoranda from various settler-farmer interests
(Nyasaland Government 1920: v). In 1946, another land commission
was set up with the remit of reporting on the needs of black peasants who were resident on lands that had been alienated to white
settlers. Clearly, the most critical question to be investigated by this
commission should have been the relative validity of the competing claims to ownership of the lands by the settlers and the black
'residents'. After all, it was the commission itself that had recognized
conflict between settlers and natives over land tenure to be a major
problem (Nyasaland Government 1946: 15). In the event, the commission preferred not to address the question, dismissing such an
undertaking as being of interest only 'to the student of history or
comparative jurisprudence' (Nyasaland Government 1946: 7). The
reforms that followed the recommendations of this report were
restricted to securing some rights of labour tenants against eviction.
Thus, they endorsed the colonial capitalist status quo.

Postcolonial land policy

The replacement of the colonial regime with a popularly elected
government in the early 1960s did not herald a transformation of
Malawi's political economy, but largely retained colonial land policies
and laws. Government policy viewed land as a commodity to be

governed by market forces, thereby encouraging entreprenuers to acquire portions of communal land and convert them into their own private lands. Predictably, the beneficiaries of this liberalization of the land market were largely indigenous capitalist farmers consisting of senior politicians and civil servants, retirees, and other formerly non-agrarian indigenous business people (Moyo 2000: 8).

Postcolonial government pursued various land reforms in the late 1960s. However, unlike in Latin America where state initiatives in land reform in the same period were instituted under conditions of grassroots pressure for revolutionary change (Veltmeyer, Chapter 10 in this volume), in Malawi the dominant driving force was the imperative of the free market and private enterprise. In addition to formally deracializing the land tenure system, the key objective of this initiative was to stimulate agricultural development by increasing the amount of land in private hands. It was argued that only private land had value as a commodity on the land market (Nothale 1984). This objective was predicated on the assumption that the reason why rural communities had hitherto not been able to gain access to commercial credit, for the development of their land, was that the customary land they occupied was not owned individually. The normative tools for pursuing the policy objectives of deracialization and individualization of title were various enactments by parliament in 1967, including the Land Act, the Registered Land Act, and the Customary Land Development Act. These laws instituted the mechanism for converting customary land into private land. This led to a dramatic increase in the number of privately owned estates, mainly dedicated to producing tobacco. Increased privatization of land for commercial purposes in the postcolonial period predictably reduced the per capita land available to peasants, smallholder farmers and communities in general.

The conflict among different class interests over land in Malawi has found normative articulation in legal regimes that have classified land ownership into three categories: public, customary and private. The law defines public land as land that is occupied, used or acquired by the government. This category of land is vested in perpetuity in the president. Customary land is land that is held under customary law, although at the same time statutory law vests it in the president and grants the power of its administration and control to the minister of lands. For its part, private land is that which is held under leasehold, freehold or Certificate of Claim title. In theory,

Table 4.1   Customary land alienation (hectares), 1983–89

Year	Customary	Public	Freehold	Leasehold	Customary lost
1983	7,459,278	1,640,594	52,058	296,811	13,057
1984	7,455,190	1,639,931	52,065	301,555	4,088
1985	7,446,705	1,641,607	52,016	308,413	8,484
1986	7,427,128	1,641,993	52,016	327,603	19,577
1987	7,398,284	1,654,953	53,903	341,601	28,843
1988	7,388,516	1,655,113	53,903	351,209	9,768
1989	7,384,484	1,655,961	53,903	355,492	4,032

Source: Malawi Government 1999, Vol. III, Part II: 9.

any parcel of land can be converted from one type of ownership to any of the other two. Historically, however, it has mostly been customary land that has registered a net loss of total hectarage to the other categories, while both public and private land have registered total net gains. Between 1967 and 1994, for example, more than 1 million hectares of customary land were lost to private and public land (Malawi Government 1999: 66). Table 4.1 illustrates this trend analytically, with reference to the 1980s specifically.

None of the reforms of 1967 addressed the legacy of landlessness and land hunger bequeathed by colonial land policy. Having deracialized land ownership and occupation at the formal level, the 1967 enactments created a normative framework for land ownership and occupation that purported to be class and gender blind. This approach obscured the class and gender character of property relations, thereby shielding class and gender inequalities from demands for their substantive transformation. Consequently, instead of facilitating the transformation of class and gender inequalities in property relations related to land, the 1967 reforms in fact only entrenched them further because, by design, they benefited only people who could afford to purchase leasehold or freehold titles to land.

In the subsequent three decades, the state further entrenched inequalities by implementing various agrarian policies relating to access to inputs, credit, marketing and agricultural services which favoured large-scale farming over smallholder farming (Mhone 1992; Pryor 1988; World Bank 1985). Even in the few cases in which smallholder farmers were targeted for policy assistance, most of the support was focused on the richest 20 per cent of the category (Malawi Government 1995: 5). The notable initiatives towards smallholders included the Integrated Rural Development Project of 1968 and the National Rural Development Project of 1977. These aimed at improving access of smallholder farmers to inputs, credit, extension services, and markets, but were unsuccessful due to insufficient funding, lack of inter-sectoral coordination, and the failure of the planners to take into account the cultural context in which the intended beneficiaries of the projects lived (Chanthunya 1999).

Besides the privatization of communal land, the state also acquired large tracts of land for a wide range of its own purposes, including the establishment of forest reserves, wildlife reserves, national parks, and environmental protection areas. It is estimated that 21 per cent of the total land area of Malawi consists of 'protected areas' – that is, national parks, game reserves and forests (Malawi Government 1983, 2001). By 2001, there were 82 forest reserves and 5 national parks and wildlife reserves scattered around the country. However, as the government observed in the early 1980s (Malawi Government 1983),

> Parks and reserves have little relevance to most Malawians. The majority of people who visit the parks are foreigners. Although it can be argued that money paid by park visitors may ultimately help finance other social services, this must, at best, seem a tenuous benefit of protected areas to most people. Most of the people who enjoy direct benefits do so illegally.

The Land Policy Reform Commission of 1999 also found that according to the Commission, 'The environmental as well as the economic importance of national parks was generally not appreciated' (Malawi Government 2000). By 2001, in addition to conservation and eco-tourism areas protected by the state, 217,651 hectares of state-owned land were used to accommodate various agricultural schemes consisting of irrigation facilities, agricultural research stations, farm institutes, livestock facilities and state farms (Malawi Government 2001).

The land question today

The alienation of peasant customary lands and their conversion to private or state ownership has progressively created and expanded a mass of land-short and landless peasants, who in effect have been presented with the following options: to continue to labour on estates; to migrate to urban centres and become part of the under-class eking out a living at the periphery of the formal market; or to engage in counter-systemic actions, such as resistance against further privatization of communal land and occupation of private or state-owned lands.

The Malawi National Land Policy of 2001 acknowledged the underlying social and economic structural determinants of the land question, and identified the key problems as follows: residual effects of colonial land policy; high population-to-land ratio; land scarcity that paradoxically coexists with idle lands; worsening land pressure; 'provocative' squatting; cross-border encroachment by immigrants; encroachment onto conservation and protected areas; uncontrolled allocation of lakeshore land; and mismanagement of land develop-ment (Malawi Government 2001: 20). What the policy omitted was the inequality in access to land; moreover, it obscured the neo-liberal policy framework, precisely that which continues to justify the commoditization of land and its appropriation by leaseholders and freeholders.

If counter-systemic actions put into motion a 'grassroots land reform', urbanization merely transfers the problem of landlessness to the urban areas. The 2002 Core Welfare Indicators Questionnaire Survey conducted by the National Statistics Office indicated that up to 46 per cent of the country's landless people live in urban centres. Here, occupations are most evident in the 'squatter settlements' of peri-urban areas, where migrants often live in very poor environ-mental and health conditions (United Nations 2001: 8). Some of the settlements have been recognized by the city and town councils as 'Traditional Housing Areas' or 'squatter upgrading' and have been provided with a modicum of social services by local government authorities (Malawi Housing Corporation 1981; Chilowa 1996).

The potential of land occupations to effect radical change in the Malawian property regime is limited by the neoliberal character of the dominant political and economic order. The constitution entrenches individual autonomy through the device of human rights norms which, as a general rule, prioritize the interests of the individual over those of the community. This system of vindicating rights undermines mass struggles, as it deliberately obscures their class character and reconstructs them as conflicts between individuals reduced to the status of 'plaintiffs' and 'defendants' (Gutto 1993).

In addition to the constitutional individualization of the land question, another relevant feature of the dominant neoliberal order is the assumption of the neutrality of adjudicative institutions. Land occupations are conflictual by nature. Their potential for effecting substantive land reform, therefore, depends critically on the predilections of the institutions that adjudicate the conflicts that land occupations represent and generate. In Malawi, the constitution empowers courts to be the final adjudicative authority. Liberal jurisprudence would suggest that courts can, and in the main do, discharge that function on the basis of objective principles (Wechsler 1959; Motala 1998). This claim is rejected by critical legal scholars of various shades who argue that such a conception of the judiciary is based on an idealization of an institution which in reality relies on a subjective legal narrative administered by judges who cannot divest themselves of subjective judgements that reflect their class, racial and gender identities (Griffith 1997). In the context of land occupations in Malawi, the judiciary has invariably upheld the right of individual owners of private land over those of the land occupiers to restitution or redistribution.

Spatial Distribution and Social Composition of Land Occupations

The first geographical factor that determines land occupations is the distribution of population density, which correlates with patterns of colonial settlement and land alienation. This situates land occupations mainly in the tea-growing districts of Mulanje and Thyolo, and areas surrounding the former colonial capital of Zomba. These districts are adjacent to Malawi's biggest industrial district of Blantyre, thereby creating the potential for alliances between land occupiers and the urban proletariat in any broad-based grassroots movement for radical social change.

The second geographical factor relates to the market-led reforms of the late 1960s which facilitated the conversion of large tracts of communally owned land to freehold estates for the cultivation of tobacco. These estates were established mainly in districts in the central and northern regions of the country including Mchinji, Kasungu, Rumphi and Mzimba. According to the report of the Presidential Commission on Land Policy Reform of 1999, land scarcity in Malawi is 'particularly serious' in the tea-growing areas of Mulanje and Thyolo; the tobacco estates in Kasungu; and Nyika, Kasungu, Lengwe and Liwonde National Parks' (Malawi Government 2000: 40).

The third geographical factor that determines the location of land occupations in Malawi is the location of nature conservation and eco-tourism areas, as well as other state lands protected by various state laws. A typical example of land occupations in nature conservation areas are those in the Matandwe Forest Reserve in the extreme south of the country. This area was occupied in 1994 by local villagers, who resisted eviction for the following eight years. In 2002, 200 of the occupiers were prosecuted and convicted of trespass. By this time, 10,000 hectares of the 26,205 hectares of the reserve were under occupation by over 5,000 local peasants, who indicated that they were prepared to resist any future attempts to evict them.[2] Another occupation of a nature conservation area involved 242 people who occupied Liwonde Forestry Reserve in the Southern Region district of Machinga in 2002. In July 2002, officials from the Forestry Department, assisted by the police, responded to the occupation by burning down the occupiers' houses, temporary shelters, and destroying farm produce. Forty occupiers were arrested and prosecuted.[3]

There have also been occupations of state lands other than game reserves or national parks. One case was that of land belonging to Lunyangwa Agricultural Research Station in the northern district of Mzuzu, which was occupied by 107 people, including a cabinet minister.[4] Another case was the occupation of lands that government had used to settle hundreds of ruling party youth – known as Malawi Young Pioneers – before their organization was disbanded as part of the democratization process in the early 1990s. Even part of the land on which the presidential palace stands has also been subjected to intermittent occupations by inhabitants of the local area, who have claimed that the government had acquired the land without paying them any or adequate compensation.

Land occupations have also occurred on private land. One example has been the occupation of a 25-hectare piece of land owned by a tea-growing company in the southern district of Thyolo. The occupiers were mainly peasants from local villages who claimed that the land in question belonged to them because it had belonged to them before it was 'stolen' by colonial settlers.[5] Other examples have been the occupation of a tobacco farm in the southern district of Zomba and of a privately owned farm in the northern region district of Rumphi. In the latter case, 800 families occupied the farm for seven years between the death of the owner and the repossession of the land by a bank, which secured a court order to evict the families.[6] Overall, land occupations of privately owned farms have covered from 5 per cent of the area of farms that are less than 20 hectares to 52 per cent for large farms of 500 hectares or more (Malawi Government 1999: 17).

Finally, there has been evidence in certain cases that have attracted media attention that land occupiers have not always been poor peasants. In a number of cases it has been reported that local traditional and other political leaders have been among those occupying government and private land. Thus, in an incident in July 2002, part of a 25,000-hectare area of land held by a government-appointed trust was occupied by a group of local people that included two of Malawi's prominent traditional chiefs and several other more junior chiefs. This was, therefore, hardly a peasant-organized land occupation movement, but one that included the elite of a social, economic and political structure based on patriarchal customary laws.

Gender dynamics are also a critical element of land occupations. Unfortunately there have been no studies to indicate how those dynamics play out in the context of Malawi. Nevertheless, there is sufficient evidence to suggest that both men and women have been involved in occupying contested land and resisting eviction.[7] However, it is equally true that the gender inequalities that characterize the Malawian political economy in general also manifest themselves in the land occupation process, particularly in terms of the limited involvement of women in the decision-making echelons of the land occupiers. It is also pertinent to note that the gender dynamics of land occupations are likely to be affected by the apparent increase in the involvement of traditional customary power structures in land occupations. Although such structures have formally been co-opted into the state since colonial times, in the context of land occupations, a number of chiefs, village heads and other traditional leaders have uncharacteristically sided with the land occupiers. This increased reliance on traditional authority structures to lead the land occupation movement is likely to reproduce in the land occupation movement the patriarchy that characterizes land occupations in general. The prospects for the quantitative and qualitative increase of the role of women in land occupations in Malawi, therefore, remains in doubt.

The growing influence of traditional authorities is also likely to affect the age differential of land occupiers. There is also a paucity of authoritative literature on the age profile of land occupiers in Malawi. It is, therefore, difficult to assess the significance of the age of land occupiers in determining various aspects of land occupation, including its geographical location, the tactics of the occupiers, the response of the authorities and the sustainability of the occupation. This is, therefore, one area that requires urgent systematic study.

Strategies and Alliances of the Landless Movement

Civil society and the land question

The role of Malawian civil society in land occupations today is best appreciated in relation to the history of Malawian civil society more generally. The imposition of capitalist relations of production by the colonial administration towards the end of the nineteenth century engendered some organized resistance among the indigenous population. In some cases, Africans used violence as a means of protest, such as during the 'Chilembwe Uprising', a series of armed attacks led by a charismatic American-trained evangelist John Chilembwe against several settler farmers (Shepperson and Price 1958). Such radicalism was, however, the exception. The more common approach taken by advocates for reform was to form 'native associations' and other pressure groups and make demands for moderate reforms in the colonial legal order without directly challenging its legitimacy or demanding self-government (van Velsen 1966). It was not until the 1950s, when the various civil society organizations coalesced around the idea of national independence, that the demands became more radical.

After independence, the organic relationship between civil society and the leading African party, the Malawi Congress Party (MCP), evolved into one in which civil society was co-opted into the state, particularly after the establishment of a highly centralized single-party constitutional regime. Thus civil society became virtually demobilized, as any political organization outside the framework of the ruling party became illegal (Chipeta 1992). The landless and land-short in Malawi historically have formed alliances with political parties and pressure groups. In fact the MCP, which spearheaded the country's independence, was founded originally as the Nyasaland African Congress in 1944, out of an alliance of civil society organizations which, among other things, advocated redress for colonial expropriation of African lands (van Velsen 1966: 400). However, as independence and victory for the MCP in the first free elections became imminent, the party began to downplay the land question. In its 1961 manifesto, for example, there was no mention of land distribution. Instead, references to agrarian issues were restricted to a commitment to modernize agriculture and commercialize it 'on a massive scale' by encouraging the growing of cash crops by the masses (Malawi Congress Party 1961).

In the early 1990s, politicians campaigning in favour of the introduction of a multiparty system of government also used land to gain the support of people, particularly in the land-hungry districts in the country's Southern Region. In this part of the country, politicians of the United Democratic Front (UDF) and the Alliance for Democracy (AFORD) promised that the introduction of multiparty politics would also bring about redistribution of land.[8] As with the linkages with nationalist politicians in the 1940s, 1950s and 1960s, the linkages with 'multiparty democrats' in the 1990s also turned out to be illusory in terms of delivering land to the landless and land-hungry. Once in power, the 'democrats' were more concerned with preserving bourgeois law and creating a conducive environment for investors based on the supremacy of market forces, as exemplified by the land policy of 2002.

Land occupations in Malawi are instructive about the limitations in the ability of civil society to effect radical social and economic change. It has been said that in Malawi, civil society is struggling to define itself, even in the minimal sense of being free associations and free of state control (Minnis 1998). Others have argued, though, that freedom from the state is not an essential condition for the existence of civil society (Sachikonye 1998), and that such a conception of civil society is peculiarly characteristic of neoliberal thinking

(Neocosmos 1996). Land occupations in Malawi appear to vindicate this view, as they expose the illusory nature of the independence of civil society from the state.

In its relation to the land question, civil society in Malawi can be categorized into three types. The first category consists of those civil society organizations that are urban-based, elite-led, and professing the philosophy of liberal democracy. The second category are those that have grassroots membership and aim to achieve a particular objective within the existing legal and policy framework that defines and governs land ownership and occupation. The third category consists of groups that organize to promote the welfare of their members by challenging current property relationships.

The first category of civil society groups consists mainly of the ubiquitous 'non-governmental organization'. Typically based in the urban centres of Blantyre, Lilongwe and Mzuzu, these NGOs are almost always exclusively funded by US or European governments and organizations. The typical NGO focuses on the advocacy of civil and political rights within the framework of a liberal democratic constitution, and does not articulate any position on land reform or participate in land occupations or any other actions aimed at effecting substantial transformation of the current property regime. The typical NGO is ideologically opposed to any substantive transformation of property relations, except in rhetoric, placing faith in market-based reforms and 'the rule of law'.

The second category of civil society groups consists of collectivities that do not display the features of the typical NGO. In this category are groupings that are more geographically diverse, with a presence that goes beyond the confines of the urban centres. The groups in this category may be further differentiated, on the basis of their relative formalization, from those that are structured like the NGOs in the first category to others that are more loosely organized. The agriculture sector in Malawi has formalized groups, with written constitutions, and a bureaucratic internal structure. These include: Kaporo Foundation for Rural Development (Karonga), Mabulabo Voluntary Transformation Initiatives (Mzimba), Mchirawengo Poor People Irrigation Development Organization (Luwelezi), Tiyende Women in Development (Balaka), Village Enterprise Zone Association (Dowa), Zipatso Association of Malawi (Mwanza) and the numerous other 'farmers' clubs' and co-operatives that operate in many of Malawi's rural areas. At the other end of the spectrum are grassroots civil society groups that are more loosely organized. These groups have relatively little bureaucracy and typically have no written constitution. Examples include the many community groups that are involved in the 'community based natural resource management' schemes under which local communities assist the state to achieve its conservation objectives for the ostensible benefit of the communities themselves. Although they operate relatively independent of the state and donors, these groups nevertheless operate within the confines of the constitution and the rule of law.

Although the second category of organizations may appear to be more structurally independent from donors and the state than the typical NGOs in the first category, the more formal among them are nevertheless also dependent on funding by the same US and European donors that fund organizations in the first category. For this reason, therefore, they are organized in accordance with the donors' requirements on internal governance and external relations, and informed by neoliberal paradigms of development and property espoused by their donors.

The third category of civil society organizations are similar to the more loosely organized groups in the second category. The critical difference between them is that groups in the former category do not accept the limitations of the constitution or other state laws. On the contrary, these groups, which include the land occupation collectivities discussed in this chapter, challenge the neoliberal legal order on the basis that it is not indigenous and is unjust because it seeks to preserve an unequal status quo in property relations.

In addition, the historical aversion of the state to labour movements has resulted in a trade union movement that is too weak and divided to galvanize unionism within the rural areas. Some of the main historical and structural barriers to the growth of such unionism have been the sectorization plan adopted after the passing of the Labour Relations Act (1996), under which the state restricted the number of sectors in which unions may organize (as of 1998 there were only 12 unions in 12 sectors); and the state's designation of the Malawi Congress of Trade Unions (MCTU) as the umbrella organization without the mandate of all the unions (Meinhardt 2003: 41–2). The result is that 'Malawi's labour movement is perhaps the least developed and weakest in the Southern African Development Community (SADC) in terms of unionization levels and material resources' (Meinhardt 2003: 41–2).

The capacity of rural civil society organizations to establish effective linkages among themselves has been adversely affected by severe limitations in the flow of information. Consider, for example, that in 1998 about half of the population of Malawi had no access to radio (Malawi Government 1998). In a country with a literacy rate of only 57 per cent, the paucity of radio severely limits mass communication, which would otherwise serve as the means by which rural communities would learn about how other communities were organizing themselves and demanding land redistribution. In this connection, it is worth noting that peasant organizations are inherently limited in their ability to have a national impact because of their dispersal (Scott 1985). A democratized mass media would be a potential tool to overcome the constraints on peasant communications nationally, although the efficacy of this would still be likely to be undermined by illiteracy, the lack of access to reading materials, lack of access to radios, and under-resourced bureaucracies (Seidman and Seidman 1994: 269).

Despite their limitations, however, some communities have used land occupations to assert their claim to a new property regime. On the basis of the reported cases, this grassroots land reform is founded on the understanding of land reform as a means of securing at least four objectives: the restitution of land that was acquired on the basis of colonial land tenure regimes; the conversion of land that is currently used as national parks and game reserves into farming land for food production; the equitable distribution of fertile lands; and the democratization of local government, including the management and administration of land. The following statements of members of groups of land occupiers exemplify this understanding:

> The land in [the government-owned Lengwe National Park] is fertile and this is why many of us prefer to farm there. After all this land belongs to us. Government took it from our forefathers and what we are doing just to farm in our own land [sic].[9]

> We want people to control the land with their own organization and not a private trust which was imposed on them…We warned [the government-appointed trust] to hand over the land to the people by March 1. They didn't want to listen, that's why the aggrieved people and chiefs have agreed to take the land which legally belongs to them.[10]

State and farmers' responses to land occupations

The radical understanding of land reform on the part of rural civil society is fundamentally different from that envisaged in the various state-led and market-assisted reforms that have been implemented to date. The neoliberal character of those reforms is typified by the National Land Policy of 2002. The policy does not suggest immediate comprehensive land redistribution or restitution. Rather it makes redistribution contingent upon the government having money with which to compensate those whose land is to be redistributed or restituted. In fact, the only specific resettlement scheme referred to in the policy is that in which the government plans to resettle approximately 20,000 people on 14,000 hectares of land at a cost of at least US$25 million (Malawi Government 2001: 55). Indeed, the policy explicitly spells out its neoliberal ethos when it states that reforms will be informed by the following credo:

> Respect for the law and protection of the integrity of accrued property rights is important for establishing a stable land tenure system. The constitutional protection of private rights and due process of law will be applied to protect investments and production factors tied to land. (Malawi Government 2001: 25)

The economic argument against land occupations suggests that land which is privately owned is more likely to be taken care of than land that has no particular owner (Hardin 1968; Leopold 1934). Yet land is not merely a commodity that gains value by reference to the market, but also a resource that has socio-cultural value in that it is an integral part of the formation, location and preservation of the social identity of communities.

The response of the authorities to land grievances and demands has been both accommodative and censorious. It has been accommodative in that the government has acknowledged the legitimacy of the demands of those who wish to reclaim land and has factored some of their demands into various land laws and policies. Thus, for example, the 2002 National Land Policy sets out, among other things, to ease growing land pressure through land redistribution and resettlement. Accommodation of the interests of those with land grievances is also attempted by co-opting local communities into structures responsible for the management of the environment, forests, and other natural resources.[11] However, the state's accommodative strategy is evident only in the context of such medium- or long-term initiatives.

On the other hand, when faced with an immediate situation of land occupation, the state has responded less benignly. Thus, in the protection of forests against occupation, the state has largely relied on policing by forest guards and scouts (Malawi Government 2001: 14). The approach of strict protection – that is, policing – is viewed negatively by the majority of the general public, who, while accepting the objectives of policing, nevertheless appear to take the view that 'the need for resources and in some cases even land [is] great enough to warrant breaking the law' (Malawi Government 2001: 14). This begs the question whether a legal order that runs counter to popular demands for social, economic and political justice can have legitimate binding authority. Positivist legal theorists would respond in the affirmative, while natural, sociological and critical legal theorists would take the opposite view (Riddall 1991).

The judiciary has played a key role in the state response to land occupations, effectively underwriting the current structure of property relations by invoking idealized conceptions of rights that generally ignore the historical nature of human rights, including property rights. In this approach, the question of the validity of the purported transfer of ownership of customary land to the colonial settlers by local chiefs is considered to be irrelevant to determining present ownership.[12] This was the position taken by the High Court during the colonial period in the case of *Supervisor of Native Affairs* v. *Blantyre and East Africa Ltd*, even as it sought to ameliorate the harsher aspects of colonial expropriation of the land of indigenous communities. It is an approach that the court has taken in numerous cases since then.

This approach is in contrast to the more historically conscious jurisprudence that has engendered the concept of aboriginal land title, which was developed in the Australian cases of *Mabo* v. *Queensland [No. 2]*[13] and *Wik* v. *Queensland*.[14] According to Judge Brennan in the former case, 'It is only the fallacy of equating [colonial] sovereignty and beneficial ownership of land that gives rise to the notion that native title is extinguished by acquisition of sovereignty' (477).[15] This position is similar to that adopted by the South African Constitutional Court in the case of *Transvaal Agricultural Union* v. *Minister of Land Affairs*,[16] in which the court observed that 'certain persons and communities have a legitimate claim to the restitution of land rights which were lost as a result of past discriminatory laws'.[17]

Landowners, for their part, have responded to occupations by invoking state intervention, which has come in the form of the application of criminal law to evict, arrest and prosecute the alleged 'encroachers'. Landowners have also resorted to the civil law to seek eviction orders and, in a limited number of cases, compensation. In a number of cases, landowners have taken the law into their own hands and used force to evict land occupiers. In one particular case, a Greek owner of a tobacco farm in the southern district of Zomba shot dead a man who was among a group of people who had occupied part of the farm.[18]

Conclusion

Land occupations in Malawi have their roots in the history of the struggle between, on the one hand, smallholder farmers on customary lands as well as farm workers, and, on the other, private landowners and the state. The neoliberal legal order that formally guarantees everyone various human rights, including the right to own property and the right to development, has been inherently incapable of empowering peasants and workers to gain access to sufficient land for their livelihood. On the contrary, the state and landowners have used the law to entrench the rights of the landowner/employer class. The response has been the emergence of land occupations as a significant means by which land occupiers challenge the legitimacy of the prevailing neoliberal economic order and its legal superstructure. Due to a number of economic, social and political reasons, however, the land occupation movement in Malawi remains largely unorganized, uncoordinated and lacking in sufficient linkages to other progressive social forces. Nevertheless, it is probably the first significant counter-systemic movement to challenge the legitimacy of the neoliberal political and economic order that has been the dominant ideology in Malawi. Landlessness and land hunger in Malawi are bound to grow in the foreseeable future. As a result, land occupations will increase in frequency and scale, thereby contributing to the struggle for substantive, not rhetorical, social and economic transformation based on the principles of restitution and redistribution.

Notes

1. The deliberate use of the law to secure black labour for exploitation by settlers included: the imposition of a hut tax at the end of the nineteenth century, which compelled blacks to seek wage employment on the plantations; the requirement by the Native Tenants (Private Estates) Ordinance (1917) that the rent on plantations could only be in the form of labour and not cash; and the prohibition by the Native Labour Ordinance (1928) of the recruitment of blacks without government permission, which was mainly aimed at preventing the depletion of the labour supply by the recruiting agents of the South African and Rhodesian mining industry.

2. *The Nation*, 25 July 2002.

3. *The Nation*, 29 July 2002.

4. *Daily Times*, 20 March 1997.

5. *Daily Times*, 3 January 1996 and 17 October 1995.

6. *The Nation*, 18 March 2003.

7. For example, in the case of the occupation of Liwonde Forestry Reserve discussed earlier, where out of the forty land occupiers arrested for violently resisting eviction by Department of Forestry officials and police officers, nine were women.

8. *The Nation*, 7 February and 25 July 2002.

9. A 34-year-old man evicted from land he had occupied in Lengwe National Park, quoted in *The Nation*, 7 February 2002.

10. Senior Chief Kaomba, quoted in *The Nation*, 7 May 2002.

11. See, for example, the Environment Management Act (1996) and Forestry Act (1997).

12. For example, see the following cases decided by the High Court: *Nchima Tea Estates* v. *All Concerned Persons* Civil Cause No. 338 of 1998; *Mwawa* v. *Jekemu* Civil Cause No. 883 of 1993.

13. (1992) 175 Commonwealth Law Reports 1.

14. (1997) 187 Commonwealth Law Reports 1.

15. See also Ng'ong'ola 1997.

16. 1997 (2) SA 621.

17. See paragraph 33 of the judgment of the court.

18. *Yiannakis* v. *The Republic* High Court Criminal Appeal No. 37 of 1994.

References

Bangura, Yusuf (1992), 'Authoritarian Rule and Democracy in Africa: A Theoretical Discourse', in *Authoritarianism, Democracy and Adjustment*, ed. Peter Gibbon, Yusuf Bangura and Arve Ofstad, Uppsala: Nordiska Afrikainstitutet.

BDPA and AHT International (1998), *Tracer Study: A Component of the Customary Land Utilisation Survey*, Volume 3, *Report of the NSSA Tracer Survey*, Lilongwe: Government of Malawi.

Chanock, Martin (1991), 'Paradigms, Policies and Property: A Review of the Customary Law of Land Tenure', in *Law in Colonial Africa*, ed. Kristin Mann and Richard Roberts, Portsmouth: Heinemann.

Chanock, Martin (1985), *Law, Custom and Social Order: The Colonial Experience in Malawi and Zambia*, Cambridge: Cambridge University Press.

Chanthunya, Charles (1999), *Financial and Economic Returns to Land: Part I of the Final Report of the Presidential Commission of Inquiry on Land Policy Reform*, Zomba: Government Printer.

Chilowa, Wycliffe (1996), 'The Role and Management of Traditional Housing Areas', Center for Social Research, University of Malawi, mimeo.

Chilowa, Wycliffe, James Milner, Blessings Chinsinga, and Ronald Mangani (2000), *Social Policy in the Context of Economic Reforms: A Benchmark Survey Report*, Harare: SAPES.

Chinsinga, Blessings (2002), 'The Politics of Poverty Alleviation in Malawi: A Critical Review', in *A Democracy of Chameleons: Politics and Culture in the New Malawi*, ed. Harri Englund, Uppsala: Nordiska Afrikainstitutet.

Chipeta, Chinyamata (1993), 'The Impact of Structural Adjustment on the People of Malawi', in *The Impact of Structural Adjustment on the Population of Africa*, ed. Aderanti Adepoju, Oxford: James Currey.

Chipeta, Mapopa (1992), 'Political Process, Civil Society and the State', in *Malawi at Crossroads: The Postcolonial Political Economy*, ed. Guy Mhone, Harare: SAPES.

Cotterrell, Roger (1992), *The Sociology of Law: An Introduction*, 2nd edn, London: Butterworth.

Freyfogle, Eric (2002), 'The Tragedy of Fragmentation', *Valparaiso University Law Review* 36: 307–37.

Gordon, Robert (1982), 'Historicism in Legal Scholarship', *Yale Law Review* 90: 1017–56.

Gray, Richard (1960), *The Two Nations: Aspects of the Development of Race Relations in the Rhodesias and Nyasaland*, Oxford: Oxford University Press.

Griffith, John (1997), *The Politics of the Judiciary*, 5th edn, London: Fontana.

Gutto, Shadrack (1993), *Human and Peoples' Rights for the Oppressed: Critical Essays on Theory and Practice from Sociology of Law Perspectives*, Lund: Lund University Press.

Hardin, Garrett (1968), 'The Tragedy of the Commons', *Science* 162: 1243–48.

Kanyongolo, Fidelis Edge (2000), 'Human Rights Jurisprudence in Polarised Societies: A Comparative Analysis of Malawi and South Africa', Ph.D. thesis, University of East Anglia.

Kelman, Mark (1984), 'Trashing', *Stanford Law Review* 36: 321.

Kelman, Mark (1987), *A Guide to Critical Legal Studies*, Cambridge, MA: Harvard University Press.

Krishnamurty, B.S. (1972), 'Economic Policy, Land and Labour in Nyasaland 1890–1914', in *The Early History of Malawi*, ed. Brigdal Pachai, London: Longman.

Leopold, Aldo (1934), 'Conservation Economics', mimeo.

Macdonald, Roderick, ed. (1975), *From Nyasaland to Malawi*, Nairobi: East African Publishing House.

MacKinnon, Catherine (1989), *Towards a Feminist Theory of the State*, Cambridge, MA: Harvard University Press.

Malawi Congress Party (1961), *Manifesto*, Limbe: Malawi Congress Party.

Malawi Government (1983), *Principal Master Plan for National Parks and Wildlife Management*, Lilongwe: Malawi Government.

Malawi Government (1987), *Statement of Development Policies 1987–1996*, Zomba: Government Printer.

Malawi Government (1993), *National Sample Survey of Agriculture*, Zomba: Government Printer.

Malawi Government (1995), *Agricultural and Livestock Development Strategy and Action Plan*, Zomba: Government Printer.

Malawi Government (1998), *Malawi Population and Housing Census*, Zomba: Government Printer.

Malawi Government (1999), *Final Report of the Presidential Commission of Inquiry on Land Policy Reform*, Vol. 1, Zomba: Government Printer.

Malawi Government (2000), *Final Report of the Presidential Commission of Inquiry on Land Policy Reform*, Vol. 2, Zomba: Government Printer.

Malawi Government (2001), *Malawi National Land Policy*, Lilongwe: Malawi Government.

Malawi Government (2001), *State of Environment Report for Malawi, 2001*, Lilongwe: Malawi Government.

Malawi Government (2002a), *National Land Policy*, Zomba: Government Printer.

Malawi Government (2002b), *Malawi Poverty Reduction Strategy Paper*, Lilongwe: Malawi Government.

Malawi Government (2003), *Core Welfare Indicators Questionnaire Survey*, Zomba: Government Printer.

Malawi Housing Corporation (1981), *Malawi's Approach to the Problems of Human Settlement*, Blantyre: Malawi Housing Corporation.

McLellan, David (1995), *Karl Marx*, London: Macmillan.

Meinhardt, Heiko, and Nandini Patel (2003), *Malawi's Process of Democratic Transition: An Analysis of Political Developments between 1990 and 2003*, Lilongwe: Konrad Adaneur Stiftung.

Mhone, Guy (1992), 'The Political Economy of Malawi: An Overview', in *Malawi at Crossroads: The Postcolonial Political Economy*, ed. Guy Mhone, Harare: SAPES.

Minnis, John (1998), 'Prospects and Problems of Civil Society in Malawi', in *Democratisation in Malawi: A Stocktaking*, ed. Kings Phiri and Kenneth Ross, Blantyre: Kachere.

Motala, Ziyad (1998), 'The Constitution is Not Anything that the Court Wants It To Be: The Mhlungu Decision and the Need for Disciplining Rules', *South African Law Journal* 115: 141–55.

Moyo, Sam (2000), 'The Political Economy of Land Acquisition and Redistribution in Zimbabwe', *Journal of Southern African Studies* 26(1): 5–28.

Munzer, Stephen (1990), *A Theory of Property*, Cambridge: Cambridge University Press.

Neocosmos, Michael (2001), 'The Post-Development State in Southern Africa: Towards Consensus as a New Mode of Legitimation', paper presented at the conference on Interrogating the New Political Culture, Harare, Zimbabwe.

Ng'ong'ola, Clement (1997), 'Land Rights for Marginalised Ethnic Groups in

Botswana, with Special Reference to the Basarwa', *Journal of African Law* 41: 1–26.

Nothale, Dailes (1984), 'The Customary System of Land Tenure and Agricultural Development in Malawi', *Journal of Social Science* (University of Malawi) 11(2): 64–76.

Nyasaland Government (1946), *Land Commission Report*, Zomba: Government Printer.

Nyasaland Government (1920), *Land Commission Report*, Zomba: Government Printer.

Olsen, Frances (1995), *Feminist Legal Theory I: Foundations and Outlooks*, Aldershot: Dartmouth.

Pryor, Frederic (1988), *Income Distribution and Economic Development in Malawi: Some Historical Statistics*, World Bank Discussion Papers, New York: Oxford University Press.

Reserve Bank of Malawi (2002), *Financial and Economic Review* 34.

Rhode, Deborah (1990), 'Feminist Critical Theories', *Stanford Law Review* 42: 617.

Riddall, John (1991), *Jurisprudence*, London: Butterworth.

Rotberg, Robert (1965), *The Rise of Nationalism in Central Africa: The Making of Malawi and Zambia, 1873–1964*, Cambridge, MA: Harvard University Press.

Sachikonye, Lloyd (1995), 'Democracy, Civil Society and Social Movements', in *Democracy, Civil Society and the State: Social Movements in Southern Africa*, ed. Lloyd Sachikonye, Harare: SAPES Books.

Sachikonye, Lloyd (1998), 'Civic Society Organisation in Southern Africa', in *Governance and Human Development in Southern Africa*, ed. Ibbo Mandaza, Harare: SAPES.

Scott, James (1985), *Weapons of the Weak: Everyday Forms of Peasant Resistance*, New Haven, CT: Yale University Press.

Seidman, Ann, and Robert Seidman (1994), *State and Law in the Development Process: Problem Solving and Institutional Change in the Third World*, London: St Martins Press.

Shepperson, George, and Thomas Price (1958), *Independent African: John Chilembwe and the Origins, Setting and Significance of the Nyasaland Native Uprising of 1915*, Edinburgh: Edinburgh University Press.

Tushnet, Mark (1991), 'Critical Legal Studies: A Political History', *Yale Law Journal* 100: 1515–44.

Unger, Roberto (1976), *Law in Modern Society*, New York: Free Press.

United Nations (2001), *Common Country Assessment of Malawi*, Lilongwe: United Nations.

Van Velsen, Jaap (1966), 'Some Early Pressure Groups in Malawi', in *The Zambesian Past: Studies in Central African History*, ed. Eric Stokes and Richard Brown, Manchester: Manchester University Press.

Wechsler, Herbert (1959), 'Towards Neutral Principles of Constitutional Law', *Harvard Law Review* 73: 1–35.

World Bank (1985), *Malawi Economic Recovery: Resource Needs and Policy Needs – An Economic Memorandum*, Washington DC: World Bank.

5

Land Occupations in South Africa

Mfaniseni Fana Sihlongonyane

The issue of land occupations has been smouldering out of view for a long time, beneath the more glaring issues of housing, employment and infrastructure. It took the highly politicized land reform in Zimbabwe during 2000–02 and the Bredell land conflict in South Africa in 2001 to bring the issue to the forefront of debate. These have been accompanied by sensational headlines in the press, referring to 'land grabs', 'Zimbabwe-style land invasions', 'landlessness and desperation', and 'hunger for land',[1] culminating in the headlines of the *New African* magazine with the warning that 'the South African land issue is a ticking bomb' (Commey 2002). This has also given impetus to a new wave of research.[2]

The debate around land occupations is intertwined with the racial politics of Southern African countries, and in turn perceptions have been largely negative. Land occupation in general is associated with disorder, political strife, economic crisis, and administrative failure on the part of blacks. In Zimbabwe, for example, the recent land occupations have been synonymous with economic crisis and political failure. In South Africa, land occupations are widely referred to as land invasions, a racist concept born of apartheid that sought to despise the efforts by dispossessed blacks to acquire land. The post-apartheid government has inherited the land problem, as well as its conceptual malaise. Besides 'invasion', the concept of 'squatting' is also used, itself born of apartheid, while 'land seizure' is even more widely used, especially by the media, to refer to a diversity of phenomena, including colonial conquest, repossession through armed liberation struggle, or simply large-scale land occupations.

Sam Moyo (2000) has identified various types of land occupation in Zimbabwe, which have a wider relevance in the region. The first is the symbolic occupation in the form of demonstrations, which is often facilitated by civic or traditional leaders, as well as war veterans in the case of Zimbabwe. A second is the intimidatory occupation, involving violence and prompting landowners to engage in the land reform process, which has been witnessed in South Africa as well. A third involves wider political mobilization and is usually associated with an electoral campaign. The Bredell case, as reflected in the media, was given some political bearing by the Pan Africanist Congress Party (PAC). A fourth is the state-led compulsory acquisition, which aims to formalize occupations after the landless have selected themselves as beneficiaries. In South Africa, especially in the urban areas where the shortage of land is very acute, there are numerous negotiated settlements under formal and informal leases, sales or quit-rent arrangements. Land occupations on white farms, backyard shacks and informal settlements are also solicited under such arrangements, often with daring agreements.[3] These types of land occupation are to be distinguished from land alienations and expropriations of the colonial and postcolonial periods, involving seizures of land by the settler state and the promulgation of racist law. The latter would include the Native Land Act of 1913, Native Administration Act of 1927, Development Trust and Land Act of 1936, Asiatic Land Tenure Act of 1946, and Group Areas Act of 1950 and 1966.

This chapter provides an analysis of the land question in South Africa, with particular interest in contemporary social mobilizations, tactics and alliances around land reform. The section below begins with an historical overview of land alienation under apartheid, and subsequent sections turn to the politics of land occupations and land reform.

Land Alienation: From Apartheid to Neoliberalism

We may identify several waves of land alienation carried out under the aegis of colonial administrations and postcolonial states. Over a period of several centuries, European imperialist agents, including white merchants, missionaries and settlers, incrementally annexed Africa and alienated land from its indigenous inhabitants. Various institutions, churches and stations were established on the native lands through numerous unscrupulous deals and treaties. The climax of imperialism occurred through the late-nineteenth-century incursions by Britain, France, Germany, Belgium, as well as Italy, Portugal and Spain. Through invasion, establishment of territorial control, and subjugation of tribes and countries, colonial land alienation was assured (see Bernstein, Chapter 2 in this volume; Davidson 1968).

In South Africa, which gained formal independence from Britain in 1912, the white supremacist government carried land alienation further, securing and safeguarding land for the white population. This process saw huge tracks of land being transferred into state control and white capital at subsidized rates, and was accompanied over time with segregationist legislation. The Native Land and Trust Act of 1936 provided for the restriction of blacks in land ownership, and substantial areas were added to the reserves that had previously been defined in the 1913 Act to eliminate various forms of black tenancy that occurred outside them (Mabin 1991). By 1950, racial restriction on access to land and housing was non-negotiable. The National Party passed the Group Areas Act, which affected Blacks, Indians and Coloureds. They were all forced to live in segregated areas, and they were not allowed to occupy land outside areas assigned to them (Festenstein 1987). This was exacerbated by the promulgation of the Prevention of Illegal Squatters Act in 1951 and the Reservation of Separated Amenities Act in 1953, which respectively gave power to remove people and demolish their places without notice and ensured the reservation of public amenities for the use of persons belonging to a particular race. It has been estimated that 3.5 million people were displaced to accommodate the white government's discriminatory laws, 670,000 'black spot' removals were carried out, and 834,000 people were displaced under the Group Areas Act (Platzky and Walker 1985; Kassier and Groenevald 1992). In one province, KwaZulu–Natal, about 13 per cent of the land was allocated to 700,000 Africans, as against 87 per cent to Europeans. The province experienced 165 black spots by 1950; 97,000 people were removed from the Bantustans between 1960 and 1970, and even more in the 1980s.

It was against this wave of land alienations that social resistance against apartheid began dramatically in the 1960s. The Liberal Party, later known as the United Democratic Front, together with churches, reacted with initiatives for social mobilization against forced removals, working closely with communities. These social groups aimed to publicize what was happening in particular communities where land was being expropriated. Resistance gained momentum in the 1980s, when the struggle against removals began to be the subject of a legalistic and human rights debate, and when the United Democratic Front (UDF) called for a stop to the demolishing of shacks with immediate effect.

The apartheid state came under pressure in the 1980s, as neo-liberalism began to impose policies on South Africa and the region at large. Under the aegis of the IMF and the World Bank, neoliberal policies advocated a minimalist state and a reassertion of the power of market forces in economic management. At the heart of these institutions was the notion that 'Government increasingly recognizes the need for more restraint and for taking "market friendly" steps to deal with problems' (World Bank 1992: 6). This meant that the apartheid state could no longer exercise a strong command over the economy. It was now faced with an ever-changing and volatile economic environment that could no longer be mastered by the regulatory and institutional mechanisms of apartheid.

Related to this condition was the growing political opposition to apartheid, which rendered the management of cities in the 1980s ever more difficult. There was a growth of civic-based resistance to apartheid policy and administration. Education, rent and services boycotts, land invasions, and resistance to removals were all developed as strategies to overthrow the apartheid regime (Bremner 1994: 39). Apartheid thus suffered a deepening crisis, and democratization was increasingly difficult to resist.

Under these circumstances, a new and most remarkable wave of urban land occupations began to take place, driven structurally by the austere economic conditions. Hendler (1992) noted that although more than 150 per cent of the land declared for African residential development between 1980 and 1989 was set aside during 1987 in the PWV region (Gauteng), from 1989 until June 1991 a further 20,200 hectares were declared as land for the development of African townships, with a balance of 23,500 hectares still to be allocated. Thus from the mid-1980s, the quantities set aside for township establishment increased so rapidly that by the turn of the decade more hectares had been allocated for township development that had originally been envisaged in the guide planned for the turn of the century (Hendler 1992: 67). The intensifying demand for a democratic society meant that the apartheid state could no longer impose planning solutions. Spatial and regulatory planning, together with forced removals, were no longer an option; instead a more progressive approach was necessary. This meant that apartheid could no longer perpetuate the 'Big Lie'.

The Sources and Composition of Land Occupations

The sources of land occupations

While land occupations became rampant in the late 1980s, the removal of apartheid laws by F.W. De Klerk also sparked a massive movement of people from neighbouring countries into South Africa, to both urban and rural areas. In the urban areas, the move was motivated by the Reconstruction and Development Programme (RDP) promissory note to provide access to land (ANC 1994: 20). To some extent, the flexible stance of government to squatter settlements – including the upgrading of informal settlements and support for green-field settlement – motivated various processes of land occupation. This was compounded by the institutional and policy vacuum in government associated with the transition period of 1990–94. This period was crisis-ridden, uncertain and inauspicious for planning (Mabin and Harrison 1997: 37). The effectiveness of government structures had declined precipitously, and bitter and often violent conflicts at local level derailed many planning initiatives. Even the image of planning had fallen into disrepute, as the general public associated planning with apartheid forced removals.

Beneath the institutional level lies the massive poverty, inequality of land access, and housing shortage bequeathed by apartheid. In 1994, South Africa ranked 86th among countries for which the Human Development Index (HDI) was measured. But white South Africans had a level of human development similar to that of Israel or Canada, while black South Africans scored lower than countries such as Egypt and Swaziland (May 2000: 22). May et al. (1996) found that 22 per cent of the rural black population fell into the lowest rank of a four-scale indicator, while 75 per cent of these households also fell below the income poverty line.

In terms of land access, approximately 55,000 commercial farmers own 102 million hectares of land, compared to 11.2 million black households with access to 17 million hectares in the former homelands (Marcus et al. 1996: 97). A rural survey made public in 1997 reported that 70 per cent of the rural population had access to land, although in the case of more than 50 per cent of this group the land size was less than one hectare (Statistics South Africa 1999).

Meanwhile, approximately 13.5 per cent of all households (or 1 million households) lived in 'freestanding' squatter settlements on the urban peripheries and in backyards of formal housing units (RSA 1994). The large and increasing housing backlog has been due to low rates of formal housing provision, coupled with an increasing number of people accessing land informally – in informal settlements, backyard shacks, in overcrowded conditions in existing formal housing, and, most contentiously, through land invasions (Royston 1998). The size of the apartheid regime's housing backlog posed one of the most significant challenges to reconstruction and development, while the democratization process itself raised high expectations. Many of those waiting patiently for delivery of the RDP promises could no longer wait, and instead took matters into their own hands and started occupying land.

The democratization process also created a regional migration dynamic, as South Africa became a 'greener' pasture in comparison with neighbouring countries. Some people returned from these countries to their land in the rural areas, following their forced removals. In some cases, they came back with others who were not necessarily part of the forced removals but who were socially related. The perceived added advantage was access to pension money for the aged or retired, which was not available in the neighbouring states. Moreover, the proportionally higher number of rural households in South Africa with access to formal income served further to attract an influx of people.[4]

The austerity policies of the 1980s intensified the sources of land occupations. These policies reduced the role of the state and destroyed the patron–client relationships that had subsidized small farmers. Bryceson and Bank (2001: 13) noted that African peasant farmers were squeezed by the rising cost of agricultural inputs including fertilizers, improved seeds, and insecticides, while cash-crop incomes fluctuated and often declined. They observed that market liberalization from the perspective of the rural consumer tended to expand choice, but at arm's length, since much of the tantalizing merchandise came at unaffordable prices. The decline of the family farm has been noted by other studies (Bryceson 1999; Meagher and Mustapha 1994). It is also reflected in the decline in the share of

agriculture in the GDP, from 17 per cent in the 1950s to around 4
per cent in the 1990s (Department of Agriculture 1995). The number
of people employed in agriculture has declined commensurately, from
a high of more than 1.5 million in the 1970s to less than 1 million
in the 1990s (Mather 2000: 151).

The decline of smallholder farming has been compounded by
declining formal-sector employment, farm evictions, and the ravages
of HIV/AIDS, which have fuelled migration to towns. People have
been left with few alternatives but to look for open land in the
peri-urban areas, near places of employment (Lahiffa and Rugege
2002). Since the urban areas have high land rates and involve the
adverse formalities of urban planning, bureaucracy, and market-related
financial responsibilities, most of the people opted for these peri-urban
areas (Holm 1992: 245). Survival strategies here have included land
occupations and informal market activities, such as beer brewing,
selling prepared snacks, hair plaiting, small-scale retailing, prostitution,
handicrafts and tailoring, many of which previously had not been
commoditized (Bryceson and Bank 2001: 14). Predictably, accommodation has been poor, non-agricultural informal sector wages low, and
food security compromised (Bishop and Scoones 1994; Shackleton et
al. 1995; Lipton et al. 1996; Shackleton and Shackleton 1997; Davies
et al. 1999). In turn, demands for security of tenure have often been
expressed as a desire for freehold rights, due to the adverse history
of relations between tenants and private landlords, and tenants and
different levels of the state (Marcus et al. 1996).

The negative effects of austerity policies have given rise to a
division of opinion between the African National Congress (ANC)
and the South African Communist Party (SACP). Whilst the ANC
seems to implement neoliberal policies without much consultation,
the SACP has been inimical to the adoption of these policies, as they
seem antithetical to the alteration of agrarian power relations and
the redistribution of the resources that underlie them. Consequently,
the land reform has been bedeviled by tension between issues of
production and those of equity, rights and historical redress; whilst
the ANC struggled to balance the two and gravitated to the former,
the SACP advocated the latter. This struggle was epitomized by the
shift from the RDP to the market-friendly Growth, Employment
and Reconstruction (GEAR) policy, with the ANC seeking to court
and involve local and foreign investors in the land reform, and the
SACP arguing for a socialist approach.

The gender composition of land occupations

Women benefit most from land occupations, especially in the rural areas (Cross 1999). Their subordinate position within traditional structures of chiefdom typically inhibits their access and control over land and its natural resources. May et al. (1995: 17) argued that, 'Of all women in South Africa, the spatial and economic marginalization of rural African women is the most severe.' Whilst women are tasked with the primary responsibility of household reproduction in an environment of economic deterioration and dwindling social support, they do not have direct title or control of land. Typically they access land rights through their husbands or families. Cross (1999: 12) stated that 'land access is closely defended by power structures and is key to the institutional processes that determine what women can and cannot do with resources in the support of their households.' Making it worse is the fact that customary tenure systems are themselves deteriorating, as corrupt administrators and developers, on the one hand, and widening differentiation within communities, on the other, fail to enforce accountable land rights (Cross 1997; Cross et al. 1996). In this context, access to land by unauthorized occupations provides women with the opportunity to meet a variety of household needs, including those that are socially identified as being the responsibility of women (Bryceson 1995).

Many women are also pushed into land occupation because they are more vulnerable to unemployment than men (Lalthapersad-Pillay 2002). Since most rural women do not have high literacy levels or specialized skills, they are rendered superfluous in the low-skilled job sector. Even in circumstances where women are employed, they tend to be drawn into the very bottom and often worst sectors of the formal economy, such as domestic service and commercial agriculture. In the informal economy, gender stratification is mirrored in the street trading of Cape Town, Durban, Johannesburg and Pretoria, where 'Male traders are more likely to have larger operations and deal in non-food items while female traders tend to have smaller scale operations and to deal in food items – the former being more lucrative than the latter' (Skinner 2002: 49). Many women also resort to hazardous informal employment, such as prostitution and night-time street vending.

Men are also highly vulnerable to the austere economic effects of, and the high rate of retrenchments in, the formal sector of the economy, estimated at half a million between 1990 and 2000 (Shackleton et al. 2000: 35). Thus men resort to the informal economy as well, including criminal and gambling activities, and they also engage in the unauthorized occupation of land, usually adjacent to the old townships created under apartheid. The common factor among these people is that all are migrants from rural areas, within South Africa or the wider region.

Post-Apartheid Land Policy

The government has not been sleeping on the land issue. The primary concern has been to ensure that it does not lead to capital flight and economic meltdown. The government has thus been very careful not to scare investors whilst feeling bound by its conscience to deliver land to the landless. A number of laws have been passed since 1990 to steer a course between the two interests; these include the Upgrading and Land Tenure Rights Act (1991),[5] the Interim Protection of Informal Land Rights (1996),[6] the Community Property Associations Act (1996),[7] as well as the White Paper on Land Policy (1997).[8]

In 1994 the government introduced a land reform programme that sought to redistribute 30 per cent of agricultural land between 1994 and 1999 through restitution, redistribution, and tenure reform programmes. However, the land reform has been largely disappointing. According to the South African Survey (SAIRR 1999/2000), by the end of December 1998, the deadline for lodging land claims, some 63,000 claims had been lodged with the Commission on the Restitution of Land Rights, and only 41 claims had been settled. The slowness of the release of land was demonstrated in the fact that, after eight years of post-apartheid government, 55,000 farmers still own more than 80 per cent of the land, some of which is not productively used. Yet more than half of South Africans are landless and need land (NLC 2001/2).

A number of explanations are advanced for the poor delivery. Kock et al. (2002: 139) argued that the commitment by the government to a neoliberal macroeconomic programme has helped to slow down land redistribution, since the latter depends essentially on state spending. The programme remains market-driven, based on the 'willing buyer, willing seller' principle, and dependent on the injection of extremely limited state resources into a stagnant land market. The relative demobilization of civil society means that demands from below are not articulated effectively, diminishing the state's incentive to release more resources, especially when facing calls for fiscal discipline. Meanwhile, communities that enter the land reform process and are willing to pool their acquisition grants become vulnerable to inflated land prices (Kock et al. 2002: 144). The market mechanisms coupled with a weak state have left power relations unchanged, as landowners are able to dominate transfer negotiations to their benefit. The R15,000 (approximately US$1,650 in 2002) Settlement/Land Acquisition Grant is limited, since it covers land acquisition and improvement, and since the high price of land is frequently insufficient to achieve the latter. Therefore, after their acquisition of land, rural people are left with little money to build shelters and plough into productive farming.

Thus the redistribution programme becomes a means of reducing South Africa's housing/shelter shortage, but does not deal with food security and rural unemployment. The Land Agriculture Policy Centre warned that 'There is a danger that the new communities established through land reform will become no more than new Bantustans, where people are dumped in settlements with no visible means of supporting themselves' (LAPC 1997 in Kock et al. 2002: 144). This is compounded by the fact that in some cases the commercial land placed on offer within the redistribution programme is of low agro-ecological value, having already experienced poor environmental management by inefficient white farmers (Fakir, personal communications). It is notable also that the scope for women to exercise power over the land redistribution process remains limited, since men typically dominate the market mechanism and the collective use of household grants with which the rural poor purchase land.

A further problem of the land reform is that the Department of Land Affairs (DLA) lacks the capacity and support from other spheres of government to pursue its programme vigorously. Thus the DLA and non-governmental organizations have failed to find effective ways of working together to empower rural society. Over time, the new government has let land reform slip down its political agenda (Kock et al. 2002: 142). This is in line with the argument of the National Land Committee (NLC) that a generally weak civil society and lack of resources for organizations are the stumbling blocs to pushing the land reform from below. It has argued that 'The rural society had been "demobilized" in the mid- to late-1990s as NGOs' leaders have moved into government positions and the trade union movement placed decreasing effort into organization of rural farm workers' (Pearce 1997).

Exacerbating the situation is the fact that evictions have continued to occur unabated. Increasingly, farmers carry out evictions as a private action with the support of the state and agricultural companies against workers who are no longer wanted on the farms. Instances of evictions of farm workers include the following: (a) upon the sale of the farm, the new owner feels no obligation towards the farm workers they inherit with the farm; (b) on farms where some form of tenancy arrangement still exists, the failure by tenant families to replace ageing workers with younger, fitter members of the family often results in a notice to vacate the land; (c) workers who complain about poor conditions or attempt to join a union are frequently dismissed for being 'troublemakers'.

The powerful position of the farmer as an employer and landowner enables him to take punitive action against workers, with expulsion the ultimate sanction at his disposal. Meanwhile, the difficulties of farm tenants in holding on to land, never mind negotiating for land in the redistribution process, are formidable. Farm tenants operate in the face of eviction orders, trespass notices, court cases, fines, bribery of law authorities by landowners, and even prison sentences; they also confront demolition of homes, the closure of access to water taps and natural resources (e.g. rivers), the barring of tenants from rearing livestock, the chasing of family members out of the family, and even demolition of tombs.[9]

Nonetheless, tenants show dogged determination and resistance in their attempts to keep their homes and way of life. It is within this context that the Bredell land occupation incident occurred, with attendant media hype and political furore.

Strategies and Alliances of the Landless Movement

The emergence of organized land struggles

Only a few non-governmental organizations, community-based organizations, research centres, and institutes exist to pursue the land agenda. Most have been active since the 1980s. They include the following: the Association of Rural Advancement (AFRA), formed in 1979 to fight evictions in the KwaZulu homeland and Natal; the Surplus People's Project (SPP), formed a year later in 1980, out of the crossroads evictions struggle in the Western Cape; the Transvaal Rural Action Committee (TRAC), which grew out of the Black Sash committee to fight forced removals; and the Grahamstown Rural Committee (GRC), now known as the Border Rural Committee (BRC). These organizations came to be affiliated to one another through the National Committee Against Removals (NCAR). The NCAR's early work was campaigning for the reprieve of communities under threat of removal and for the return of communities that had already been removed from their land. In 1990, the NCAR was renamed the National Land Committee (NLC). The NLC participated in the debate on restitution and redistribution with the ANC affiliates, and made policy proposals.

Since then, the NLC has promoted the creation of a new and unified network of national rural social movements in the belief that pressure from below is the most effective mechanism to galvanize more effective state action on land. Other important network partners now include the Group for Environmental Monitoring, the Land and Agricultural Policy Centre, the Centre for Rural Legal Studies, the Centre for Legal Studies at the University of Witwatersrand, and the Programme for Land and Agrarian Studies at the University of the Western Cape (Kock et al. 2002).

In 1993, when several displaced communities rejected the apartheid government's land reform body, the Advisory Commission on Land Allocation (ACLA), the NLC launched the 'Back to the Land Campaign'. The NLC led representatives from 80 rural communities across the country in protest against the property rights clause of the fledgling constitution. This led to increased affiliation to the organization. Subsequently, in 1994, before the country's first non-racial elections, the NLC organized a land summit that was attended by some 400 civil society and land organizations. The summit produced a land charter, which was circulated to all political parties. The charter motivated the rural social movements to consider expropriation as a lever to force the pace of reform (Pearce 1997).

In 1999, the NLC joined forces with other rural-orientated NGOs and community-based organizations to launch the Rural Development Initiative (RDI) in a Land and Agrarian Reform Conference (LARC). The LARC was a one-off initiative held in

Pretoria, co-organized by the NLC and the Programme for Land and Agrarian Studies (PLAAS), a research and policy institute based at the University of the Western Cape. The LARC convened a range of national and provincial actors, NGOs, and representatives from community-based organizations (CBOs), and assessed the progress of land and agrarian reform in the five years of democracy (Hargreaves 1999: 43).

The Rural Development Initiative is driven by a number of NGOs, namely the NLC, the Rural Development Services Network (RDSN), the Trust for Community Outreach and Education (TCOE), the Initiative Participatory Development (IPD), and the South African NGO Coalition (SANGOCO). It organizes through clusters across provinces and regions, and steering committees have been established to coordinate activities at all levels. The RDI National Steering Committee developed a gender strategy in November 1998, and a small working group known as the Gender Task Team (GTT) was formed.

The RDI also produced a Rural People's Charter and Rural Development Policy Framework and Implementation Plan. The charter was drafted in a convention in Bloemfontein at which representatives of more than 600 rural communities across the country were present. In the process, the RDI sought to lay the groundwork for rural social movements. It also convened policy task teams comprising NGOs with experience in rural development to evolve policy for an integrated rural development strategy framework (Greenberg 1999). The NLC also mobilized its affiliates to advocate the rights of the landless through its Land Rights and Advocacy Department (LRAD), which is responsible for lobbying, advocacy and policy. A number of conferences have been hosted, which have led to the formation of the Land Access Movements of South Africa (LAMOSA), concerned with strengthening community structures.

In 2000 the NLC convened a summit of land organizations. This was intended to get actors outside government to reflect upon the new Integrated Programme on Land Redistribution and Agricultural Development (IPLRAD) and come up with a joint response. The organizations involved were the Congress of South African Trade Unions (COSATU), the South African Council of Churches (SACC), the Centre for Applied Legal Studies, the Legal Resources Centre, and the Programme for Land and Agrarian Studies. In addition, a number of community organizations made contributions, including the Labour Tenants Committee in Johannesburg, consisting of labour tenants from the Wakkerstroom district in Mphumalanga (NLC 2000/01: 13). Through NLC support, the organizations managed to organize a picket at the Department of Land Affairs in Pretoria.

The NLC subsequently organized a national training workshop for its affiliates. Planact, an allied NGO, was asked to facilitate the workshop. The NLC and the Border Rural Committee (BRC) conducted training on Integrated Development Plans (IDPs) for AFRA. The BRC shared its experience on the IDP process in the Willowvale District of the Eastern Cape. Another training workshop, on local government budgeting, was held in August 2000, facilitated by IDASA, and all IDP information acquired from Planact was given to the NLC IDP task team to be distributed to its affiliates. In addition, the NLC involved itself in a collaborative research initiative with Food First/Institute for Food and Development Policy in the USA. As part of its collaborative endeavour, the NLC, Rural Development Services Network (RDSN), and Centre for Applied Legal Studies (CALS) made a joint submission to traditional leaders and institutions.

The NLC was responsible in particular for the collaborative Southern African Network on Land (SANL), established in 1998 to ensure coordination and cooperation in the land and rural development sector in the region. The SANL consists of the Forum for Sustainable Agriculture (FONSAG) for Botswana, the Namibian NGO Forum (NANGOF), the Zimbabwe Environmental Regional Organization (ZERO), Organização Rural de Ajuda Mútua (ORAM) for Mozambique, the Lesotho Council of NGOs (LCN) on Land Agriculture and Environment, the Coordination Assembly of NGOs (CANGO) for Swaziland, and the National Land Committee for South Africa. The SANL is seen as a vehicle for sharing experiences and expertise, and for creating a common platform for advocacy. Thus the NLC is not only a national but also the regional hub of Southern Africa. As such, it has also facilitated the Agrarian Reform Network (ARNET), a programme of the Popular Coalition to Eradicate Hunger and Poverty. It is also part of the Land Rights Network of Southern Africa (LRNSA). Furthermore, strategic partnerships and international links have been forged with the Oxfam (UK) Land Rights Unit, the UK Department for International Development, the Southern African Regional Poverty Network, and the Southern African Human Rights NGOs network.

Parallel recognition should be given to Zimbabwe as a regional force, since it has achieved a remarkable shift in property rights, outside the above networks. This shift raises insightful contrasts with South Africa. Whilst in South Africa the land reform is orderly and planned, in Zimbabwe the planned land reform failed to avoid a 'tinderbox' effect. Whereas Zimbabwe had primarily depended for its market-based land reform on the flow of international funding, with some state funding, South Africa mainly uses internal budgets, with some funding from the World Bank. The Zimbabwean Constitution and the Land Acquisition Act of 1992 allowed for compulsory acquisition and called for limitations on farm size and various types of ownership (multiple, absentee and foreign), while the opposite is true in South Africa, where property rights are protected in the country's constitution of 1996. It is this that has, remarkably, enabled Zimbabwe to transfer a huge amount of land to black people through a fast-track process despite the political upheavals around the land issue.

The issue has become a breeding ground for confusion and contradictions among the alliances created at both national and international levels. Whilst some organizations are 'anti-Mugabe', others are in favour, as demonstrated by the opposing chants at the earth summit in Johannesburg where some shouted 'Up with Mugabe!' and others 'Down with Mugabe!' Intriguingly, the Landless People's Movement (see below) condemned and disassociated itself from the Zimbabwean land occupations. But, despite the divisions, this has not deterred the formation of international links.

The trend towards creating supra-national groupings has seen increasing collaboration at international levels on common issues of development. A Landless People's Charter was adopted in August 2001 in Durban, in a Landless People's Assembly during the United Nations World Conference Against Racism (NWCAR). More than 3,000 landless delegates from communities across South Africa, and their landless allies from around the world, took part in the adoption. The charter declared, 'We are the people who have borne the brunt of colonialism and neocolonialism, of the invasions of our land by the wealthy countries of the world, of the theft of the our natural resources, and of the forced extraction of our labour by the colonists.' This initiative was also linked to the NWCAR's 'Landlessness = Racism' campaign, which was carrying forward the 1994 demands of the Community Land Charter (NLC 2001/2).

Immediately prior to the Durban conference, the Landless People's Movement (LPM) was formed, out of the NLC framework. The LPM convened the 'Day of the Landless', with the support of the NLC. The LPM was formally launched in August 2002, during the WSSD in Johannesburg. The LPM has become the most visible rural social movement, struggling to organize and unite all the landless people of South Africa, around the motto 'Land Now! Organize and Unite!'

These various networks of the NLC have served to motivate joint ventures with other national and international NGOs. Joint work with the Urban Sector Network (USN) has begun following the urban forced removals in Gauteng as a part of the government's 'Urban Renewal Programme'. Notably, a visit by the Brazilian MST to South Africa was coordinated by Nkuzi and the NLC. This led to several public-speaking engagements, including the Landless People's Assembly during the WCAR, the World Rural Women's Day Workshop in Kimberly, the WSSD preparatory meeting of the Civil Society Indaba, and the NLC Annual General Meeting. Finally, even the Church has since been motivated to lend its support to the plight of the landless. Churches have been involved in several ways in the campaign for land restoration, and many fieldworkers from the Council of Churches and individual churches have supported communities returning to the land.

The rise of these networks occurs in a context where there is a convergence between globalization, social crisis and democratization. This unsettling combination has generated a reaction from groups that is best described as loose constellations of left-leaning community-based social movements. They vary in size, focus and influence, but what unites them is their common objective to help the poor and downtrodden, and their resentment of hierarchies, bureaucracies, corporate power and the profit motive in an unfettered market.

Looking to the future

A number of issues are shaping the struggle for land, especially within the emergent social movements.

First, the struggle for land is largely defensive in nature. It is not underwritten by a coherent political programme for social change. It is reactive and casual, having lost the supporting thrust of civic organizations, labour and students, as well as the zest that drove the anti-apartheid struggle in the 1980s. These organizations have now been caught up in anti-globalization struggles, and their support for land remains largely rhetorical. Most NGOs have also chosen to focus on more fashionable and politically rewarding issues, such as HIV/AIDS, poverty and the environment, at the expense of politically sensitive issues such as land.

Second, the nature of the struggle has also changed. It no longer operates within electoral politics and the traditional unions and civics but is driven by community-based organizations that are directly affected by land issues. These include people who opposed not only apartheid but also the injustices of the post-apartheid system. Thus the new tide of land struggles that have emerged seem to be inimical to the interests of both government and its partners, such as COSATU and civics. Yet the land struggle now finds itself in a new relationship with the anti-globalization movement, from which it draws financial and technical, but not ideological, support. This creates an ideological vacuum, since the membership of grassroots movements, as of the LPM, is largely illiterate and barely familiar with the economic dynamics of globalization. In this regard, Bond (2000) has noted that an elitist transition managed by the ANC–COSATU–SACP alliance has created a dampening of the protest spirit and orchestrated a containment of the revolutionary struggle.

Third, the struggle for land is fragmented. There is a lack of co-ordination and synthesis. Whilst instances of collaboration are apparent, and common objectives, programmes and grievances recognizable, there is no clear common enemy. Whereas some attack government at national level, others attack it locally, others at the provincial level, while others blame privatization/globalization. This creates a sense of confusion and uncertainty about the nature of the struggle and the means of achieving its objectives. Most of the organizations seem to be mere pressure groups without ideological direction and without the structural means to pursue their goals. Some appear to have a detached and casual attitude, others are ambiguous and shifting in their relations with government.

Relatedly, there is also uncertainty in the relations between movements and NGOs, and indeed among themselves. In some cases, an organization is not clear itself whether it is an NGO, a CBO, simply a pressure group, or a weapon for social mobilization. Even more noticeable is the range of agendas. Whilst some have a technical support inclination, others see themselves as political mobilizers. Tensions often develop between original objectives and subsequent developments. Exacerbating this are complex issues of ideological inclination and political imperative, where white-led NGOs seek to champion the needs of the black majority. Notably, the white technical staff tend to align themselves with government and seek to operate within its framework, while the grassroots want to operate outside.

The LPM has promise. It provides a good basis for the creation of a solidarity struggle for land among different people involved in land reform advocacy. Yet the challenges it still faces are great: harmonization of the different perspectives on land reform; the shaky organizational structure of some of the players; the superficial nature of the networks and partnerships; lack of resources; generating the political will among all concerned to push the land issue forward. An effective communication plan, able to deal with ideological, language, gender and geographical barriers, is critical to success. Such a plan must focus internally on mobilizing and strengthening grassroots structures and reaching out to the most marginalized, especially women. Yet the struggle must also extend internationally, for the fight is against a common system that has ravaged black people in the region and the landless in the world as a whole. There is a need to develop a global struggle beyond the rhetoric of the 'WSSD show of struggles'. This struggle must be underwritten by a practical, implementable plan to change people's lives. Thus the alliances that the NLC has made with organizations such as the MST should be developed into a worldwide struggle against landlessness.

In relation to the actual land reform process, the method of land reform must be recast to consider the needs of the people rather than the market. The land movement must develop tactical interventions that take into account the diversity of land issues in the various parts of the country, instead of relying on a blanket strategy. The historical and political–economic dynamics of the particular context must determine the kind of actions to be taken. Whilst one situation may warrant land seizure, another may need mere negotiation to acquire a piece of land. A range of strategies therefore needs to be developed. Moreover, the practice of land reform requires the creation of a structure for mediation. Currently the mediation organ is only targeted at the land claims, while the conflicts that occur at local levels are left to legal and policy enforcement procedures. A tense environment is thus created, which stifles any move to procure land within the land reform programme.

Finally, the movement lacks adequate information on which to base land claims. There is an urgent need for a land audit, focusing on land ownership per province, land use patterns, and land capacity for production per province and per farm. Moreover, there is need for a database of information on land demand, focusing on land right demands (related to forced removals), economic demands of various types, and traditional and religious land demands. In turn, education about the land reform should be undertaken in a more radical manner.

Conclusion

The land question is a long-standing issue in South African politics and is fundamental to the human rights, development and prosperity of the people. It is the basis on which political and economic changes, especially in developing countries, are determined. Land has been a dynamic factor in imperialism, colonialism and neocolonialism, and has had repercussions for the determination of power in the processes of production, distribution and exchange. Nevertheless the issue has been overshadowed by politically more vital issues, such as housing, employment creation and infrastructure.

The Zimbabwean and Bredell land occupations, ahead of the conference of the Non-Aligned Movement in Durban, brought the issue to the fore, accompanied by talk of 'Seattle-style resistance', 'Genoa, the repeat', and the sense of anxiety for resistance politics. The government, for its part, has been concerned with fostering a stability that conforms to its market-friendly programme. This has resulted in strong tensions between state and society, which have taken various forms, around issues of funding, alliance, support and technical assistance. Many movements are at pains to redefine their stance vis-à-vis the government, while others are experiencing fraught alliances, doubts and a tendency to introspection.

What is certain is the groundswell of grassroots demands for land. As variegated as these demands may be, they have common points of convergence, especially against the destructive effects of neoliberalism. They have also differences in approach, strength and attitudes towards government and towards one another. This suggests that the social movements in South Africa have some considerable way to go before they find the unity and resolve to identify and fight their common enemy.

Notes

1. *Newsweek*, 16 July 2001; *Cape Argus*, 29 August 2001; *Cape Times*, 6 July 2001; *Newsweek*, 16 July 2001; *Natal Witness*, 17 August 2001; *Sowetan*, 16 July 2001.

2. Deborah James (2001: 94) has located the stimulus for research within the 'regional setting' cum 'neighbour syndrome'.

3. This is relatively legitimate between the parties involved, especially in cases where government formalizes occupations that have been seen as informal settlements. Moyo (2000) views this as a legitimizing process. This problem is widely acknowledged in Lesotho (Shale 1997) and Swaziland (Sihlongonyane 2001).

4. Reportedly, 94.9 per cent of households in South Africa as a whole had access to formal income (May 1996), while 20 per cent in Namibia (Ashley and LaFranchi 1997) and 43 per cent in Zimbabwe (Bradley and Dewees 1993).

5. This brings the Act into line with government policy on the conversion of rights in land.

6. Protects the interests of people who have informal rights to land while an investigation is in progress.

7. Provides a legal mechanism to accommodate the needs of those people who wish to hold land collectively.

8. This created the framework of the land reform and its three programmes, tenure reform, redistribution and restitution.

9. Interview with the chair of the Landless People's Movement, December 2002.

References

ANC (African National Congress) (1994), *Reconstruction and Development Programme*, Cape Town: Umnyango Publishers.

Ashley, Caroline, and Christopher LaFranchi (1997), *Livelihood Strategies for Rural Livelihood in Caprivi: Implications for Conservancies and Natural Resource Management*, DEA Research Discussion Paper No. 20, Winkhoek: Ministry of Environment and Tourism.

Bishop, Joshua, and Ian Scoones (1994), *Beer and Baskets: The Economics of Women's Livelihoods in Ngamiland, Botswana*, IIED Research Series, Volume 3, London: International Institute for Environment and Development.

Bond, Patrick (2000), *Elite Transition: From Apartheid to Neo-liberalism in South Africa*, London: Pluto Press.

Bradley, Philip N., and Peter Dewees (1993), 'Indigenous Woodlands, Agricultural Production and Household Economy in Communal Areas', in *Living with Trees:*

Policies for Forest Management in Zimbabwe, ed. P.N. Bradley and K. McNamara, World Bank Technical Paper No. 10, Washington, DC: World Bank.

Bremner, Landsay (1994), 'Development and Resistance: The Lessons for the Planners of Phola Park', *Urban Forum* 5(1): 23–44.

Bryceson, Deborah Fahy, ed. (1995), *Women Wielding the Hoe: Lessons from Rural Africa for Feminist Theory and Development Practice*, Oxford: Berg.

Bryceson, Deborah Fahy (1999), 'Sub-Saharan Africa Betwixt and Between: Rural Livelihood Practices and Policies', African Studies Centre, Working Paper No. 43, Leden: African Studies Centre.

Bryceson, Deborah Fahy, and Leslie Bank (2001), 'End of Era: Africa's Development Policy Parallax', *Journal of Contemporary African Studies* 19(1): 5–23.

Commey, Pusch (2002), 'South Africa, Land: A Ticking Time Bomb', *New African*, November: 12–16.

Cross, Catherine (1997), 'Rural Land Tenure Reform: Surrounded by Hungry Allocators', *Indicator South Africa* 14(2): 72–8.

Cross, Catherine (1999), 'Women and Land in the Rural Crisis', *Agenda: Empowering Women for Gender Equity* 42: 12–27.

Cross, Catherine, Tobias Mngadi, Sipho Sibanda and Jama Victoria (1996), 'Making a Living under Land Reform: Weighing Up the Chances in KwaZulu-Natal', in *Land, Labour and Livelihoods in Rural South Africa*, Volume II, ed. Michael Lipton, Frank Ellis and Merle Lipton, Durban: Indicator Press.

Davidson, Basil (1968), *African History: Themes and Outlines*, London: Weidenfeld & Nicolson.

Davies, J., M. Richards and W. Cavendish (1999), *Beyond the Limits of PRA: A Comparison of Participatory and Conventional Economic Research Method in the Analysis of Ilala Palm Use in Southeastern Zimbabwe*, London: Overseas Development Institute.

Department of Agriculture (1995), *Abstract of Agricultural Statistics*, Pretoria: Department of Agriculture.

Department of Land Affairs (1995), *Land Policy Framework Document: Consultant Document*, Pretoria: DLA.

Festenstein, Melville (1987), *Land and Race: South Africa's Group Area and Land Act*, Johannesburg: South Africa Institute of Race Relations.

Fikir (1985), Personal Communications (an Interview), in L. Platzky and C. Walker, *Surplus People's Project: Land Restitution in South Africa – Alternative Forms of Compensation*, Cape Town: SPP.

Greenberg, Steve (1999), 'Building a People Driven Rural Development Strategy: Lessons from the RDI', paper presented to the 'Land and Agrarian Reform' conference, Alpha Training Centre, Broederstroom, Pretoria, 26–28 July.

Hargreaves, Samantha (1999), 'Land Reform: Putting Gender in the Centre', *Agenda* 42: 42–8.

Hendler, Paul (1992), 'Living in Apartheid's Shadow: Residential Planning for Africans in the PWV region, 1970–1990', *Urban Forum* 3(2): 39–80.

Holm, Magens (1992), 'Survival Strategies of Migrants to Makambako – An Intermediate Town in Tanzania', in *The Rural–Urban Interface in Africa: Expansion and Adaptation*, ed. Jonathan Baker and Poul Ove Pedersen, Seminar Proceedings, No. 27, Uppsala: Scandinavian Institute of African Studies.

James, Deborah Fahy (2001), 'Land for the Landless: Conflicting Images or Rural and Urban South Africa's Land Reform Programme', *Journal of Contemporary African Studies* 19(1): 93–109.

Kassier, Eckart, and Jan Groenewald (1992), 'Agriculture: An Overview', in *Wealth or Poverty: Critical Choices for South Africa*, ed. R. Shrineled, Cape Town: Oxford University Press.

Kock, Eddie (1996), *Land Reform in South Africa: Buoyed by Restitution and Redistribution a Phoenix Arises*, Ford Foundation Report, New York: Winter.

Kock, Eddie, Peter John Massyn and Andrea van Niekerk (2002), 'The Fate of Land Reform in Southern Africa: The Role for the State, the Market and Civil Society', in *Whose Land? Civil Society Perspectives on Land Reform and Rural Poverty Reduction: Regional Experiences from Africa, Asia and Latin America*, ed. K.B. Ghimire and B.H. Moore, Geneva: UNRISD.

Lahiffa, Edward, and Sam Rugege (2002), 'A Critical Assessment of State Land Redistribution Policy in the Light of the Grootboom Judgment', *New Agenda: South African Journal of Social Policy and Economic Policy* 3(7): 48–67.

Lalthapersad-Pillay, Pinky (2002), 'The Effects of Poverty on Women', *Africa Insight* 32(1): 37–44.

LAPC (Land Agriculture Policy Centre) (1997), 'Review of Land Reform in South Africa', unpublished report, Johannesburg.

Lipton, Michael, Frank Ellis and Merle Lipton, eds (1996), *Land, Labour and Livelihoods in Rural South Africa*, Volume II, Durban: Indicator Press.

Mabin, Alan (1991), 'The Impact of Apartheid on Rural Areas of South Africa', *Antipote* 23(1): 33–46.

Mabin, Alan, and Philip Harrison (1997), 'Ideas, Philosophy and Personality in the History of KwaZulu-Natal's Town and Regional Planning Commission', *South African Planning Journal* 42 (June): 22–42.

Marcus, Tessa, Kathy Eales and Adele Wildschut (1996), *Land Demand in the New South Africa*, Durban: Land and Agriculture Policy Centre, Indicator Press, University of Natal.

Mather, Charles (2000), 'South African Agriculture and Rural Livelihoods in the Era of Liberalisation', in *At the Crossroads: Land and Agrarian Reform in South Africa into the 21st Century*, ed. Ben Cousins, Braamfontein: PLAAS and NLC.

May, Julian, Deborah Posel and Michael Carter (1995), *The Composition and Persistence of Poverty in Rural South Africa: An Entitlements Approach to Poverty*, Research Report No. 15, Land and Agriculture Policy Centre, Johannesburg: LAPC.

May, Julian (1996), 'Assets, Income and Livelihoods in Rural KwaZulu-Natal', in *Land, Labour and Livelihoods in Rural South Africa*, Volume II, ed. Michael Lipton, Frank Ellis and Merle Lipton, Durban: Indicator Press.

May, Julian (2000), 'The Structure and Composition of Rural Poverty and Livelihoods in South Africa', in *At the Crossroads: Land and Agrarian Reform in South Africa into the 21st Century*, ed. Ben Cousins, Braamfontein: PLAAS and NLC.

May, Julian, Heido Atwood, Peter Ewang, Francie Lund, Andy Norton and Wilfred Wentzel (1997), *Experience and Perceptions of Poverty in South Africa:*

An Entitlement Approach, unpublished report to the World Bank, Government of Netherlands and ODA, Data Research Africa, Durban.

Meagher, Kate, and Abdul Raufu Mustapha (1994), 'De-agrianisation in Rural Housaland: Flexibility or Fragility?', in *De-Agrianisation in Africa*, ed. D. Bryceson and C. van der Laan, Working Paper No. 20, Leiden: Africa Studies Centre.

Moser, Caroline (1996), *Confronting Crisis: A Comparative Study of Household Responses to Poverty and Vulnerability in Four Poor Urban Communities*, Washington, DC: World Bank.

Moyo, Sam (2000), 'The Political Economy of Land Acquisition and Redistribution in Zimbabwe', *Journal of Southern African Studies* 26(1): 5–28.

NLC (National Land Committee) (2000/01), *Annual Report* Johannesburg: Media Unit of the National Land Committee.

NLC (National Land Committee) (2001/2), *Annual Report*, Johannesburg: Media Unit of the National Land Committee.

Pearce, Brendan (1997), 'Overview Paper on Land Reform in South Africa', December, mimeo.

Platzky, Lanine, and Walker Cherryl (1985), *The Surplus People's Project: Forced Removals in South Africa*, Johannesburg: Ravan Press.

Royston, Lauren (1998), *Urban Land Issues in Contemporary South Africa: Land Tenure Regulation and Infrastructure and Services Provision*, No. 87, Development Planning Unit, University College London.

RSA (Republic of South Africa) (1994), *White Paper: A New Housing Policy and Strategy of the Government of National Unity*, Pretoria: Government Gazette.

SAIRR (1999/2000), *South Africa Survey*, South African Institute of Race Relations: Johannesburg.

Shackleton, Sheona Elizabeth, J.J. Stadler, K.A. Jeenes, S.R. Pollard and J.S.S. Gear (1995), 'Adaptive Strategies for the Poor in Arid and Semi-arid Lands: In Search of Sustainable Livelihoods. A Case Study of Bushbuckridge District, Eastern Transvaal, South Africa', unpublished report produced for the IIED and Wits Rural Facility, Klaserie.

Shackleton, Charles Michael, and Sheona Elizabeth Shackleton (1997), 'The Use and Potential for Commercial of Veld Products in the Bushbuckridge Area', unpublished report, DANCED Community Forest Project, Department of Water Affairs and Forestry, Nelspruit.

Shale, Pheelo (1997), 'Illegal Land Occupation in Maseru, Lesotho', M.Sc. dissertation, Faculty of Architecture, University of Witwatersrand.

Sihlongonyane, Mfaniseni F. (2001), 'Rural–Urban Encounters In Swaziland: The Case of Manzini City', paper presented at the DPU International Conference on 'Rural–Urban Encounters: Managing the Environment of the Peri-Urban Interface', London, 9–10 November.

Skinner, Caroline (2000), 'Getting Institutions Right: Local Government and Street Traders in Four South African Cities', *Urban Forum* 11(1): 49–71.

Statistics South Africa (1999), *Rural Survey*, www.statssa.gov.za/relsched/releases/p0360/p0360/htm.

Surplus People's Project (1985), *Forced Removals in South Africa*, Cape Town: Ravan.

World Bank (1992), *Governance and Development*, Washington, DC: World Bank.

6

Land Occupations and Land Reform in Zimbabwe: Towards the National Democratic Revolution

Sam Moyo and Paris Yeros

The land occupation movement in Zimbabwe has achieved the first major land reform since the end of the Cold War.[1] It has also been the most important challenge to the neocolonial state in Africa under structural adjustment, and, if judged by its effectiveness in acquiring land, it has also been the most notable of rural movements in the world today.

Yet it has proved an intellectual challenge and a matter of political ambivalence. On the one hand, the land reform process has raised fundamental analytical questions regarding peripheral capitalism, the state and nationalism. On the other hand, neither academia nor 'progressive' political forces have risen to the task. Most have readily denounced the land reform process as 'destructive' of the state, and its nationalism as 'authoritarian' or 'exhausted' (i.e. belonging to a previous era); others have gone the other way, celebrating the land reform as the culmination of 'black empowerment' or 'economic indigenization'.

The polarization of the debate has less to do with the peculiarities of Zimbabwe and more to do with the state of academia in the 1990s. This has been marked by a diversion into rarefied debates over 'identity politics', nationally and internationally, and the generalized embourgeoisement of nationalist intellectuals. Certainly, twenty years ago, radical land reform in Zimbabwe would have received a different response. While the event would have presented considerable analytical difficulties even then, progressive intellectuals would have proceeded to debate the relevant issues rigorously, and these would have concerned the nature of the neocolonial state, inter-capitalist conflict, peasant–worker relations, the class struggles within the land occupation movement, and the direction of the national democratic revolution.

Why such a change in just twenty years? Is it that neocolonialism is no longer relevant? Did structural adjustment deliver national democracy? Or is it that the national form of sovereignty itself has been superseded by neoliberal globalization? Nothing, of course, could be further from the truth. The answer lies precisely in the co-optation of both academia and 'oppositional' politics, to the point where imperialism has become mystified, national self-determination demoted, the state obscured, and the agrarian question abandoned.[2] Such intellectual reversals have had real political effects, perhaps most clearly in relation to Zimbabwe, whose radical nationalism and land reform have proved unpalatable to the 'civic' and 'post' nationalisms of domestic and international social forces.

The Political Economy of Neocolonialism

The political economy of Zimbabwe is comparable to that of other African, Latin American and Asian states that have remained in a disarticulated pattern of accumulation with unresolved agrarian questions. This persisting underdevelopment is part and parcel of the neocolonial situation – that is, the failure of juridically independent states to complete the national democratic revolution. This remains the case despite complete transitions to capitalism in the twentieth century.

The case of Zimbabwe, and of Southern Africa more generally, consists in a subtype of neocolonialism, deriving from the white-settler colonial experience. One crucial aspect of white-settler colonial capitalism was that, periodically, it manifested strong contradictions between introverted and extroverted capital accumulation strategies. This was especially the case in Zimbabwe upon the emergence of an industrial bourgeoisie in the course of the two world wars. In this sense, the historical experience of Zimbabwe (together with South Africa) can be understood as comparable to 'semi-peripheral' Latin American countries. A second aspect of white-settler capitalism, however, was that, in the organization of the labour process, white capital exercised both 'direct' and 'indirect' power over the indigenous black population. This contrasts with recent interpretations regarding the primacy of 'indirect' rule in Africa (Mamdani 1996), and it also contrasts with Latin American historical experiences in which the post-slavery *latifúndio-minifúndio* system did not institutionalize racial segregation. These two aspects of white-settler capitalism have given a particular shape to neocolonialism in Zimbabwe, notably in its dynamics of class, race and nation.

The white-settler colonial state

The political economy of colonial Zimbabwe began to exhibit its peculiar tendencies early in the twentieth century, as the initial speculative incursion by mining capital gave way to the establishment of a white agrarian bourgeoisie with a partial interest in the home market. The ensuing years were marked by an intensifying inter-capitalist conflict between white agrarian capital, on the one hand, and mining capital and London-based finance, on the other (Arrighi 1973). This culminated in 1923 in the establishment of white 'self-government' in the colony of 'Southern Rhodesia', by which the white agrarian bourgeoisie both established its political leadership and struck a compromise with extroverted capitals.

Also established under the leadership of white agrarian capital was the institutionalization of racial segregation. In itself, this was a profound contradiction to whatever designs white agrarian capital may have had for the development of the home market. For the vision of the 'home market' held by white agrarian capital would thereafter be confined to the white-settler element, and would only partly be challenged in due course by the emergence of a white industrial bourgeoisie. This white supremacist framework was to leave an indelible mark on the development of capitalism in the white-settler colonial state. From an early stage, white agrarian capital demonstrated that, while it was 'more than comprador', it was 'less than national' (Phimister 1988: 180); and, over time, while inter-capitalist conflict would challenge the foundations of racial segregation, it would never do so to the point of becoming properly 'national' – that is, of producing an alliance between white industrial capital and popular nationalist forces for the concerted development of the home market.

The seeds of black capitalism were also sown from the early days of the white-settler colonial state. In the interwar years, the state allowed for the creation of a small black agrarian capitalist class outside the communal areas – in the 'Native Purchase Areas' – as a means of cultivating a bourgeois alliance across the racial divide. But this project remained insignificant, as the white-settler colonial state refused to support black capital for its expansion and, indeed, competition with white agrarian capital. Beyond Purchase Area farmers, a small black bourgeoisie also developed within the communal areas, together with the development of commodity production, but this too was to be prohibited from dynamic development.

The labour process in colonial Zimbabwe came to be characterized by an enduring contradiction between proletarianization and a politically engineered functional dualism, by which petty commodity production in the communal areas, and especially unwaged female labour, would subsidize the social reproduction of male labour-power on mines and farms. This contradiction would produce neither a settled industrial proletariat nor a viable peasantry, but a workforce in motion, straddling communal lands, white farms, mines and industrial workplaces. This was the 'semi-proletariat', the aggregate of peasant-worker households, differentiated by gender, and torn between ethno-linguistic particularities and a developing sense of nationhood (Yeros 2002b). Under such conditions, trade-union organization was an onerous struggle. The obstacles inherent in semi-proletarianization – migration, rural–urban duality, poverty, ethnic and gender cleavages – were compounded by state repression and, in the postwar period, by the onset of divisive tactics by international trade unionism (Raftopoulos 1996). Nonetheless, soon after the end of World War II, trade unionism in the white-settler colonial state did make advances, even to the point of mobilizing successful country-wide strikes in 1945 and 1947.

The mode of rule in colonial Zimbabwe combined direct and indirect forms, for indirect rule in itself was far from self-contained or sufficient to organize the labour process. The segregationist project of white agrarian capital proceeded actively after 1923, in the combined form of territorial segregation, notably by the Land Apportionment Act (1930), and, even more crucially, *legal* segregation. As the institutional lynchpin of African-style functional dualism, this consisted in the transfer of judicial authority within communal areas to chiefs, under the Native Affairs Act (1927) and the Native Law and Courts Act (1937), while its social linchpin was the binding of women to the land by kinship relations, adjudicated by chiefs

(Schmidt 1990). Beyond this 'indirect rule', white agrarian capital continued to exercise direct power over the vast tracts of 'European' land that it appropriated; and there it reproduced relations of personal dependence vis-à-vis black tenants and labour (Palmer 1977). For its own part, mining capital would perfect the 'compound system', by which labour would be bound to the mining compounds by means of a variety of economic and extra-economic instruments (Van Onselen 1976). The power of the central state would also be used to undermine African agriculture systematically, taxing it and manipulating it, most notably by the Maize Control Acts (1931, 1934), for the purpose of subsidizing white agrarian capital and reinforcing its economic-structural supremacy; while agrarian, mining and, later, industrial capitals as a whole resorted systematically to the deployment of the security forces of the state to suppress trade-union organization – notably by the Industrial Conciliation Act (1937, 1937) and the Sedition Act (1936) – as well as, in due course, nationalist mobilization.

World War II and its aftermath brought about a restructuring of the economy, in two important ways. First, industrial capital embarked on a spectacular growth path, expanding output fivefold between 1939 and 1948 – in such industries as food-processing, construction, textiles and clothing (Phimister 2000: 32–3) – and maturing politically to pose a new challenge to functional dualism. Second, agrarian capital redirected its accumulation strategy resolutely to the external market, by the conversion of its farmland from maize to tobacco (Arrighi 1973: 350–58). Thereafter, inter-capitalist competition would produce a closer alliance between mining and agrarian capital against the industrial bourgeoisie.

Between the late 1940s and the late 1950s, a new compromise was struck among white capitals to broaden further the home market, by two means: first, by the Native Land Husbandry Act (1951), whose intention was to reorganize the communal areas along capitalist lines and to create a settled urban proletariat; and second, by enlarging the sphere of influence of white-settler capital beyond Southern Rhodesia to colonial Malawi and Zambia (Nyasaland and Northern Rhodesia) by means of the establishment of the Central African Federation. This process was accompanied by limited reforms in labour relations, as well as in the electoral system, intending to co-opt black labour and the petty bourgeoisie within the framework and ideology of racial 'partnership'.

The reforms and the partnership did not succeed or survive. By the late 1950s, the perennial constraints of disarticulated accumulation were imposing themselves on the Federation, thrusting its balance of payments into crisis; by 1958, class balances and capitalist alliances were entering a new period of reconfiguration. On the one hand, black trade-union organization was continuing to advance, now resonating with the popular anti-colonial nationalism spreading across the continent. On the other hand, a black bourgeoisie did not emerge in time under the wing of white capital to defend a neocolonial solution. Instead, the white-settler colonial state became polarized between a cross-class African nationalism, led by the black petty bourgeoisie, and a cross-class white supremacism, led by white agrarian capital (Arrighi 1973). In the following years, nationalist organization was suppressed and driven underground, decolonization was aborted, unilateral independence declared (UDI) in 1965, and, ultimately, the transition to neocolonialism postponed. With the collapse of the Federation in 1963, Zambia and Malawi would make their neocolonial transitions on their own.

Under UDI, the white-settler colonial state went from boom to bust. It experienced rapid industrial development, as all capitals, including industrial capital, closed ranks under a highly interventionist capitalist state, to be steered into an introverted white-supremacist survival project. This would be facilitated by UN-sponsored international sanctions that were permeable by design, de facto allowing for the financing of Rhodesia by Western banks, the importation of oil, military aid, and direct investment by transnational capital – the latter expanding its capital stock by 37 per cent in 1966–76 (Clarke 1980). Until 1974, 'sanctions' and state dirigisme would drive an annual average industrial growth rate of 9 per cent. However, by the mid-1970s, the white-settler economy was once again overheating, as its unresolved internal and external constraints were re-imposing themselves on the accumulation process. For the state never broadened the home market beyond the settler element, even as it turned inwards; instead, it reinforced functional dualism in its segregationist form and relied on the super-exploitation of black labour for rapid capital accumulation. The crisis was compounded politically and economically by the reorganization of the nationalist movement in two parties, ZANU and ZAPU, and the launch of armed struggle in the countryside, with the support of China and the Soviet Union, respectively.

The remaining years of colonial occupation were riven by guerrilla warfare in a Cold War context. By the late 1970s, British and American foreign policies were becoming intensely preoccupied with the possibility of radical outcomes in southern Africa, henceforth focusing their energies on a negotiated transition to neocolonialism. In 1979, after years of guerilla warfare, and under a Patriotic Front (PF) coalition, the liberation movement would sign up to the neocolonial transition at Lancaster House in London.

From liberation to liberalization

The independence of Zimbabwe was celebrated on 18 April 1980. At long last, Zimbabwe was embarking on a nation-building project of its own. But in the new state, the national democratic revolution would remain a matter of social struggle. The 'post-white-settler colonial state' was a particular variety of the neocolonial state, for formal power had not been ceded to a black petty bourgeoisie alone; instead, the aspiring black bourgeoisie would share power with the established white-settler capital (Mandaza 1986a, 1986b). Ideologically, this political dispensation was cast in the form of 'reconciliation', an echo of postwar 'partnership', consisting effectively in a reconciliation *not* 'between the races' but 'with capital' (Sibanda 1988). Economically, industrial and mining interests remained wholly owned by local white and foreign capital, under monopoly conditions. For its own part, the white agrarian bourgeoisie, some 6,000 farmers at independence, retained 39 per cent of the land, amounting to 15.5 million hectares of prime agro-ecological farmland, while 1 million black households remained consigned to 41.4 per cent of the land, or 16.4 million hectares of marginal land (Moyo 1995). In all, the white minority, at below 3 per cent of the population, commanded nearly two-thirds of national income; while the black majority, at 97 per cent, took the remaining one-third. Constitutionally, the Lancaster House agreement established the 'willing-buyer, willing-seller' principle as the basis of land transfers, with an expiration date of 1990; and it reserved 20 per cent of parliamentary seats for the white community of 3 per cent, with an expiration date of 1987.

The Zimbabwean economy at this time was the second most industrialized in sub-Saharan Africa, following South Africa. Zimbabwe inherited the UDI agro-industrial complex, characterized by significant articulation between the sectors (almost half of agricultural output was feeding domestic industry), and diversified production of 7,000 commodities, ranging from food and clothing, to fertilizers and chemicals, to metal products, electrical machinery, and equipment, even to locally assembled automobiles; manufacturing accounted for 25 per cent of GDP and earned 40 per cent of foreign exchange (Mlambo 2000: 80). Yet, the economy remained in a fundamentally disarticulated pattern of accumulation, and the home market a luxury market, effectively restricted to less than 15 per cent of Zimbabwe's 7 million people. Moreover, agriculture remained the most important sector, accounting for 40 per cent of GDP and employing 70 per cent of the population (Stoneman and Cliffe 1989: 43).

Nation-building was rightly cast as a matter of endogenizing the economy – that is, deepening sectoral and social articulation. Yet, under the new political dispensation, facilitated not least by the ongoing organizational weakness of the semi-proletariat (to which we will soon turn), the national plan invoked the reformist UN language of the 1970s, labelled 'Growth with Equity' in the case of Zimbabwe, by which redistribution would be subordinated to the growth/stagnation of industry. In turn, the latter would be seen as the leading developmental sector – not as auxiliary to the technical development of agriculture.

Inter-capitalist conflict in the neocolonial state began to manifest new tendencies and alliances. The conventional conflict between intro-verted and extroverted capitals was compounded by new sources of conflict, namely between the aspiring black bourgeoisie and white capital, but also *within* the black petty bourgeoisie itself. Racial conflict was to produce a particular scenario, marked by deep resentment *and* instrumentalization of race by both whites and blacks – the latter to extract concessions, the former to 'window dress' monopoly capital-ism with black managers. Meanwhile, intra-black petty-bourgeois conflicts intensified rapidly, and tragically. The black petty bourgeoisie – effectively shut out of the white private sector – was to redirect its accumulation strategies through the state and, moreover, resort to the instrumentalization of ethnicity. This would culminate in a violent crackdown by the state in the southern provinces of Matabeleland, in the period 1983–87, pitting the ruling ZANU–PF party against dissident former PF–ZAPU guerillas. As was astutely observed at the time, under neocolonialism 'ethnic diversity becomes employed not to enrich the cultural heritage of the nation but to advance the class interests of groups or segments. The racial divisions are utilized not to entrench national unity but to consolidate class domination and exploitation' (Sibanda 1988: 266–67).

Yet, of most immediate concern to imperial power was the more conventional conflict between introverted and extroverted accumulation strategies. This concern synergized with the distrust of black majority rule generally, and of the ruling party specifically, which continued to profess Marxism–Leninism, despite its 'Growth and Equity' programme. In this sense, the Lancaster House constitutional provisions would not be sufficient to quell Anglo-American fears of African nationalism. The imperial task hereafter would be to ensure that extroverted capital would prevail in national politics, and this meant focusing political energy and finance on the co-optation of industrial capital, as represented by the Congress of Zimbabwe Industries (CZI); the other sectors, mining, commerce and agriculture, were already inclining back to an extroverted alliance with transnational capital, given that the white supremacist guardian state had been defeated.

The imperialist campaign was led by the World Bank and the IMF: the former focusing on industry specifically, by establishing an 'export-revolving fund' for the sector in 1985; the latter focusing on gaining leverage over the government by means of debt. At independence, Zimbabwe was seen as 'underborrowed', with a debt-service ratio of only 10 per cent, which would soon change. Zimbabwe re-entered a balance-of-payments crisis as early as 1982, and this was quickly seized upon (Chimombe 1986; Stoneman 1989; Bond 1998). 'Within a year of joining [the IMF] from an "underborrowed" position, Zimbabwe was drawing on a stand-by agreement and was, therefore, in the position of being dictated to in its economic policies' (Stoneman 1989: 41). The debt-service ratio soon ballooned to 32 per cent. But this was not yet the launch of structural adjustment, only its postponement, as government opted instead for 'self-imposed' austerity, in the form of cutbacks in rural development, including land acquisition and resettlement.

A limited amount of land reform took place in the 1980s under the market mechanism. In all, government resettled 58,000 on 3 million hectares of land, reducing the white commercial farming sector to 11 million hectares, 29 per cent of agricultural land. As we will see, this was far short of the targeted 162,000 families for resettlement, while the land acquired was largely of low agro-ecological value (Moyo 1995). Under the Lancaster House constitutional constraints, more emphasis was placed on rural development in the peasant sector – on research, extension services, roads and marketing depots – with a budget increase of 37 per cent annually in 1980–85, plus heavy spending on education and health (Bratton 1987). These would be complemented by rising producer prices in the same period for the main commodities (maize, wheat, beef), such that by 1985 peasants were producing 45 per cent of marketed output (up from 8 per cent in 1980), although differentiated in terms of agro-ecological region and class (Cliffe 1988). But in the second half of the 1980s, under economic austerity and industrial stagnation, rural spending would enter a process of reversal. At the same time, the division of labour in agriculture would also shift, with peasants specializing in maize and cotton, and large-scale farmers in the high foreign-exchange earners, tobacco and coffee, as well as maize and cotton. One important political result was that large-scale farmers once again became more clearly extroverted and with an interest in dismantling – liberalizing – the price-support systems that were being used by the state to transfer income, through infrastructural development, back to the peasant sector (Skålnes 1995).

Industry remained in a state of overcapacity, and by the late 1980s was being co-opted into export markets. Indeed, by 1988 all capitals across sectors had realigned behind a common policy stance of extroversion, specifically the liberalization programme promoted by the World Bank. Importantly, this realignment was matched by the ongoing embourgeoisement of the black elite, whose accumulation strategies were still operating on the fringes of monopoly capitalism – in petty commerce, real estate and the hospitality industry – and with the assistance of the state, the process known as 'corruption'. It was also in an advanced stage of 'compradorization', as a small but powerful group established itself within the white-dominated financial circuit (Bond 1998). After 1987, with the end of the Matabeleland violence via the Unity Agreement, and consequently the absorption of PF–ZAPU into the ranks of ZANU–PF, nationalist elites would finally set aside their ethnicized divisions and clear the way for a joint strategy of accumulation (Raftopoulos 1992). In the following year, discussion would begin for the foundation of the Indigenous Business Development Centre (IBDC), a black business lobby aiming at a better deal against white capital (CZI), and it would soon turn its lobbying energy on 'affirmative action' in the course of liberalization. Importantly, the whole process of embourgeoisement, compradorization and national unification was accompanied by a new political project to establish, by constitutional amendment, a 'one-party state' – that is, a dictatorship of the bourgeoisie stripped of its democratic formalities. As we will see, this would ultimately be defeated, by popular mobilization led by the Zimbabwe Congress of Trade Unions (ZCTU).

If in the rest of the periphery structural adjustment was being imposed by means of the balance-of-payments crisis (Gowan 1998; Haggard and Maxfield 1996), in Zimbabwe it occurred by co-optation of its domestic capitals. Although Zimbabwe was pursuing austerity policies, and was running on industrial overcapacity, it was not yet in a payments crisis (Bond 1998). The change of economic direction was further enabled by political transformation in the global arena, specifically the collapse of the Soviet Union, which translated locally into a collapse of legitimacy for statist economic policy. Thus events moved rapidly: in 1989 a liberal Investment Code was implemented; in 1990 the foreign exchange allocation system was replaced by an Open General Import Licence; and, finally, in 1990, the Economic Structural Adjustment Programme was launched; this involved the standardized recipe of cuts in public spending, currency devaluation, and the liberalization of prices, interest rates and trade, followed by deregulation of the capital account and labour relations.

The liberalization programme was implemented fully over the next few years, and led to the standard stagflationary effects. By 1992, the trade deficit had ballooned, inflation had tripled to 42 per cent, and monetary authorities were implementing 'sado-monetarism' (Bond 1998). The economic results were as follows. Between 1991 and 1995, deindustrialization would set in, with a new round of downsizing and bankruptcies, involving the closure of one-fifth of the clothing sector. Utilization of industrial capacity was further reduced to 65 per cent, while by 1998, the contribution of manu-facturing to GDP had fallen to 17 per cent, down by one-quarter (ZCTU 1996; UNDP/UNCTAD 2000). By 1993, real wages had fallen by two-thirds; by 1995, job losses in both public and private sectors amounted to 45,000; meanwhile the share of wages in the national income had dropped from 64 per cent to 40 per cent, as against the increase in the profit share from 37 per cent to 60 per cent (ZCTU 1996; Kanyenze 1996).

Agricultural policy underwent similar reversals. Marketing boards were commercialized or privatized; extension services, subsidies and credits were reduced, all of which produced an adverse synergy with currency devaluation, to the effect of raising the cost of production for petty-commodity producers and hence eroding farm incomes (ZCTU 1996; UNDP/UNCTAD 2000). The focus of ESAP agricultural policy was the promotion of traditional exports (tobacco, cotton, beef, etc.), plus 'non-traditional' export activities (specifically ostrich husbandry, horticulture, and wildlife management), the latter peddled as Zimbabwe's 'comparative advantage' and tailored exclusively to large-scale farmers, who rapidly expanded operations to the new activities. By mid-decade, about one-third of commercial farmers had taken up horticulture and ecotourism, and to a lesser extent ostrich husbandry, while only 10 per cent of smallholders had become involved in these non-traditional land uses (Moyo 2000).

Finally, land policy entered a period of ambiguity and new contradictions. On the one hand, the Lancaster House constitutional safeguards for market-based land transfers expired in 1990; on the other hand, the liberation movement had, by this time, been co-opted into structural adjustment, a macroeconomic policy framework that would submerge the land reform agenda. The contradictory result would be a series of constitutional amendments (1990, 1993) and a new Land Acquisition Act (1992) that hereafter would enable the state to designate and acquire land compulsorily; but such legislation retained the principles of legal recourse for landowners and compensation, and, importantly, it would not renounce the 'willing-buyer, willing-seller' method. For the next several years, the two methods (state and market) would coexist constitutionally, and the constitutional framework for compulsory acquisition would effectively remain dormant. In 1992–97, about 800,000 hectares were acquired, the bulk of which is in less fertile regions (Moyo 1995; GoZ 1999).

Structural adjustment had a devastating effect on Zimbabwe, economically and politically. The second most industrialized country in Africa entered into rapid deindustrialization, while the post-independence social gains in the fields of health and education began to be reversed (UNDP/PRF/IDS 1998). The burden of adjustment was carried by the peasant-worker household, and particularly women, whose productive and reproductive labour was, by necessity, intensified. To make matters worse, ESAP would act in synergy with the onset of the HIV/AIDS pandemic. Thus, deteriorating physical capacity, loss of employment, erosion of real wages, declining farm incomes – all would put pressure on the semi-proletarianized peasantry and force it deeper into marginal economic activities, illegality and social conflict. Politically, the meaning of national liberation, and the land question specifically, would be transformed by aspiring black capital into a project of 'indigenization', in effect 'a racial substitution formula for the development of capitalist farming' (Moyo 1995: 7). In the 1990s, the IBDC and other lobbies would demand that government 'set aside' land for 'indigenization', but generally to little effect, as the economy was in a downward spiral. By this time, black agrarian capital amounted to only about 350 farmers who had purchased land, plus 400 farmers leasing 400,000 hectares of land (Moyo 2001b). Henceforth, inter-capitalist conflict would not be one of introversion/extroversion, but more clearly racial. And nationalism would be animated by more pronounced class contradictions, but also, as it would soon emerge, by the possibility of a cross-class nationalist alliance on land.

Civilizing society

Inter-capitalist conflict is a natural driving force of capitalist society; the other is class struggle. Interpreting class struggle is a challenge of a different order, given its diverse manifestations, from its 'hidden' forms to the more overt and organized, and across its fractures of gender, generation and ethnicity. The challenge is greater in semi-proletarianized societies, where the labour process aggregates capitalist and ostensibly 'non-capitalist' forms, and where politics are split between town and country. An even greater challenge is to understand class within the wider context of imperialism and its nationalist antithesis – that is, to link class struggle to the principle of national self-determination. In Africa, analysis of class and nation historically has been among the most insightful (Fanon 2001; Cabral 1979), although over the years such analysis has been overtaken by those who have tended either to see nationalism uncritically, or not to see it all. Upon Zimbabwe's independence, the study of nationalism set off on a new course of critical engagement, especially among Zimbabwean intellectuals. This produced robust debate, focusing on elite politics (Mandaza 1986b), urban and organized working-class politics (Raftopoulos 1992, 1999, Raftopoulos and Yoshikuni 1999), and rural and low-profile working-class politics (Moyo 1995, 1999, 2000, 2001a).

In the 1990s, the study of nationalism dovetailed with liberalization and the new preoccupation with 'civil society'. A landmark in the

African debate was the publication of Mahmood Mamdani's *Citizen and Subject* (1996), which successfully brought back the agrarian question to the civil society debate. As pathbreaking as this would be, it nonetheless fell short of robust political economic analysis: it reduced the agrarian question (classically understood as a transition to modern statehood) to a mere question of local government, and it confined the national question (the fulfilment of national self-determination against imperialism) to the realm of peasant–state relations. By consequence, a whole series of crucial issues were either left aside, including the organization of the labour process as a whole (the labour question) and inter-capitalist conflict (whether introverted/extroverted or racial), or they were obscured, most notably by the removal of the state and civil society from their specific *neocolonial* context. Our analysis of the case of Zimbabwe serves as a counterpoint.

It is well acknowledged that the liberation struggle in Zimbabwe was a mass popular uprising with far-reaching international implications. It is also well acknowledged, however, that the movement never attained a clear class understanding of itself or an articulate socialist project (Mandaza 1986b). Its petty-bourgeois leadership, acting as the fulcrum between imperialism and the semi-proletariat, was never tilted decisively in favour of the latter, which in turn remained organizationally and ideologically dependent: trade unionism in the urban areas was chronically fragmented and subsumed during the war under the competing nationalist parties; while rural mobilization was undertaken directly by the parties themselves. In turn, the primary social base of the liberation struggle was located in the countryside, where the war was fought, and included mainly peasant-workers but also the rural petty bourgeoisie, while its ideological structure was anti-colonial, with a strong emphasis on land and its repossession. This ideological structure of Zimbabwean nationalism and its rural base were to continue to exercise power of judgement over the fate of national liberation, especially in the course of its embourgeoisement.

Upon independence, Zimbabwe was riven by an outburst of wildcat strikes in the urban areas (200 strikes in 1980 alone) and widespread land occupations in the countryside, in what was described as a 'crisis of expectations' (Sachikonye 1986; Wood 1988). These were compounded, as we have seen, by an elite split in Matabeleland. In the event, the civilization of society to the requirements of neocolonialism was swift, as the ruling party moved to 'put a rein on its mass base' (Mandaza 1986b). The tactics pursued consisted, first, in the splitting of the semi-proletariat organizationally between town and country; second, in the corporatization of political expression through ruling party channels; and third, in the use of the Rhodesian state apparatus to suppress dissent, most violently in Matabeleland. Yet neocolonialism also exhibited its 'schizophrenia', by proceeding to deliver a number of social goods, especially in rural development, and including land reform. In fact, neocolonialism would never rest at ease against the semi-proletarian masses, whose land occupation tactics, outside civil society, would compel the government from early on to implement an 'accelerated resettlement programme' involving lands abandoned by white farmers during the war.

It is often posited that civil society in Zimbabwe was subordinated to the 'state'. But this is to fall into the liberal trap of dichotomizing state and civil society. First, the state is the institutional expression of the *capital–labour* relation (Marx 1975): not only is the state inseparable from society; it is also active in its 'civilization' to the requirements of capital. Second, the state is the *local* institutional expression of capitalist society, within a larger capitalist society that transcends the state and that operates through a states-system (see Moyo and Yeros, Chapter 1 in this volume). Three implications follow: (a) while the resulting world order is formally 'anarchical', 'multilateral' and founded on the principle of national sovereignty, it remains imperialist in substance, in violation of national sovereignty; (b) the sources of 'civilization' to capital are 'state', 'supra-state' and 'trans-state', to include *inter alia* international finance, covert and overt military operations, donor agencies, and international trade unionism; and (c), and most crucially, breaking with the state is not a sufficient condition for autonomous self-expression; breaking with the civility of *capital* is the requirement, and this is a much more demanding task. In the case of Zimbabwe, such 'incivility' has been present throughout the post-independence period, but has generally been fragmentary, low profile, loosely organized and inarticulate. How this 'uncivil society' obtained radical land reform *through the state* and *against imperialism* is a question that challenges the prevailing wisdom.

The civilization of society in Zimbabwe was led by the neo-colonial state and assisted by international agencies, always through tensions and contradictions. In labour relations, the state proceeded to corporatize trade unionism, by separating public- and private-sector workers institutionally, under the PSA (Public Service Association) and the ZCTU, respectively, imposing a client leadership, and intervening in wage determinations. In the case of the ZCTU, its inauguration in 1981 was sponsored by the ICFTU and the US-led AALC (the AFL–CIO's regional body), in a message clearly targeted at international capital. Real wages remained virtually unchanged for the next five years, while in the agricultural and domestic sectors they remained below the poverty datum line (Wood 1998). Over these years, the ZCTU remained under the wing of the state, while also receiving funding from both the ICFTU and the Soviet-led WFTU.

But by the mid-1980s, the national labour centre would begin to assert its independence from the state and embark on a collision course with capital. Between 1984 and 1988, the centre purged corruption within its ranks, elected an independent leadership, implemented an internal recruitment and democratization campaign, and entered a new era of adversarial labour relations. The latter included not only concerted demands for collective bargaining but also national mobilization against the 'one-party' state and, ultimately, against structural adjustment. But the shortcomings of the labour centre were also clear: it still lacked strong links to the shop floor, remained financially weak and dependent, and confined to the formally employed workers, largely in urban areas; the labour centre had no organizational links to rural areas, except on commercial farms where workers remained weakly organized and in semi-servile conditions.

These shortcomings were the Achilles heel of the labour centre, and were to bring about its 're-civilization'. While in the first half of the 1990s it led a defiant campaign against liberalization, by mid-decade it was seen moderating its stance, technicalizing its development language, and calling for 'social dialogue'. This transformation was due to the combination of state repression to which it was subjected and the wholesale adoption of the labour centre by the ICFTU and other donor agencies in the wake of the Soviet collapse. By the late 1990s, the ZCTU was dependent for two-thirds of its income on foreign sources. By this time also, it had abandoned the task of establishing organizational links with the unemployed and the communal areas, and instead was challenging the ruling party on the grounds of 'good governance', the language of late-twentieth-century imperialism. This was also to become the ideological structure of the new party to which the ZCTU would give birth, the Movement for Democratic Change (MDC), to challenge ZANU–PF in the millennium elections (Yeros 2002a, 2002b).

In the rural areas, the process of civilization was no less tense and contradictory. On the one hand, the ruling party proceeded to implement 'accelerated' land reform under pressure from mass land occupations; for 'land redistribution was a key demand of the government's most populous constituency and, at least initially, people had access to powerful patrons and the space to act outside state structures' (Alexander 1993: 185). Moreover, government established modern political structures to replace chiefdom, in the form of village, ward, district and provincial development committees; and it amalgamated the previously segregated European and African areas into Rural District Councils (RDCs). On the other hand, government would soon proceed to *re*-subordinate local government to central government and to the requirements of neocolonialism. 'In theory, government had established democratic, secular, and non-racist channels of popular participation in planning and policy-making from village to provincial level'; in practice, these structures were marginalized and regarded by central government 'primarily as policy implementing, not formulating, agencies'; in due course, even chiefdom was resurrected, to regain control of courts and thus to reinforce patriarchal order (Alexander 1993: 168–73). Besides local government, the ruling party succeeded in corporatizing farming interests, with the exception of the white Commercial Farmers' Union (CFU). The strategy here would be to merge all farmers into one union, and thereby to dilute class and racial cleavages; the result in 1991, was the merger only of black small-scale commercial farmers and communal area farmers into the Zimbabwe Farmers' Union (ZFU), under the control of bourgeois farming interests, while the CFU would remain independent (Bratton 1994).

By the 1990s, both urban and rural organizations, whether or not under the wing of the state, had been well civilized to the requirements of neocolonial capitalism; this would also give rise to a gaping political vacuum, which would be compounded by the ESAP-induced economic decline. By the late 1990s, no civic organization could claim to have a class project to unify the semi-proletariat, none had organizational links to the countryside outside commercial farming, and none could claim financial independence – even the formally democratic ZCTU. Whatever advocacy for the land question existed among civic organizations, it was ambiguous and rhetorical, and submerged in 'good governance' and liberal 'human rights' language.

By 1999, the collectivity of Zimbabwe's civil society – the largely urban-based and/or bourgeois/petty bourgeois civic organizations, including labour, churches and NGOs – proceeded to unify itself into a 'National Working Peoples' Convention', to discuss and ultimately found a new political party, the MDC.

Yet the land cause had never been abandoned by the semi-proletariat itself. Throughout the independence period the landless and landshort continued to pursue land occupations (Moyo 2000, Yeros 2002b). These were generally low profile and diffuse but, in aggregate, presented a grave threat to the legitimacy of the ruling party. As an internal memorandum in the Ministry of Local Government noted as early as 1988,

> It is needless to emphasise that, bearing in mind the century-long Land Question, the severity and centrality of the squatting problem has its own inertia. That is, squatting generates itself as a pressing priority on the agenda before our national leadership. At the moment, there are about 100 squatter concentrations of proportions enough to merit urgent attention and these concentrations comprise thousands of persons who have already tasted battle with the authorities.

Land occupations were to intensify over the decade of structural adjustment. And whatever action would thereafter be taken on land, this would happen outside the civic network.

Land Occupations and Land Reform

Land occupations were the driving force of land reform throughout the independence period, despite the official land acquisition model. The latter remained committed to the market principle, at first in accordance with the Lancaster House constitutional provisions, and then with the terms of the structural adjustment programme. Nonetheless, with the expiry of the Lancaster House provisions, the government began to redefine the official model by enacting legislation in 1992 that would enable compulsory acquisition, but without, in effect, implementing such acquisition or replacing the market method. The three models – popular, market and state – would interact dynamically over the decade of structural adjustment (Moyo 2003).

The land reform process may be usefully divided into three periods: 1980–92, characterized by the relatively secure predominance of the market method; 1992–99, characterized by the beginning of an official challenge to the market method, and leading to a real threat of compulsory acquisition in 1997, in the context of deepening social and political crisis; and 2000–02, the period in which the market method was resolutely abandoned and replaced by radical, compulsory acquisition.

The interaction of land reform models

The first period can be further subdivided into two, 1980–85 and 1985–92: in the first, political emphasis was placed on engaging actively with the market and delivering land to the peasantry; while in the second, land redistribution tapered off, alongside the deteriorating fiscal status of the state and the embourgeoisment of the liberation movement. As such, the first sub-period was also the one in which the ruling party sought to appease its main constituency, while in the second the social base of the ruling party shifted to the aspiring black bourgeoisie and a rift emerged between the ruling party and the countryside.

Yet the land occupation tactic was not be relinquished from one period to the next; it was only modified in form. The early independence years were characterized by 'low profile, high intensity occupations' (Moyo 2001b), which received sympathetic support and even encouragement by political leaders at the local level of the ruling party, mainly in Manicaland province. And in these years the pace of land acquisition and redistribution through the market was relatively rapid, totalling approximately 2,200,000 hectares, at 430,000 hectares per year. This included land that had been abandoned by white landowners in the liberated zones of the war, and hence was more easily acquirable. In Matabeleland the land occupations and the land reform process itself would fall victim to the ZANU–ZAPU power struggle and the security crackdown by the state; it was only after the Unity Accords in 1987 that the political climate in Matabeleland would begin to tolerate land reclamations, but again to little effect, as the land posture of the state was already under transformation.

From 1985 to 1992, the country-wide pace of acquisition diminished dramatically to 75,000 hectares per year, and to a total of about 450,000 hectares. This deceleration was accompanied by a reversal of the political response to land occupations at the local level, including the Mashonaland provinces, as well as by a transformation of land occupations to what we may term 'normal low intensity' (Moyo 2003). Significantly, from 1985 onwards, the state resorted to the establishment of a 'squatter control' apparatus at the local level, through Squatter Control Committees accountable to the Ministry of Local Government, for the purpose of monitoring illegal self-provisioning of land and carrying out mass evictions (Alexander 1993; Moyo 2000; Yeros 2002b). What this meant in effect was that, on the one hand, the semi-proletariat lost whatever informal influence it may once have had over national land policy; but on the other hand, the state itself would not succeed, even through squatter control, in stemming the process of land self-provisioning. Thus a political stalemate in the battle over land would set in, and form the background of structural adjustment.

Over the period 1980–92, market-driven land reform proved its inability to deliver on Zimbabwe's land question. The process was not only slow and incremental; it also delivered land of low agro-ecological value and imposed onerous fiscal demands on an already financially constrained state. As has been noted elsewhere (Moyo 2002), only a small proportion of the land acquired (19 per cent) was of prime agro-ecological value, the rest being in the less fertile regions. By the mid-1980s, the state realized that it was facing diminishing returns on its resources devoted to land acquisition. This was the case despite the fact that the United Kingdom, as the former colonial power, provided financing for land reform on a matching-grant basis. On the whole, Britain contributed US$44 million to land reform, an amount grossly inadequate to the resolution of Zimbabwe's land question. The slow and mistargeted nature of the land reform process would become, from the mid-1980s onwards, a source of bitter diplomatic conflict between the governments of Zimbabwe and the United Kingdom (Matondi and Moyo 2003). This was compounded by the gradual emergence of black large-scale commercial farmers, who had also benefited from the market method.

This conflict intensified upon the expiry of the Lancaster House provisions for 'willing-buyer, willing-seller' land transfers and the enactment of constitutional provisions for compulsory acquisition. In 1990, despite the launch of structural adjustment, the government signalled a change of direction on land policy, and in 1992 it proceeded with a new Land Acquisition Act, legalizing compulsory acquisition with provisions for compensation and legal recourse, and without displacing the market principle. Hereafter the market method would continue to prevail in the political process, as structural adjustment submerged the land question resolutely, but the two methods (state and market) would enter a period of open competition. Importantly, compulsory acquisition was the favoured principle not only of the semi-proletariat but, more immediately, of the aspiring black capitalist class. In fact, black capital in the 1990s would enhance its presence in the large-scale commercial farming sector, such that by the end of the market-based reform period about 800 black commercial farmers had emerged, either through land purchases or leases on approximately 10 per cent of large-scale commercial farmland. But in all, the pace of land reform remained slow. In 1992–97, about 790,000 hectares of land were acquired, at a pace of 158,000 hectares per year; this involved the resettlement of 600 peasant families displaced by the construction of the Osborne Dam.

The combination of structural adjustment and 'indigenization' of the land question had as its corollary the intensification of low-profile land occupations. As private and public sector jobs were shed, real wages reduced, and farm incomes undermined, the demand for land and its natural resources increased among the semi-proletarian households, in both rural and urban areas (Moyo 2000). Thus several new squatting trends emerged in the 1990s. In one trend, squatting spread from large-scale commercial farming areas to other land tenure regimes, to such an extent that the bulk of officially recognized squatters were now in communal areas (33 per cent), plus resettlement areas (12 per cent), urban areas (10 per cent), and state lands (31 per cent), and only a minority (14 per cent) on commercial farms (Moyo 1998). In another trend, land sales and rental markets deepened *within* communal and resettlement areas. Title to such land is legally vested in the state and administered 'customarily' by traditional authorities in the first instance. But in the 1990s, communal land was increasingly commoditized by payment of fees or political obligation to local MPs, ruling party members, chiefs, headmen and spirit mediums. In turn, land conflicts among 'villagers' and 'squatters' also intensified.

These new squatting trends rendered 'squatter control' ever less effective, though the apparatus continued to be applied with vigilance. In 1992, the squatter control policy was reconstituted within the

Ministry of Local Government to establish a hierarchy of national, provincial and district squatter control committees, and to grant 'the land authority or owner' the legal power to evict. In effect, this meant that the national land problem would be 'parochialized' on communal land and 'privatized' on commercial farms. And on this basis, mass evictions were repeatedly implemented under structural adjustment, in some cases involving hundreds of squatter families at a time, in a manner reminiscent of the methods of the white-settler colonial state (Yeros 2000b).

Nationalism and land reform re-radicalized, 1997–2002

By the end of the first structural adjustment programme in 1996, national politics had come to the boil, and the legitimacy of the ruling party as the 'guardian' of the nation was under severe challenge. Strike action would spread from private- to public-sector workers, whose union (the Public Servants' Association) would even become affiliated to the ZCTU, in open defiance of the government's divide-and-rule tactics. In 1997, strikes would grip several industries, including construction, commercial, hotel and catering, clothing, cement and lime, railways, urban councils, and post and telecommunications. In all, the year saw more than 230 strikes in 16 sectors. Most notably, farmworkers downed tools for the first time, in what appeared to be a wildcat strike, in protest over poor working conditions and wages, which stood at less than one-sixth of the poverty datum line.

Yet the ruling party was not only being challenged from the outside. It was also entering a new period of internal polarization, marked by the open return of war veterans to national politics, through the National War Veterans Liberation Association. Precipitated by a financial scandal and collapse of the state-sponsored War Veterans Compensation Fund, the war veterans demanded that the state compensate them from the national budget. While this appeared to be a 'self-serving' demand – for both media and academic analysis – it was indicative of a class split within the ruling party, between the elites at the forefront of 'indigenization', on the one hand, and the lower echelons, on the other, which had never been accommodated by the post-independence state and many of whom were indeed living in poverty. Moreover, the demands resonated with a re-radicalized nationalism and discontent with the fate of national liberation. In the event, the government succumbed to their demands and disbursed a large compensation package which had not been foreseen in the national budget. Moreover, the government would turn its sights back to the land question and designate 1,470 white commercial farms for compulsory acquisition, promising 20 per cent to the war veterans. These moves, in turn, sent the economy into a downward spiral, led by a crash in the Zimbabwe dollar of 74 per cent in one day (14 November). These moves, too, appeared as 'self-serving' – in this case on the part of President Mugabe – but in fact the war veteran challenge was of a different magnitude, for the war vets were also firmly embedded in the state apparatus and, indeed, were in charge of security, including the president's office.

Thereafter, events in Zimbabwe began to move in a markedly different direction. The second structural adjustment programme (ZIMPREST) was abandoned, balance-of-payments support from the IMF was suspended, and the economy continued on a rapid decline. But this was not yet the time of radical land reform and structural change. For the white farms listed by the government were not acquired. Instead, the threat of compulsory acquisition would galvanize the land question nationally, and even internationally, giving rise to a new round of negotiations with foreign donors, including the World Bank and the British government. In 1998, a Donors' Conference was held in Harare, where a tense agreement was reached to proceed with both compulsory and market acquisition, as well as other complementary approaches. Importantly, on the eve of the conference, a wave of high-profile land occupations swept through the country, for the first time since the early years of independence. This was loosely organized at the local level, by dissident ruling party politicians, traditional leaders, displaced workers, and the war veterans' association, further demonstrating the class cleavages within the ruling party (Moyo 2001a). This wave of land occupations was intermittently condoned and used by the government as an instrument against the donors, but it was clear that government was not firmly in control. Not before long, the government would resort to the use of force to control the occupiers, together with promises to accelerate land reform. The peasants in turn agreed to 'wait'.

Between 1998 and 2000, no progress was made on the land question, despite the conference agreements. Instead, national politics continued to boil more fervently, especially with the launch of the MDC and the euphoria over the prospect of defeating the ruling party at the millennium elections. Indeed, by 2000 the ruling party was in its most severe crisis of legitimacy since independence. And it was at this time that the balance of class forces within the ruling party was tipped in favour of radical nationalist solutions. In February 2000, mass land occupations, led by war veterans, began in the southern province of Masvingo and spread to every province, such that at their height in June about 800 farms had been occupied and government was implementing compulsory land acquisition and mass redistribution. By the end of 2002, 'fast track' land reform had compulsorily acquired some 10 million hectares of land – approximately 90 per cent of white commercial farmland – and redistributed most of it to 127,000 peasant households and 8,000 middle capitalist farmers (discussed below). In the course of this rebellion, national elections were manipulated and civil society subjected to violence, resulting in over a hundred politically related deaths between 2000 and 2002. Violence would also lead to deaths on the farms (including six white farmers and eleven farmworkers) and would involve cases of rape and torture.

As national politics boiled over, international politics also entered a period of renewed conflict, including an international propaganda war, a financial boycott, and regional instability. The private national press and international media networks, led by the British, denounced the land reforms as 'land grabs' and the ruling party as a 'corrupt and brutal dictatorship', even likening President Mugabe to 'Milošević'. The MDC and the ZCTU joined the imperial repertoire, demanding 'free and fair multiparty elections' and joining in an alliance with white commercial farmers against the land reform. Foreign donors and their funds fled the country to begin a long international boycott, except for 'humanitarian' purposes. And regional states and civil societies themselves were forced to choose sides, with the former cautiously backing the land reform, the latter generally condemning it. For its own part, the new Landless Peoples' Movement of South Africa entered the realm of civil society and was immediately confronted with the contradiction of forming civil alliances and supporting a radical nationalist strategy on land; in the event, the LPM defended the occupations.

There is certainly much to criticize in Zimbabwe's land reform process. But this would be impossible without identifying its class structure and dynamics, its weaknesses and failures, but also its successes and, indeed, its fundamentally progressive nature.

The structure of the land occupation movement

The land occupations unfolded in a complex way, driven by local and regional peculiarities, but they shared a common social base – that of the rural semi-proletariat – across gender and ethno-regional cleavages. The strengths of the land occupation movement are to be found precisely in this social base, and, moreover, in its militant commitment to land repossession – a commitment which no other civic organization had ever been willing to make. Over time, this social base expanded to include urban poor and petty-bourgeois elements, who were also co-opted into the fast-track redistribution programme. This would strengthen the movement, especially by bridging the organizational divide among the rural and urban poor, while the petty-bourgeois overture would not threaten, as yet, the overall class content of the movement. The movement was also strengthened in its momentum by the endorsement of the process by the black capitalist lobby and, ultimately, by the stitching together, through the war veterans' association, of a tense but resolute cross-class nationalist alliance on land. In this case, too, the black capitalist lobby would not yet threaten the working-class content of the movement. In all, this cross-class nationalist alliance would stand opposed to the cross-class 'post-national' (or 'civic national') alliance of civil society, including the MDC, trade unions, NGOs and white farmers.

The land occupation movement was organized and led by the war veterans' association. This was also a profound source of strength, combining militancy on the land question with an organizational structure permeating state and society. The war veterans activated their organizational roots as much in rural districts, through the local branches of the association, as in all levels of the state apparatus, including local and central government, the police, the military, the Central Intelligence Organization, the state media (print, television, and radio) and the ruling party. This pervasive web-like structure would contain the unique potential to mobilize both the rural areas and the state apparatus behind the land cause.

The bureaucratic elite, however, would seek to develop hegemony over the land occupations and even own the land reform. And this would occur through the control of the ideological content of media representations of the 'Third Chimurenga' (Uprising); insistence on the use of a state right, legislatively defined (i.e. through amendments to the Constitution and the Land Acquisition Act), to expropriate the occupied lands and the larger areas required by an expanding movement; and by its custody of land reform policy as defined in the fast-track programme documents and of oversight of implementation at both central and provincial levels. This way the land occupation movement gradually became 'programmatized'.

In this context, the war veterans' association would also become a source of weakness for the movement, for several discernable reasons. First, the war veterans' association emerged as a 'single issue' movement, focusing exclusively on the immediate question of land repossession and not on longer-term political economic questions, particularly the post-fast-track phase. Relatedly, the war veterans' association would not seek to establish self-sustaining, democratic peasant-worker organizational structures, with a view to preparing for longer-term class-based political education and ideological struggle. Third, while its nationalism was itself organic and indispensable, its class content was not clearly articulated. The movement sustained a militant anti-colonial nationalism, focusing organizationally and ideo-logically on land repossession; and as effective as this would prove for land repossession, the class direction of the movement would remain threatened by the direction of class conflict within the war veterans' association itself, the ruling party and the bureaucracy.

The principal tactic of the movement was the land occupation. This tactic built upon the previous sporadic and scattered land occupations, specifically those that unfolded during the 1998 Donors' Conference. The new, and much larger, wave of land occupations began in February 2000, following a pre-election referendum on constitutional reform in which the proposal of the ruling party was defeated, thereby signalling the 'end game' for the liberation movement. Land occupations began in Masvingo but spread to the Matabeleland and Mashonaland provinces, at a slower pace in the former and a faster pace in the latter, which would soon become the epicentre (Alexander and Macgregor 2000; Moyo 2001a). Land occupations focused on white farms, but also sporadically on farms owned by black capitalists and the political elite. In the beginning, land occupations focused on underutilized land, but this too would change to include productive land, especially land which fitted other criteria, such as multiple ownership, foreign ownership and contiguity to communal areas. Land occupations also expanded to peri-urban areas, upon the entry of urban poor and petty-bourgeois elements. In a few cases, leadership of the land occupations was not provided by war veterans but by individual MPs and traditional leaders, who in turn sought to 'formalize' their occupations by appealing to war veterans. There were also instances of antagonism between the local initiatives and the higher echelons of the war veterans' command structure, which would cause frictions within the movement. And violence occurred on an estimated 300 farms, depending on the response of the farmers as well as relations with farmworkers.

Farmworkers in some cases supported and joined the land occupations, while in many other cases they resisted the land occupations and violence and evictions were used against them. This would prove another weakness of the land occupation movement: its rapid emergence, without a pre-existing process of political education and mobilization on the farms, would pit the landless workers against the farmworkers, in a climate of distrust, in which the latter would be perceived as having been mobilized by landowners to vote against the government's constitutional proposals. On the one hand, the farmworkers had never been mobilized by their trade-union representatives towards land repossession, who instead had always focused on reformist workerist issues (wages and conditions of employment). On the other hand, war veterans had an ambiguous, even arrogant, posture towards farmworkers, viewing them as incapable of nationalist political consciousness. In a tense conjuncture, farmworkers were faced with the choice of either defending their jobs and employers, or joining the land occupations and staking their hopes on accessing land either through the war veterans directly or through family links in the communal areas. A minority of farmworkers of non-Zimbabwean origin were in a particularly precarious situation; and so were women farmworkers, the majority of whom were employed casually on the farms and had weak access of their own to the land application process in the rural areas. Farmworkers thus found themselves in a confounding antagonism in which their erstwhile employers and exploiters – the landowners – were defending them, and vice versa, in opposition to land redistribution. And this contradiction was not resolved by initiative of the war veterans, who did not see it fit to win over the farmworkers by providing them with adequate access to land – that is, beyond 5 per cent of the 150,000 displaced workers (discussed below).

Finally, the strategy of seeking land reform through the ruling party and the state was also both a strength and a weakness of the land occupation movement. On the one hand, the ruling party proceeded rapidly with constitutional reforms to expedite compulsory land acquisition procedures, modifying existing provisions for compensation by limiting it to improvements on the land and explicitly relegating any other responsibility for compensation to the British government. These were complemented by presidential decrees, under the Presidential Powers Act, to amend the Land Acquisition Act (2000) several times so as to postpone compensation and remove legal recourse and other procedural impediments to land acquisition. Thereafter, the ruling party passed the Rural Land Occupiers (Protection from Eviction) Act in 2001, by which the landless would be afforded legal protection from eviction. These legislative changes were conducted through repeated confrontation with the High and Supreme Courts responsible for the protection of private property. In the countryside, the security apparatus of the state (police, military and CIO) would intervene to provide logistical support to the land occupation movement, as well as protection against possible militarization on the part of the landowners and other violence outside its control. Finally, the state also entered the propaganda war vociferously through the state media, even to the point of threatening the existence of private media (followed, in late 2003, by the shutting down of the leading private daily newspaper, the *Daily News*).

On the other hand, the fundamentally bourgeois structure of the bureaucracy would not be dissolved. That is, the leadership of the land occupation movement remained unable, even unwilling, to wrest control of the ruling party and state from the black elite. On the contrary, the black elite employed the state apparatus to retain its power and prepare the ground for its reassertion in national politics. And here the basic tactic was the same as that employed throughout the colonial and neocolonial periods: the splitting of the semi-proletariat organizationally between town and country. Besides facilitating and protecting the land occupation movement, the leadership of the ruling party used the state apparatus to drive a forceful wedge between organized urban workers and their rural counterparts, by repressing urban working-class demonstrations, persecuting trade-union leaders, and disorganizing trade-union structures. The immediate objective of this instrumentalization of violence would be twofold: the safeguarding of the land reform process against reactionary trade unionism; and the securing of the parliamentary (June 2000) and presidential (March 2002) elections against the 'post-national' alliance. This practice, however, would survive both fast track and the elections, to the point of undermining systematically any source of working-class organization outside elite ruling-party control, in both town and country.

It is in this contradictory process that the class balances within the nationalist alliance would also begin to shift against the semi-proletariat. The black elite exercised its bureaucratic power not only to make room for the urban petty bourgeoisie on 7,260 small/middle capitalist farms but also for itself, appropriating 150,000 hectares (0.5 per cent of the acquired land) for the benefit of an estimated 178 elites. It also steered the land reform process away from several key agro-industrial estates of private (individual and corporate) and state ownership and, in all, ensured that lands redistributed to the semi-proletariat would be largely confined to those of relatively lower agro-ecological potential and with limited access to irrigation infrastructure. The urban working class was further segmented by the offer to over 10,000 families of small (3–20 hectares) plots in the peri-urban zones, and the initiation of land reform for housing among the homeless and others who pursued this new entitlement through urban land occupations. Moreover, with the end of fast-track land redistribution and the withering away of the land occupation movement under the single-issue leadership of the war veterans' association, there would remain only a minimum of organized political structures among the peasantry to exercise influence over the post-redistribution phase of agrarian reform.

We may conclude that the strategy of pursuing land reform through the ruling party and the state did not go far enough *within* the ruling party and the state to safeguard the peasant-worker character of the movement, or to prepare the semi-proletariat organizationally against the reassertion of the black bourgeoisie, especially in the post-fast-track phase. Despite this, however, we must also conclude that the land occupation movement succeeded in compelling the expropriation of over 90 per cent of commercial farmland, broadening substantially the structure of the home market, removing the racialized structure of class struggle, and laying the necessary foundations for the next phase of the national democratic revolution.

The National Democratic Revolution at a Crossroads

The academic debate over the land reform has largely failed to identify the class dynamics of the process, pitting two camps against each other, the 'civic/post-nationalists' and the 'indigenizationists', both including liberals and self-professed Marxists, but all reproducing the categories of bourgeois social science. The former camp has proceeded to denounce the land reform merely as an 'assault on the state', without a class analysis of the neocolonial state specifically, or civil society, or the land occupation movement and its nationalism (Hammar, Raftopoulos and Jensen 2003; Bond and Manyanya 2002); while the latter camp has defended the land reform but obscured the class struggles within the liberation movement and celebrated fast track as the culmination of 'black empowerment', in line with the accumulation priorities of the indigenization lobby.

Neither of these two positions can properly serve the next phase of the national democratic revolution. This remains at a crucial juncture and requires ongoing critical analysis. The immediate result of the land reform is clear and urgent, marked by worsening poverty and the inability to restore the supply of food to the population. On the one hand, imperialism continues to exercise its financial power deliberately to isolate Zimbabwe and smother the process of agrarian reform, such that the currency has hyperinflated to 500 per cent, recovery of agricultural production has been severely impeded – compounded by two years of regional drought – and the urban and rural population has been relegated to a state of 'humanitarian aid'. For its own part, the state has not yet devised a coherent plan for reconstruction and development, given that it cannot cajole private capitals into a national plan of introverted accumulation. This situation lingers on due to the absence of working-class unity across town and country (further undermined by the fall in food production), and is compounded by the ongoing repression of civil society and the emerging dominance of the black bourgeoisie in the policymaking process, against the interests of peasants and workers. The danger is full reversal into a process of re-compradorization and recolonization under a dictatorship of the bourgeoisie, and ultimately the failure to fulfil the developmental potential of the new agrarian structure.

The new agrarian structure

A full analysis of the new agrarian structure is not possible here (see Moyo, forthcoming). In what follows, we provide a condensed overview. Our data derives from the Presidential Land Review Committee (PLRC), which reported in July 2003. The Committee was appointed by the president in response to continuing pressure

Table 6.1   Fast-track land reform: land allocation pattern, 2000–03

Land tenure	Settlers (farm households)		Farm area targeted		Land take-up rate
	(No.)	(% total)	(Ha)	(% total)	(%)
A1 (peasant)	127,192	93.7	4,231,080	40.7	97
A2 (capitalist)	7,260	5.3	2,198,814	21.1	66
Remaining white LSCF	1,332	1.0	1,175,607	11.3	
Total land allocated (as of July 2003)			7,605,501	73.1	
Land unallocated (as of July 2003)			2,800,000	26.9	
Total	135,784	100.0	10,405,501	100.0	

Note: *A1 tenure* consists in use rights to a family plot plus common grazing land; family plots are inheritable but non-marketable; *A2 tenure* consists in leasehold title with a proposed option to buy; *LSCF (large-scale commercial farming) tenure* consists in individual freehold title.

Source: Calculated from PLRC 2003.

from within the ruling party to establish the facts on the ground, including the status of farmworkers and the misappropriation of land by elites. Table 6.1 provides the land acquisition and redistribution figures for the fast-track land reform; the table is organized in terms of Zimbabwe's land tenure regimes. Table 6.2 combines these figures with pre-existing or remaining landholding patterns to provide the holistic picture of the agrarian structure today; this table is reorganized to capture, as much as possible, the emerging *class* structure, which is not well grasped by reference to tenure type and farm size per se.

Re-peasantization has been the dominant phenomenon under fast-track land reform: the new petty-commodity-producing establishments account for 93.7 per cent of total new farming establishments, thus far on 40.7 per cent of the land acquired; nearly all (97 per cent) have taken up their lots. The large majority of the beneficiaries had their origin directly in the communal areas. This process has combined with a renewed 'merchant path' of urban professionals, petty bourgeois and bureaucrats, amounting to 7,260 small, middle, and large farmers, on 21 per cent of the acquired land and with a lower take-up rate (66 per cent). Urbanites have also entered the A1 model, such that we may estimate that urban beneficiaries make up approximately 20 per cent of the total. The land reform process has also proceeded to downsize and retain (as opposed to fully expropriate) 1,332 white large-scale commercial farms. We note also that as of July 2003, a large amount of land (26.9 per cent) had not yet been allocated, and remains subject to the political process.

Further analysis of the figures (Moyo, forthcoming) shows that war veterans received less land than originally targeted and that women and farmworkers were more severely prejudiced. War veterans received less than the 20 per cent threshold set by government after the initial listing of farms in 1997. Tentative estimates suggest that a possible maximum of 25,000 war veterans, ex-detainees, and *mujibhas* (youth collaborators in the liberation struggle) received 10 per cent of total land, the majority on A1 tenure and at a national average below 50 hectares per war veteran. In turn, women received titles of their own at a low national average rate of 16 per cent; the false assumption here has been that heads of household are typically men, and that women in need of land are married or otherwise access land through various family links.

The case of farmworkers has presented analytical and empirical difficulties, given their dual 'identity' as migrant workers (national and foreign) and communal area farmers. Prior to fast track, the large-scale commercial farming sector (LSCF) employed 350,000 workers, of whom 75 per cent were of communal-area origin. If we were to add official fast-track figures of declared 'farmworkers' and fieldwork estimates of farmworkers applying for land as 'landless peasants' via communal areas, it is probable that they account for 5 per cent (or 8,750) of total beneficiaries. What this also means, as recent studies have shown (Magaramombe 2003; Chambati and Moyo 2003, Sachikonye 2003), is that a large number of farmworkers were stranded. Of the original total of 350,000, half were part-time/casual workers (largely consisting of women), the other half being permanent workers (mainly men). Of the permanent workers, over 50 per cent (85,000) retained employment positions, largely in the agro-industrial estates (specializing in sugar, coffee, tea and forest plantations) that were not expropriated, while the other half generally lost employment, with some providing labour to new farmers. Of the part-time and casual workers, approximately 80,000 continue to provide labour on the remaining LSCF farms. The general estimate is that about 90,000 farmworkers were completely stranded, with women being

Table 6.2 Emerging agrarian class structure

Class	Land tenure	Households/farms		Farm area		
		(No.)	(% total)	(Ha)	(% total)	(Ave.ha)
Proletariat in transition (employed, casuals, unemployed)	Resident on farms; relocated to CAs; stranded	(350,000)	n.a.	n.a.	n.a.	n.a.
Peasantry (semi-proletariat, small capital)	CAs and A1	1,300,000	98.6	20,631,080	66.6	13.0
Small/middle capital	Old SSCF	8,000	0.6	1,238,700	4.0	155.0
	New A2	5,760	0.4	1,798,814	5.8	312.0
	Subtotal	13,760	1.0	3,037,514	9.8	
Large capital	Large A2	1,500	0.1	400,000	1.3	267.0
	Black LSCF	1,440	0.1	938,723	3.0	651.9
	White LSCF	1,332	0.1	1,175,607	3.8	882.6
	Subtotal	4,272	0.3	2,514,330	8.1	
Corporate capital	Corporate	743	0.06	1,365,173	4.4	1,837.4
	Parastatal	153	0.01	572,786	1.8	3,743.7
	Church	64	0.005	41,902	0.1	654.7
Land in transition	Unallocated			2,800,000	9.0	
	Total	1,318,992	100.0	30,962,785	100.0	

Note: Peasants: land sizes range between 1 and 30 ha, depending on natural region, with family arable land ranging from 0.2 to 5.0 ha, plus common grazing land. 'Communal' land and A1 are of the same tenure type; the former refers to pre-existing lands, the latter to resettlement lands. *Small and middle capitalists*: comprise 'old' farmers from the colonial period and 'new' black farmers, including those with post-independence allocations on 'small-scale commercial farms' (SSCF) and the fast-track beneficiaries. 'Small capitalist' farms range between 30 and 100 ha, depending on natural region, while 'middle capitalist' farms range between 40 and 150 ha, again depending on natural region. *Large capitalists*: farms range from 150 to 400 ha in NR I/II to 1,500 ha in NR IV. *Corporate farms*: range from 1,000 to 1,500 ha, but few are near the lower hectarage mark.

Source: Calculated from PLRC 2003.

most severely affected; the stranded workers have either remained on their residential plots on the farms, or relocated to the communal areas, or formed new 'informal settlements' under desperate conditions. A related result is that employment conditions on new farms have deteriorated, with piecework and casualization on the rise.

The external financial punishments imposed on the Zimbabwean economy, combined with internal policy incoherence and ongoing repression, will continue to aggravate the living and working conditions of the urban and rural proletariat and semi-proletariat. Persisting landlessness, unemployment, casual employment, poor working conditions and incomes, low peasant farm incomes, and food shortages will all remain pressing economic and political issues for the foreseeable future. Meanwhile, the new peasantry on A1 farms will itself maintain the dual semi-proletarian income strategy of petty-commodity production and wage labour, especially as differentiation proceeds apace.

In Table 6.2, we seek to estimate the emerging agrarian class structure. This is by nature an imprecise task, and more so in the absence of new census data and household surveys. But the task remains essential, and its objective is to capture the differential capabilities (and vulnerabilities) of capitalists in the accumulation process. The basic criterion is land size, which is then adjusted to account for tenure type, agro-ecological potential and technical capacity. Tenure type becomes particularly significant in accounting for the disadvantages of Communal and A1 tenure in the mobilization of resources. Agro-ecology varies in Zimbabwe between five Natural Regions (NR I–V), from the more fertile lands of relatively lesser hectarage per farm and intensive cropping, to the less fertile lands of larger farm sizes and extensive cropping (small grains) and livestock/wildlife management. The level and type of technology thus also differs across the natural regions.

The 'peasant' category refers to petty commodity production on Communal and A1 resettlement land; this now accounts for 98.6 per cent of total farms, or 66.6 per cent of total land. There is class differentiation within this category, which is not captured here, and which is driven *inter alia* by agro-ecological variation, off-farm incomes, and local political power. Whether under adverse or positive economic conditions, this differentiation is expected to continue, as is the operation of informal land markets under the aegis of traditional authority. It is notable that the institution of chiefdom has not been challenged in the process of mobilization for land reform.

While 'small capitalists' historically comprise below 10 per cent of the peasantry in communal areas and employ substantial non-family labour from other peasants and the remaining landless there, we have not segmented them into the category due to insufficient data. We may only note here that they would be of great political significance, as they are likely to return to dominate the Zimbabwe Farmers' Union, together with the small capitalists on A2 land. What we have also done tentatively is merge the 'small capitalist' category with that of 'middle capitalists' as there is much overlap across the natural regions. Generally, small capitalists range from 30 to 100 hectares, and middle capitalists from 40 to 150 hectares, and they employ substantially more hired labour than provided from their own family. The important point to note is that there is likely to be ongoing reconfiguration of these two categories, as the two compete. Notably, middle capitalists have great advantage in the land bidding and accumulation process, by virtue of their better access to other means of production (credit and technology), to contacts and information, and to the policymaking process itself.

'Large capitalist' farms range from 150 to 1,500 hectares, depending on natural region, and enjoy even better access to economic and political resources. At present, middle and large capitalists are in political alliance under the banner of 'indigenization', seeking to appropriate the remaining land and also to tailor the agricultural policy framework to their needs. Their vision is of a differentiated agricultural sector, in which middle/large capitalists specialize in the production of high-value commodities for export (tobacco and hybrid beef), and peasants produce grain for domestic consumption. The contradictions between small and middle/large farmers and between internal/external orientation will thus accentuate as they bid over public and private resources (infrastructure, water, credit) and policy instruments (interest rates policy, foreign exchange allocations). It is important finally to note that there is a significant process of reorganization of capital under way across the economic sectors, by which the emerging agrarian bourgeoisie is joining forces, economically and politically, with the nascent indigenous bourgeoisie in transport and retail, and most importantly with finance, which has seen the emergence of a dozen new indigenous institutions. Together, they recognize the significance of agricultural production and distribution to their own reproduction.

Importantly, the entire range of these capitalist farmers pay wages (whether below or above regulated minimum rates) that are well below the current poverty datum line (see also Kanyenze 2004). Such labour is procured from the retained and retrenched former LSCF workers, unemployed relatives from communal area households, and growing unemployed urban workers.

The picture therefore that is emerging is of a significantly broadened home market, including an enlarged peasantry and an enlarged black capitalist class. Further research would need to examine three interrelated process: agro-industrial reorganization and consolidation of the black capitalist class; differentiation within the peasantry, including the trajectories of rich (small capitalist) and poor (semi-proletarians) peasants; and the labour process which underpins both the above and which will continue to be characterized by functional dualism. This process will become more entrenched, the more that black capital, together with its downsized white counterpart, succeeds in re-entrenching a disarticulated pattern of accumulation.

The new challenges

In the best of strategies, national development should prioritize agricultural reconstruction with an emphasis on the development of the home market – that is, with the aim of sectoral and social articulation (Amin 1981). Agriculture indeed carries the heaviest of burdens, including production for domestic food consumption (food security and self-sufficiency), production for domestic industrial consumption, and production for the earning of foreign exchange. Industrial development should be seen as auxiliary to the technological upgrading of agriculture and to the production of mass consumer goods; while finance should be firmly subordinated to the long-term investment requirements of introverted agro-industrial development. Such a strategy would require careful control of imports and currency allocations, and, importantly, repudiation of debt, as well as deconcentration of mining rights, and guarding against the institution of land property rights that can promote the re-concentration of land and agrarian capital against the accumulation needs and social reproduction of small farmers and rural workers.

The fate of such a strategy, however, will remain subject to the correlation of political forces, between the proletariat/semi-proletariat and capital, and between national self-determination and imperialism. In this sense, the national democratic revolution is at a critical juncture. The organizational task remains the reconstitution of the working class across the rural–urban divide, independently of the state and capital, and at arm's length to the 'civility' of international trade unionism; the political objective remains to compel the state to commit to the development of the home market, against the comprador aspirations of the new agrarian bourgeoisie and the aspirant middle classes, who are advocating the return to neoliberalism and narrow liberal democratic reforms.

The reinstatement of civil and political liberties is central to this process, but it also presents the challenge of overcoming the (reactionary) civilizing forces that will be unleashed. As the comprador bourgeoisie consolidates itself across party political lines, it will seek to enlist the state to its own accumulation strategy and employ its repressive and co-optation tactics towards the splitting of the semi-proletariat across the rural–urban divide and the corporatization of political expression. The further expansion of traditional authority to the resettlement areas will itself be central to this process. Resisting the repressive tendencies of both central and local government and advocating the entrenchment of a redistributive framework of national resource allocation should remain the priority for advancing the national democratic revolution.

The emerging labour process, grounded in the formal and informal, rural and urban sectors, is most inauspicious. It requires a long-term, systematic commitment on the part of trade unions to extricate themselves from current alliances with capital and sink new roots on the new farms and rural areas more broadly and to confront the new black employers and traditional authority. In this regard, the new labour process will also present a new ideological space to be conquered, namely the reassertion of a new class-based nationalism against the racialized, bourgeois nationalism of the 'indigenization' lobby, and against neoliberal democracy politics. Indeed, with the removal of the hegemony of the white agrarian bourgeoisie, the anti-colonial claims of the black bourgeoisie will become tenuous and implausible, as class assumes importance – but also, notably, while the spectre of ethno-nationalism remains a threat. The added challenge to new working-class organization will be to create commensurate space for women peasants and workers, to make itself relevant to their specific demands, and to provide for the ascendance of women to leadership positions within its ranks. As distant as this struggle may appear at present, it is an essential requirement in confronting the strategies of the agrarian and wider bourgeoisie and traditional authority.

On the international front, working-class organization must confront the Eurocentrism of international trade unionism and the anti-globalization movement. The agrarian question is far from resolved in Zimbabwe, despite radical land reform. Introverted accumulation requires the articulation of a new development vision which not only condemns neoliberalism but formulates clearly an economic framework for sustainable accumulation in the periphery as a whole, as well as a political strategy for its realization. It is only then that the principle of national self-determination will begin to be wrested from its imperial grip.

Notes

1. We wish to thank Henry Bernstein for comments on an earlier draft. Errors of fact and interpretation remain our own.

2. For two of the starkest examples, see Hammar, Raftopoulos and Jensen 2003 and Bond and Manyanya 2002.

References

Alexander, Jocelyn (1993), 'The State, Agrarian Policy and Rural Politics in Zimbabwe: Case Studies of Insiza and Chimanimani Districs, 1940–1990', D.Phil. thesis, Oxford University.

Alexander, Jocelyn, and JoAnn McGregor (2000), 'Elections, Land and the Politics of Opposition in Matabeleland, Zimbabwe', mimeo.

Amin, Samir (1981), *The Future of Maoism*, trans. Norman Finkelstein, New York: Monthly Review Press.

Arrighi, Giovanni (1973), 'The Political Economy of Rhodesia', in *Essays in the Political Economy of Africa*, ed. Giovanni Arrighi and John S. Saul, New York: Monthly Review Press.

Bond, Patrick (1998), *Uneven Zimbabwe: A Study of Finance, Development, and Underdevelopment*, Trenton, NJ, and Asmara: Africa World Press.

Bond, Patrick, and Masimba Manyanya (2002), *Zimbabwe's Plunge: Exhausted Nationalism, Neoliberalism and the Search for Social Justice*, Scottsville, London, and Harare: University of Natal Press/Merlin Press/Weaver Press.

Bratton, Michael (1987), 'The Comrades and the Countryside: The Politics of Agricultural Policy in Zimbabwe', *World Politics* 39(2): 174–202.

Bratton, Michael (1994), 'Micro-Democracy? The Merger of Farmer Unions in Zimbabwe', *African Studies Review* 37(1): 9–37.

Cabral, Amilcar (1979), *Unity and Struggle*, New York: Monthly Review Press.

Chambati, W., and Moyo, Sam (2003), 'Land Reform and the Political Economy of Agricultural Labour', Harare: African Institute for Agrarian Studies, mimeo.

Chimombe, Theresa (1986), 'Foreign Capital', in *Zimbabwe: The Political Economy of Transition, 1980–1986*, ed. Ibbo Mandaza, Dakar: CODESRIA.

Clarke, D.G. (1980), *Foreign Companies and International Investment in Zimbabwe*, London and Gwelo: Catholic Institute for International Relations and Mambo Press.

Cliffe, Lionel (1988), 'Zimbabwe's Agricultural "Success" and Food Security', *Review of African Political Economy* 43: 4–25.

Fanon, Frantz ([1961]2001), *The Wretched of the Earth*, Harmondsworth: Penguin Books.

Gowan, Peter (1999), *The Global Gamble*, London and New York: Verso.

Government of Zimbabwe, Ministry of Lands and Agriculture (GoZ) (1999), *National Land Policy Framework Paper*, November.

Haggard, Stephen, and Sylvia Maxfield (1996), 'The Political Economy of Financial Liberalization in the Developing World', in *Internationalization and Domestic Politics*, ed. Robert O. Keohane and Helen V. Milner, Cambridge: Cambridge University Press.

Hammar, Amanda, Brian Raftopoulos and Stig Jensen, eds (2003), *Zimbabwe's Unfinished Business: Rethinking Land, State and Nation in the Context of Crisis*, Harare: Weaver Press.

Kanyenze, Godfrey (1996), 'Labour Markets and Employment During ESAP', mimeo.

Kanyenze, Godfrey (2004), 'Giving Voice to the Unprotected Workers in the Informal Economy in Africa: The Case of Zimbabwe', in *Restart: Our Path to Social Justice – The MDC's Economic Programme for Reconstruction Stabilisation Recovery and Transformation*, Harare: MDC.

Magaramombe, G. (2003), *Resource Base and Farm Production: Farm Labour Relations, Use and Needs*, African Institute for Agrarian Studies (AIAS), Harare, mimeo.

Mamdani, Mahmood (1996), *Citizen and Subject: Contemporary Africa and the Legacy of Late Colonialism*, Princeton, NJ: Princeton University Press.

Mandaza, Ibbo (1986a), 'The Political Economy of Transition', in *Zimbabwe: The Political Economy of Transition, 1980–1986*, ed. Ibbo Mandaza, Dakar: CODESRIA.

Mandaza, Ibbo (1986b), 'The State and Politics in a Post-White Settler Colonial Situation', in *Zimbabwe: The Political Economy of Transition, 1980–1986*, ed. Ibbo Mandaza, Dakar: CODESRIA.

Marx, Karl (1975), 'Critique of Hegel's Doctrine of the State', in *Early Writings*, introduced by Lucio Colletti, Harmondsworth: Penguin.

Matondi, Prosper, and Sam Moyo (2003), 'Experiences with Market Based Land Reform in Zimbabwe', in *The Negative Impacts of World Bank Market Based Land Reform*, ed. Flávia Barros, Sérgio Sauer, and Stephen Schwartzman, Brasília: Rede Brasil.

Ministry of Local Government, Rural and Urban Development (1998), *Discussion Paper on Squatter Policy*, Memorandum, 15 August, Ref: C/54/10, Ministry Archives, Harare.

Mlambo, A.S. (2000), 'Manufacturing in Zimbabwe, 1980–90', in *Zimbabwe: A History of Manufacturing, 1890–1995*, ed. A.S. Mlambo, E.S. Pangeti and I. Phimister, Harare: University of Zimbabwe Publications.

Moyo, Sam (1995), *The Land Question in Zimbabwe*, Harare: SAPES Books.

Moyo, Sam (1998), 'ESAP, Land Policy, and Land Markets', mimeo.

Moyo, Sam (1999), *Land and Democracy in Zimbabwe*, Monograph Series, Harare: SAPES Books.

Moyo, Sam (2000), *Land Reform under Structural Adjustment in Zimbabwe: Land Use Change in the Mashonaland Provinces*, Uppsala: Nordiska Africainstitutet.

Moyo, Sam (2001a), 'The Land Occupation Movement and Democratisation in Zimbabwe: Contradictions of Neoliberalism', *Millennium: Journal of International Studies* 30(2): 311–30.

Moyo, Sam (2001b), 'The Interaction of Market and Compulsory Land Acquisition Processes with Social Action in Zimbabwe's Land Reform', public lecture, Millennium Lecture Series, London School of Economics, 2 May.

Moyo, Sam (2003), 'The Interaction of Market and Compulsory Land Acquisition Processes with Social Action in Zimbabwe's Land Reform', in *Pan-Africanism and Integration in Africa*, ed. Ibbo Mandaza and Dani Nabudere, Harare: SAPES Books.

Moyo, Sam (forthcoming), *Fast-Track Land and Agrarian Reform in Zimbabwe*.

Palmer, Robin (1977), *Land and Racial Domination in Rhodesia*, London, Ibadan, Nairobi and Lusaka: Heinemann.

Phimister, Ian (1988), *An Economic and Social History of Zimbabwe, 1890–1948*, London and New York: Longman.

Phimister, Ian (2000), 'From Preference Towards Protection: Manufacturing in Southern Rhodesia, 1940–1965', in *Zimbabwe: A History of Manufacturing, 1890–1995*, ed. A.S. Mlambo, E.S. Pangeti, and I. Phimister, Harare: University of Zimbabwe Publications.

Presidential Land Review Committee Report (PLRC) (2003), *Report of the Presidential Land Review Committee under the Chairmanship of Dr Charles M.B. Utete*, Volumes I and II: *Main Report to His Excellency the President of the Republic of Zimbabwe*, August 2003.

Raftopoulos, Brian (1992), 'Beyond the House of Hunger: Democratic Struggle in Zimbabwe', Parts I and II, *Review of African Political Economy* 54: 59–74; 55: 57–66.

Raftopoulos, Brian (1996), 'Labour Internationalism and Problems of Autonomy and Democratisation in the Trade Union Movement in Southern Rhodesia', mimeo.

Raftopoulos, Brian, and Tsuneo Yoshikuni, eds (1999), *Sites of Struggle: Essays in Zimbabwe's Urban History*, Harare: Weaver Press.

Sachikonye, Lloyd (1986), 'State, Capital and Trade Unions', in *Zimbabwe: The Political Economy of Transition, 1980–1986*, ed. Ibbo Mandaza, Dakar: CODESRIA.

Sachikonye, Lloyd (2003), *The Situation of Commercial Farmers after Land Reform in Zimbabwe*, report prepared for the Farm Community Trust of Zimbabwe.

Schmidt, Elizabeth (1990), 'Negotiated Spaces and Contested Terrain: Men, Women, and the Law in Colonial Zimbabwe, 1890–1939', *Journal of Southern African Studies* 16(4): 622–48.

Sibanda, Arnold (1988), 'The Political Situation', in *Zimbabwe's Prospects: Issues of Race, Class, State and Capital in Southern Africa*, ed. Colin Stoneman, London: Macmillan.

Skålnes, Tor (1995), *The Politics of Economic Reform in Zimbabwe*, London: Macmillan.

Stoneman, Colin (1989), 'The World Bank and the IMF in Zimbabwe', in *Structural Adjustment in Africa*, ed. Bonnie K. Campbell and John Loxley, London: Macmillan.

Stoneman, Colin, and Lionel Cliffe (1989), *Zimbabwe: Politics, Economics and Society*, London and New York: Pinter.

UNDP, Poverty Reduction Forum (PRF), and IDS (1998), *Zimbabwe Human Development Report 1998*, Harare: UNDP, PRF and IDS.

UNDP/UNCTAD (2000), *Zimbabwe: Globalization, Liberalization and Sustainable Human Development*, Country Assessment Report, first draft, mimeo.

Wood, Brian (1988), 'Trade-Union Organisation and the Working Class', in *Zimbabwe's Prospects: Issues of Race, Class, State and Capital in Southern Africa*, ed. Colin Stoneman, London: Macmillan.

Van Onselen, Charles (1976), *Chibaro: African Mine Labour in Southern Rhodesia, 1900–1933*, Johannesburg: Ravan Press.

Yeros, Paris (2002a), 'Zimbabwe and the Dilemmas of the Left', *Historical Materialism* 10(2): 3–15.

Yeros, Paris (2002b), 'The Political Economy of Civilisation: Peasant-workers in Zimbabwe and the Neo-colonial World', Ph.D. thesis, University of London.

ZCTU (1996), *Beyond ESAP: Framework for a Long-term Development Strategy in Zimbabwe Beyond the Economic Structural Adjustment Programme*, Harare: ZCTU.

PART II

ASIA

7

Rural Land Struggles in Asia: Overview of Selected Contexts

Filomeno V. Aguilar, Jr

Some of the most dramatic episodes of land redistribution in the twentieth century have been witnessed in Asia. But large disparities in access to land continue to pervade its wide expanse. Struggles over rural or agrarian land ownership, control and possession continue to be waged in many places, but of late these have not attracted regional, much less global, attention. The end of the Cold War, along with the spread of nascent industrialism in many parts, has removed the intense ideological context of earlier movements to gain land for the dispossessed. Yet, amid globalism and the influence of neo-liberal strategies, land struggles persist in many varied settings, some of which are distinct to the late-twentieth century, such as the collapse of collectivized agriculture, while others are logical extensions to expand and deepen earlier land reform programmes begun under the aegis of state developmentalism (see Bernstein 2002).

Given the diversity and extensity of the geographical area under discussion, and my own limited specialization, this chapter does not aspire to completeness. It covers only certain types of contemporary land struggles, and its approach is to elaborate upon a basic classificatory grid. For heuristic purposes, these struggles can be understood according to a number of factors: as either organized movements with leaders and political entrepreneurs, or as spontaneous actions; as occurring either through state mechanisms, or outside of them, such as through a land market that may be either formal or informal; and as directed either against hegemonic or non-hegemonic entities, such as state and social classes, actors or groups. A case of land struggle can be characterized by a combination of any of these factors. This approach is consistent with what the introduction to this volume posits: that the political engagement of peasants is extremely varied at any one time and over time. In all cases, however, the emphasis is on direct action on the land through initiatives that, despite their diverse and multiple impulses as well as ramifications, come largely from the grassroots. These struggles are characterized by the goal of acquiring a piece of cultivable land and, where it has been denied, the right to control production and the disposal of the output.

Land Occupations:
Moving to the Highlands

In the same vein that James Scott (1985) has called attention to everyday forms of resistance, thus alerting us to events other than organized protest actions and revolutions: the first place to search for peasant land struggles and land occupations is in the everyday spontaneous actions of peasants who seek to claim land in areas that are legally considered forestlands or areas subsumed by the state's claim to eminent domain. De facto claims to forestland, largely by individuals or small groups, are made and asserted probably on a daily basis, although such spontaneous actions are of the type that eludes official surveillance. Corporate capitalist interests gain access to large tracts of public land, but such actions are often legitimated by recourse to legal measures, such as through a mining permit or timber concession, and a scientific discourse of conservation with doubtful results (Cooke 1999). The quiet and largely unheralded occupation of upland tracks by the marginalized rural poor, which in aggregate has produced a burgeoning sector, occurs outside the state, and thus constitutes a form of challenge to state power. The expansion of a substantially enlarged upland population has been blamed for widespread deforestation caused by highland peoples' shifting cultivation practices, which is a highly contentious assertion. But because states are unable to remove the increasing numbers of upland occupants, states have been compelled, since the 1980s, to accept their presence and resort to the 'regulation' of their agricultural practices. Because of the causal link between secure tenure and conservation of natural resources, states have even begun to issue various forms of legal instruments that recognize the landholding rights of upland cultivators. Thus the current popularity of so-called community-based forest management (Poffenberger 1999).

Accurate statistics are unavailable, but indicative figures suggest that massive land occupations have transpired on the highlands. For instance, in the Philippines, the total population in forestlands (defined as lands with slopes in excess of 18 per cent, regardless of actual forest cover) was estimated at around 14.4 million persons in 1980, a figure that rose to 17.8 million by 1988; during the same period, the migrant population in highland areas was estimated as rising from 1.9 million in 1980 to 2.6 million in 1988 (Cruz, Zosa-Feranil and Goce 1988: 18–19). These estimates have been updated, and the total upland population has been placed at approximately 24 million in 2000, or roughly 31 per cent of the country's total population (Beasca and Borrero 2003). As underscored by Beasca and Borrero (2003: 1), the annual population growth rate in the Philippine uplands from 1995 to 2000 was about 2.5 per cent, which surpassed the national rate of population increase of 2.3 per cent during the same period. In northern Thailand, the highland population was placed at 272,568 in 1972; by 1985–87 the number had risen to 495,353; by 1991 the figure had jumped further to 749,353 (Kanok 1996). While the annual population growth rate of the whole of Thailand was around 1.1 per cent, the highland population of the northern region grew by 6 per cent every year from 1986 to 1991 (Kanok 1996). By 1995 the total upland population of Thailand was placed at 10 million; the estimate for Vietnam was 25 million, and for Indonesia 60 million (Poffenberger 1999: 36).

Evidently, the tremendous increase in the upland population of Southeast Asia cannot be accounted for solely by 'natural' increase owing to existing fertility patterns. Rather, the higher-than-average annual population increments have been spurred by the growing numbers of peasants who have been trekking upwards in search of land on which to grow basic subsistence as well as cash crops. In some areas, it is not difficult to imagine an intensifying competition among land claimants. A case in point is the Central and Western Visayas regions of the Philippines, which have registered the country's highest population densities at about two to three times the national forest population density of 1.9 persons per hectare, as suggested by a World Bank study (1989). In those circumstances, even the amount of cultivable sloped land 'open' for occupation has been dwindling, and peasants claiming land must be increasingly competing among themselves over whatever land they can find in such fragile environments.

There are various reasons for the upward migration of landless and near-landless peasants, who have added their numbers to indigenous communities that have had a long history of settlement on highland regions. For the lowland-to-upland movers, occupation and acquisition of a piece of land within state property can be seen as a defence against immiseration, in the face of loss of farmland or the collapse of rural peasant or artisanal petty commodity production systems in the lowlands. Given increasing population numbers and congestion in the lowlands, peasants who cannot subsist through rural wage work, or migrate to urban centres where casual work will be their likely lot, resort to this strategy of staking a claim on forestland. The struggle to acquire a piece of land in the uplands, and maintain a peasant petty commodity mode of existence, can be seen as a decision to ward off full- or semi-proletarianization. And land occupants succeed because of the incapacity, and perhaps also unwillingness, of the state to prevent 'trespassing' and completely enclose forest and highland zones. Despite the absence of an estimate of the upland population in forestlands across Asia, what is evident is that, through spontaneous migration and occupation of state lands, innumerable households have resisted de-agrarianization.

The strategy of moving into the interior is far from novel. Retreat into the hinterland away from the arm of the state occurred repeatedly during the colonial period, although the reasons then might have differed from the current conjuncture. Still, such movements bore traces that resonate with contemporary patterns. In the colonial era migration to the hinterland away from the reach of the colonial state was a strategy to avoid subsumption to the colonial state or to foreign imperial capital (Aguilar 1998; Peluso 1992).

From the peasant actors' point of view, these land occupations may be an enactment of what James Scott (1976) calls the moral economy of the peasant, conjoined with the fact that the state's claim may not be seen as legitimate, or with indigenous concepts of usufruct rights to open space belonging to no one but nature. Utilizing state land may be deemed defensible because of the moral imperative of the subsistence ethic. Nonetheless, these acts occur outside the formal structures of legality, and may be construed as acts of opposition against the social order established by hegemonic classes. Since the 1980s, however, populist and conservationist forces

– which intersected with the international indigenous peoples' movement – have resulted in changes in forestland laws, which have made room for some form of legal and official recognition of the rights of upland claimants. In the Philippines communal land title certificates are available to indigenous communities that are able to formulate a land use and natural resources development plan – suggesting the critical role of NGOs in assisting these communities to undergo a formal planning exercise. Long-term stewardship certificates have also been issued to individual land occupants. In effect, the state 'has been brought back in' to the highlands, where previously its role was not much more than a pronounced absence. The new upland policies make the state the final arbiter of land tenure and possession, thus inadvertently laying the basis for the emergence of a land market in the uplands.

Land Struggles and the Collapse of Collective Agriculture

The everyday strategies employed by peasants in acquiring land through spontaneous colonization of forestlands have also been evident in the quiet struggles over land and produce that were to lead to the official termination of collective agriculture in China and Vietnam. Although the collapse of collectivization is not usually framed as a struggle over land, and despite the specificities of the Chinese and Vietnamese cases, historical analyses of events leading to the breakdown of socialist agriculture suggest that control over land, labour and the distribution of produce was a central concern of peasant producers. Struggles to acquire and cultivate private plots – with yields exceeding those of collective farms – transpired outside of the state-sanctioned framework and, although largely uncoordinated, constituted actions that effectively challenged the hegemony of the state. In China's case, the unravelling of collective farming coincided with a period of growth and a predisposition from the top leadership, while in Vietnam's case the situation veered to the opposite scenario.

In the mid-1950s, China's collectivization programme reduced villagers' autonomy and increased the state's control over markets and surplus production, although in this initial period individual households were allowed to work discrete plots of land that clearly identified individual effort and contributions (Kung and Putterman 1997). The collectivization programme was carried to the extreme in the Great Leap Forward of 1958–60, which resulted in massive famine (Kerkvliet and Selden 1998: 41). Those disastrous years were followed by successful state campaigns to develop rural infrastructure and launch a green revolution. By the late 1970s, China's grain output per capita had risen to a level that could assure peasants of their subsistence, even as the surplus extracted from the countryside fuelled China's industrialization programme. But because of widespread poverty, stagnant incomes and chronic underemployment, 'Without fanfare, villagers in the late 1970s, sometimes supported by local and regional officials, pressed to expand the scope of the household and market' (Kerkvliet and Selden 1998: 48). Quiet pressure from below coincided with a new philosophy that emerged with the rise of Deng Xiaoping after Mao's death in 1976. Within four years, between 1978 and 1982, land cultivation rights were returned to peasant households.

Private land ownership, however, has not been officially reinstituted in China. Ownership is vested in villages, whose officials assign land rights to specific households for extended periods. These long-term use rights to lands are subject to periodic adjustments to account for changes in household size (Kerkvliet and Selden 1998: 50–51). Since the 1990s, however, the peasant land market, especially in coastal and suburban areas, has begun to exhibit trends similar to what may be found in other peripheral capitalist settings. Villagers with off-farm incomes, and especially those with lucrative industrial jobs, have become a sort of absentee landowner class. They sublet their land-rights or they hire labourers, often migrant workers, to cultivate the land. In some cases, the hired cultivators are contracted to do so on behalf of the whole village. About a quarter of former production teams are said to have retained or reinstituted collective farming activities. In many other cases, however, land is being privately tilled (Kerkvliet and Selden 1998: 52). At the same time, the Chinese state continues to impose quotas for essential crops that are bought at below-market prices, just as the state controls the supply and price of critical farm inputs. The various land-use arrangements make for an extremely complex situation in which landholder and labourer may take various forms of contradictory relationship, even as the state acts as both economic exploiter and protector of the peasant population.

In Vietnam, collectivization was introduced in the North in the late 1950s, but the state's cautious approach did not see collectives becoming widespread until the late 1960s. After the war the collectivization drive accelerated, but agriculture did not post any significant gains. Collectively held land did not lead to high productivity, which thwarted state objectives. Peasants were determined to concentrate their energies on the cultivation of their private plots, which initially comprised 5 per cent of arable land and whose produce could entirely be kept by peasants. Private plots yielded rice and other produce that were at least double that of collectivized land. Peasants prioritized labour on their tiny private plots in the face of stagnating or even deteriorating living conditions, the inequitable share received by non-cultivating communist cadres and officials, the large bureaucracy that sought to regulate and regiment their lives and farms, and the impersonality of large cooperative systems (Kerkvliet 1995: 402–4). Peasants showed little enthusiasm for working on collectivized land, resorting to foot-dragging and, sometimes, total abandonment of the land.

Although officially outlawed, family farming began to emerge in northern and central Vietnam by the mid-1960s through to the late 1970s in the form of so-called 'sneaky contracts' that tinkered with production arrangements without calling attention to the rather dramatic experimentation that went on within some communes (Kerkvliet 1995: 406–7). In one of the biggest such experiments, in Hai Phong, an area with over 90,000 hectares, several stages of rice production were turned over to individual families, who were permitted to keep any surplus beyond the required quota. Although higher officials stopped analogous experiments in other places, the Hai Phong experiment produced very impressive results and, in 1980, it became the official model for the region. Also during the 1970s, the Vietnamese state began to relax its monopoly control over the market, with quotas being discussed with, rather than imposed on, cooperatives.

Amid a worsening economy and urban shortages, recognition of individual household production started in the early 1980s. Cooperatives were authorized to enter into 'family contracts' that assigned land parcels directly to individual peasant households, which could keep or sell everything beyond the contracted amounts. Finally, the debate on the very notion of a centrally planned economy led to the admission of mistakes, culminating in 1986 in the adoption of the policy of *doi moi*, the building of a mixed economy. As in China, private ownership continues to be illegal, but peasants are now entitled to 'use rights' for twenty years, and these rights are renewable, transferable to heirs, and can be sold and mortgaged. These changes were legislated by a law passed by Vietnam's National Assembly in 1993. There is no upper limit on the possession of land-use rights, but the amount of land a household can directly cultivate is capped at 3 hectares for annual crops and 10 hectares for perennial crops (Otsuka 2002). A new type of struggle within the peasantry has thus emerged around the market for land-use rights. The state can continue to influence this market by its power to determine the classification of specific land areas (as agricultural, rural residential, urban, special-use, or unused land), which sets a ceiling on the price of land-use rights. Nonetheless, a landless class is being formed out of peasants whose indebtedness due to natural disasters and the low prices of farm produce have compelled them to sell land-use rights. In Can Tho province, the landless comprise more than 10 per cent of rural households (Otsuka 2002: 126), resulting in proletarianization in a regime that is officially communist.

The end of collectivization was wrought by, among other factors, the familiar strategies of everyday resistance which, in the end, transformed state policy. The success of seemingly uncoordinated acts of individual peasant households suggests some form of mass movement, although not of the type involving clearly identified political entrepreneurs. Starting from acts outside the parameters of the state, peasant actions have invaded centre stage, resulting in the triumph of individual petty commodity production and the official celebration of small family farming. Is this the revenge of the peasant? Unavoidably, Chayanovian views of the peasant economy have been rekindled by this historical outcome. Yet, as Kitching's (1998) study of the failure of collectivization in Russia suggests, the Chayanovian response may have been implicated in peasants' insistence on tilling their own private plots, but this behaviour must be understood within its wider context. In the Russian case, the generation was gone that deemed individual land ownership and family farming as essential to peasant identity, which might have exacted the peasant revenge. On the contrary, at the demise of socialist agriculture, small private farms and large collectivized land operated in symbiosis rather than in competition, and peasants themselves would appear to have preferred to become industrial workers, if only the state-controlled economic infrastructure had allowed that desire to be fulfilled.

The experiments in China and, certainly, in Vietnam did not share the comparative historical length of Russia's socialist agriculture. But field data suggest that the struggle for private land in Vietnam and China did not mean that peasants did not care about equitable land distribution – they did. Hence, the peasant 'revenge' in these two countries did not signify a desire to return to the huge land disparities of the past. Rather, it could only mean that specific historical conditions did not allow the dream of equitable land distribution to prosper. The dictates of sheer survival, and a rational assessment of the wider context with its free riders, inequities and alienating systems (Popkin 1979), pulled them back to private plots. Now that there is a de facto land market in these countries, inequalities are being reintroduced and a class of landless peasants or a class of rural proletarians is being formed. Commodity relations have been allowed a rather free rein in these formerly centrally planned economies, and the simple reproduction squeeze yields its predictable victims (Bernstein 1981).

Land Occupations within Agrarian Reform Programmes

Instances of land occupation pursued within state parameters have also achieved some success. Reformist state policies, no matter how flawed, have provided the legal framework for these land occupations to occur. The case studies from India (Pimple and Sethi, Chapter 8 in this volume) that have transpired in the course of the twentieth century attest to the significance of state policies by which minority ethnic groups have found an avenue to lay claim to land. Regardless of whether the land-to-the-tiller programme was a product of the developmentalist phase, or of recent modifications since the late 1980s, as in the post-Marcos Philippines (because of the clamour for change in the context of the widening of the democratic space), agrarian reform legislation appears to provide a basis for land occupations. Direct action on the land, as the following discussion drawing mainly on Philippine experiences shows, have occurred when organized peasant groups exploited cracks and obstructions in the implementation of agrarian reform to claim possession of land they believe is rightfully theirs. While the object is clearly control of land, peasant groups have had to contend with a range of opposing forces, from corporate interests and recalcitrant landowners to competing claimants among the rural poor. In any event, the decisive intervention of sympathetic state actors and of NGOs in assisting the organizing of agrarian reform beneficiaries and their takeover of land has been crucial. However, despite points of intersection with the revolutionary movement of the Communist Party of the Philippines (CPP), and despite nationwide coordination of land struggles (as discussed by Feranil, Chapter 9 in this volume), these land occupations remain essentially localized and disjointed struggles for land. Nonetheless, they carry the potential to become part of a large-scale social movement.

A successful attempt at land occupation pursued within the agrarian reform framework of the Philippines involves the 817-hectare Pecuaria Estate in Bula, Camarines Sur province, on the main island of Luzon (Abelardo 1997). Formerly owned by a Greek national, the estate passed into the hands of two Filipino landowners after the Second World War. By 1972, it was operating as a corporate farm with over seventy employees involved in raising pigs and cattle, and planting rice, corn and sugar cane. Its workforce eventually expanded to include some 500 farmworkers. In 1985, the company became insolvent, and a year later the estate's workers were made redundant. Threatened by the CPP's New People's Army, which operated in the area, the owners decided in 1988 to turn over the property to the government's agrarian reform programme under the Voluntary Offer to Sell (VOS) scheme. With force looming in the background, land reform in this estate was driven neither by the market nor by altruism. What is more, chaos arose as the opportunity to acquire a piece of the large estate prompted competition among several interested groups, precipitating an overt, even violent, struggle.

A total of 1,000 individuals applied for land in the Pecuaria Estate, but initial screening by the Department of Agrarian Reform (DAR) trimmed down the potential beneficiaries to 620. The estate's former workers strengthened their group, and made a strong bid for the land with the support of the owners, whose role had changed from employer to patron. Confident that they would be allocated land, 100 former estate workers and 136 residents of a nearby village entered the property and occupied the best portions of the land in 1988. But DAR officials warned them they could be disqualified because proper procedures were not followed; the occupants retreated. After a major typhoon in 1989, 36 individuals entered a seemingly abandoned estate, but they were neither former estate workers nor residents of nearby villages. More illegal occupants entered the estate, their number burgeoning to over 250. By 1990, the situation was getting out of control. Some of the original applicants began to cordon off the area to deter new entrants, but thugs among the latter continued incursions. To avoid violence, a non-governmental organization teamed up with the DAR to start a process of consultation with various parties to help settle the conflicting claims. The 'rightful' beneficiaries had to be identified based on the government's criteria and screening procedures. Of the original 620 applicants, only 480 were deemed qualified. Illegal occupants were placed in the lowest priority, aggravating the tension among claimants. In 1992, both sides began to stage public rallies to air their demands; later that year the DAR decided to allocate a contiguous 100-hectare area within the estate in favour of what were known as 'illegal entrants'.

Meanwhile, by 1991 the original competing groups that pitted former estate workers against 'landless' claimants from three nearby villages decided to coalesce in a major alliance against the 'illegal' occupants who had come from other places. In 1992, this group was registered as the Pecuaria Development Cooperative, Inc. (PDCI). Because a portion of the estate had been allocated to the 'illegals', government officials decided to relocate them and provide areas that could be used by PDCI members. The relocation in May 1993 resulted in heated arguments, and some illegals refused to cooperate. At the end of that year, however, 202 PDCI members were in possession of 47 per cent of the estate. Tensions did not ease. In April 1994, Pablito Dante, leader of the PDCI, was stabbed to death in the course of a heated argument. A more concerted intervention by NGOs ensued, and a 'festive' relocation was planned with military precision. Nevertheleess, 50 of 114 illegal occupants refused monetary assistance and relocation to the designated site. After more dialogues, some illegal occupants agreed to move, but a sizeable number were recalcitrant. The available data for early 1996 indicated, however, that 426 PDCI members had been able to claim land parcels that averaged 2 hectares in each case, in addition to a residential lot each measuring 600 square metres.

The case of the Pecuaria Estate demonstrates a state-sanctioned land takeover that had to confront not hegemonic classes, but 'internal' struggles within the peasantry. The former estate workforce – an agrarian proletariat – sought to become peasant landowners; when it became apparent that their group interest would not prevail, as peasants-in-waiting they entered an alliance with other peasants desiring to acquire land of their own. Given the great need for land, the contest with other peasants was almost inevitable, especially since information on the Pecuaria Estate's 'availability' was not hidden from the mass media. The competition for land took place on a 'first past the post' basis. Peasants who had originated from other places daringly sought to occupy land, thus posing a threat to the locally established peasantry that would appear to have had a 'prior claim' to the land. The apparently conciliatory intervention of agrarian reform officials in allocating land to 'illegal occupants' went a long way in resolving a highly conflictual situation. State regulations prevailed in determining the 'rightful' beneficiaries. However, there remains the challenge posed by some 20 per cent of the PDCI membership, who have been granted land but have not occupied it. In the long struggle, many of them had moved on or migrated to urban centres. The 'illegal occupancy' rate could increase, and similar conflicts could re-emerge. The land struggles in this estate are far from over.

Another instance of land occupation within the agrarian reform framework of the state is illustrated by the case of the Philippine Agro-Industrial Corporation (PAICOR) Estate in Baungon, Bukidnon province, on the island of Mindanao (Cabanes 1997). Measuring 464.5 hectares, the PAICOR Estate was originally part of the public domain that individual peasants claimed and cultivated on usufruct basis, in a process not unlike that described in the first section of this chapter. An enterprising local trader began to purchase the cultivated land, until he and his kin amassed a huge property. The PAICOR acquired the property and started cassava starch milling in 1978. But cassava monoculture depleted the soil's nutrients, and in a few years the company faced huge financial losses. In 1987, it decided to shift to corn production and, the following year, after declaring bankruptcy, dismissed all but sixty of its farmworkers. As a corn-growing area, the estate fell under the scope of the Comprehensive Agrarian Reform Program, but the corporation did not wish to sell the land voluntarily. In April 1989, the DAR proceeded to expropriate and forcibly transform the estate into a land reform area, but the corporate owners filed a petition to defer reform for ten years, citing especially that the change of crop was a temporary measure. The petition was rejected, but the company made several appeals.

Despite the appeal, the DAR collected over 500 names of potential beneficiaries, and it went ahead with the screening process involving government and NGO representatives, and those of potential beneficiaries. The list was pared down to about 300 names, most of whom were company employees who had been dismissed. After further public hearings, the impending beneficiaries began to be organized and mobilized with NGO help. In September 1992, thirteen land certificates covering 143 hectares – representing 47 per cent of the agrarian reform area within the estate – were set to be awarded to the organized beneficiaries. The PAICOR protested, and a legal order was issued to suspend the reform process. The case remains pending.

Because the land transfer was stalled by the court case, the beneficiaries decided they could not wait years for the justice system to resolve the issue. Besides, the eventual decision might not be in their favour. With the assistance of partner NGOs, the agrarian reform beneficiaries conceived a systematic three-day land invasion plan, which entailed fencing off the area and immediately starting farm work. The invasion was made to coincide with a peasant congress that was to be held adjacent to the contested site. The occupation was scheduled for 14 March 1994. However, the company found out about the plan and sent its security guards to patrol the area. The occupation was postponed by a couple of days. In the presence of NGOs, media reporters and local police officers, the invasion took place and, despite some skirmishes with company guards, proceeded generally peacefully. As expected, the company objected, but the agrarian reform beneficiaries were armed with their own legal counsel, hence they could not be moved from the land. A case of 'forcible entry' was then brought to court.

Interestingly, the land occupants, most of whom were redundant company workers, had to square off with the company workers, whose union was affiliated with the nationwide Association of Labor Unions–Trade Union Congress of the Philippines (ALU–TUCP). The workers' union insisted they were the rightful beneficiaries of the whole estate. After a lengthy dialogue, the workers' union settled for 113 of the remaining 159 hectares that had not been allocated to individual recipients.

While the resistance of corporate capital to agrarian reform is understandable, the case of the PAICOR Estate is instructive of the conflict between various stakeholders who occupy different class positions before the land occupation. In this instance, a plantation workforce, backed by a large industrial working-class organization, was pitted against the re-peasantized redundant workers and other peasant claimants of the land. The company union was seen as a major obstacle to the land occupation, because it wanted to benefit from both the company as its job provider and from the agrarian reform law, should reform eventually come to pass. In this case, a plantation proletariat was ranged against a peasantry composed mainly of petty commodity producers. In contrast to the Pecuaria Estate, where segments of the peasantry literally fought over the limited land available, in the PAICOR Estate two agrarian classes were in competition. These conflicts among non-hegemonic classes epitomize the social class fragmentation in the countryside as various groups and classes seek to secure the material base for petty commodity production. Although various forms of compromise have been reached, these were necessarily to the exclusion of other peasants who also needed land.

It must be stressed that the occupations and contestations all occur within the framework of the state, in the first instance within its agrarian reform legislation and bureaucracy, and later within the broader legal and judicial complex of the state apparatus. Working within state parameters may be a tactical or strategic move. Nevertheless, land occupations pursued within the reformist space of the state ultimately rely upon the state and state institutions to settle competing claims and issues of legality. Certainly, there are nuances in battles, strategies and outcomes, but the state becomes the key institution.

In Sumilao, also on the island of Mindanao, peasants confronted large corporate capital when the ten-year lease of Del Monte Philippines over 144 hectares of prime agricultural land expired in 1993. The 137 peasant members of the Mapalad Cooperative competed with the Norberto Quisumbing, Sr. Management and Development Corporation, which sought to convert the area into an agro-industrial site. Insisting that the area had long been covered by a notice of compulsory acquisition, the DAR sided with the peasants, and the certificate of land ownership was issued to the Mapalad peasants in September 1995. But the Quisumbing company had appealed the DAR's decision to the Office of the President, whose Executive

Secretary reversed the DAR's decision and approved the company's conversion plan in March 1996. Despite the filing of various motions for reconsideration, in July 1997 seventy-eight Mapalad peasants entered the property and began farming. But, confronted by systematic harassment and violence, the peasants were compelled to give up their land occupation. With NGO and Catholic Church support, twelve Mapalad peasants, three of whom were women, journeyed to the national capital in October of that year to stage a hunger strike in front of the main DAR office. The hunger strike, which lasted twenty-eight days, attracted considerable media attention. The intense publicity constrained then President Fidel Ramos to form an independent commission and to eventually grant 100 hectares to the Mapalad Cooperative (*Mapalad Agrarian Reform Monitor* 1998).

The first two cases of land reform-cum-occupation mentioned in this chapter exemplified the situation in which peasants dealt with agrarian corporate capital that had been weakened by bankruptcies. In that context, various fragments of non-hegemonic classes struggled among themselves for a share of the land. In the third case, peasants confronted a rather strong, well-connected corporate capitalist interest. As we see in Feranil's account (Chapter 9), struggles with hegemonic classes risk harassment, reprisals and counter-reform. In the last case presented here, but also in the earlier two, the peasant cause benefited from the intervention of sympathetic actors within the agrarian reform bureaucracy who gave (tacit) approval and legitimacy to the planned land occupations. Given the prevailing democratic space, peasant determination and intense public and media attention constrained the state to accede eventually to its reformist arm. Because of the contentious legal context, and the desire of peasants to secure their claim to land within the law, peasant mass actions were carefully orchestrated and planned, with the aid of NGOs, legal practitioners, and strategically placed agrarian reform advocates within the bureaucracy. Far from spontaneous, these land occupations benefited from the fact that the state is not monolithic.

The Dull Compulsion of the Market

Any discussion of struggles over agrarian land ownership, possession and control must take into account the range of market-based land transactions that actually occur in the countryside. The market is seldom seen as offering the possibility of providing land to the landless, and of arriving at a fair redistribution of land and agricultural assets. Eloquent proof is the operation of the market in the post-socialist agricultural contexts of China and Vietnam, where a subtle jostling for land leaves some with no land to till while others acquire more land than they can personally cultivate. In other Asian contexts, land reform legislation has not stopped market mechanisms from concentrating land in the hands of the relatively well-off. This group includes rich peasants who are able to augment their landholdings due to petty capitalist accumulation within agriculture or probably with assistance from external sources, including remittances by kin involved in international labour migration; and segments of the rural petty bourgeoisie, such as traders and low-skilled professionals, who decide to invest their earnings and savings in land that would most likely be sub-let. Land is generally acquired from smallholding peasants who dispose of their meagre lots, induced by indebtedness that is the product of commodity relations that extend and deepen the simple reproduction squeeze. Others sell their land before migrating to the city. The dull compulsion of economic forces further skews the already unequal distribution of land.

Thus, the results of a study in West Bengal come somewhat as a surprise. Vikas Rawal (2001) examined land sales in two villages from 1977 to 1995, and found that land markets contributed to redistributing tiny plots of land to poor peasants who otherwise would have been landless. West Bengal, along with Kerala, is exceptional in India for the way it implemented and gave substance to land reform. After the political struggles of the 1960s and 1970s, a coalition of left-wing parties, dominated by the Communist Party of India, came to power in 1977. The land reform programme that was implemented after 1977 gave permanent cultivation rights to about 1.4 million sharecroppers; expropriated 1.26 million acres of land, most of which was distributed to some 2.5 million households; imposed a ceiling on holdings; and distributed state land to the landless. The local government units – the Panchayats – as well as rural mass organizations became active participants in the land reform process. These reforms boosted West Bengal's agricultural production and productivity rates, leading to its designation as a 'success story'. This context is important in understanding the dynamics of the land market in the two villages in the Bankura district studied by Rawal, where cropping intensities and rates of production growth were even higher than the state averages. In the two villages the volume of land sales was also remarkably higher than in other parts of India. But most notable was the fact that serious land reform and agrarian change influenced the behaviour of the land markets.

In the two study villages, 40 per cent of households bought cultivable land between 1977 and 1995, while 24 per cent had remained landless. During this period the land reform programme provided land to 15.3 per cent of currently landowning households that were landless in 1977. Land transactions became the means of acquiring land on the part of 17.2 per cent of currently landowning households that were landless in 1977. In total, 32.5 per cent of landowning households in 1995 had belonged to the landless category in 1977. Many of those who had purchased tiny plots of land through cash transactions belonged to scheduled caste and scheduled tribe communities. The land sellers were mainly non-resident landowners and a resident big landowner. Of the 68 households that were landless in 1995, only two owned land in 1997 and were forced to sell the land in the interim. Rawal (2001) attributes these unexpected outcomes to the improvement, albeit small, in the purchasing power of poor and landless peasants, owing to higher real wages and increased days of work, which were made possible by improved agricultural productivity after land reform. The process of land reform implementation itself had also convinced landowners with land in excess of the ceiling that it would be more advantageous for them to sell than hang on to surplus land. The land reform law also took a strong stand against absenteeism. In this setting, the twice marginalized agricultural proletariat (twice, owing to cultural proscriptions and the economic structure) utilized their small savings to purchase tiny plots of land in which owners had basically lost interest. The market has far from effected a radical redistribution of land, but the historical context made it achieve, at least in this corner of India, a quite unexpected result. The peasant action of buying small parcels of land may have been spontaneous – that is, not classifiable as an organized movement – but it could not have happened without the appropriate state framework and the supportive role of rural mass organizations.

Peasants are also acquiring and losing cultivable land through informal market transactions that take the form of land pawning contracts. The borrower loses the land when the debt is not paid within a prearranged period. These arrangements have been reported in several Asian countries, particularly in Bangladesh, India, Indonesia, Thailand and the Philippines. Where land values are low, and the land market, as well as the financial market, is riddled with imperfections, land pawning becomes prevalent. In Muslim countries land pawning is a way of circumventing the prohibition against charging explicit interest rates (Ghate 1988). In any event, the arrangement is a socially accepted mechanism of providing and securing loans. In the Philippines, despite the provision in the agrarian reform law against the selling or pawning of reformed land within the first ten years of its acquisition, such transactions have been widespread in some areas. Even in earlier periods when share tenancy was the accepted norm, peasants bought and sold tenancy rights.

These informal arrangements may well lead to a concentration of land in the hands of wealthier peasants, as indebtedness may cause poor peasants to lose land entered as collateral. Fukui's (1995) study suggests, however, that a worsening of land distribution need not be the necessary outcome. In one village in Nueva Ecija province in the Philippines, where a quarter of the households were engaged in pawning contracts, Fukui found the average farm size of the pawner (2.53 hectares) was larger than the average farm size of the pawnee (0.89 hectare). In addition, the average asset of the pawnee was about six times that of the pawner. Most of these transactions were good for one-and-a-half to three years. Thus, Fukui interprets the situation in this village as one in which a peasant household with a small area of land to cultivate but with surplus funds (obtained from either an efficient production system or off-farm income sources) enters into a land pawning contract as a way of acquiring cultivation rights over an enlarged area. They acquire the pawned land from peasants with relatively large landholdings but lower assets; these peasants temporarily let go of a portion of their land in order to acquire funds for investment that is likely to be a non-agricultural venture deemed to yield a higher profit than farming. Pawning thus appears to be a mutually beneficial arrangement. To what extent Fukui's finding is generalizable is uncertain. Yet, in this instance at least, a flawed market enabled peasants to take direct action on land, resulting in a temporary reallocation of this basic means of production, contrary to the dictates of the state but according to the requirements of petty agrarian capital.

Supporters of the neoliberal approach of developing formal rural land markets (through financial institutions and corollary activities such as the titling of land and rationalized land records management), and those advocating the use of agrarian reform land in formal land transactions, cannot use the cases outlined here to buttress their position. From Nueva Ecija to West Bengal, the results are highly contingent upon historically specific factors. An unrestrained land market will wreak havoc on poor peasants, who are unlikely to emerge triumphant in this struggle, landlessness and proletarianization being the fate that most likely awaits them. On the other hand, it cannot be denied that the commoditization of peasant land is clearly advancing apace, in both post-collectivized and never-collectivized settings. There is a certain inevitability about the commoditization of land, even in cases that started out through land occupations.

At the same time, where profitable off-farm incomes are found, such as in rural industries, peasant households appear to have improved their socio-economic status even without a change in the distribution of agricultural land. This trend appears to be occurring in some parts of Southeast Asia, although the overall trend remains unclear because of extremely uneven conditions. In such instances, Rigg (2002) observes, land is 'no longer the strategic resource' that it once was. In localities where peasants are able to derive comparatively high incomes from a combination of farm and off-farm sources, but with the latter proving to be the more significant income source, he argues that poverty can now be delinked from the inequitable distribution of land. As Fukui's study suggests, smallholding peasants may have more disposable income than those with larger landholdings. This pattern has been actualized in some parts of the capitalist periphery in Asia, not only because of an emerging industrialization but also because of the phenomenon of overseas labour migration and employment, which is discussed in the next section. What is apparent is that land struggles assume a diversity of forms – including reliance on non-agrarian activities and, for some, eventual departure from the land. Given their specific historical conditions, peasants adopt a range of strategies to gain security and improve their economic conditions, strategies that ultimately locate them within simultaneously contradictory and increasingly transborder class relations and positions.

Global Migration and Rural Land Ownership

In another study of land pawning in the Philippines, Nagarajan et al. (1992) found that peasants resorted to pawning contracts as an informal credit instrument. Poor peasants tend to pawn out land to fund medical emergencies and vital consumption needs. But the predominant pattern in the study by Nagarajan et al. was the use of pawning contracts as a way of raising capital for investment in off-farm activities that were expected to yield returns higher than in agriculture. These peasants tended to invest in human capital, through the education of children, and in securing overseas employment.

Labour migration, which in Southeast and South Asia has undergone a trend toward feminization in recent years, with most migrant women finding overseas employment in paid domestic work (Aguilar 2002; Battistella and Paganoni 1996; Chin 1998; Constable 1997), has injected a totally new force into the rural countryside. Village studies have shown that remittances of overseas labour migrants worsen income stratification, but they afford peasant households that possess negligible assets and resources to be catapulted into the upper reaches of the village social structure. In fact, the household may adopt a strategy of disposing of some or all of its landholdings precisely to invest in overseas employment – for men, mostly in seafaring and construction work – which usually, but not always, leads to significantly higher incomes (Bautista 1989). Others may already have generated the wherewithal to obtain overseas contracts through petty capitalist accumulation, made possible by general agrarian change (including gains from the green revolution) and returns from non-agrarian economic activities. In this situation we observe the other end of the spectrum of land struggles, characterized by flight from land as peasants decide to leave agriculture behind to become proletarians in another nation-state. Thus sizeable pockets in the countryside exist where the struggle is not to acquire and own land but to move out of the agrarian field altogether. In these instances, land ownership is no longer the desired goal. The lack of an emotional bond to land may be a startling observation, as peasants seem ready to explore options outside of agriculture. But in Southeast Asia, at least, peasants historically did not posses a 'natural inclination' to be attached to land that European colonial authorities expected them to exhibit. On the Malay peninsula, for instance, colonial legislation in the late nineteenth and early twentieth centuries was a record of difficult efforts and failed attempts to bring into existence a class of landholding peasant cultivators who remained more or less permanently settled in one location tending a fixed plot of land (Kratoska 1985). That peasants are not by nature attached to land – many see it in instrumental terms, in contrast to some land reform advocates who view land with an almost sacred reverence (Aguilar 1992) – will illuminate the strategies adopted by contemporary peasants as they seek economic advancement beyond the agrarian field.

Peasants who may begin with very few resources but somehow manage to send a child overseas have experienced dramatic leaps in the life chances of household members. Fuwa (1996) describes the case of a family whose male head had inherited half a hectare of land but lost all of it, presumably to finance subsistence needs. They derived their income from the 'informal sector', until he obtained cultivation rights as a share tenant in the early 1980s. In 1986 a high-school-educated daughter applied for and obtained a job as an 'entertainer' in Japan, with a starting salary of US$350 per month that gradually rose to US$1,050 per month by 1993. Her remittances have since contributed the bulk of her household's income in the Philippines. The father continues to be a share tenant, but has invested in an irrigation pump and a hand tractor, in addition to improving the household's physical dwelling place. Subsequently, with the disposable cash, a son was able to find employment as a factory worker in Saudi Arabia, augmenting the remittances received by the household in the Philippines. Although the gains from global migrations are not entirely clear, the case described here is not uncommon. Income from overseas has allowed peasant households to acquire land, sometimes more than the family can cultivate; these land parcels are then sub-let on a sharecropping basis to poorer peasants.

In rural Egypt, Weyland (1993) has found that international labour migration is used as a strategy for social reproduction in the literal sense, for without the male's earnings from contract employment in another state it would be difficult to raise the bride price needed for marriage and the establishment of a family. Wives may also prod husbands to become migrant workers to obtain resources in order to establish an autonomous household, avoiding the frictions that usually arise when living with the in-laws. Migration as a household strategy should therefore not imply a homogeneity of goals and interests within the household unit. More importantly, Weyland (1993) points out, international labour migration does not lead to the disintegration of the peasant household and production system. The higher incomes are used to purchase land and draught animals that perpetuate the peasant mode of life, although now inseparable from a modernizing ethos. Certainly, landless wage labourers have become landowners. If anything, therefore, global migrations prop up peasant petty commodity production, even as it elevates the individual household's social status and class position in the locality.

While some peasants desire to leave agriculture by working overseas, other peasants generate capital from overseas employment to persist in agriculture and even invest in it. Overseas remittances thus significantly complicate the hybrid forms of class relations and overlapping circuits of exploitation that make and define rural class structures in Southeast Asia (Aguilar 1989; Turton 1989). Remittances may transform the subsistence peasant household into a capitalized family farming unit. The peasant may rely primarily, or even completely, on hired hands to cultivate the land, acquiring the class position of a petty capitalist employer of a rural proletariat. The capitalized farm owner may then decide to work off-farm, deriving cash income from waged work elsewhere (a proletarian position) or to engage in a small enterprise (a self-employed or petty-bourgeois position). Through monetary infusions, peasant migrants as members of the global proletariat, or the global underclass, directly stimulate peasant capitalism and rural micro-capitalist industry. The rural economy, in the process, becomes directly imbricated with the contradictions of global capital accumulation (Aguilar 2003). The resulting multiple and contradictory class positions and relations inevitably complicate the political field, subtly affecting the land struggles in the countryside. Although for many the desire may still be to own a piece of land, to be wrested from big landlords, corporate capital, or the state, increasing numbers may seek a literal way out through global migration. The force fields of globalization thus impinge upon local land struggles, crosscutting the contradictions within nation-states.

Conclusion

The struggles for land in Asia are as diverse as its political-economic and cultural landscape. These take many forms: individual or group action; through state mechanisms or through formal or informal land markets; and against the state or hegemonic classes, or in competition with other peasants and members of the rural proletariat. Land struggles range from individual land occupations in highland areas and individual manoeuvring in and around collective agriculture to prioritize private plots, to well-organized land occupations that seize the fissures in the state's implementation of land reform. A large-scale movement as the communist revolutionary forces in the Philippines has also been engaged in land occupations. But evidently everyday forms of resistance predominate.

Regardless of the type of land struggle, the preponderant aim appears to be the establishment or preservation of petty commodity production, subject to historically specific conditions that vary by region, country and even locality. But regardless of how the land is acquired or occupied, commodity relations almost inexorably spread and take root. At the same time, petty commodity production implies a very unstable existence, with some eventually falling into the landless and dispossessed class of proletarians. Ironically, the best defence of petty commodity production is its combination with off-farm income, whether in waged work or self-employment. With global labour migration, petty commodity production takes two routes: either the household leaves agriculture altogether (freeing the land for use by another peasant or capitalist farmer) or it evolves into capitalized family farming, with the peasant becoming a petty capitalist and employer of rural labour.

Consequently, land struggles and their outcomes are best understood in the broader context of the multiple and contradictory class positions occupied by various members of the peasant household, which give rise to a highly complicated process and structuring of class differentiation. The stability and seeming permanency of hybrid forms of national and transnational labour encapsulate the structural 'fragmentation of labour' which characterizes contemporary capitalism (Bernstein 2002: 453). Directly globalized relations render the classic agrarian question, defined in national terms, redundant. Nonetheless, specific contexts require their own appropriate solutions and responses. Aspects of neoliberalism, including the global integration of labour, may be beneficial to some rural producers, but not to others; rotate and expand the axes of struggle; and, in any case, require some form of fundamental transition as a precondition for agrarian transformation (Kay 2002). In a situation of economic chaos and untold complexity, the moral imperative of sharing land with the needy appears to be the only unifying impulse, drawing NGOs and bureaucrats to support and organize land occupations. The neo-populist dream of advocating economically superior small-scale production ultimately is not dissociated from a morally grounded populism. The politics of the struggle for land cannot be distanced from this necessity, and

neither ought we to forget that every struggle is partial. We need
to learn from peasants who find and exploit the cracks.

References

Abelardo, Ma. Theresa (1997), 'Land Tenure Improvement in the PECURIA
    Estate', in *Making Agrarian Reform Work: Securing the Gains of Land Tenure
    Improvement*, Quezon City: Philippine Partnership for the Development of
    Human Resources in Rural Areas (PhilDHRRA).
Aguilar, Filomeno, Jr. (1989), 'The Philippine Peasant as Capitalist: Beyond the Cat-
    egories of Ideal-Typical Capitalism', *Journal of Peasant Studies* 17(1): 41–67.
Aguilar, Filomeno, Jr. (1992), 'Pitfalls of Theory and Evidence of Practice: Notes
    on Land Reform as a Populist Ideal', *Philippine Sociological Review* 40: 1–23.
Aguilar, Filomeno, Jr. (1998), *Clash of Spirits: The History of Power and Sugar
    Planter Hegemony on a Visayan Island*, Honolulu and Quezon City: University
    of Hawaii Press and Ateneo de Manila University Press.
Aguilar, Filomeno, Jr. (2002), *Filipinos in Global Migrations: At Home in the World?*,
    Quezon City: Philippine Migration Research Network and the Philippine
    Social Science Council.
Aguilar, Filomeno, Jr. (2003), 'Global Migrations, Old Forms of Labor, and New
    Transborder Class Relations', *Tonan Ajia Kenkyu (Southeast Asian Studies)*
    41(2): 137–61.
Battistella, Graziano, and Anthony Paganoni, eds (1996), *Asian Women in Migration*,
    Quezon City: Scalabrini Migration Center.
Bautista, Cynthia B. (1989), 'The Saudi Connection: Agrarian Change in a Pam-
    pangan Village, 1977–1984', in *Agrarian Transformations: Local Processes and the
    State in Southeast Asia*, ed. Gillian Hart, Andrew Turton and Benjamin White,
    Berkeley, Los Angeles and Oxford: University of California Press.
Beasca, Joel, and Ted Borrero (2003), 'An Evaluation of the Upland Resource
    Management and People's Development Assistance Project of the Upland
    NGO Assistance Committee (UNAC)', Quezon City: Optima Management
    and Development.
Bernstein, Henry (1981), 'Concepts for the Analysis of Contemporary Peas-
    antries', in *The Political Economy of Rural Development: Peasants, International
    Capital, and the State*, ed. Rosemary Galli, Albany, NY: State University of
    New York Press.
Bernstein, Henry (2002), 'Land Reform: Taking a Long(er) View', *Journal of
    Agrarian Change* 2(4): 433–63.
Cabanes, Leonora (1997), 'Land Tenure Improvement in the PAICOR Estate',
    in *Making Agrarian Reform Work: Securing the Gains of Land Tenure Improve-
    ment*, Quezon City: Philippine Partnership for the Development of Human
    Resources in Rural Areas (PhilDHRRA).
Chin, Christine B.N. (1998), *In Service and Servitude: Foreign Female Domestic Workers
    and the Malaysian 'Modernity' Project*, New York: Columbia University Press.
Constable, Nicole (1997), *Maid to Order in Hong Kong: Stories of Filipina Workers*,
    Ithaca, NY and London: Cornell University Press.

Cooke, Fadzilah Majid (1999), *The Challenge of Sustainable Forests: Forest Resource Policy in Malaysia, 1970–1995*, St. Leonards, NSW, and Honolulu: Allen & Unwin and University of Hawaii Press.

Cruz, Ma. Concepcion, Imelda Zosa-Feranil and Cristeta Goce (1988), 'Population Pressure and Migration: Implications for Upland Development in the Philippines', *Journal of Philippine Development* 15(1): 15–46.

Fukui, Seiichi (1995), 'The Role of Land Pawning in Securing Loans: The Case of *Sangla* in the Philippines', *Developing Economies* 33(4): 397–409.

Fuwa, Nobuhiko (1996), 'Social Stratification and Mobility in a Pangasinan Barrio, 1962–1994', *Pilipinas* 26 (Spring): 33–66.

Ghate, P.B. (1988), 'Informal Credit Markets in Asian Developing Countries', *Asian Development Review* 6(1): 64–85.

Kanok Rerkasem (1996), 'Population Pressure and Agrobiodiversity in Marginal Areas of Northern Thailand', in *Population, Land Management, and Environmental Change: UNU Global Environmental Forum IV*, ed. Juha I. Uitto and Akiko Oho, Tokyo: United Nations University Press.

Kay, Cristóbal (2002), 'Chile's Neoliberal Agrarian Transformation and the Peasantry', *Journal of Agrarian Change* 2(4): 464–501.

Kerkvliet, Benedict (1995), 'Village–State Relations in Vietnam: The Effect of Everyday Politics', *Journal of Asian Studies* 54(2): 396–418.

Kerkvliet, Benedict Tria, and Mark Selden (1998), 'Agrarian Transformations in China and Vietnam', *China Journal* 40 (July): 37–58.

Kitching, Gavin (1998), 'The Revenge of the Peasant? The Collapse of Large-Scale Russian Agriculture and the Role of the Peasant "Private Plot" in that Collapse, 1991–97', *Journal of Peasant Studies* 26(1): 43–81.

Kratoska, Paul (1985), 'The Peripatetic Peasant and Land Tenure in British Malaya', *Journal of Southeast Asian Studies* 16(1): 16–43.

Kung, James K.S., and Louis Putterman (1997), 'China's Collectivisation Puzzle: A New Resolution', *Journal of Development Studies* 33(6): 741–63.

Mapalad Agrarian Reform Monitor (1998), 'The Mapalad Hunger Strike and Agrarian Reform', *Mapalad Agrarian Reform Monitor*, January: 1–7.

Nagarajan, Geetha, Cristina David and Richard Meyer (1992), 'Informal Finance through Land Pawning Contracts: Evidence from the Philippines', *Journal of Development Studies* 29(1): 93–107.

Otsuka, Naoki (2002), 'Land-use Rights and Its Transfer in Changing Vietnam: A Case Study at Mekong Delta Region', in *Agrarian Transformation and Areal Differentiation in Globalizing Southeast Asia*, ed. Hiromitsu Umehara, Tokyo: Rikkyo University Centre for Asian Area Studies.

Peluso, Nancy (1992), *Rich Forests, Poor People: Resource Control and Resistance in Java*, Berkeley: University of California Press.

Poffenberger, Mark, ed. (1999), *Communities and Forest Management in Southeast Asia*, Berkeley, CA, and Gland: Asia Forest Network and IUCN–World Conservation Union.

Popkin, Samuel (1979), *The Rational Peasant: The Political Economy of Rural Society in Vietnam*, Berkeley, Los Angeles and London: University of California Press.

Rawal, Vikas (2001), 'Agrarian Reform and Land Markets: A Study of Land Transactions in Two Villages of West Bengal, 1977–1995', *Economic Development* and Cultural Change 49(3): 611–30.

Rigg, Jonathan (2002), 'Land and Livelihoods in Southeast Asia: Breaking the Bond?', in *Agrarian Transformation and Areal Differentiation in Globalizing Southeast Asia*, ed. Hiromitsu Umehara, Tokyo: Rikkyo University Centre for Asian Area Studies.

Scott, James (1976), *The Moral Economy of the Peasant: Rebellion and Subsistence in Southeast Asia*, New Haven, CT, and London: Yale University Press.

Scott, James (1985), *Weapons of the Weak: Everyday Forms of Peasant Resistance*, New Haven, CT, and London: Yale University Press.

Turton, Andrew (1989), 'Local Powers and Rural Differentiation', in *Agrarian Transformations: Local Processes and the State in Southeast Asia*, ed. Gillian Hart, Andrew Turton and Benjamin White, Berkeley, Los Angeles and Oxford: University of California Press.

Weyland, Petra (1993), *Inside the Third World Village*, New York: Routledge.

World Bank (1989), *Environment and Natural Resources Management Study: A World Bank Country Study – Philippines*, Washington, DC: World Bank Group.

8

Occupation of Land in India: Experiences and Challenges

Minar Pimple and Manpreet Sethi

Land, in its most comprehensive interpretation, which includes water, forests, mountains and mines, is the basis of all human life. It provides for the fundamental needs of food, clothing and shelter. Even more significantly, for the 70 per cent of the Indians primarily dependent on agriculture, land is not just the means of sustenance but also a way of life. And even for those who are landless, it is a source of livelihood and the means of their survival.

Given this importance of land, its ownership and usage patterns impact heavily upon the economic well-being of a nation, as well as the social well-being of its people. Historically, land as a key productive resource has been the basis of capital accumulation, which was a pre-requisite for industrialization throughout the world. In fact, the value of land lies not only in its food-producing potential but also in its capacity to energize economic and social mobility. This potential assumes greater significance in a caste society such as India's, which is socially and economically structured in a hierarchical fashion.

The caste system that evolved as a means of division of labour several centuries ago predetermined an individual's status and occupation in society at birth. This then decided his or her access to natural, material and even spiritual resources.[1] The two higher castes, comprising the *Kshatriyas*, the ruling class, and the *Brahmins*, the priestly class, enjoyed the greatest access to land and knowledge, the two determinants of social status. The *Vaishyas*, or the trading class, came next, while the *Shudras*, the backward classes, were mostly artisans and producers, and the *Atishudras*, or untouchables, were at the lowest rung of the social ladder. While the hold of the caste system has today largely shrivelled away in the urban areas, the countryside is still largely in its grip. Even today, the higher that one is positioned in this social pyramid of caste, the greater is one's power and control over those below, and over the access to natural and other resources. Furthermore, in India as in many other societies, ownership of land is held and inherited largely by men. This is true in spite of the significant role women play in making land productive, nurturing it and harvesting the diverse produce from it. But, for them, access and control over land is determined by their caste status as well as by their gender. Therefore ownership of land determines access to political and economic resources and governs social, productive and reproductive relations.

These relations find expression in modern statutory laws and property regulations, which now identify strict patterns of ownership and even land usage. In fact, under the doctrine of eminent domain, the state has now assumed complete proprietorship of the geographical expanse of the country and it alone has the power to provide the right of possession of land to its citizens, including over resources beneath and above it. The exclusive right over a piece of land, however, embodies a concomitant dispossession of land to others. While elaborate property rules and regulations govern this possession, and the rule of law is deemed a sign of civilized society, the fact remains that even in democracies laws are often mere creations of an economic and social elite, aiming to preserve the status quo, or at least ensure that reforms and other progressive legislation do not rock the boat too dangerously.

Land Policies and Reforms

Historical background

As the basis of all economic activity, land can either serve as an essential asset for the country to achieve economic growth and social equity, or it can be used as a tool by the elite to hijack a country's economic independence. During the two centuries of British colonial subjugation, Indian traditional land ownership and land-use patterns were changed to facilitate acquisition of land at low prices by British entrepreneurs for mining, plantations, and other economic pursuits.

The widespread introduction of private property delegitimized traditional community ownership systems of indigenous communities. With the introduction of land tax under the Permanent Settlement Act of 1793, the British encouraged a semi-feudal agrarian system. The ownership and control of land were highly concentrated in a few landlords and intermediaries, whose main intention was to extract maximum rent, either in cash or in kind, from tenants. Under this arrangement, the sharecropper or the tenant farmer had little economic motivation to develop farmland for increased production. Naturally, a cultivator who did not have security of tenure, and was required to pay a high proportion of output in rents, was less likely to invest in land improvements, or use high-yielding varieties or other expensive inputs likely to yield higher returns. At the same time, neither was the absentee landlord particularly concerned about improving the economic condition of the cultivators. As a result, at Independence, agricultural productivity was low and oppression of tenants was high. This also gave rise to numerous land struggles by tenants in various parts of India, contributing significantly to the larger freedom movement against British colonial rule.

In the years immediately following India's independence, a conscious process of nation-building turned to the land question with pressing urgency. In fact, the national objective of poverty abolition was hinged on simultaneous progress on two fronts: enhancing agricultural productivity and undertaking equitable distribution of land. In this schema, land reforms were visualized as an important pillar for a strong and prosperous country committed to social justice. The first few five-year plans allocated substantial budgetary amounts for the implementation of such reforms. A degree of success was even registered in certain regions and states, and especially in the realms of abolition of intermediaries, protection of tenants, rationalization of different tenure systems, and the imposition of ceilings on land holdings. Half a century later, however, the land question remains far from resolved. Most legislation for land reform has always stopped short of completely dismantling the possessions of the landed elite. Redistribution of land acquired by the government through the imposition of the ceiling rules, or through the voluntary Bhoodan (land donation), or otherwise, has never reached a substantive scale.[2] Rather, landlessness has been in the ascendant due to multiple factors, resulting into growing unemployment, a decline in food security, and poverty. The vested interests of the landed elite and their powerful nexus with the state bureaucracy have seemed to block meaningful land reforms and/or their earnest implementation. The oppressed have either been co-opted with some nominal benefits, or further subjugated, as the new focus on liberalization, privatization and globalization has altered government priorities and elite perceptions. As a result, we are today at a juncture in the land question, where land has increasingly become a matter of housing, investment and building of infrastructure for the urban, educated elite, who are also among the powerful decision-makers. Thus, the notion of land as the basis of subsistence, survival, social justice, and human dignity has largely been lost.

Neoliberalism and land

The implementation of the neoliberal model has left no economic factor of production untouched. Land and other issues related to it have also been affected. With land being valued primarily as a crucial productive asset, it is treated as a commodity to be traded for maximization of efficiency and profit. Consequently, there has been a transformation in land tenure arrangements in favour of privatization, with most activities associated with land turning into commercial ventures. In a bid to maximize yield per hectare through the increased use of external inputs, or its use for other commercial purposes, more land is being alienated with little regard for those that may have traditionally subsisted on it, often without legal ownership.

The consequences of these trends, however, are widespread and profound. On the one hand, the small farmer becomes the victim of global economic forces that peg his/her survival to the ability to adapt to the demands of market agriculture. She or he is encouraged to turn to commercial crops in order to fetch higher prices and to seek agricultural credit to be able to afford the expensive external inputs, such as fertilizers and pesticides. But this large-scale commercialization of agriculture, the introduction of multinational corporations into agriculture, and the extensive use of external inputs (including, credit, seeds, fertilizers and pesticides), erodes the viability of subsistence farming, leading to the abandonment of agriculture and the depressed sale of the land. From a socio-economic point of view, the repercussions of this are visible in the increasing inequalities in concentration of land. Data provided by the National Sample Survey of 1999 indicate that nearly 63 per cent of the population dependent on agriculture own smallholdings of less than 1 hectare, while the large parcels of 10 hectares of land or more are in the hands of less than 2 per cent of the population. The absolute landless, or the near landless (those owning up to 0.2 hectares of land), account for as much as 43 per cent of total peasant households (NIRD 2000).

At another level, with more land being consumed for purposes of housing, industry, infrastructural development, entertainment complexes and natural preserves, without adequate attention paid to the rehabilitation of the displaced, the number of poor and landless is on the rise (NCAS 2001). Losing control over their livelihood, the dispossessed either continue to look for means of employment and survival in rural/forest areas or migrate to urban areas. Obviously this involuntary migration results in overpopulation and burdening of the – often unplanned – city infrastructure. Thus, slums proliferate and cities expand, encroaching upon surrounding land with little regard for its cultivable or other ecological value.

In any case, under the modern laws of the Indian constitution – which proclaims commitment to an egalitarian socio-economic order – the dispossessed and the landless are treated as encroachers, as they either move into cities and occupy urban land, or move onto village common property resources, such as grazing lands, burial grounds, or some other patch of forest or wasteland. The modern law of the state is also in conflict with customary law. Under the application of neoliberal land policies, including the regularization of land records systems and the implementation of cadastral surveys to establish undisputed land ownership, traditional occupiers of land under customary law confront the prospect and reality of becoming illegal encroachers on lands they have cultivated and sustained for generations. They are vulnerable and subject to summary eviction.

State-led Land Alienation

The forceful alienation of land by the state in the name of development, 'public purpose'[3] or public enterprises has severe repercussions on the livelihoods of the poor and the landless. In India, three types of public land are especially under contestation: forests under state control, village commons (such as pastures and local woodlands), and public spaces within village settlements.

The area under forest and village commons, and the extent of people's access to them, have declined steadily, particularly since neoliberal policies have been vigorously pursued. Given the high dependency of the rural populace on these lands for fodder, fuel, supplementary food and other basic items, this decline has substantially weakened the livelihood security systems of poor rural households. This has led to their being termed encroachers on government land. On the other hand, encroachers on state land are often also large capitalists with expansion plans, including rich plantation owners or ministers in the government (Sharma 2003).

Forests and tribals

Until the end of the nineteenth century, land and forests almost throughout India belonged to tribal communities. The lands were administered by village elders, bestowing usufruct rights on separate families. There was no concept of 'exclusive title or possession' within the community. Ownership was best understood as 'mutual respect and recognition of the access of an individual or family to a separate plot of land to be used for "special requirements of the family"' (Prabhu 2002: 249).

The Indian Forest Act of 1878, however, empowered the government to declare any land covered with trees or brushwood as government forest and to make rules for its management. Forests were divided into village, reserve, and protected lands, with several use restrictions being imposed on the last two. Thus the Act radically altered the nature of common property and, in several cases, even appropriated land used by tribal communities. The emphasis, rather, was on exploiting forests to augment state revenue.

Under the Indian Constitution, certain areas have been specially designated as Tribal Areas in the north-eastern region and as Scheduled Areas in the rest of the country. These provisions were originally incorporated for the welfare and advancement of the Scheduled Tribes and were an acknowledgement of the fact that these communities had some special requirements. But, over time, state legislatures have gone on extending general administrative laws to these areas, thereby denying the tribals the need for special institutional structures. This has resulted in a conflict between the traditional systems and the formal institutions, especially with regard to the rights of the tribal people over the land and resources on which they might have subsisted for centuries without a formal ownership deed. Beginning with colonial forest policy and continuing under the postcolonial state, the intrusion of the formal economy, which privileges 'individual right' and the profit motive, has systematically undermined the informal system of the tribals and their livelihood.

The conflict has been further aggravated by the influx of non-tribals into tribal areas and their assuming ownership of land. Certain regulations under the Fifth Schedule[4] do not permit the sale of tribal land to outsiders, except to a government body or a tribal cooperative. Yet, in the absence of a comprehensive framework, this has not been completely effective. Rather, short-sighted government schemes aimed at developing infrastructure to improve access and develop tribal regions have been particularly disastrous; as investments have increased manifold, so have outsiders, while the rights of the tribals over their resources have gone on shrinking.[5]

The loss of tribal control over traditional natural resources has occurred through five means of land alienation. First is the reservation of forests. By declaring large tracts reserved or protected forests, the government has expanded its control over several areas. Many village lands too have been included in reserved forests and the inhabitants evicted.[6] This trend in fact started in the late 1800s under British rule, when villages in forests were marked off in blocks, including cultivable and wastelands, and declared out of bounds of the tribals. Outside the blocks lay the protected forest areas in which rights were regulated, even curtailed. In some cases, forest villages have been permitted to remain by the Forest Department, but in most cases the tribals end up serving as free and cheap labour for the forest officials. The situation is worsened by the fact that the forest administrators often also enjoy judicial and police powers.

In a recent case, in 1998, involving a World Bank-supported project of the Joint Forestry Management, an attempt was made to regularize encroachments in forest villages. But even in this case, the fundamental problem of state control over tribal lives was not allayed. Upon announcement of the regularization project, 476,596 people presented their applications for regularization, but subsequently only 148,000 were identified as eligible for land possession papers, while these too would have to be expressly permitted by the central government under the Forest Conservation Act of 1980 (Ramanathan 2002: 212).

The second means of land alienation is the leasing of forest lands to industrialists for timber felling, regeneration, agribusiness or tourism ventures. An important example of the leasing of waste land

and degraded forest for industry has been in Karnataka, where in 1977 the state gave 30,000 hectares of fallow land to two companies, Mysore Paper Mill and Karnataka Pulpwood. The purpose was to undertake the regeneration of forest land so as to produce raw materials for the paper industry. As the government started transferring land according to this agreement, the tribal people subsisting on the land were denied access to their pasture lands and forests, which had been providing them with their daily requirements of fuelwood and fodder. More such instances are now coming to light as the overall economic trend towards privatization is tempting state governments.

A third means of land alienation is enabled by the land acquisition Amendment Act, which simplifies the procedures for the acquisition of land by state-controlled or -owned enterprises on the grounds of serving a 'public purpose'. While the landowner and other 'persons interested', defined under the Act, receive some compensation for the acquisition of land, the landless labourers, artisans and forest land cultivators are not considered 'persons interested' and hence are not entitled to compensation for their resulting loss of earnings.

The fourth means is the exclusion from forest areas, an issue that has acquired more stridency in national parks and wildlife sanctuaries. Under the Wildlife (Protection) Act of 1972, national parks and sanctuaries have become the zone of contention between environmentalists and tribals. The enclosure of areas demarcated as national parks and sanctuaries invariably displaces communities that may have long lived on or off that land. It also displaces their traditional rights, which in turn are converted into 'licences' that permit them limited access. Even this is seen as unacceptable by environmentalists, who have in various court cases described the tribals as threats to the biodiversity and ecology of the area. In fact, the redefinition of the tribal as the 'enemy' of ecology and the outsider as 'protector' has become a widespread part of current thinking.

A fifth and final experience of alienation comes in an unofficial, extortionary form. In Dang district of Gujarat, which is mainly inhabited by tribals, the Forest Department extracts rents from the tribals in exchange for permission to remain on the land. At the same time, the Forest Department denies the existence of 'encroachments' on forest land. No official figures for the scale of encroachment are available, given that it is not recognized, but according to a survey carried out in 1995–96 it was estimated that some 726 Bhil tribals were cultivating 4,493 acres of land in 18 villages (Engineer 2002: 312–14).

The overall result of state alienation of land is that the rights traditionally held by the forest communities have been progressively curtailed. It is hardly surprising, therefore, that social unrest has emerged in the areas affected, in the form of grassroots forest protection movements which adopt tracts of forest for their preservation and regeneration.

Village commons and dalits

Common property resources – defined as 'community natural resources where every member has access and usage facility with specified obligations, without anyone having exclusive property rights over them' (see Ramanathan 2002) – are an integral aspect of the social and institutional arrangements made to meet the everyday requirements of village communities. They are of particular relevance to the landless, agricultural labourers and the rural artisans. *Dalits* (formerly untouchable communities) constitute the largest category of landless people in the agrarian sector. Studies of the states of Bihar and Uttar Pradesh point out that the *dalits* are concentrated among the agricultural labourers, since even under the traditional caste system they have been excluded from ownership of land. Consequently, their survival strategies have drawn on common property resources. For instance, in one study conducted in seven states in the semi-arid regions of India the village commons were seen to account for 9–26 per cent of the household income of the landless and marginal farmers, 91–100 per cent of their firewood needs, and 69–89 per cent of their grazing needs (Jodha 1986). However, with commonly held land and livelihood resources becoming increasingly scarce through state possession or privatization, the *dalits* are facing an even more difficult situation, as is brought out in the two examples detailed below.

The first is the case of the 'Maharvatan lands' in the Western Maharashtra region. During the feudal days of the Nizam, the Mahar communities, one of the castes earlier treated as untouchables, were provided land in villages for the scavenging services they rendered. However, there were no written records to this effect, and over subsequent years the Mahars were often evicted or denied control over their lands. It is estimated that the strong and powerful have grabbed nearly 24,000 acres of these lands. Struggles to secure permanent possession of these lands for the Mahar community – including the initiatives of prominent Mahar member and legislator Dr Ambedkar[7] – resulted in the enactment of legislation on Maharvatan lands by the government of Maharashtra, but this has not affected the huge acreage already taken over by other sections of society. In fact, the state government published the report prepared by the Patil Commission on this issue after more than a decade of struggle.

In another, more recent, instance the Tamil Nadu government has initiated a wasteland development programme that will pave the way for the entry of large corporate interests into the state's agricultural sector, and is likely to deprive thousands of farmers of their land and livelihood (Vishwanathan 2003). The Tamil Nadu Watershed Development Agency (TAWDEV) has been constituted to implement the programme, which has two components: a participatory watershed development scheme and a plan to develop government wasteland by involving the corporate sector, small companies and co-operatives. In none of the government orders (GO) issued on the subject has there been a clear definition of wasteland. The first GO in September 2001 stated that the scheme would only cover waste and fallow lands that are cultivable, leaving out permanent pasture land. The second GO of May 2002 stated that the first component of the programme would cover 'an estimated watershed area of 2.15 lakh hectares', while the third GO of July 2002, stated that the programme was meant to develop 'cultivable wastelands' and added that the 'unique' programme involving the corporate sector would be taken up in blocks of land lying 'waste and fallow'. In many places even grazing lands have been identified as wasteland. For instance, of the nearly 10,000 hectares of land identified as wasteland by the Kancheepuram district administration, about 8,000 hectares are grazing land (Vishwanathan 2003).

In fact, over the years, large tracts of land declared in government records as 'wastelands' have been brought under the plough by thousands of small and marginal farmers on the basis of assurances from government officials that *pattas* (land ownership documents) would be issued to them in due course. In the Kilapaakkam-Vellappandal village, for instance, the *dalits* claim that Panchami land to the extent of about 1.5 lakh hectares had been assigned to them decades ago. These *dalits* are the descendants of 200 families, each of which was given government land measuring 44 cents (0.2 hectare) in the early

1960s on the strength of a resolution passed by the local Panchayat (village elders with power of adjudication over local matters). But over the years no legal documents were made available to them, rendering their land vulnerable to being identified as wasteland and threatened by corporate acquisition.

Over 200 corporations across the country, including some industrial giants, are keen to participate in the programme. They are among the over 1,500 applicants for a package scheme that offers not only land on long lease at cheap rates but also governmental assistance in forward linkages to market facilities. The entry of companies into agriculture will pose a threat to the right to livelihood of the people and their right over and access to natural resources. At the same time, they are likely to sink deep wells, which will lower the groundwater level and cause acute water scarcity, with adverse effects for small farmers. In all, the inability of small farmers to compete with larger capital is set to result in further land alienation.

Further threats derive from the violation of the Tamil Nadu Land Ceiling Act and other legislation pertaining to land and tenure. While the Land Ceiling Act has fixed the ceiling of land one can possess at 15 standard acres (6 standard hectares), the programme intends to hand over hundreds of hectares of land to corporate bodies. The programme also envisages the leasing of common land in villages by the government, a step that is in violation of the Panchayat Act, under which *panchayati raj* institutions have the right and control over common land. According to critics of the programme, the *dalits*, who form a significant percentage of the 86.55 lakh landless labour in the state, will be the worst hit, most of them impoverished further by the loss of employment.

The Dynamics of Land Occupations

Unlike the experiences in several Latin American and African countries, land occupations in India have been less organized and smaller in scale. As traditional occupiers of common property resources, forests and other village commons are expelled in the course of state-led land alienation, the tendency of the evictees is to relocate to other areas in search of a livelihood. There have been few en masse premeditated occupations of land. There may be many reasons for this.

First, in Indian culture, perhaps more than in many others, land is not perceived in a detached fashion as just a means of production.

Rather, it provides a more religious, spiritual and cultural rooting and identity to the individual or the community. Therefore people find it difficult not only to abandon the land of their ancestors, towards which they have a sense of belonging, but also to occupy other land elsewhere with which they have no such bonding.

Second, despite the country's large size, but probably because of its huge population pressures, not enough unoccupied land is available for occupation in India. This is in marked contrast to the situation in countries such as Brazil, where huge tracts of land estimated at over 60 per cent of the farmland are believed to be lying idle (Frank 2002).

Third, stringent land laws and policies have made land occupation difficult. Under the doctrine of eminent domain, the state claims ownership of all land not under private ownership, and hence the scope for occupying unoccupied land is extremely limited.

Fourth, the strong nexus between the landed elite, politicians, lawmakers and bureaucrats often makes it extremely risky for the landless to occupy land. In fact, given the caste factor in rural politics, the landlord and the politician is often the same person.

Fifth, instances of regularization of occupied land have been few and far between, dissuading others from taking the step. In some countries, there is a process whereby the continued occupation of land, after a specified period, leads to the acquisition of full title of the land. In India, too, this is envisaged as a legitimate process for bringing security to those unable to prove original ownership, and acts regularizing tenancy have been based on this premiss. However, in recent times, sometimes even despite government orders to that effect, regularization has not been implemented. Even where state governments have stipulated dates up to which land encroachments may be regularized, the implementing authorities have refrained, for one reason or another, from providing ownership deeds to the occupants.

Sixth, there is a lack of adequate country-wide political mobilization among the landless. Instead of being united on the basis of class, the landless are severely fragmented along caste, ethnic and religious lines. Moreover, land struggles tend to differ significantly: for example, the *dalits* strive for land ownership, while tribal/indigenous communities strive for protection of their existing land and homesteads. Such struggles also differ from those of small and middle farmers, who strive not only to retain their land but also to make it more productive and to acquire or enhance their political clout. Interestingly, in areas where communist parties were actively involved in organizing the landless and marginal farmers during the pre- and post-independence periods, class consciousness is most pronounced, while in other areas the caste or ethnic undertones of land struggles are predominant.

While the above reasons, in varying measures, may explain the relative weakness of land occupations in India, there are some isolated, though militant, instances of land occupation. Wherever these have been undertaken, it has been an attempt to push reforms from below with the twin objectives of reasserting people's right to own land and challenging state authority and its mechanisms. Some of these are discussed briefly in the following sections.

Jabran jot (cultivation by force), Vidarbha, Maharashtra

This struggle dates back to the pre-independence period, when landless people in the Vidarbha region of the present Indian state of Maharashtra began occupying land, primarily in forest areas, for cultivation. However, even after years of cultivating the same piece of land, sometimes over generations, no legal ownership could be established due to the non-availability of any land deed or document. Soon after independence, in 1947 and in 1952, *pattas* (land ownership documents) were distributed by the government to some people, but the process was never completed and a majority of the people still do not have any such ownership deeds.

In the 1960s, another wave of occupation took place in the districts of Bhandara, Gadchiroli, Chandrapur, Gondia and Nagpur. In 1972 the government decided to conduct land surveys, including through the use of NGOs, to establish the names of those cultivating occupied lands and providing them with *pattas*. In 1980, under the rule that became famous as 'One Kayda' (one law), it was decided that no further encroachment would be honoured, but those who had occupied the land earlier would be regularized. However, in most cases the land documents have still proved elusive, since the onus of proof of continuous cultivation is placed on the land occupant. The occupant is to provide this through favourable evidence provided by the village revenue officer, forest officer, headman, police and neighbours. Vested interests, and lack of availability of one or another of these officials, have often dragged cases out. It is also possible

for an occupier to substantiate his claim to land by showing proof
of continuous cultivation through a document filed by him to the
revenue officer at the time of each harvest showing his produce.
But in many villages, soon after the 'One Kayda' order was passed,
government officials had stopped accepting these documents from
the farmers. As a result, the occupiers remain illegal encroachers,
deprived of legal documentation despite a government order seeking to regularize occupation, and they continue to live under the
threat of eviction.

Pardi Ghasia satyagraha[8] *(struggle of the Pardi Ghasia tribe),*
Valsad district, South Gujarat

Launched in the early 1950s, this struggle continued for fifteen years
in the Pardi region, which has an overwhelming majority tribal
population. In 1952, approximately one hundred landlords owned
three-quarters of the total cultivable land of Pardi (Desai 2002: 320).
These landlords, however, were interested not in agriculture but in
commerce. Rather than cultivating the land, they preferred to leave
a large portion of the land waste so that grass could be harvested
annually for the profitable fodder trade. This did not simply make
the original tribal inhabitants landless labourers; in most cases, due
to the growing of grass, even employment as wage labour was lacking for most of the year. Moreover, not only was land fraudulently
acquired from the tribals and turned into grasslands, but their cattle
were denied access to the grass too.

The struggle to redeem this situation was launched in 1953.
The prime objective of the movement was to grow food crops on
grasslands, since they considered it a sin to grow grass on cultivable
land when humans were starving. The movement did not seek to
challenge the existing socio-economic structure itself, categorically
declaring that the question of unequal land ownership, and hence the
redistribution of land, were not on their agenda. In September 1953,
after having served prior notice to the government, the *satyagraha* was
started in Dumlav village, where about 1,050 tribals, including 95
women, entered the private plot of a landlord and started tilling the
land. As expected, the *satyagrahis* were arrested. But over the weeks,
the movement witnessed immense political mobilization, including a
successful call to boycott all grass-cutting work. In 1955, the Bombay
government, succumbing to the social pressure, made a budgetary

allocation for a three-year period aiming to bring grasslands under various food crops. Later, in 1967, an agreement was also reached with the landowners, whereby they would surrender 14,000 acres of land to the government for distribution among the landless tribals (Desai 2002: 332–33).

Bodhgaya struggle, Bihar

The Bodhgaya land struggle was waged with the objective of establishing the rights of the landless to their own lands in the district of Bodhgaya, one of the most backward regions in Bihar. Some 125 villages from four blocks participated in the struggle in the late 1970s. The struggle was waged to reassert rights over land captured by a Hindu religious order to establish a *math* (temple monastery), supposedly to counter the influence of Buddhism.[9] Using religion and force, the *math* succeeded in alienating most of the land of the poor and marginal farmers in 120 villages. Only the richer peasants and upper-caste people retained their ownership. Later, the alienated land was allotted in the name of a number of fictitious trusts. It was against these that the Bodhgaya labourers waged their struggle.

The mobilization of peasants and workers was initiated in 1978 and a year later they were fully organized to press their demand through the physical occupation of land. Over the following eight years, the programme of collective land occupation was pursued in all four blocks. At the same time, the people also realized the benefits of collective cultivation over the collectively occupied land. The struggle brought forth the slogan *Jote-boye-kate dhan, khet ka malik vahi kisan* (the land belongs to the peasant who tills the land, sows and harvests the crop).

The struggle was waged for ten long years before the people finally managed to get their land. Another important consequence of the struggle was that women too acquired the right to own land. This led to a rise in their status and in the overall level of prosperity in the region.

Chattisgarh land satyagraha, Chattisgarh

This ongoing land *satyagraha* in some 700 villages of Raipur district of Chattisgarh raises several related land problems. The first one pertains to the landless who have been provided with land ownership

documents (*pattas*) by the government but have no physical occupation of that piece of land. In some cases they do not even know
where the land is located, though the government claims them as
beneficiaries of its land distribution scheme.

A second land struggle involves those who have been forcibly
occupying and cultivating a piece of government land but have no
pattas. In a survey of tribal hamlets in the Bundelkhand, Baghelkhand,
Chhattisgarh, Mahakaoushak, Malwa and Chambal regions of Madhya
Pradesh, it was discovered that this problem was rife over 11,000
acres of land (Parishad 2002). By contrast, it was also discovered that
similar forcible occupation of government open spaces by the rich
and powerful has been regularized!

A third struggle involves those who have been subsisting on a
piece of revenue land[10] that the government later declared as forest
land even though it had no tree cover. People who have been cultivating this land for years are subject to harassment by the forest
officials and often suffer evictions. At times, ruling parties have played
manipulative electoral politics and provided *pattas* to the settlers, but
successive governments have not always honoured these, leaving the
issue unresolved. For instance, *pattas* given during the Janata Party
rule in the state in 1977–80 were cancelled when the Congress (I)
came to power in 1980 (Singh 2002; Sail 2002).

The people have been waging their struggle against these injustices.
Their case has been strengthened by a scientific survey of land in
the region. Parallel land records have been created and made available to the people to challenge the fraudulent and false land records
maintained by the revenue officials. One of the prominent slogans of
this land *satyagraha* is *Zamin ka faisla, Zamin par hoga* (All land issues
will be settled on the very land itself). This was coined to address
in particular legal delays and to reduce the time and resources lost
by the poor in travelling to courts in places far away from their villages. Another important slogan that has come from land struggles in
Madhya Pradesh, defying the legitimacy of the state itself is *Zameen
hamari, Kagaz tumhara* (Land is ours, the paper is yours). This slogan
exposes the fraudulent practices in favour of the rich and powerful
in manipulating land records, and asserts that the people would not
honour any papers that go against their legitimate claims.

In another notable act of defiance in July 1995, people chose to
plough the very same fields that they were being debarred from
cultivating. In all areas, poor landless and small farmers went in large

numbers with their ploughs and bullocks to register their claim over the ancestral land. Such programmes of collective cultivation were declared well in advance and officials concerned were informed of the intention. This direct action brought mixed results. In some places, people were able to gain and register their control over land. In others, officials resorted to repression through the filing of false criminal cases against the activists and the people themselves. The struggle continues. In fact, the land *satyagraha* has triggered a new momentum among the people to take control of their resources. The land struggle is being coupled with a campaign for natural farming methods, against the use of high-yielding-variety seeds and chemicals. People have opened indigenous seed banks to promote the use of local varieties. Therefore a more holistic approach to the issues of land is now visible.

National and international alliances

In India there is a large diversity of movements agitating for a wide range of causes. There are those that are based in rural, coastal and tribal areas fighting for the empowerment of their social constituencies. These range from groups of fish workers, tribal, landless, marginal farmers, middle peasantry, *dalits*, caste-based organizations, women's organizations, students and youth organizations, and those fighting for regional/local autonomy. These organizations deal with multiple issues, including the demand for access to, and control and conservation of, marine resources against commercial trawling; for water (drinking, irrigation) and electricity (domestic and farm) at affordable rates; and for the establishment of social infrastructure, such as health, education, communication, transportation and roads. They deal also with issues of displacement caused by various developmental projects and they demand input subsidies in the form of fertilizers, seeds, agriculture credit and crop insurance, as well as minimum support prices for agricultural produce with state purchase guarantees. There are also movements dealing with issues of corruption, caste discrimination and atrocities, violence against women; and beyond this there are broader campaigns supported by local mobilization, such as the right to work, to food, to information, to democratic governance and democratic participation.

These struggles take the form of mass-based movements or trade unions, either established by, or affiliated to, communist or social-democratic parties, or they are new social movements, such as Narmada Bachao Andolan (Save Narmada Campaign), Chhatis-garh Mukti Morcha (Chhatisgarh Liberation Front), Ekta Parishad, Nimaad-Malwa Sangharsh Samittee, Adivasi Gothra Sabha (Tribal Grand Council), among many others across the country. They co-ordinate at the national level in various formations, such as the National Alliance of Peoples Movement, the National Coordination Committee for Rights of Rural Workers, Bharat Jan Andolan (Indian Peoples Movement), Mines, Minerals and People, and the Housing and Land Rights Committee of the Habitat International Coalition.

Many of these movements and organizations have taken the lead in organizing the Asian Social Forum in 2003 and the World Social Forum in 2004. Their aspirations were aptly captured by the statement of the Asian Social Mass and Peoples Movements and Organizations during the Asian Social Forum in Hyderabad (January 2003), which resolved to 'assert people's right to work, energy, food, water, land, other natural resources, education, health and public transport'. This resolve will be further consolidated through large-scale coalition-building activities that are taking place among the mass organizations affiliated to communist and socialist parties and new social movements represented by various coalitions such as the National Alliance of Peoples Movement and Bharat Jan Andolan.

The initiation of the Asian Social Forum in India, along with hosting the World Social Forum in 2004, is for the first time bring-ing together in an important way all organizations and social move-ments that oppose imperialist globalization, privatization of public resources, assets and services, market liberalization, sectarian violence and fundamentalism, casteism and patriarchy, and that believe that 'another world is possible'. These movements are optimistic about carrying this 'anti-globalization' project forward.

Conclusion

Land access for the poor is restricted in India not only by physical constraints, but more so by the legal and institutional mechanisms that are designed to deprive the majority of land. As such, the land question remains fundamentally a matter of political economy. It follows that the formulation of land policy is a political process and that land redistribution challenges the existing structure. It also

follows that a programme of equitable distribution of
justice must have the support of organized and c(
movements.

Mere physical occupation of land will be perceiveu as __
ment under the rule of law unless it is substantiated by legal deeds
and entitlements. Therefore there is an urgent need to build the
social legitimacy of the right to land. This requires the transformation of institutional structures of subordination through large-scale
changes in the laws, civil codes and property rights that precisely
underwrite elite control and privileges. As Amartya Sen (1999) has
argued, most cases of starvation and famine in the world are not the
result of people being deprived of what they are entitled to, but as
the result of people not being entitled, within the prevailing legal
system of institutional rights.

In an agrarian country like India, land circumscribes the individual's and the community's existence as an extension of their collective
consciousness, and particularly for the country's substantial tribal
population. It has not merely economic significance as a resource
for survival and a political significance as the material basis for
power; it also has a social basis as the person's sense of belonging
to a specific cultural community, and it establishes a cultural link to
traditions, ethos and way of life. A just and fair distribution of land
resources, therefore, is of the utmost importance. While redistribution
by the government remains the preferred mode, where this is not
forthcoming forcible physical occupation may be the only way. The
alliance that is emerging between landless movements in India and
the MST in Brazil, as well as with Vía Campesina, is a new sign
of global solidarity that hinges on a new vision of a humane new
world. Yes, another world is possible.

Notes

1. Caste developed into a sophisticated filigree of social interconnections
and divisions, even enjoying religious sanction, whereby responsibility for social
wrongs and oppression is deflected away from individuals and diffused in a
metaphysical universe.

2. The Bhoodan movement was started by Acharya Vinoba Bhave, who
exhorted the landed elite to surrender voluntarily their land in excess of the
ceiling so that it could be redistributed to the poor and landless. He started the
movement in the Telangana region in 1951. He travelled over 80,000 kilometres

on foot all over India with this demand until 1969. He received land donations of nearly 17 million hectares from half a million donors. However, only about half of this land could be redistributed, since the rest was either unfit for agriculture, or had been encroached upon, or because relevant documents were not available; see Das 2000.

3. Over the years, 'public purpose' has acquired a measure of immunity from challenge in court. Courts have generally sustained the view that a state's perception of what constitutes 'public purpose' is above judicial review.

4. An important feature of the constitutional provisions under the Fifth Schedule is that the legal and institutional frame for the tribal areas be so designed as to be in consonance with the people's institutions in these areas.

5. In West Bengal, Karnataka, Kerala and Tamil Nadu, the process of scheduling has not yet begun, even though the tribal sub-plans have been operating there for over the last twenty years; see Sharma 1997.

6. A clear example of this illegal inclusion of villages in reserved forests is that of Bihar. The Forest Department of the state has drawn new maps that include two tribal villages from the Porahat Pargana region of the Singhbhum district as reserved forests; while the village maps of 1932 clearly show them as lands belonging to the villagers.

7. Chairman of the drafting committee of Indian Constitution, first Law Minister of India, and member of the Mahar caste community, who became a major leader of the all-India movement against caste oppression.

8. The word *satyagraha* was popularized by Mahatma Gandhi during the independence struggle, as a form of non-violent civil disobedience; literally, it means the 'struggle for truth'.

9. At Bodhgaya, the founder of Buddhism, Gautama Buddha, is believed to have attained enlightenment.

10. The Revenue Department of the government of every state owns revenue land. In contrast, forestland is owned by the Forest Department, and this land is generally occupied by the landless in the hope of getting *pattas* in the future.

References

Agarwal, Bina (1994), *A Field of One's Own*, Cambridge: Cambridge University Press.

Das, Sukumar (2000), 'A Critical Evaluation of Land Reforms in India, 1950–55', in *Land Reforms in India: An Unfinished Agenda*, Volume V, ed. B.K. Sinha and Pushpendra Singh, New Delhi: Sage Publications.

Desai, Kiran (2002), 'Land Reforms through People's Movements', in *Land Reforms in India: Issues of Equity in Rural Madhya Pradesh*, Volume VII, ed. Praveen K. Jha, New Delhi: Sage Publications.

Engineer, Irfan (2002), 'Struggles of Dangi Adivasis for Livelihood and Land', in *Land Reforms in India: Issues of Equity in Rural Madhya Pradesh*, Volume VII, ed. Praveen K. Jha, New Delhi: Sage Publications.

Fernandes, Walter, and S. Anthony Raj (1992), *Development, Displacement and Rehabilitation in the Tribal Areas of Orissa*, New Delhi: Indian Social Institute.

Frank, Jeffrey (2002), 'To Models of Land Reform and Development', *Activism Online* 15(11), www.activismonline.org.

Government of Maharashtra, Directorate of Economics and Statistics (2002), *Economic Survey of Maharashtra, 2001–02*, Mumbai: Directorate of Economics and Statistics, Planning Department, Government of Maharashtra.

Hiremath, S.R., ed. (1997), *Forest Lands and Forest Produce: As If People Mattered*, Dharwad: NCPNR.

Jha, Praveen K., ed. (2002), *Land Reforms in India: Issues of Equity in Rural Madhya Pradesh*, New Delhi: Sage Publications.

Jogdand, P.G., ed. (2000), *New Economic Policy and Dalits*, Jaipur and New Delhi: Rawar Publications.

Jodha, N.S. (1986), 'Common Property Resources and Rural Poor', *Economic and Political Weekly* 21: 27.

Kulkarni, Sharad (2000), 'The Plight of the Tribal', *Seminar* 492 (August): 37–9.

Lobo, Brian (2002), 'Land Reforms: Turning the Clock Back', *Economic and Political Weekly* 37(5): 529–32.

NIRD, National Institute for Rural Development (2000), *India Rural Development Report*, Hyderabad: NIRD.

NCAS, National Centre for Advocacy Studies (2001), *Fact Sheet on Land Reform and Land Alienation*, Pune: NCAS.

Parishad, Ekta (2002), 'A Perspective on Lands and Forests in Madhya Pradesh', in *Land Reforms in India: Issues of Equity in Rural Madhya Pradesh*, Volume VII, ed. Praveen K. Jha, New Delhi: Sage Publications.

Prabhu, Pradip (2002), 'Land Alienation, Land Reforms and Tribals in Maharashtra', in *Land Reforms in India: Issues of Equity in Rural Madhya Pradesh*, Volume VII, ed. Praveen K. Jha, New Delhi: Sage Publications.

Ramanathan, Usha (2002), 'Common Land and Common Property Resources', in *Land Reforms in India: Issues of Equity in Rural Madhya Pradesh*, Volume VII, ed. Praveen K. Jha, New Delhi: Sage Publications.

Sail, Rajendra K. (2002), 'People's Struggle for Land: A Case Study', in *Land Reforms in India: Issues of Equity in Rural Madhya Pradesh*, Volume VII, ed. Praveen K. Jha, New Delhi: Sage Publications.

Sen, Amartya (1999), interview, 15 December, available on www.theatlantic.com/unbound/interviews/.

Shah, Ghanshyam, and D.C. Shah, eds (2000), *Land Reforms in India: Performance and Challenges in Gujarat and Maharshtra*, Volume VIII, New Delhi: Sage.

Sharma, B.D. (1997), 'The Scheduled and Tribal Areas: Omissions, Neglect and Illusive Strategies', in *Forest Lands and Forest Produce: As If People Mattered*, ed. S.R. Hiremath, Dharwad: NCPNR.

Sharma, Ravi (2003), 'Eating Up Forest Lands', *Frontline* 20(6), www.hinduonline.com.

Singh, Anoop (2002), 'The Land Question in Chattisgarh', in *Land Reforms in India: Issues of Equity in Rural Madhya Pradesh*, Volume VII, ed. Praveen K. Jha, New Delhi: Sage Publications.

Sinha, B.K., and Pushpendra Singh, eds (2000), *Land Reforms in India: An Unfinished Agenda*, Volume V, New Delhi: Sage Publications.

Upadhyay, Sanjay, and Bhavani Raman (1998), *Land Acquisition and Public Purpose*, New Delhi: The Other Media.

United Nations Center for Human Settlements (1985), *Land for Public Purposes: Guidelines*, Nairobi: United Nations.

Vishwanathan, S. (2003), 'Land Reforms in Reverse?', *Frontline* 20(5), www.hinduonline.com.

9

Stretching the 'Limits' of Redistributive Reform: Lessons and Evidence from the Philippines under Neoliberalism

Salvador H. Feranil

In the era of neoliberal reforms, land reform has taken a back seat. Not only has poverty discourse among the multilateral institutions moved towards 'enlarging' the pie rather than redistributing it (Herring 2001), but discussions among academics and policymakers have also tended to point to the increasing difficulty of redistributive reforms in countries beset by agrarian conflicts. However, the persistence of agrarian conflicts reveals the continuing need to address the land question (Kay 2000) and search for solutions that take cognizance of the political, economic, social and cultural dimensions of the rural world (El-Ghonemy 1999). Peasant uprisings and mobilizations in Asia, Africa and Latin America from the 1980s to 1990s, and the more recent land occupations in Zimbabwe, demonstrate that land reform remains a central issue among developing countries.

The profound political, economic and social changes that have taken place in the world over the last two decades have been accompanied by an agrarian reform model that has emphasized the rolling back of the state and the replacement of redistributive reform by market-led agrarian reform (MLAR). Despite the existing critiques of the model, the MLAR talks of advantages related to land pricing, claim-processing and cost-effective administration, which make the 'demand-driven' model more 'viable' than the 'supply-driven', state-led agrarian reforms of the past.

The emerging debate between state-led and market-led land policy tends to create bipolar tendencies in viewing current agrarian reform implementation across countries. But agrarian reform and its outcomes are not simply determined by institutions like the state or market alone. Public policy is a dynamic political process that takes place through power struggles, while changes in the balance of power in society create profound effects on the outcomes of reforms (Sobhan 1993). Current debate tends to neglect the fact that policy outcomes are located within arrangements that are invariably re-examined, revised and even overturned (Kerkvliet 1993). Thus an analysis that examines the interaction of state and social actors within an existing socio-political and economic context would offer more incisive explanations of current land reform experiences.

The case of the Philippines provides interesting insights on this interaction between the state and the landless and rural poor on agrarian reform. In the mid-1980s, non-governmental organizations (NGOs) and people's organizations (POs) engaged pro-reform legislators in a process that resulted in the formulation of the Comprehensive Agrarian Reform Programme (CARP), covering all agricultural lands in the country. Yet, the CARP continued to be resisted by big landlords, even despite the existence of market-friendly mechanisms and components in the programme, including cash incentives for willing sellers, land valuation based on land productivity, and priority for landowners in agribusiness ventures. Thus the socio-political dynamics of the process have continued to shape reform outcomes. In particular, state–society interaction on agrarian reform has demonstrated variegated tendencies, including successes and failures in land redistribution, across time, land types and geographic locations.

Redistributive agrarian reform in the Philippines has been beset with problems for more than a decade. The limitations, difficulties and seemingly bleak prospects of agrarian reform were initially attributed to flaws in policy design (Hayami et al. 1990), existing structural and institutional constraints which derived from the influence of landowning elites on state policies and decisions (Putzel 1992), the limited political will of the government to implement redistributive reforms (Kasuya 1995), and the inherent resource limitations of the programme (Riedinger 1995). Generally, the current land reform experience in the Philippines was understood to have failed in meeting the demands for social justice and in altering the structures that perpetuate rural inequality.

Such initial views on the 'limits' of agrarian reform, however, were overtaken by the results of CARP implementation from the mid-1990s onward. Official figures from the Department of Agrarian

Reform (DAR) in 2001 have illustrated that more than 80 per cent of close to 4 million hectares of agricultural lands targeted by the programme had been redistributed to landless peasants and farmworkers. Though a closer scrutiny of government figures could possibly reveal lower land redistribution outcomes, the accomplishment far exceeds the pessimistic predictions of CARP critics (Borras 2002). Despite doubts raised about policy outcomes, the initial and concrete victories achieved by local peasant organizations that engaged the state under the CARP demonstrate that structural and institutional constraints to land reform could be significantly overcome by autonomous peasant mobilizations from below, combined with initiatives from reformists within the state institutions, or what can be termed the *bibingka* strategy (Borras 1998).

Nonetheless, a closer examination of CARP outcomes also demonstrates that the programme did have weaknesses in significantly redistributing contentious private agricultural landholdings owned by despotic landlords. Among the sectors that continue to face stronger resistance from landowners is the commercial farms sector that is composed of landholdings devoted to both traditional and non-traditional agricultural exports. Even though the 10-year deferment provisions of CARP[1] were lifted in 1998, large private landholdings have remained in the hands of landowners and agribusiness companies, while some of those distributed earlier have experienced second-generation problems, such as conflicts among beneficiaries. Though social mobilizations in the mid-1990s fuelled some of the reform initiatives related to land reform, anti-reform currents in both state and society continue to pose serious threats to the potential of peasant mobilizations and collective action aimed at further stretching the reform limits of CARP. Against this background, this chapter intends to look at the emerging strategies and potentials of local peasant collective action and land occupations in challenging the limits of land reform implementation in the Philippines.

The Political Economy of the Philippines

Democratization and agrarian reform

Poverty and landlessness are widespread in the Philippine countryside. Official government figures in the year 2000, which are not entirely reliable, indicate that 4.3 million Filipino families – 34 per cent of Filipinos (26.5 of the 77.9 million total population) – are 'poor'.[2] Independent observers estimate that roughly two-thirds of the country's poor are rural poor (Borras 2001b).[3] A Gini coefficient of 0.647, based on government data from a pre-CARP census of 1988, indicates a high degree of inequality of land ownership; in 1988, 65 per cent of landowners (or 1 million out of 1.5 million) owned only 16.4 per cent of total farm area in holdings of less than 3 hectares (Putzel 1992). Even these data, however, are to be taken with caution, given the limitations of the data-gathering method, which in effect allowed landowners to under-report the full extent of their holdings.[4]

The skewed land ownership has had a profound impact on the political composition of Philippine society. Rural politics are dominated by agrarian political elites who compete for political office by utilizing complex patronage networks (Anderson 1988), electoral machineries, 'official socio-economic organizations', conservative local churches and private armies (Lara and Morales 1990), and who are able to control political processes and outcomes in their own political fiefdoms (Sidel 1989). The agrarian oligarchy continues to rely on its traditional economic power for the exercise of its political power, although its position has been challenged by modernizing landlord-entrepreneurs in the non-traditional export sector. The latter manifested their influence on political institutions and in policymaking processes when Congress approved the deferment provisions in CARP exempting commercial farms from land redistribution for a period of ten years. Compared with traditional agrarian oligarchs who reject land reform outright, modernizing landlords who seek ways to maximize land productivity through modern agriculture tend to be more open to reform arrangements that open the possibilities for cooperation between reform beneficiaries and enterprising landowners.

Past cycles of peasant uprisings and mobilizations – including the peasant-based revolution initiated in the late 1960s by the Communist Party of the Philippines (CPP) and the New People's Army (NPA) – have produced only intermittent concessions from the state. The response of the agrarian elite has traditionally been a combination of repression and limited land reform (Borras 1998: 270). Thus, although previous land reform programmes, not least under the authoritarian government of Marcos in the 1970s, have sought to put an end to land-based conflicts and uprisings, reform outcomes generally failed to do so.

The transition from an authoritarian to an electoral regime in 1986 did not result in complete democratization of the countryside. Despite the apparent democratization initiatives sweeping the country at the national level from 1986 onward, local authoritarian enclaves persist and entrenched political elites continue to dominate the rural polity (Franco 2000). Although reform openings encouraging wider civic and political participation were initiated by some state reform-ists after the promulgation of CARP in 1988, such opportunities did not translate into substantial gains for the marginalized rural sectors. Peasant mobilizations and collective action that pressure the state to remain firm in its commitment to a redistributive agrarian reform continue to mount, while land redistribution continues to be resisted by despotic landowners in different parts of the country.

The promulgation of the Republic Act 6657, otherwise known as the Comprehensive Agrarian Reform Programme (CARP), has been a landmark in the country's history of land reform. First, it heralded an official land reform programme that was a product of interaction among organized sections of the peasantry, agrarian re-form advocates, non-governmental organizations and state elites. In 1987, the organized peasantry coalesced with different land reform advocates and groups to form the Congress for a People's Agrar-ian Reform (CPAR) and submit their proposed People's Agrarian Reform Code to the Aquino government. Although the CARP was far less radical than the proposal of the CPAR, the coalition's interaction with legislators during policy formulation did have an influence on the state, and in particular on the passing of a redistributive land reform policy designed to benefit millions of landless rural poor in the country.

Second, the agrarian reform programme became the centrepiece of the Aquino administration's strategy to spur development and democratization in the Philippine countryside. Though most CARP critics claim that the policy has contained loopholes that compromise the interests of the landless rural poor in relation to the landowning class (discussed below), the CARP has provided significant openings for the landless to engage the state and challenge policy. The exist-ing policy follows a 'land to the tiller' principle. Selection of reform beneficiaries prioritizes landless peasants and farmworkers who actually occupy and till the land, and in commercial plantations those who have worked on the land within the 1988–98 period. The policy disquali-fies applicant beneficiaries whose work tenure in plantations expired prior to the promulgation of CARP. Other landless applicants who are not actual tillers on CARPable lands are considered only when there is an excess in the minimum 'one hectare, one beneficiary' ratio in a particular landholding. The exclusionary practice within CARP suggests that other interested landless rural poor could become beneficiaries only when a landholding is large enough to accommodate those who are not actual tillers or occupants of the land.

Third, while previous land reform policies covered limited lands, the CARP marked a significant shift by including all public and private agricultural lands (regardless of tenurial relations) in its coverage. The expanded coverage of 10.3 million hectares of farmland offers opportunities for millions of landless rural poor to benefit from the policy. Finally, the policy has illustrated the role and obligations of the state not only in relation to land redistribution but also in providing post-distribution support packages that include infrastructure and other support services necessary to augment the productive capacities of reform beneficiaries.

On the other hand, the official agrarian reform policy has also incorporated market-friendly provisions that provide room for land-owners and investors to benefit from the programme. First, far from being a radical state-led land reform programme that expropriates and freely distributes lands to the landless rural poor, CARP employs a 'just compensation principle' that provides payment to landowners. Land valuation is based on the land's average production per hectare over the last three cropping seasons. Payments are given to landowners both in cash and in bonds that mature over time. As an incentive to landowners, the cash portion is subsequently increased when lands are voluntarily offered for sale to the government. Second, the policy allows a market-based Voluntary Land Transfer that directly transfers lands to beneficiaries under mutually agreed terms between landlords and peasants. Under this mechanism, the state simply facilitates the process for land transfer while negotiation outcomes are virtually left to landlords and beneficiaries.

Third, previous landowners and investors could enter into joint-venture arrangements after lands have been redistributed to beneficiaries. Though such arrangements could be forged only after land redistribution, policy implementation tends to reveal that landowners, in collusion with corrupt government officials, bind land redistribution to post-distribution agribusiness arrangements that tend to disadvantage reform beneficiaries. In extreme cases, these arrangements virtually lack the transfer of effective land control to beneficiaries. Fourth, the policy is to be complemented by a pending law that suggests the use of farmlands as collateral in accessing loans from banks and other private financial institutions. While such a proposal supposedly provides leverage for beneficiaries in accessing the necessary capital to augment land productivity, it opens up the possibility for landowners to regain land ownership should beneficiaries fail to pay their debts.

As argued earlier, policy alone does not determine outcomes. Policy and its implementation are shaped by political dynamics at the national and local levels, deriving from the balance of social forces. Before analysing this process more closely in the next section, we turn here to the national development policy framework and its transformation in the 1990s.

Agriculture and liberalization

The importance of the agricultural sector in the national economy has had a heavy influence on the course of land reform, despite the diminishing size of the sector in relation to the rest of the economy. In the late 1980s, the contribution of agriculture to GDP amounted to 27 per cent, while agro-industry amounted to 41 per cent of GDP (Putzel 1992). In addition, roughly one-third of labour employed in the service sector was in agroindustry, making agriculture-based activities the main source of employment, approximately 60 per cent of the total (Borras 1998). And if we consider that a good proportion of the service sector – whether in wholesale and retail trade, transport and storage, or government and private services – is directly related to agribusiness activity, the total contribution of agriculture is even higher (Putzel 1992: 17).

From 1992 to 1998, the Ramos administration actively implemented neoliberal reforms, in a strategy intended to spur economic growth and raise the performance of the industrial sector in particular. These reforms were continued by the Estrada administration after 1998. This outward-looking policy orientation has entailed a shift of emphasis towards high-value crops, through the Medium Term Agricultural Development Plan (MTADP), together with efforts to increase foreign direct investment as well as foreign exchange remittances by Filipino workers overseas. State support for low-value, high-volume crops was increasingly withdrawn.

This development strategy resulted in modest economic gains, as foreign direct investments began to flow in and foreign exchange earnings from dollar remittances of overseas Filipino workers contributed approximately 10 per cent of total GDP (Borras 2001b: 249). The average GDP growth rate of 3.5 per cent from 1990 to 1999 more than tripled the average growth rate of 1.0 per cent between 1980 and 1990. However, despite the higher aggregate growth rate, the performance of the agricultural sector grew 1.5 per cent in 1990–99, up only slightly from the 1.0 per cent growth rate in 1980–90, and much lower than the service sector, which manifested a steady upswing throughout the 1980s and 1990s. Although agriculture's contribution at 19 per cent of GDP in 1997 (NSCB 2000) is not far from its 15 per cent contribution in 1998, the slow growth of the sector is reflective of the bias against agriculture in the new development strategy.

The policy bias has been in favour of merchandise exports that are deemed more capable of generating capital accumulation. In the period of neoliberal reforms, the total amount of merchandise exports in the country soared from US$8.07 billion in 1990 to US$29.44 billion in 1998 (World Bank 2001). The manufacturing sector, which previously accounted for only 38 per cent of exports in 1990, comprised 90 per cent of total exports in 1998. Meanwhile, agricultural product exports grew from US$5.44 billion (1991–94) to US$7.15 billion (1995–98). But while agricultural exports appear to be growing, the larger picture in agriculture shows that imports of agricultural products almost doubled from US$5.70 (1991–94) to US$10.50 billion (1995–98), posting an agricultural trade deficit of US$257.47 million and US$3.35 billion for the respective periods. It is no surprise, then, that despite the tremendous increase in the volume of international commerce within the Philippine economy, the country has continued to experience a trade deficit through the years, as imports have far exceeded exports in the national balance sheet.

The country's agricultural exports, which include traditional export crops like sugar cane and coconut, and non-traditional exports like banana and pineapple, have significant influence on the implementation of land reform. Traditional exports like sugar cane had declined dramatically from US$1.82 billion in 1979–82 to an average of just below US$400 million in 1987–98. Coconut exports, on the other hand, remained steady, averaging US$2 billion in 1983–94 and reaching a peak of US$3.1 billion in 1995–98. Meanwhile, export winners like banana, pineapple and mango composed the bulk of non-traditional agricultural exports. For the twenty-year period of 1979–98, banana exports remained the biggest dollar earner for the non-traditional sector, generating more than US$3 billion. In the period 1995–98, the earnings of banana exports surpassed by more than 30 per cent the earnings of coconut exports. Compared to coconut, which covers approximately 3 million hectares, banana covers only 50,000 hectares of land across the country. In turn, the most contentious private landholdings in the agrarian reform programme have been located in the banana plantations, but also in those which cultivate the traditional export crops of sugar cane and coconut.

Agrarian Politics before and after CARP

Engaging the state on policy formulation

The upsurge of radical peasant mobilizations and collective action in various parts of the country in the 1980s, backed by the entire National Democratic (ND) movement, paved the way for the revival of the land question in Philippine politics. By the time the Aquino government came to power, land reform had become one of the more pressing issues that demanded immediate state legislation. The newly installed administration was compelled to pursue land reform immediately as a means to restore and maintain political stability in the countryside after the EDSA uprising.[5] With the national democratic movement gaining ground both in the cities and in the countryside, land reform was perceived not only as an instrument that could unleash the productive capacities of the countryside (Hayami et al. 1990), but also as a socio-political measure that could strengthen the Aquino administration's legitimacy among the landless rural poor. Apart from the fact that land reform constituted an important aspect of Aquino's presidential campaign in 1986, it was also perceived as an extremely important reform measure for any government in quelling the rural insurgency.

Given the opportunities for enlarging the political space and for pushing redistributive reforms within a government-in-transition, the Kilusang Magbubukid ng Pilipinas (KMP, Philippine Peasant Movement) proved crucial in lobbying the Aquino government for a progressive agrarian reform policy that would end landlord domination. During the 1986–88 democratic transition, the KMP could be considered as the most important peasant organization, succeeding in mobilizing high-profile demonstrations and submitting a comprehensive and detailed land reform proposal as early as June 1986, before the government was able to draft its own plan.

The Aquino government's indecisiveness in drafting and enacting immediately a land reform policy compelled the KMP to intensify further its mobilizations. On 22 January 1987, tens of thousands of KMP members, together with their urban allies, marched to the Mendiola Bridge near the President's Palace to press for land reform. However, instead of heeding the legitimate demands of the KMP, the phalanx of military units deployed at the bridge opened fire at the demonstrators, killing thirteen civilians and wounding several more. While legislative processes on land reform were hastened thereafter, there were already clear indications from this bloody incident and the debates in the Philippine legislature that the Aquino government would not draft a land reform policy that would challenge outright the agrarian oligarchy.

With legislative initiatives subsequently under way in Congress, peasant organizations from various political blocs converged to form the Congress for a People's Agrarian Reform in order to push for their own version of agrarian reform. Composed of thirteen national rural organizations of different political persuasions, representing landless peasants, peasant women, small farmers, farmworkers and fisherfolks, the CPAR provided a vehicle for agrarian reform advocates from civil society groups to work with pro-reform state legislators in influencing the processes and outcomes of Aquino's agrarian reform policy. Although these initiatives were spearheaded by social democrats (SDs), the ND rural peoples' organizations joined the coalition. The KMP, as the biggest and broadest national campaign centre of local and regional peasant organizations operating around the country, with a membership of some 800,000 members (Weekley 2001), was among those in the forefront of legislative debates on agrarian reform. In contrast to the liberal and social-democratic groups that espoused a compensatory land reform, the KMP advanced a more radical position calling for a 'genuine' agrarian reform that would involve 'free land distribution' among the rural poor. Yet the anti-reform forces in the Aquino administration, especially in Congress, managed to overcome the radical interventions, and the Aquino government succeeded in having the loophole-ridden CARP proposal approved by Congress and promulgated in June 1988. CARP was far from their ideal agrarian reform model, and most organizations across the political spectrum rejected it. For its own part, the KMP declared CARP to be anti-peasant and pro-landlord, particularly the clauses on 'just compensation', the 5-hectare retention limit, and the deferment of land redistribution in commercial plantations.

Land occupations and Total War policy

Land occupations are a symptom of the deep malaise in Philippine society (Putzel and Cunnington 1989). If the government were committed to a genuine and redistributive agrarian reform, peasants would not have to resort to land occupations. The Aquino government continued to be dominated by the landowning class (Borras 1998), and clearly landowning interests would prevail in any state-legislated land reform program. Hence, while the political transition in 1987 could have been an opportune time to address the land question and restructure Philippine society, the president remained captive to the interests of the landowning class by relegating the whole issue to an elite-dominated legislature. In this context, land occupations became a necessary political tactic, manifesting the determination of landless peasants to implement land reform with or without the state's intervention.

Simultaneously with campaigns for a genuine agrarian reform, popular initiatives and massive land takeovers on the ground were launched by local KMP chapters (sometimes backed by the NPA) in different parts of the country (Kerkvliet 1993). KMP members occupied idle public lands and took over those that were either abandoned by Marcos's cronies or foreclosed on by banks in various parts of the country. In Negros Occidental, in the western part of the island of Visayas, the efforts of KMP to intensify land occupations reached approximately 75,000 hectares of agricultural lands and benefited some 50,000 landless households.[6] The breadth and scale of these occupations far surpassed previous occupations by the National Federation of Sugar Workers, who had attempted to take over lands left idle and abandoned by the sugar planters at the height of the crisis in the sugar industry in the mid-1980s.

Land occupations, however, were short-lived as the Aquino government began to implement a Total War policy against the CPP–NPA and its continuing armed struggle. With the resurgence of authoritarian tendencies in the Aquino government, landowners were able to regain idle and abandoned lands occupied by the landless peasants of KMP. Borras (1998: 56) points out that while land takeovers in the second half of the 1980s contributed in keeping land reform on the national agenda, it failed as an alternative land reform programme implemented outside the state:

> First, most of the areas were heavily militarized and so the peasants could not resume their normal farming activities; second, almost no government or private institution wanted to lend credit to the peasants occupying the lands; third, the pool of cadres, peasants or otherwise, assigned in their communities were trained as political activists and not as business entrepreneurs or development activists who could help these communities organize profitable farming enterprises ... fourth, the majority of the occupied lands were marginal; fifth, and perhaps a summary of the earlier factors, was that when the communities started to be militarized, the peasants normally did not make an exhaustive effort to stay, perhaps because they felt there was not much at stake in the land: no legal titles and productive activities.

The Total War inflicted serious damage on the organized peasantry as military operations in the countryside completely overran peasant communities. The shift in Aquino's political stance against the left likewise paved the way for the consolidation and restrengthening of the landowning class within the state. Thus, far from the common claims and beliefs that democratization efforts had been sweeping the country after the downfall of Marcos, local authoritarian enclaves continued to persist despite the political reforms initiated by the Aquino government.

The intensification of Aquino's Total War policy constricted the activities of the democratic movement. For one, the military teams deployed in the countryside would not make a distinction between underground operators and legal personalities representing open legal organizations. During military offensives, communities (suspected of being a revolutionary base) were attacked regardless of whether the people in these areas were hardcore revolutionaries, supporters of the CPP–NPA, or civilians who had long been residing or cultivating in the area. At the height of the implementation of the counter-insurgency strategy, legal mass organizations, and especially their leaders, were subjected to harassment from military teams deployed in the countryside. Further, the Total War policy generated support from rural households that became victims of the excesses of the CPP–NPA during the purge period in the Party. Thus, apart from the internal debates that haunted the whole revolutionary movement in the early 1990s, the increased militarization of the countryside and the reconsolidation efforts of the landowning class contributed to the decline and fragmentation of the progressive peasant movement.

Cleavages in the peasant movement

The debates on agrarian reform resulted in cleavages within the broad coalition of civil society organizations engaging the state on its land reform policy. Hence, while the radical KMP decided to launch massive initiatives to counter CARP and call for genuine agrarian reform, certain sections of the previously CPP-led peasant movement began to work the system by engaging the Aquino government in CARP implementation. This manifested a clear deviation from the previous strategy of the CPP-led left, whose organizing strategy operated within the framework of the national democratic revolution. The shift in orientation and strategy towards an open peasant mass movement stirred debates within the CPP and consequently led to the formation of various legal peasant organizations that were increasingly autonomous from the dictates of the Party and more open in working with non-aligned organizations in their engagement with the state.

While the KMP decided to continue pressing for genuine agrarian reform and worked largely outside the system, some of those who saw reform opportunities in CARP engaged the state in its 'tripartite strategy' of CARP implementation. Within such strategy, reform initiatives of government, non-governmental organizations (NGOs), and people's organizations (POs) converged towards a common direction and outcome. The convergence initiatives among different reform-oriented groups stemmed largely from the efforts of the Department of Agrarian Reform (DAR), under the administration of Ernesto Garilao, to harness the wider participation of civil society organizations in CARP implementation. These initiatives later translated into a policy whereby Tripartite Partnership for Agrarian Reform and Rural Development (TriPARRD) projects were implemented in selected parts of the country.[7] Though the real impact created by TriPARRD, especially in moving contentious private landholdings and in propelling autonomous mobilizations from below, raised doubts among civil society organizations, the strategy could be perceived to have served its purpose of harnessing civil society participation in the state's reform programmess and in enlarging the political space available for subaltern groups in the Philippine countryside.[8]

From the early 1990s, autonomous peasant organizations, previously associated with the CPP-led Left, used a variety of tactics to keep the pressure on CARP implementation, including mass demonstrations, pickets and land occupations. Though such actions are similar to previous forms used by left organizations, the novelty lies in the new political context characterized by the existence of reform-oriented individuals strategically located within the state bureaucracy who would exert pressure of their own. Thus, parallel pressures from state reformists complemented pressures mounted by peasants from below. The correlation of forces was later termed the *bibingka* strategy, whereby the interaction of agrarian reform initiatives 'from below' and 'from above' tilted the balance of forces in favour of agrarian reform (Borras 1998, 2001a).[9]

Reform initiatives from above have been perceived as a crucial factor in the CARP implementation process. It was these perceived reform openings in the DAR that changed the strategic complexion of NGOs and POs, and opened the way for engagement with the state on land reform. In the process, formal and informal alliances between civil society organizations and reformists at the DAR created a national momentum which, in turn, put pressure on local-level DAR officials to respond more favourably towards land reform, against local-level obstacles.

Despite reformist pressure from above, however, local autonomous peasant organizations continue to face resistance from landowners during CARP implementation. For this reason, local autonomous organizations have sought to go beyond the local confines of their mobilizations and build national-level federations and organizations that construct the broadest possible alliances among pro-reform actors across state and civil society. The Pambansang Ugnayan ng mga Nagsasariling Organisasyon sa Kanayunan (UNORKA, the National Coordination of Autonomous Rural Organizations), as we will see below, is one among other current initiatives of the landless to build national organizations.

Such organizations are now facing a changing political environment at the national level as well. While the *bibingka* strategy resulted in concrete gains in the redistribution of contentious private land-holdings during the time of the Garilao and Morales administrations of the DAR (Borras 1998), the end of the 1990s witnessed a shifting alignment of forces within the state and society, which has reversed the reform openings within the bureaucracy and, hence, challenged the rationality of the *bibingka* strategy itself. The constriction of reform openings in the Braganza administration of the DAR, as manifested by the minimal movement of lands in CARP in 2001–02, together with emerging counter-reform initiatives in Congress (e.g. the cutting of the budget allocated for land acquisition and distribution, the impending 'Farmland as Collateral' bill), have compelled the landless to rethink their political strategies. The unfolding of recent events in the national political situation suggest that the *bibingka* strategy needs to be re-examined and restructured to confront a new situation, in which reformism 'from above' is receding and landlord power re-asserting itself at various levels of Philippine society.

Exploring a rights-based approach to reform

A strategy that is emerging from the recent experiences of autonomous peasant organizations in 'stretching' reform potential may be termed the *rights-based* approach. This approach invokes the rights of landless peasants as legitimate members of the polity, emphasizing the right to food and, by extension, the right to land as a basic resource. The approach emanates from the initiatives of civil society to provide equal weight to the economic, social and cultural rights of the people as part of the whole bundle of human rights to be enjoyed by every citizen. Within this approach, mobilizations and collective action are geared not only towards engaging the state on its reform programme but also to pushing the state to recognize, fulfil and protect the constitutional rights of the landless. The strategy seeks to expand the available political space by collectively asserting the rights of individuals and subaltern groups as legitimate members of the political community (Harvey 1998).

The emerging rights-based approach has developed into what sections of the organized peasantry call *rightful resistance,* to refer to the innovative use of laws, policies and other officially promoted values to defend their lawful rights and interests. As a term developed by the American scholar Kevin O' Brien (1996: 33) in his study of rural politics in China, rightful resistance refers to a form of popular contention that operates near the boundary of an authorized channel, employs the rhetoric and commitments of the powerful to curb political or economic power and hinges on locating and exploiting divisions among the powerful.

Rightful Resistance: The UNORKA Experience[10]

Autonomous mobilization and collective action

Among the various peasants' organizations that engaged the state on CARP implementation in the 1990s have been the local peasant organizations and federations belonging to UNORKA, such as the Kilusang Magbubukid ng Bondoc Peninsula (KBMP, the Peasant Movement in Bondoc Peninsula), the Ugyunan ng Mangunguma kag Mamumugon sa Negros (UMMA, the Federation of Peasants and Farmworkers in Negros), and the United Floreindo Employees Agrarian Reform Beneficiaries Association (UFEARBAI) in Davao. Local federations operate within their specific political settings, and most, if not all, challenge landlord power in local authoritarian enclaves. For example, in 1997, the inter-municipal federation of KBMP started to challenge the political and economic powers of the Chinese–Filipino Reyes–Uy clan that is believed to own and control an estimated combined total of between 18,000 and 20,000 hectares of agricultural lands across different municipalities in Southern Quezon (or Bondoc Peninsula).[11] In Negros Occidental, UMMA members are currently engaged in more than 5,000 hectares of agricultural landholdings owned and controlled by former Marcos cronies Roberto Benedicto and Eduardo Cojuangco. In Mindanao, UFEARBAI remains in a struggle against the state to redistribute more than 5,000 hectares of banana plantations owned by kingmaker and Marcos crony Antonio Floreindo. These landlords have in various ways strengthened their political and economic clout in the country through their ties with former Philippine dictator Ferdinand Marcos. Elsewhere in the country, UNORKA-affiliated organizations continue to push for land distribution in contentious landholdings (private and public) in landlord-dominated enclaves. These engagements form part of UNORKA's initiatives to push the state to redistribute close to 200,000 hectares of private agricultural landholdings around the country.

Landlord domination provides both the context and the object of autonomous peasant mobilizations. UNORKA's mobilizations are a reaction to harsh and unjust treatment from landlords, and they are directed towards the lands owned by these landlords. Though autonomy is a matter of degree and claims for absolute autonomy could be problematic, UNORKA's mobilizations have so far been free from the dictates, prompting and support of the CPP–NPA, or from the political manoeuvrings of officials and parties seeking to build and strengthen their electoral base. UNORKA's contentious political actions stem largely from the landless rural poor's strong desire to end landlord rule in the country. Thus, UNORKA members, in the belief that reform is possible, mobilize and assert their rights by working the system to effect changes in both property and power relations in the Philippine countryside.

Despite the perceived structural and institutional constraints to reform, UNORKA continues to challenge landlord power through official state policy. While remaining critical of the anti-poor provisions of CARP and the landlords' influence on policy implementation, local UNORKA-affiliated organizations participate in state-initiated activities on agrarian reform. Interactions with reform-oriented DAR officials and non-governmental organizations, such as those belonging to the Philippine Ecumenical Action for Community Empowerment (PEACE) network, further strengthen the resolve of local peasant organizations to take active participation in shaping CARP processes and outcomes and subsequently strengthen the landless rural poor's stake in rural democratization and development.

Reform initiatives, however, are also confronted with counter-reform initiatives – including evictions from land, the use of violence and terror against leaders and organization members, co-optation of parallel organizations with promises of improved tenurial and labour relations – and these, in turn, can threaten reform-seeking organizations with fragmentation. In such cases, the support base of a given organization must be strong enough to endure challenges and organizational cleavages that could lead to a complete dissolution of autonomous peasant initiatives. UNORKA has so far endured the counter-reform tactics of landlords (and those of DAR). Thus, despite all the organizational casualties suffered by UMMA (including several injuries and the death of one member) in confronting the Benedictos and other landlords since 1998, landless peasants continue to assert their rights to land through contentious political actions. In Davao, the forceful eviction of forty farmworker households from Floirendo's plantation in May 2000 and the shooting of UNORKA farmworker militants at the gates of the DAR Office in June 2001 did not discourage local UNORKA organizations from pressurizing DAR to persist with the redistribution of Floirendo-owned plantations. In Bondoc Peninsula, where the Reyes–Uy clans sowed terror among the landless peasants through the brutal killing of pro-reform mayoral candidate Felicito Mendenilla and KBMP peasant-leader Edwin Vender in 1998, UNORKA-affiliated organizations continue to wage radical mass actions against the landlords. Instead of being cowed and demoralized by the counter-reform actions of landlords, UNORKA's militancy has increased over the years.

Direct political action against the state and landowners characterizes UNORKA political tactics. Besides land occupations against landlords, UNORKA has repeatedly organized rallies, demonstrations, and even the padlocking of government offices in pressing local and national DAR officials to act on their demands. For example, in June 2001, member organizations of UMMA in Negros Occidental padlocked the DAR office in La Carlota City and Bacolod City to press for the immediate redistribution of lands belonging to the Benedictos and Cojuangcos[12] and other prominent landlords in the province. In August of the same year, UMMA members launched a human padlocking of the DAR provincial office, again to press the DAR further to expand land redistribution in other haciendas in the province. Protesting workers and peasants blocked the gates of DAR by forming human chains that prevented entry to the compound. In the same month, around 500 peasant leaders from UNORKA, from Bondoc Peninsula and other provinces in Central and Southern Luzon, stormed the Office of the Secretary of the DAR in Quezon City to engage DAR Secretary Hernani Braganza in dialogue in order to resolve 519 agrarian disputes involving nearly 100,000 landless peasant households. Despite the violent threat of dispersal from the elite police contingent of the Special Weapons and Action Team (SWAT), the UNORKA members refused to vacate the DAR premises and continued to press for an audience with Braganza, who in turn refused to meet with them. For two nights and three days the UNORKA stood their ground, and lifted their barricades only after getting a written promise from the DAR leadership on the mechanism on how to resolve the 519 land disputes. In Davao City, UNORKA-affiliated organizations dumped a truckload of bananas in front of the DAR office in 1996 and forcibly padlocked DAR gates in June 2001 to press the agency to act on their demand for land redistribution in various commercial plantations in Southeastern Mindanao Region. Between February and May 2002, UFEARBAI militants from Davao went to Manila and staged their protests against DAR – pickets, hunger strikes, chaining themselves to the gates of the Department of Justice – for its inaction on distributing plantations contracted by the Davao Penal Colony to the Floirendos since the 1960s.

While mass mobilizations are able to get the attention of the state elites, who subsequently issue directives to address policy problems, there are instances when political actions fail to mount the kind of pressure that moves the state to heed demands of the landless rural poor. During more intense engagements, UNORKA's collective actions shift to more radical forms of mobilization such as land occupations. For example, UMMA and KBMP pursued land takeovers in their respective provinces towards the end of 1990s to further assert their rights over CARPable landholdings. UMMA's land occupations in the towns of Pontevedra, Bago City and La Carlota City in the late 1990s compelled the DAR to redistribute more than 300 hectares of agricultural lands to landless peasants and farmworkers. Though limited in scope when viewed against the close to 300,000 hectares of CARPable lands in Negros Occidental, UMMA's land occupations demonstrate the potential of radical political action within rightful resistance. In Bondoc Peninsula, despite the fierce resistance against peasant collective actions, land occupation initiatives of the KBMP member-organization Samahan ng Magsasaka sa Catulin (SAMACA) on 30 June 1998 compelled DAR officials to recognize the organization's right over the 174-hectare property of Domingo Reyes. On 9 September 1998, DAR Undersecretary Conrado Navarro (backed by thirty soldiers from the Philippine Army and twenty police from the Regional Command in Lucena, Quezon) supported the peasants in claiming the property of Reyes and thereby served justice to the long struggle of the landless peasants.[13] UNORKA's land occupations demonstrate the potential of rightful resistance in land reform implementation.

Working the legal system

UNORKA's rightful resistance focuses on confronting various legal provisions that surround CARP and its implementation. Landlords often contest demands of peasant petitioners within the CARP either by circumventing the law to delay if not prevent land redistribution, or by filing cases against petitioners in the whole course of struggle. With the loopholes in CARP, landlords often question the qualifications of beneficiaries representing autonomous organizations. When this fails, landlords contest every DAR ruling that leads to land transfer by filing restraining orders in various courts at different levels of the judicial system. With the inefficiency of the Philippine judiciary, land cases often take years to be resolved in court, and in some cases landlords elevate their cases to higher courts each time a ruling is more favourable to peasant-petitioners. When these tactics fail, landlords question land valuation or file charges against DAR officials based on alleged technical and procedural errors committed in the processing of land claims, thereby ensuring that land transfers are stalled, if not totally blocked, beyond all legal remedies.

The legal system is thus an important arena of the land struggle, but also one that tends to be biased against peasants. Legal cases filed by landlords are part of the repertoire of harassment intended to compel peasants to back down from their land cause. This is further illustrated by the legal 'punishment' tactics of landlords against peasants, as narrated by Carranza of PEACE:

> between 1995 and 1996 one frustrated murder, one arson and two theft cases had been filed by landowners against four tenant-petitioners at the Superior-Agro estate in San Narciso. Between 1995 and 1997 a total of 102 counts of *estafa* had been filed against 28 farmers in the Aquino property in Cambuga, Mulanay. By 1997, two more farmers were charged with estafa in the Samuel Uy property in Sitio Libas, San Vicente in San Narciso, as was another in the Marasigan property in Lilukin, Buenavista. The following year, twelve farmers were charged with qualified theft after collectively harvesting coconut in the Ribargoso estate in San Juan, San Narciso, and another was charged with qualified theft in the Quizon property in Talisay, San Andres.

Working the legal system requires landless peasants to become acquainted with the law and to make innovative use of law and other prescribed values by the state in confronting various legal cases filed by landlords against them. With the limited resources of peasant organizations, allies become crucial in land struggles. Thus, since the 1990s, local UNORKA-affiliated organizations have been building alliances with pro-reform lawyers in their respective provinces in order to confront landlord resistance and engage them in legal battles every step of the way. Apart from this, PEACE Foundation has also been conducting para-legal training and seminars among UNORKA leaders to capacitate them in confronting legal cases and in exploring various alternatives in the use of the law to their advantage. The innovative use of laws among UNORKA-affiliated organizations complements contentious political actions in challenging landlord rule in defined landholdings. Despite institutional constraints in working the system, such as the judiciary's inefficiency and its tendency to be corrupted and influenced by elites, the innovative use of laws has contributed in strengthening more than five hundred UNORKA legal claims of landless peasants over contentious private landholdings around the country.

Building allies for reform

The importance of alliances in the struggle for land reform cannot be underestimated. Especially in contested large private landholdings, local peasant organizations often need to achieve a considerable breadth and scope in their mobilizations to confront counter-reform initiatives of landlords. The entry of community organizers in UN-ORKA areas under the auspices of the PEACE network have served a number of objectives: (a) to inform the landless rural poor about their rights under the CARP and other aspects of the law; (b) to facilitate the development of horizontal linkages among peasants and to share with them organizing and organizational management techniques; (c) to help extend and broaden the reach of their collective actions beyond their existing geographical, political, and institutional limits; and (d) to teach the tenants the art of 'tacticizing' (or crafting of various approaches and actions to effect land redistribution). Through allies such as the PEACE network, vertical and horizontal linkages with groups advocating social reforms help strengthen and broaden collective action. Thus, despite the specificity of contexts among different landholdings, common struggles and concerted efforts are elevated and waged at the regional or the national level. For example, the nationally coordinated campaigns launched by UNORKA in October 2001 and 2002, which witnessed landless peasants and farmworkers from different provinces around the country barricade the DAR Central Office, partly pushed the DAR Secretary Braganza to take immediate and concrete action on highly contentious private landholdings covered by CARP. Though the national DAR leadership had a differential take on the various agrarian cases bannered by

UNORKA in these mobilizations, the actions propelled land reform into the national debates conducted by policymakers.

Linkages with international groups that garner critical support and resources for peasant mobilizations provide additional leverage for local peasant organizations to challenge resource-strong landowners resisting reform. Though still limited, UNORKA'S alliance-building at the international level has provided new opportunities for up-grading collective action and for pressuring state elites to place land reform onto the state agenda. Such had been the experience of UNORKA in working with the Philippine section of the FoodFirst Information Action Network (FIAN). From 1996 until the present, FIAN representatives have been conducting fact-finding missions in various UNORKA-covered provinces where contentious political actions of landless peasants have been met with human rights viola-tions. Through these missions, issues that beset UNORKA-affiliated organizations in their land struggle against despotic landlords draw international pressure on the state and generate favourable public opinion. In most cases (Bondoc Peninsula, Negros and Davao), FIAN's initiatives helped compel DAR officials to address the concerns of struggling landless peasants.

Conclusion

The novelty of peasant collective action that has been emerging in the Philippines resides in the strategic shift to open engagement with the state, and thereby the use of available policy and legal procedures to expand reform possibilities within the state's reform programmes. The fundamental importance of locating and integrat-ing the struggle for land within a rights framework is to be found in the potential it creates for shifting the priorities in the political economy of resource allocation and distribution in favour of people living in poverty. These actions are not simply aimed at getting the attention of big landowners by utilizing the 'weapons of the weak' in their everyday resistance (Scott 1985); nor are they considered as peasant rebellions bent on seizing state power. The whole reper-toire of emerging peasant collective actions lies between these two poles, focusing specifically on open engagements with the state on its proclaimed reform programme and by pushing the boundaries of authorized channels (O'Brien 1996). Hence, while the trajectory of peasant collective action works within the course prescribed by CARP, UNORKA constantly engages local and national DAR officials to review and revise policy based on what transpires in its implementation. By pressing both national and local DAR officials to stretch the reform potentials of CARP, landless peasants and farmworkers are able to build a momentum of peasant collective action that challenges the gap between what was promised in a state's reform programme and what is being delivered.

These mobilizations are perceived to broaden reform possibilities within existing structural and institutional arrangements. Hence, despite the political constraints inherent in local authoritarian enclaves, state elites are constantly pressured to respond to the rightful claims of peasants. These actions against local and national elites may not automatically and immediately translate into far-reaching gains for the landless, and in extreme cases they may even be met with violence. However, critical engagements with the state allow landless peasants to build on their gains and expand citizens' participation in policy implementation. Grounded in the existence of laws and policies that aim to recognize, fulfil and protect the rights of the landless, land reform is being reasserted by local peasant organizations through official state policy in an effort to make the state more accountable to its citizens.

The experience of mobilization and collective action by UNORKA provides useful comparative insights into rightful resistance. First, it illustrates that contentious political actions, ranging from rallies, demonstrations, pickets and strikes to radical land occupation, remain important in engaging the state on its reform policy. Further, experience reveals the need to intensify such political actions in the light of diminishing reformist spaces within the bureaucracy. Second, while contentious political actions often involve actions that stretch beyond the rule of law, legal remedies utilized by landlords to weaken autonomous peasant initiatives could be confronted by making innovative use of laws to curb the political and economic power of the landed elites. Third and last, though peasant mobilizations and collective action have been increasingly met with coercion, the support of allies from local to international levels provides additional strength in confronting anti-reform currents in both state and society.

Notes

1. This provision had deferred land acquisition and distribution of private commercial farms for ten years, in order to allow big landowners and agribusiness corporations to recoup their investments from the plantations.

2. www.nscb.gov.ph/poverty/2000/00povin1.asp.

3. According to the United Nations Development Programme in the Philippines, three-quarters of the poor live in rural areas, where 68 per cent of the population are poor; www.undop.org.ph/emp_security.htm.

4. Indeed, only 90,000 landowners – or a meagre 5.8 per cent of the total – reported holdings of more than 12 hectares.

5. EDSA is the Epifanio De los Santos Avenue, site of the famous 'People Power' uprising that toppled the late dictator President Ferdinand Marcos in 1986.

6. Figures based on interviews conducted among peasant cadres who formerly belonged to national and regional peasant secretariats of the Communist Party of the Philippines.

7. TriPARRD was the brainchild of a group of agrarian reform advocates led by the Philippine Partnership for the Development of Human Resources in Rural Areas (PHILDHRAA). The core idea was to explore areas of collaboration or coordination among NGOs, POs, donor agencies and the government in the implementation of agrarian reform.

8. A review of TriPARRD strategy reveals that only 5,000 hectares of lands were redistributed in adopting the strategy. A total of 50 per cent of these lands were acquired through a voluntary offer for sale (VOS) scheme on the part of the landowners, which virtually commands better compensation than that provided by a Compulsory Acquisition (CA) adopted in some contentious landholdings.

9. The main theoretical framework of the *bibingka* strategy drew on the work of Jonathan Fox (1992) on Mexico, and specifically on the 'sandwich strategy' of pushing distributive reforms (i.e. village food councils) in the early 1980s.

10. The data used here had been collected by Jennifer Franco, Romulo de la Rosa and Salvador Feranil for the research project on Philippine Contemporary Social Movements (to be published by the Institute for Popular Democracy, Quezon City).

11. Data were based on Franco's fieldwork from 1998 to 2002.

12. Roberto Benedicto and Eduardo Cojuangco had previously been appointed by former president Marcos to manage the national sugar and coconut industries, respectively. Both cronies utilized their direct and powerful connections to the president to amass lands in Negros Occidental.

13. Based on fieldwork findings of Franco.

References

Anderson, Benedict (1988), 'Cacique Democracy in the Philippines: Origins and Dreams', *New Left Review* 169, May–June.

Borras, Saturnino, Jr (1998), *The Bibingka Strategy in Land Reform Implementation: Autonomous Peasant Movements and State Relations in the Philippines*, Quezon City: Institute for Popular Democracy.

Borras, Saturnino, Jr (2001a), 'State–Society Relations in Land Reform Implementation in the Philippines', *Development and Change* 32(4): 545–75.

Borras Saturnino, Jr (2001b), 'The Philippine Agrarian Reform: Relatively Vibrant Land Redistribution Amidst Less-than-Dynamic Agricultural Transformation', in *Power in the Village: Agrarian Reform, Rural Politics, Institutional Change and Globalization*, ed. H. Morales Jr and J. Putzel, with F. Lara Jr, E. Quitoriano and A. Miclat-Teves, Quezon City: Project Development Institute.

Borras, Saturnino, Jr (2002), 'Problems and Prospects of Redistributive Land Reform in Mindanao, 1972/1988–2001', *Mindanao Focus*, 1, Davao City: Alternate Forum for Research in Mindanao (AFRIM).

Deininger, Klaus (1999), 'Making Negotiated Land Reform Work: Initial Experience From Colombia, Brazil and South Africa', *World Development* 27(4): 651–72.

El-Ghonemy, Riad (1999), *The Political Economy of Market-Based Land Reform*, UNRISD Discussion Paper No. 104, Geneva: United Nations Research Institute for Social Development.

Franco, Jennifer Conroy (2000), *Campaigning for Democracy: Grassroots Citizenship Movements, Less-than-Democratic Elections, and Regime Transition in the Philippines*, Quezon City: Institute for Popular Democracy.

Fox, Jonathan (1992), *The Politics of Food in Mexico: State Power and Social Mobilization*, Ithaca: Cornell University Press.

Harvey, Neil (1998), *The Chiapas Rebellion: The Struggle for Land and Democracy*, Durham, NC, and London: Duke University Press.

Hayami, Yujiro, Ma. Agnes Quisumbing and Lourdes Adriano (1990), *Toward an Alternative Land Reform Paradigm: A Philippine Perspective*, Quezon City: Ateneo de Manila Press.

Herring, Ronald (2001), 'Beyond the Political Impossibility Theorem of Agrarian Reform', in *Power in the Village: Agrarian Reform, Rural Politics, Institutional Change and Globalization*, ed. H. Morales Jr. and J. Putzel, with F. Lara Jr, E. Quitoriano and A. Miclat-Teves, Quezon City: Project Development Institute.

Kasuya, Yuko (1995), *The 'Failure' of Agrarian Reform in Transitional Democracy, Philippines 1986–1992*, ISS Working Papers, No. 194, The Hague: Institute for Social Studies.

Kay, Cristobal (2000), *Conflict and Violence in Rural Latin America*, ISS Working Papers, No. 312, The Hague: Institute for Social Studies.

Kerkvliet, Benedict (1993), 'Claiming the Land: Take-overs by Villagers in the Philippines with Comparisons to Indonesia, Peru, Portugal and Russia', *Journal of Peasant Studies* 20(3): 459–93.

Lara, Francisco, and Horacio Morales (1990), 'The Peasant Movement and the Challenge of Rural Democratization in the Philippines', in *The Challenge of Rural Democratization: Perspectives from Latin America and the Philippines*, ed. Jonathan Fox, London: Frank Cass.

NSCB (2000), *2000 Philippine Statistical Yearbook,* Makati City: National Statistics Coordination Board.

O'Brien, Kevin (1996), 'Rightful Resistance', *World Politics* 49 (October): 31–55.

Putzel, James, and John Cunnington (1989), *Gaining Ground: Agrarian Reform in the Philippines,* London: WOW Campaigns.

Putzel, James (1992), *A Captive Land: The Politics of Agrarian Reform in the Philippines,* London and New York: Catholic Institute for International Relations and Monthly Review Press.

Riedinger, Jeffrey (1995), *Agrarian Reform in the Philippines: Democratic Transitions and Redistributive Reform,* Stanford, CA: Stanford University Press.

Scott, James C. (1985), *Weapons of the Weak: Everyday Forms of Peasant Resistance,* New Haven, CT, and London: Yale University Press.

Sidel, John (1989), 'Beyond Patron–Client Relations', *KASARINLAN* 4(3).

Sobhan, Rehman (1993), *Agrarian Reform and Social Transformation: Preconditions for Development,* London and Dhaka: Zed Books and University Press.

Weekley, Kathleen (2001), *The Communist Party of the Philippines 1968–1993: A Story of Its Theory and Practice,* Quezon City: University of the Philippines Press.

World Bank (2001), *World Bank Development Report 2000/2001: Attacking Poverty,* New York: Oxford University Press.

PART III

LATIN AMERICA

I O

The Dynamics of Land Occupations in Latin America

Henry Veltmeyer

The problem of landlessness has always been the basis for a politics of land invasions and occupations, a problem that has its genesis in what Marx defined in terms of a process of 'primitive accumulation' – the separation of the direct producers or workers from their means of social production – or, in more historically specific terms, the expulsion of peasant farmers from their land. This problem was once posed as a matter of land hunger and cultural identity: that is, the presumed need for peasants and other rural producers and workers to be reconnected to the land as a source not only of productive activity but of everything that gives meaning to their lives. In the more recent context of the changes that have ensued since World War II, with particular reference to the launching of the 'development project' (Sachs 1992), the problem has generally been redefined as a matter of social exclusion and poverty: that is, the inability to meet the basic needs of the population, as well as a matter of regaining or improving the access of rural groups and communities to society's productive resource in land – or land reform.

The dynamics of land reform in this and other contexts are very complex and varied, and can best be understood in political terms – that is, in terms of a protracted struggle of peasant farmers and other rural groups for land and land reform, and in terms of the reaction of the dominant landholding class to this struggle, as well as the workings of the state. The purpose of this chapter is to place these dynamics of land reform in historical and theoretical perspective. In this context land occupations take form as a tactic of class struggle and direct collective action, a fundamental strategy for gaining access to land.

The chapter is organized in two parts. The first part reviews in historical terms the dynamics of class struggle entailed in land occupations. The second part then considers three basic paths towards reform traced out in the contemporary period, the reference point being the Cuban Revolution of 1959. The Cuban Revolution created an entirely new context both for a new wave of revolutionary movements in the countryside of Latin America, characterized by the occupation of unused land on the peripheries of the cities, and for a new cycle of state-led land reforms. In the wake of these developments, and in a new and entirely different context, one created by the widespread implementation of a 'new economic model' and a process of democratization, the stage was set for another wave of peasant-led grassroots revolutionary movements as well as a new twist in the land reform programme – the transition from a state-led land reform programme to a new market-assisted reform programme. Many analysts saw this transition as 'the death of land reforms'. We view it differently: as a new twist in the reform option presented to a new generation of revolutionary peasants by governments as well as by the bilateral and multilateral institutions that provide overseas development assistance. The tactic of land occupations acquires its political significance in this context.

Posing the Problem: Primitive Accumulation, Landlessness and Rural Poverty

The peasantry and the state in historical context

The institution of a capitalist mode of production, as Marx analysed so well in the European context, is predicated on a process of 'primitive accumulation' designed to create a class for hire, a proletariat or wage-labouring class. In its historical context, 'primitive accumulation' denotes a process of separating the direct producers from their means of production, usually in the form of the violent seizure or expropriation of native communal landholdings. As Marx saw it, this process allowed for the conversion of money, accumulated in and by diverse ways and means – including pillage, theft, mercantile trade, and the enslavement of Amerindians – into 'capital' and the transformation of various modes of pre-capitalist production into capitalism. Both in the 'old world' of Europe and what would emerge as the 'new world' of the Americas this process can be traced back some five hundred years to an extended period of colonial rule in the new world and the rather abrupt destruction and transformation of pre-capitalist and pre-colonial indigenous societies into proto-capitalist class-divided and dominated forms of transplanted European societies.

The period of colonial rule, from the 'discovery' of 'the new world' in the fifteenth century and the 'conquest' of the indigenous population to a process of national independence in the nineteenth century, entailed a history of land expropriation and 'primitive accumulation'. However, there was another side to this process. From the outset, there was widespread resistance, with numerous outbreaks of peasant rebellion and even the institution of state-led agrarian reform laws that consolidated the gains achieved by the peasantry, who constituted the major social and political force in the largely rural society, through a process of land occupation. A major case in point was the Tupac Amaru rebellion in the eighteenth century and the subsequent land reform laws of the 1820s (Jacobsen 1993).

In the aftermath of the national independence movements, various forms of class struggle ensued in the newly independent or self-proclaimed nation-states. In colonial Peru, Haiti and Mexico the enslaved, indentured, enserfed and semi-proletarianized rural workers (most self-identified as peasant farmers) throughout the eighteenth and early nineteenth centuries challenged the power of the colonial state. In the late-colonial or postcolonial liberal reform period in Central America (El Salvador, Honduras, Nicaragua, Guatemala), the state instituted legislative, policy and repressive measures to bring into line (squash labour disorders involving) the rebellious peasants, indigenous peoples and landless rural workers, in favour of the semi-feudal landed oligarchy (Wheelock Román 1985; Gould 1993; Amador 1990; Mahoney 2001).

At issue in these class struggles was property in the means of production, namely land, the basic productive resource available, which for some (a small landed oligarchy) would be the source of personal fortune and relations of privilege and power, and for others (the vast majority of workers and producers, and indigenous communities) their primary source of livelihood. This land struggle pitted a semi-feudal landed propertied class, with a preponderant political influence over the state apparatus, against a rural population largely composed of peasants and serfs, a vast proletariat of dispossessed (landless or near-landless) rural workers, and, in some contexts, indigenous communities of peasant producers.

On the one side of this class struggle was a semi-feudal or mercantile propertied class in a position to control not only the government of the day but other parts of the state, such as the judiciary and the security apparatus, all of which were brought into play in the land struggle (Harris et al. 1978; Lindqvist 1979; Orlove and Custred 1980; Vilas 1995). On the other side were organized groups of peasants and a large semi-proletariat who utilized all the weapons and tactics at their disposal, notably land occupations and direct actions against the holders of political and economic power or their agents (Fogel 1986; Foley 1991; Heath 1969; Katz 1988; LeGrand 1983; Loveman 1976; Horton 1998). Those engaged in this struggle were caught up in and represented diverse relations of production. They ranged from enslaved plantation workers to producers enserfed under the production relations of the *encomienda* system (land tenancy, debt peonage, indentured servitude, labour rents), from sharecroppers to a semi-proletariat of seasonal rural workers/subsistence farmers, and from a rural proletariat of landless workers to indigenous communities of peasant farmers.

The history of the land struggle took diverse forms in different places and engaged diverse groups of 'peasants' whose struggle was not only generally sporadic but localized. As yet there does not exist any systematic study of the class dynamics of these struggles (which particular groups participated, how and under what conditions), but it is clear enough that, more often than not, diverse categories or groupings of 'peasants' and landless rural workers would join the land struggle and acts of rebellion in diverse conjunctures and situations.[1] The tendency for diverse groupings and categories of 'peasants' to join the struggle was encapsulated by the Mexican Revolution, which not only won for peasants and indigenous communities the rights to large tracts of land expropriated from them in previous decades and centuries but established a watershed in peasant–state relations throughout Latin America (Petras and Veltmeyer 2002).

In the wake of the Mexican Revolution – and the October Revolution in Russia – the state in Latin America, under pressure for more revolutionary change, was reoriented towards programmes of land reform, designed not only to improve access to land for various categories of dispossessed or landless producers and workers ('peasants') but also to keep the social peace.

In the 1930s, significant peasant-based mass movements emerged in Mexico, El Salvador, Nicaragua, Colombia, Brazil and Peru.[2] In the Caribbean, rural workers, particularly sugar workers in modern plantations in Cuba, the Dominican Republic and Puerto Rico, as well as Guyana and elsewhere, engaged in class warfare. In each instance, either extremely violent and repressive measures were taken by the state to suppress or to destroy these rural rebellions, or – as in the exceptional case of Mexico under Cárdenas – agrarian reform was extended to include hundreds of thousands of poor rural families. In El Salvador, the peasant uprising was crushed and some 30,000 were killed (Dunkerley 1992: 49); a similar event in Ecuador under almost identical circumstances had the same devastating effects on an incipient class struggle. In Nicaragua, the Dominican Republic and Cuba, the US occupation army and its newly anointed tyrant-presidents – Somoza, Trujillo and Batista – slaughtered thousands, decimating the burgeoning peasant and rural workers' movements. In Brazil, the Vargas regime defeated Prestes's rural-based guerrilla army while pursuing a strategy of national industrialization; in Chile, the Popular Front of radicals, socialists and communists aroused – and then abandoned – the peasant struggle, together with demands for agrarian reform in an implicit gentlemen's pact with the traditional landed oligarchy (Castells 1976; Kay 1981; Loveman 1976).

In the best of cases, peasant-based revolutions were able to secure institutional reforms in the agrarian sector – that is, land redistribution – but these reforms often followed a process of de facto land occupations. The government, in effect, was compelled to legalize the status quo as well as dampen pressures for more radical land redistribution. In the case of Mexico, this process began in the early 1900s and reached its high point in the 1930s.[3]

In the subsequent fifty years, particularly in the 1960s and 1970s, virtually all of the national governments in Latin America used the power of the state to alter the distribution of land for different categories of producers and households, and to redefine the right to land for those given access in the process. This happened regardless of the complexion of the regime in power. In 1952 in Bolivia a revolution of miners and peasants led to a sweeping agrarian reform that resulted in the expropriation of most of the large estates (Beltrán and Fernandez 1960; Dandler 1969; Dunkerley 1984; Lora 1964; Malloy and Thorn 1971). In Cuba, the victory of the 26th of July movement in 1959 resulted in the confiscation of most of the US-

and Cuban-owned plantations, the land being either collectivized or distributed to smallholders (McEwan 1981). Substantive land reforms also took place in Peru from 1958 to 1974, in Brazil from 1962 to 1964, in Chile from 1966 to 1973, in Ecuador from 1964 to 1967, in El Salvador from 1980 to 1985, in Guatemala from 1952 to 1954 (and again after the civil war following the peace accords), in Honduras in 1973, and in Nicaragua from 1979 to 1986. These reforms were state-led, regardless of the form of the state (authoritarian, military, liberal reformist, proto-revolutionary), but in all cases undertaken in response to mass peasant mobilizations and a general threat of 'social revolution' (Blanco 1972; Cotler 1978; De Janvry et al. 1998; Kay 1981, 1982; Midlarsky and Roberts 1995; Vilas 1995).[4]

Rural and urban dynamics of land occupations

In spite of these efforts, many categories of rural households remained – and remain – landless or near-landless. As late as 1998, 90 per cent of all arable land in Latin America was concentrated in large holdings that account for 26 per cent of all farmers, the lion's share of total land and farm production. In the case of Brazil, which since 1988 has undergone land reform programmes both 'from below' and 'from above', as well as a rural exodus of staggering proportions (30 million over the past twenty-five years), 3 per cent of the population still own two-thirds of the country's arable land and there remain upwards of 4.8 million families in rural areas without any access to land.[5] In addition, in the case of Brazil and virtually every other country in the region, the majority of those who do have access to some land are barely able to eke out a subsistence-level existence let alone make a commercial living. The smallest 50 per cent of all production units or 'farms' in the region, with barely 2 per cent of the land, entail economically marginal operations, allowing only for the subsistence of the families that remain on the land.

In response to this situation – a historic and contemporary product of what Marx, in a different context, had identified as a process of 'primitive accumulation' – vast numbers of a dispossessed rural proletariat have been forced to migrate to the urban centres and cities, resulting in one of the major upheavals and social transformations in modern times: capitalist development of urban-based economic activity and the associated makeover of a rural peasantry into an urban proletariat. Today, all countries in the region are at least 50 per cent urban in terms of residence and economic activity – in a number of cases, such as Argentina, up to and over 80 per cent. One of many consequences of this 'great transformation' (industrialization, modernization, urbanization, capitalist development) is that the rural land struggle, and land occupations, have been transferred from the rural sector to the periphery of the new urban metropoles. This process was particularly pronounced in the 1960s and 1970s, when up to a quarter of the rural population migrated to the urban centres in search of waged employment and housing. Most of this housing was constructed on a self-help basis by communities of rural migrants who invaded and 'settled' – illegally occupied and squatted on – unused urban land areas, creating in the process the *pueblos jovenes* of Lima, the *favelas* of Rio de Janeiro, the *rancherias* of Caracas and the *poblaciones* of Santiago, Chile. Because of this urbanization process, up to 60 per cent of the urban population live in precarious housing conditions (Guimarães 1997: 191).[6]

As a result of these and related developments, land occupations took place in a new urban context, replicating some of the dynamics of the rural struggle for land but in different form – land invasion, squatting, negotiations with the municipal government for services and legal title to their 'property', and, through grassroots organizational efforts, upgrading these neighbourhoods into the working class *barrios* that surround so many Latin American cities today. The social dynamics of this process are complex and variegated, with diverse dimensions that include the break-up and division of many families, with some of the women staying behind to tend subsistence plots of land and many of the men involved in seasonal outmigration from these plots or work within the 'unstructured' informal sector of the urban labour market (Portes et al. 1989; PREALC 1993). Under these conditions, many landless workers are unable or unwilling to break their connection to rural society, even without access to land or other means of social production. Nevertheless, the structure of landholding continues to reproduce the conditions of rural poverty and to fuel a process of outmigration by large numbers of dispossessed 'peasants' or 'landless rural workers'.

As recent as 1997, over 60 per cent of all rural households in Latin America were mired in poverty – 40 per cent overall – and for 60 per cent of these households this poverty was 'extreme' (ECLAC 1998). Some of the conditions of this poverty were 'new', in the sense that they derived from a structure put into place by a neoliberal programme of policy reforms – privatization of the means of production and public enterprises, liberalization of trade and the flow of investment capital; deregulation of capital, product and labour markets; and a retrenchment of the state vis-à-vis social programmes (Bulmer-Thomas 1996;Veltmeyer and Petras 1997, 2000). However, some forms and conditions of this poverty preceded this 'development' and are entrenched in the structure of land owner-ship in the rural areas. In this connection, not even the relatively 'radical' or extensive land reform programmes in some countries had managed to change substantially the structure of land ownership; in the cases of Chile and Nicaragua, the programmes were reversed. In Brazil, land concentration and landlessness in the countryside have continued to accelerate despite years of land reform. In 1970, estates of over 1,000 hectares, representing 0.7 of the total farms, accounted for 40 per cent of the land; in 1996, 1 per cent of the landowners with farms of over 1,000 hectares owned 45 per cent of the land. At the same time over 4 million farm workers were without any land at all while large numbers are near landless. Another example can be found in Honduras where 409,000 hectares were redistributed (120,000 hectares between 1973 and 1977, the heyday of agrarian reform) to beneficiaries who constituted only 13 per cent of the total rural population. In this situation, over 200,000 families (equivalent to 44 per cent of the rural population) still have no access to land, or have very little. These families, as elsewhere in Latin America, continue to live in very poor conditions and constitute the nucleus of 'extreme poverty'.

Another reason for the persistence of rural poverty – even with-out regard to what has been termed 'the new poor' – is that even where significant gains were made in the course of state-led land reform programmes, in the medium and long term these gains were eroded, with the peasants and rural landless workers suffering a series of setbacks. In the case of Chile, the substantive gains made by peasant producers in the 1960s and early 1970s were arrested and reversed by the Pinochet regime, which in 1975 initiated what for Latin America amounted to a counter-revolution. A few years later, one astute analyst of agrarian development, Lehmann (1978), with particular reference to Brazil, could write of the death of land reform, a view echoed by others such as Kay (2000) and De Walt et al. (1994). Under conditions of neoliberal adjustment – and the counter-revolution – the process of state-led land reform was over.

The state was in retreat, and where not in retreat had an entirely different agenda. With the capture and death of Che Guevara in Bolivia and the destruction and containment, if not defeat, of most of the guerrilla armies for national liberation in the region (with the exception of the FARC–EP), the threat of social revolution had evaporated and with it a major wave of peasant rebellion.

Disappearance of the peasantry?

The central protagonist in Latin America's class struggle over land has been the peasantry. However, both the nature of the peasantry as a socio-economic and political category and its role in contemporary struggles over the land have been subject to considerable reconcep-tualization and ongoing debate. First of all, the precise meanings of the terms 'peasant' and 'peasantry' are at issue in regard to social and economic considerations – as a socio-economic category (Kearney 1996). A second set of debates surrounding the peasantry have to do with an assessment of its role in the political struggle. On this issue, recent research and analysis have tended to oscillate between two competing conceptualizations and political perceptions. On the one hand, the peasantry is regarded more or less as a passive entity, the disempowered object of various kinds of state agency (legis-lation, taxation, agricultural production regimes, systems of regula-tion, macroeconomic planning, etc.). Most sociological studies in the structuralist tradition of modernization theory take this view, which is also reflected in the writings of historians such as Hobsbawm who see the peasantry as a category of declining numerical and thus political significance, defeated by the process of modernization and change (Bryceson et al. 2000). On the other hand, there is an alternative perception of the peasantry as an active and empowered force that continues to contest the terrain of struggle over the land (see, in particular, Petras 1997a, 1997b).

This difference in perception is also reflected in the epistemological debate between proponents of 'structuralism' as a mode of analysis and those who reject all forms of structuralism in favour of 'grassroots postmodernism' (Esteva and Prakash 1998) and 'discourse analysis' (Escobar 1995).[7] For structuralists generally, including Marxists, the peasantry is an economic and political category that corresponds to a transitional organizational form, destined to disappear into the dustbin of history, whose presence on the world stage is effected now

in other disguises – as a rural proletariat, as an urban lumpenprole-
tariat trapped in a proliferating informal sector, or as 'wage-labour
equivalents' (Bryceson et al. 2000; Kay 2000).[8]

The dynamics of this process have been generally analysed in
terms of expropriation, land concentration, rural outmigration and
land invasions on the periphery of the large urban centres, settlement
on these lands, and gradual incorporation of the rural migrants into
the structure and life of the city. The end result of these processes,
in theory, is a numerically reduced peasantry as an economic agent
and a political force for change, a traditional social category deci-
mated by the processes of modernization, urbanization, and capitalist
development of urban-centred industry (Bartra 1976; Cancian 1987;
Kay 2000). This is one perspective on the peasantry, argued with
numerous permutations and closely associated with views about 'the
end of land reform'.

Yet it is by no means the only one. For one thing, some analysts
have in certain contexts detected a trend in the reverse direction,
namely peasantization (Bakx 1988). There is also the perspective on
agrarian transformation articulated by James Petras, among others.
In this perspective, the peasantry cannot be understood purely in
numerical terms, as a percentage of the labour force or by the
size of the peasant sector of the economy. The peasantry, it is
argued, remains a force whose weight and significance is out of
proportion to their number. Indeed, in the Latin American context
it constitutes the most dynamic force for anti-systemic change,
found on the crest of a new wave of class struggle – and of indigenous people for land, land reform, autonomy, social justice and
democracy. The Ejército Zapatista de Liberación Nacional (EZLN)
in its political irruption in 1994 can best be understood in this
way, rather than, as Burbach (1994) does, as the 'first postmodern
movement in history'.

Three Paths towards Reform

In 1948 the project of international cooperation for development
was born – invented, in the words of Sachs (1992) and his associates
in postdevelopment. It was designed, in the first instance, to prevent
those countries regarded as 'economically backward' and recently
liberated from the ties of European colonialism from succumbing

to the lure of communism and treading a socialist path in their national development. In the 1960s, in the wake of the Cuban Revolution, this project was redesigned so as to inhibit movements for radical change and social revolution in many rural parts of the 'Third World'. In the 1970s, however, this 'project' (reform and development) was challenged from both the left and the right, leading to various calls for an alternative project – social revolution in the one case, a conservative counter-revolution in the other. The agency for revolutionary change generally took the form of social movements rooted in either the working class or the peasantry, while the agents of counter-revolution turned towards the state to implement a neoliberal model of free-market capitalist development and globalization – to create what George Bush Senior termed 'the New World Order', releasing thereby what George W. Bush Junior, ten years later, in his 2002 National Security Report, termed 'the forces of freedom, democracy and free enterprise'. In the context of this conservative 'counter-revolution', and on the basis of an experiment in Chile (namely, the Pinochet military regime) with a neoliberal model of macroeconomic policy reforms, the World Bank designed the 'structural adjustment programme' – a set of policy reforms based on what in Latin America was termed the 'new economic model' (Bulmer-Thomas, 1996).

Implementation of this model has created an entirely new context for the dynamics of the land struggle in different parts of the world. A number of analysts in this context invoked the 'death of land reform', while some, such as Gwynne and Kay (1999) and Kay (2000), write of an 'agrarian transformation' process. As to the nature and dynamics of this transformation, de Janvry et al. (1997) write of the transition from 'state-led to grassroots-led land reform', while others highlight the transition to a 'market-assisted' approach to land reform. In this same context, James Petras (1997a, 1997b) and this author (Veltmeyer 1997) point to the emergence of a new wave of peasant-based and -led movements that push beyond land reforms towards more revolutionary or radical changes in government policy, as well as the neoliberal model behind it and the 'system' created by the implementation of this model. In effect, it is possible to identify three divergent paths towards land reform, each characterized by a distinct overall strategy and a mixed bag of tactics: (a) state-led land reform (expropriation with compensation, land redistribution, rural development); (b) market-assisted land reform (titling, commodification and land banks); and (c) grassroots land reform (occupations, negotiation and struggle).

State-led land reform

It is a commonplace that in Latin America, as elsewhere, the state has been essential to the maintenance or defence of the dominant social relations of production. In each specific form of agricultural production over the years, the state has been instrumental in the foundation, extension, reproduction and transformation of the system involved, benefiting some classes – most often the large landowners – and disadvantaging mainly workers and peasants (Feder 1971; Huizer 1973). The theoretical point here is that the growth of 'the market' is inexorably linked to an 'activist state', as is the process of agrarian reform. The state has been the central institution in the process of changing the dominant relations of economic production and the class systems based on this process. The repressive apparatus of the state has been brought into play in numerous occasions, in different historical contexts, to maintain the existing regime of property in the means of production. The judiciary also has been called upon to play its part in this regard. Thus, for example, in the land struggle of the MST in Brazil the state has been active in the trial and imprisonment of MST activists, while the actions of the propertied class in 'defence' of their property rights, even when involving murder or massacre, have been met with legal impunity. The powerful links that exist between the large proprietors and the judiciary – and Brazil is no exception to the rule – is demonstrated by the fact that between 1985 and 1999 1,158 rural activists were assassinated in land disputes, but only 56 gunmen were brought to trial and only 10 were convicted. Since F.H. Cardoso came to state power in 1995, 163 MST activists have been assassinated, and yet not one of those responsible was brought to legal account (Figueres 1999: 40; MST 2002). Sixteen MST activists were assassinated with virtual impunity in 2001. In 2003, this policy of repression of the MST where and when it refused to toe the government line (to have patience and support the government's land reform programme) has been continued under the PT (Partido dos Trabalhadores) regime of Luiz Inácio Lula da Silva. What is more, the government has even sent in the military police to surround the MST headquarters and intimidate the leadership.

As for the process of land reform, particularly in the twentieth century, the major agency involved has also been the state but in the form of the government of the day, acting on the basis of legislation in which the propertied groups in the dominant class generally have had the predominant influence. State-led agrarian reform over the years has entailed a protracted struggle, first, to have the reforms implemented, and then to consolidate the gains made.[9] In most cases, under the conditions of this struggle, the advances made by peasants and rural workers were preserved if not consolidated. In some cases, however, as in Chile with the ascendancy of Pinochet to state power, the gains made in a process of land reform were halted and reversed. The essential factor in determining the outcome of the struggle, as always, has been the relation of the peasant movement to the state. Thus, in Mexico, Bolivia and Peru a prolonged process of state disinvestment in the reform sector culminated in legislation that provided incentives to agroexport monopolies, alienating community lands (the *ejido* in Mexico) and stimulating cheap (i.e. subsidized) imported foodstuffs. The politics of alliances, in which the peasantry has generally been subordinated to the urban petty bourgeoisie and bourgeoisie, has often secured an initial round of redistributive reforms and state assistance. But subsequently peasant movements have tended to fragment and divide along an 'official' and 'oppositional' line in which the former have become a transmission belt for state policy.

When programmes of land reform in the 1960s were initiated by the state they were essentially defensive responses to the lessons of the 1959 Cuban Revolution, and thus designed to prevent the emergence of more radical demands for change. In this political climate the government in almost every country initiated a broad programme of agrarian reform, an additional political objective being to incorporate the peasantry within a dual agenda: not just to divert existing and future dissent into constitutional channels, where it might more easily be co-opted by the state, but also to bring smallholders into the orbit of capitalist development, offering them thereby an alternative to systemic transformation or socialism.

Generally speaking, under the rubric of agrarian reform legislation designed to modernize agriculture, the ownership of productive tracts of land has been further concentrated, redistribution occurring only within the peasant sector itself, leading to a process of internal differentiation.[10] The latter has involved the emergence of a small stratum of rich peasants, some of whom are converted into rural capitalists; a somewhat larger middle stratum of self-sufficient 'peasant farmers' with productive capacity vis-à-vis the domestic market; and a rural proletariat, composed of a huge mass of semi-proletarianized (landless or near landless) migrant workers. In most contexts, however, these attempts at accommodation and co-optation, including unionization from above and the setting up of parallel or government-controlled peasant organizations, either failed or were only partially successful. Usually they tended to unleash class conflicts that continued into another and more radical phase of land reform (Kay 1981). For this and other reasons, Latin American governments instituted a land reform programme but then devoted their energies to preventing its radicalization, using a combination of strategies ranging from corporativism (unionization from above), attempts at controlling peasant organizations, co-opting their leadership, to outright repression.

In each phase of capitalist modernization the state has played a crucial role in promoting, financing and protecting the dominant 'modernizing' classes from the threat of peasant and rural worker movements, forcing the rural proletariat and peasantry to bear the costs of 'transition'. These dynamics, for example, reappeared in the 1980s, in the context of a transition towards a neoliberal 'new world order' facilitated by a process of structural adjustment and 'globalization' (Gwynne and Kay 1999; Kay 1999; Thiesenhusen 1989, 1995). Among those disadvantaged by the application of neoliberal measures, the peasantry and rural workers figure prominently, as evidenced in the virulence of their opposition and periodic outbreaks of rural violence (Barry 1987; Veltmeyer and Petras 2000).

Market-assisted land reform

In the 1960s and 1970s, the state in its various parts (government, legislature, judiciary, forces of internal order) was the dominant agency for agrarian and rural development, including the implementation of land reforms. These reforms were instituted under conditions of pressure for revolutionary change exerted from the grassroots. In the 1980s, conditions were generated for an alternative path towards agrarian development by the actions of the state in response to the requirements of the 'new world order' based on the workings of the free market and private enterprise (Deininger 1998). We can identify two responses to these requirements and the institution of the new economic model: (i) the emergence of a new wave of peasant-based and -led anti-systemic socio-political movements oriented towards direct action; and (ii) the evolution of a market-assisted approach towards land and agrarian reform. This approach, advocated by the World Bank and other ODAs has dominated government policy throughout the 1990s.

In this new context a debate on alternative forms of agrarian and land reform ensued in policymaking and academic circles across the region. At the centre of these discussions and debates was the issue of promoting land markets as a means of improving the access of poor households to society's 'productive resources' – to expand use of the market mechanism in the process of agrarian development (Ghimire 2001). The dominant model of rural development, one still very much in use today, is predicated on the accumulation of 'social capital' rather than the natural capital embedded in the land (Coleman 1988; Chambers and Conway 1988; Helmore et al. 2001; Woolcock and Narayan 2000). With this focus on social capital, which, in theory, is abundantly given to the poor in the form of their capacity to network and act cooperatively, the pressure on governments to expropriate and redistribute land was reduced if not eliminated. Similarly, class or state power, always a central issue in the land struggle, is depoliticized – transmuted into a question of 'social empowerment' (Amalric 1998; Brockett 1998; Veltmeyer 2003). Nevertheless, landlessness and lack of access to productive land remained an issue, leading the ODAs, particularly the World Bank, to advocate policies to 'modernize' agriculture and stimulate the growth of a land market. These policies include land titling – giving legal title and security of tenure to those with access to land, eliminating landholdings that prevented individuals from buying and selling land, and establishing land banks (Bromley 1989; World Bank 1996, 1997).

With regards to land banks, the World Bank has instituted pilot projects in Brazil, Colombia and the Philippines. The aim of this policy, and market institution, was not only to promote a market in land – and to create a 'new rural world' – but, at least in the case of Brazil, to counteract the tactic of land occupations used by grassroots organizations and social movements. The aim, in other words, was to stimulate utilization of 'the market mechanism' (UNRISD 2000) in lieu of what the leaders of these movements take to be 'the broader class struggle' (Stédile 2000).

Hardly a country in Latin America with a significant agricultural sector has escaped this drive to create a land market. In the early 1990s, country after country in the region instituted 'agrarian modernization' or reform law in one form or another but invariably designed to promote a land market. In Mexico and Ecuador this meant the abolition of constitutional protection of indigenous communal lands, a policy that was successfully instituted in the case of Mexico (1992), where the dominant peasant federation was in the pocket and under the control of the government, but that in Ecuador hit a political snag in the form of an 'indigenous uprising'. More generally, countries in the region shifted their prior focus on land redistribution towards the provision of legal security of land tenure and managed to institute a programme of land titling. This programme provided the infrastructure for a market-assisted approach towards land reform, which was further advanced via the institution of a land bank, to provide the rural poor landholders with access to credit and thus the capacity to purchase land or access other 'productive resources', such as new technology.

The context for this path towards land reform was provided by the widespread implementation in the 1980s of a neoliberal policy programme of adjustments to the economy (Veltmeyer and Petras 1997, 2000). By the end of the decade there were only four hold-outs in this 'reform' process – Brazil, Peru, Argentina and Venezuela – and these in relatively short time came on board in the 1990s, with some of the most radical forms of structural adjustment programme instituted anywhere in the world (Petras and Veltmeyer 2002).

Between 1991 and 1994, at the behest of the World Bank and within the framework of a neoliberal policy reform agenda, the governments of Mexico, Ecuador, Bolivia, Peru, and a number of other countries in South and Central America, turned towards a market-assisted approach to agrarian reform. This approach was based on legislation that included the abolition of the constitutional or legal protection of communal property and legal entitlement to land worked by smallholders, increasing their capacity to sell their land and, in the process, to build a land market, as well as, supposedly, increasing the 'efficiency' of production.[11] However, combined with the elimination of subsidies to local producers, the commercialization of credit, the reduction of protective tariffs, and in many cases an overvalued currency, these measures (land titling etc.), rather than resolving the agricultural crisis, have created what analysts have termed a 'difficult environment' for various categories of producers of tradable products, especially 'small scale peasant producers' (Crabtree 2003: 144). The latter, as Crabtree observes concerning Peru (though the point is generalizable), have been 'extremely vulnerable to the inflow of cheap agricultural products'. Not only has this increase in agricultural inputs and products undermined or destroyed local economies, forcing large numbers of local producers into bankruptcy or poverty, but at the same time it has brought about or accelerated a fundamental change in production and consumption patterns away from traditional crops, especially grains like quinoa, kiwicha, coca, alluco, beans, and potatoes. The impact of this change and its implications have yet to be evaluated.

In the case of Peru, the abolition of ECASA, one of a number of government marketing boards and agricultural price support institutions, liberalized the national market in rice, removing an organization that, like its counterparts in other countries in the region, had maintained price stability for the benefit of local producers. Some of the functions of ECASA were taken over by PRONAAA,[12] a government-subsidized food programme for the poor that bought directly from small-scale producers. However, such an institutional change – replicated in the other countries in the region – had relatively little impact on the poorest farmers, many of whom had never benefited from government programmes of any sort (Crabtree 2003: 147). As for those producers who managed to integrate themselves into the competitive local urban markets, the disappearance of Banco Agrario meant that they were forced to rely on various agro-industrial firms for commercial credit. This credit was extended to the same producers only under the most onerous terms, with rates that in the case of Brazil under F.H. Cardoso reached 20 per cent a month, given the enormously 'high risk' taken by the creditors. These creditors are extremely reluctant to lend, even to larger-scale, more prosperous landowners with privileged market access. When they do lend, the interest rates charged reflect the perception of high risk involved in lending to smaller-scale producers. Their appetite for lending is also reduced by the incidence of bankruptcies in sectors, such as asparagus, that had briefly seemed to offer endless possibilities (Crabtree 2003: 145–7).

In many cases, as in Mexico and Peru, the result of these and other such 'institutional changes' and the recourse to 'the market mechanism' has been a drastic deterioration in the market situation of small producers, forced to sell their products at prices below the cost of production, accruing enormous debts and in many cases pushed into bankruptcy. In Mexico, this situation has generated one of the largest mass movements in a long history of land struggle – a million-strong organization of highly indebted 'independent' family farmers (El Barzón). As for the peasant economy in Peru, Ecuador, Mexico, Central America and elsewhere in the region, it has been devastated, forcing large numbers to flee the countryside in the search of wage employment in the cities and urban centres. The only alternative was – and remains – rural poverty.

Studies that have been undertaken in this area point towards a pattern of increased social inequality and rural poverty – in the not atypical case of Peru, from 41.6 per cent of rural households in 1985 to 54.1 per cent in 2000, after a decade of agricultural modernization and capitalist 'free market' development (Crabtree 2003: 148). The same study shows a pattern of decline in extreme poverty, from 18.4 to 14.8 per cent, but no analysis or explanation – probably to be found in the World Bank's methodological approach, which is to reduce poverty by statistical fiat (defining it in terms of earnings of less than \$1 a day).

Peasants in action: grassroots land reform and the occupation tactic

In the 1960s and 1970s, the struggle for land and land reform was at the very epicentre of the class struggle in Central and South America. This struggle had taken shape and assumed diverse forms in previous decades, but the Cuban Revolution gave it a new impetus. The protagonists in this struggle were, on the one hand, the state, generally acting on behalf of the propertied class, those with landed property in the means of production, and access to the capital needed to expand production. The state was fundamentally concerned to avoid another Cuba taking form. The other major protagonists in struggle were organizations and communities of peasant producers and a rural landless or near-landless proletariat, organized in the form of social movements. For the most part, these were oriented towards land reform and, in the process, engaged in a multifaceted relation of struggle with the state, responding to diverse strategies of the government of the day to accommodate them, incorporate them, co-opt their leadership, and employ outright repression against them. Some of the peasant-based social movements, however, took a more radical stance and, with reference to the Cuban experience, were oriented towards various form of revolutionary struggle based on direct action in land invasions and the use of armed force in relation to the state.

By the 1980s, in a very different context – characterized by debt, neoliberalism, redemocratization in the form of civilian rule, decentralization of government decision-making, and the emergence and strengthening of civil society – the land struggle, in both its reformist and revolutionary forms, subsided and gave way to a new wave of social movements and struggle. In these 'new' social movements, the major protagonists were no longer peasants, nor workers, but the urban poor and diverse issue-oriented social organizations (Ballón 1986; Brass 1991; 2000; Calderón and Jelín 1987; Escobar and Alvarez 1992; Slater 1985, 1994).

In the 1990s, however, these 'new social movements' began to give way to a third wave of socio-political movements that were both peasant-based and peasant-led and, in some contexts, rooted in the struggle of indigenous communities for land, territorial autonomy and democracy, if not social justice. The most dynamic of these movements is generally held to be the MST (Movimento dos Trabalhadores Rurais Sem Terra), a national organization of Brazilian peasants ('rural landless workers') formed in the context of a broad civil struggle to establish 'the new republic', and the formation of PT (Workers' Party), whose leader, Lula, was elected to the presidency in 2003. However, similar movements were formed in similar contexts, notably in Mexico (the EZLN) and Ecuador (CONAIE).

Collectively, these and other such movements – in Paraguay, for example, the Federación Nacional Campesina – have formed and employed direct action land occupation tactics, combined with confrontations with the state to legalize and finance agricultural credits and inputs (Fogel 1986). In Bolivia, Colombia and Peru peasant movements have been in the forefront of the struggle to develop or maintain alternative crops as a source of livelihood in the face of neoliberal policies that have inundated local markets with cheap imports. All of them are peasant-based and peasant-led, different in this regard from the peasant movements in the wave that spread throughout Latin America in the 1950s and 1960. Many of these movements were peasant-based but not peasant-led.

In this context, direct action by grassroots movements in the 1990s took a number of diverse forms, which were combined in what MST leader João Pedro Stédile (2000) terms 'the broader class struggle'. However, as in the class struggle of Tupac Amaru in the late eighteenth century in what is now Peru, land occupations are at the centre of the strategy for direct action and radical reform, and figure prominantly in the arsenal of tactics of the MST. The strategy of the MST for land reform and direct action in this context has been 'occupation, negotiation and production'.

The basis for the land occupation tactic in Brazil is the agrarian reform legislation that was established in the land reform programmes of the 1960s, which, similar in form to the legislation established in the state-led land reform programmes of the 1960s and 1970s, calls for the expropriation of large landholdings deemed to be 'unproductive' – to have no 'social use'.[13] In Brazil and elsewhere (El Salvador and Honduras, for example), this law has provided the legal basis for a programme of state-led legal expropriation and land redistribution. However, as noted by Thiesenhusen (1995), among others, by the 1990s little land had actually been so transferred, leading the reorganized peasant movements to take action in diverse political and legal forms – in the case of El Salvador to pressure the government to act upon its own legalization. Other movements, however, particularly the MST in Brazil, adopted the direct-action tactic of land occupations in the context of a broader class struggle (Stédile 2000). In this context, the MST mobilized its membership to take direct action in the form of large-scale land occupations that typically mobilize between 1,000 and 3,000 families. Upon occupation of the land, the leadership of the movement on behalf of the encamped settlers immediately enters into negotiations with the government for legal title to the land under its own legal provisions for expropriation of landed properties that do not have 'social use'.

In the case of Brazil, this strategy has been so successful that the government has been forced to revive and step up its own land reform programme, including the implementation of a new World Bank programme based on the 'market mechanism' – begun in 1997 as a pilot project (named Cédula da Terra) in the northeast of the country and generalized in 1999 in the form of the land bank (Banco da Terra). The aim of this 'market-supported' land reform was to redistribute land not to the tiller but to 'the most productive'. Consequently, the actual acreage of land transferred via this mechanism under this programme is relatively modest, if not small. Today, after fifteen years of struggle and a revamped state-led land reform programme, 3 per cent of the population still owns two-thirds of the country's arable land, much of which continues to lie idle.

The rhythm of MST occupations has been maintained over fifteen years of struggle, averaging 345 a year and resulting in the settlement of over half a million families (569,733) on 25,598 hectares of land (Dataluta 2002). In just four months in 1999, at the height of the MST's conflict with the Cardoso government and its alternative 'official' land reform programme, over 155 large estates were occupied by 22,000 families organized by the MST and the Confederação Nacional de Trabalhadores na Agricultura (CONTAG). By mid-1999, over 72,000 families – over 350,000 farm people – were 'encamped' on land awaiting a response by the government and action in the form of legalizing the de facto 'expropriation' of the occupied land. However, some families continued to live in the temporary settlements or camps for up to four years and more. By withholding federal funds, and launching a programme to offer loans to small farmers for the purchase of land, the Cardoso regime hoped – in vain – to discourage the land occupiers and to undermine public support for the MST (Stédile 2000; see also Fernandes and Mattei, Chapters 11 and 12 in this volume).

In the course of fifteen years of struggle, the MST has mobilized up to half a million families of rural landless workers to occupy land, negotiate its legal expropriation and put it into production. During its thirty years of existence, INCRA, the institution established by the government under the agrarian reform law, has expropriated very few landholdings and settled fewer than 7 per cent of the landless rural families – some 330,000 out of 4 million. As a point of fact, most land settlements were initiated by MST-organized occupations that were later legalized by INCRA.

Social Movements in Latin America, Old and New

The struggle for social change in Latin America has taken various forms, including, most importantly, the emergence of social movements, which in the Latin American context were formed on the crest of three distinct waves. The first of these hit Latin America in the 1960s in the wake of the Cuban Revolution. The most important and dynamic movements were formed by organized workers in the urban centres and by peasant organizations that in their revolutionary form (guerrilla armies of national liberation) were generally led by urban middle-class intellectuals. Both the urban-centred labour movement and the peasant-based struggles for land and social change made substantial gains, improving the general situation of their members and advancing the class struggle. However, by the end of the 1970s most had been either defeated or destroyed in a complex process of implementing state-led projects of community-based 'development', the accommodation or corruption of the movements' leaders, or, when and where required, outright repression (Petras and Veltmeyer 2000).

In the 1980s, in a very different urban context (debt crisis, a new economic model, a state in retreat, a process of democratic renewal), Latin America was hit by a second wave of social movements that emerged from within 'civil society' – both in its popular sector (the urban poor) and the middle class. Well into the decade, sociologists and other analysts armed with a poststructuralist and a postmodernist perspective (Slater 1985, 1994; Calderón 1995; Calderón and Jelín 1987; Escobar and Alvarez 1992) dubbed these movements 'new' in regard to the subjectivity and heterogeneity of conditions that gave rise to them, their broad social base and their fundamental concerns. In this context these movements were conceived of as a new social actor on the political stage, rather than in class terms. However, no sooner had these new social movements been so constructed in theory than they disappeared into the political spaces within the structure of political and economic power – spaces created by the process of democratization and alternative development. The social basis of these 'new social movements' was the emergence and then strengthening of 'civil society' in the context of a retreating state and a push to democratize its relation to civil society in the interest of establish-ing 'good governance' – political order with minimum government and the participation in public policy formation of representative civil society organizations (Dominguez and Lowenthal 1996). The nongovernmental organizations were enlisted in this process to help secure not only 'good governance' but the proposed marriage of capitalism (free markets) and democracy (free elections)

In the ebb and flow of changing political tides towards the end of the 1980s, there emerged another wave of social movements, which included Brazil's MST, the most dynamic and successful among them. Unlike the 'new' movements of the 1980s, these movements were formed in the rural sector and were both peasant-based and peasant-led. A number of them also had an ethnic character and social base in the indigenous communities of peasant farmers. This was the case, for example, in Mexico (Zapatista Army of National Liberation), Ecuador (CONAIE), Bolivia (the Cocaleros, an organization of 30,000 coca-producing peasants).

Although the dynamics and future of these movements in the twenty-first century remain uncertain, and require further study, what is clear is that in a number of respects they can be viewed as 'new', which is to say different from their predecessors. What is not new is the fundamental dynamic of their struggle for land and land reform. What *is* generally new in these movements can be summed up in the following terms. First, unlike the revolutionary peasant-based movements of the 1960s and 1970s (with the exception of FARC–EP), these movements are peasant-led. Second, not only is the leadership composed of peasants but leaders maintain close links to their rural social base and the membership of the movement. In this regard, the austerity of conditions that they share with the membership is striking. Compared with the labour movement, there is no question among the new rural movements of the formation of a well-paid bureaucratic organizational elite that would be structurally related to government, which in the case of labour has been a major factor in the general decline and virtual demise of the movement. Among the rural movements, including the MST, critical decisions as to strategy and tactics are always made in close consultation with the members, generally in the form of popular or community-based assemblies.

Other new features are also notable, such as gender equity and autonomy from political parties and the state. Regarding the latter, the MST has maintained its autonomy as a social movement vis-à-vis the PT, with which it has always maintained cordial relations and tactical, even strategic, alliances. To what degree these relations have changed with PT in government is an open question, but it is certain that, with regard to autonomy, the other peasant-based and -led movements in the region have generally followed suit. As regards gender, changes within the MST in particular include an internal shift towards gender parity at all levels of the movement. Other rural social movements have not been as quick to follow the MST's lead in this area, which may be a reflection of the greater willingness of the MST to work with, and accept the support of, the international NGOs that are generally committed to the principle of incorporating women into the development process, if not gender parity. At the same time, it seems that both the FARC–EP and the EZLN, particularly the latter, have developed a revolutionary gender line in their politics, probably with an eye on the Cuban model.

Finally, as of the mid-1990s, another change has been in process, namely the formation of strategic alliances with urban civil society and class organizations to build public support for the movement. This is a process that has extended beyond states, leading to the formation of intra-regional organizations of peasant producers and international advocacy groups. In this connection, the MST has become a critical component of the World Social Forum, and by this means the worldwide anti-systemic/anti-globalization movement.

Conclusion

Land invasions and occupations have been a major political development since the 1990s, both in Latin America and, under different political conditions, in Asia and southern Africa, most particularly Zimbabwe. The Latin American experience suggests that this phenomenon of land occupations can best, if not only, be understood as a protracted and ongoing class struggle in the countryside. The historical conditions, political dynamics, and forms of this struggle are variable and contingent. But it is clear that land occupations are part of a broad land reform strategy that privileges direct action, within a wider context of worldwide class struggle against capitalism and neoliberalism. In the particular context of Latin America, the driving force behind this strategy is the peasantry, a socio-economic and political category that has been dismissed by many as a bygone political actor and force for revolutionary change. Our analysis suggests that this view is mistaken, that in the contemporary era of neoliberal capitalist development and globalization the peasantry remains a significant factor of social and political change in rural society.

Notes

1. The theoretical issues involved in categorizing peasants in terms of class are outlined by, among others, de Janvry (1981), Brass (1991, 2000) and Kearney (1996). In Latin America, a rural petty bourgeoisie composed of independent

farmers did not develop to the same extent that it did, under very different conditions, in North America. The Latin American trajectory has been characterized by a politically weak and subjugated peasantry and by the predominance of the *latifúndio*. On the issue of the alternative paths of agrarian development in Latin America, see De Janvry 1981 and Kay 1981.

2. See, *inter alia*, the relevant sections in the important collections edited by Stavenhagen (1970), Landsberger (1969, 1974), and Roseberry et al. (1995).

3. Early and still useful accounts that chronicle this process include Simpson 1937; Whetten 1948 and Tannenbaum 1968.

4. The literature on the dynamics of these agrarian reforms is voluminous but see, *inter alia*, Gutelman 1974, and, more broadly, de Janvry 1981 and Stavenhagen 1970. With respect to Chile specifically, a number of commentators have identified up to three different agrarian reform programmes: the first, from 1982 to 1967, being pre-capitalist in form; the second, under Frei and Allende, 1967 to 1973, involving a transition towards a capitalist agriculture; and a third, from 1973 onwards, based largely on the return of landed properties to their former owners, many of whom were converted into capitalists of the Junker variety.

5. The rural census of 1986 estimated the rural population at 23.4 million people. By 1995, the rural population had declined to 18 million, pointing towards a massive exodus of over 5 million people. Because of declining revenues, the compression of prices to below production costs, and massively increasing indebtedness among producers an additional 800,000 families – that is, over 2 million persons – are estimated by IBGE (the Brazilian Institute of Geography and Statistics) to have abandoned the countryside in just five years (from 1995 to 1999) because of the lack of land, credit and/or low prices.

6. IBASE, a research centre in Brazil, has studied the fiscal impact of legalizing MST land occupations-cum-settlements compared to the cost of services used by equal numbers of people migrating to urban areas. When landless workers occupy land and force the government to legalize their holdings, it implies costs: compensation to the former owner, credit for the new farmers, etc. But the total cost to the state to maintain the same number of people in an urban shanty town, including the services and infrastructure used, exceeds in one month the yearly cost of legalizing land occupations.

7. On this debate vis-à-vis Latin America's 'new social movements' and alternative approaches to development, see Veltmeyer 2002.

8. For a less metaphorical and more analytic review of this debate *vis-à-vis* the peasantry, see Petras and Veltmeyer 2002. This rural-to-urban movement was the effect of a proleterianization process that proceeded apace with the advance of capitalism into the countryside (Bartra 1976; Cancion 1987). The transition towards full proletarianization went ahead slowly and unevenly, with extra-economic coercion persisting well into (and in some cases beyond) the 1960s in most Latin American nations. By 1970, a large part of the rural population in many countries was partially or wholly proletarianized, a situation which generated a new wave of political protest and peasant insurgency. As pointed out by Paige (1975) and discussed below, different categories of peasants (tenants, sharecroppers, rich/middle/poor cultivators) responded differently to this process; thus the key issue in rural struggles might be land, land reform, access to credit

or technology, higher wages and better working conditions, or indeed any combination thereof.

9. As de Janvry et al. (1998: 5ff) outline, this land reform programme was implemented in stages: (i) the placement of the modernized estates in the non-reform sector under threats of expropriation, providing land ceilings for the non-reform sector, organizing the reform sector into communal or state collective form (*ejidos*, etc.) and distribution holdings as individual tenures; (ii) individual titling of collective lands, *ejidos* and state farms; and (iii) providing rural development for individual beneficiaries and access to idle lands for the landless and the micro-landholders (*minifundistas*).

10. To take the not atypical and well-studied case of Chile, in the mid-1960s the Inter-American Committee of Agrarian Development published a survey (CIDA 1966) that showed the inequality both of the land tenure system and of income derived from rural property ownership. In this survey the *latifundistas*, or landowning oligarchy, represented barely 2 per cent of the rural population but received a third of all income; rich peasants, or the rural bourgeoisie, represented 7 per cent of the population and received 15 per cent of total income. Middle peasants, however, constituted 21 per cent of the population but received only 12 per cent of total income, while various forms of smallholder made up the remaining three-quarters of the rural workforce but accounted for less than a third of total income. The question is, what impact has the land reform programme had on this social structure and pattern of income distribution? Indications are, and several partial studies suggest, that the overall impact of the land reform programmes of the 1960s and 1970s on this structure has been negligible; see Barraclough 1973, de Janvry 1981, Ghimire 2001.

11. In a number of systematic studies into the productivity of small versus large highly capitalized farms the general finding has been that in all cases relatively smaller, less capitalized farms are much more productive per unit area – 200 to 1,000 per cent greater – than the larger ones (Rosset 1999: 2).

12. Fujimori's poverty relief programme was similar to Salinas's PRONASOL (1992) in that it served primarily as an electoral mechanism for securing the rural vote.

13. Inefficient or unproductive use of land is rooted in a pattern of land tenure where 9 per cent of the landowners own nearly 78 per cent of the land, while at the other extreme 53 per cent of the rural population have little or no land (less than 3 per cent, according to IBGE 1989). The IBGE estimates that less than 20 per cent of Brazil's arable land is cultivated in any form, which leaves 80 per cent without a productive function, and hence a target for legal expropriation with compensation.

References

Amador, F. (1990), *Un siglo de lucha de los trabajadores en Nicaragua*, Managua: Centro de la Investigación de la Realidad de América Latina.

Amalric, Frank (1998), 'Sustainable Livelihoods, Entrepreneurship, Political Strategies and Governance', *Development* 41(3): 31–8.

Bakx, Keith (1988), 'From Proletarian to Peasant: Rural Transformation in the State of Acre, 1870–1986', *Journal of Development Studies* 24(2): 141–60.

Ballón, Eduardo (1986), *Movimientos Sociales y Democracia: La Fundación de un Nuevo Orden*, Lima: DESCO.

Barraclough, Solon L. (1973), *Agrarian Structure in Latin America, A Resumé of the CIDA Land Tenure Studies*, Lexington: Lexington Books.

Barry, Tom (1987), *Roots of Rebellion: Land and Hunger in Central America*, Boston: South End Press.

Bartra, Roger (1976), '¡Si los campesinos se extinguen!', *Historia y Sociedad* 8 (Winter): 71–83.

Beltran, Fausto, and José Fernández (1960), *¿Donde va la reforma agraria Boliviana?*, La Paz: Talleres Gráficos Bolivianos.

Blanco, Hugo (1972), *Land or Death: the Peasant Struggle in Peru*, New York: Pathfinder Press.

Brass, Tom (1991), 'Moral Economists, Subalterns, New Social Movements and the (Re) Emergence of a (Post) Modernised (Middle) Peasant', *The Journal of Peasant Studies* 18(2): 173–205.

Brass, Tom (2000), *Peasants, Populism and Postmodernism: The Return of the Agrarian Myth*, London and Portland, OH: Frank Cass.

Brockett, Charles D. (1998), *Land, Power and Poverty: Agrarian Transformation and Political Control in Central America*, Boulder: Westview Press.

Bromley, D. (1989), 'Property Relations and Economic Development: The Other Land Reform', *World Development* 17(6): 867–77.

Bryceson, Deborah, Cristóbal Kay and Jos Mooij, eds. (2000), *Disappearing Peasantries? Rural Labour in Africa, Asia and Latin America*, London: Intermediate Technology Publications.

Bulmer-Thomas, Victor (1996), *The New Economic Model in Latin America and its Impact on Income Distribution and Poverty*, New York: St. Martin's Press.

Burbach, Roger (1994), 'Roots of the Postmodern Rebellion in Chiapas', *New Left Review* 205 (May–June): 113–24.

Calderón, Fernando (1995), *Movimientos Sociales y Política*, México: Siglo XXI.

Calderón, Fernando, and Elizabeth Jelin (1987), *Clases y Movimientos Sociales en América Latina. Perspectivas y Realidades*, Buenos Aires: Cuadernos CEDES.

Cancian, Frank (1987), 'Proletarianization in Zinacantan 1960–83', in *Household Economies and Their Transformation*, ed. Morgan Maclachan, Lanham MD: University Press of America.

Castells, Manuel (1976), *Movimientos Sociales Urbanos en América Latina: Tendencies Históricas y Problemas Teóricos*, Lima: Pontífica Universidad Católica.

Chambers, Robert, and Gordon Conway (1998), 'Sustainable Rural Livelihoods: Some Working Definitions,' *Development* 41(3).

CIDA (1966), *Chile: Tenencia de la tierra y desarrollo socio-económico del sector agrícola*, Santiago de Chile: Talleres Gráficos Hispano Suiza.

Coleman, James Samuel (1988), 'Social Capital in the Creation of Human Capital', *American Journal of Sociology* 94, Supplement: 95–120.

Cotler, Julio (1978), *Clases, estado y nación en el Perú*, Lima: Instituto de Estudios Peruanos.

Crabtree, John (2003), 'The Impact of Neo-Liberal Economics on Peruvian Peasant Agriculture in the 1990s', in *Latin American Peasants*, ed. Tom Brass, London: Frank Cass.

Dandler, Jorge (1969), *El Sindicalismo Campesino en Bolivia*, Mexico: Instituto Indígenista Interamericano.

Dataluta (Banco de dados de luta pela terra) (2002), *Assentamentos rurais*, São Paulo: UNESPI/MST.

Deininger, Klaus (1998), 'Implementing Negotiated Land Reform: Initial Experience from Colombia, Brazil and South Africa', in *Proceedings of the International Conference on Land Tenure in the Developing World with a Focus on Southern Africa*, 27–29 January, University of Cape Town.

de Janvry, Alain (1981), *The Agrarian Question and Reformism in Latin America*, Baltimore, OH: Johns Hopkins University Press.

de Janvry, Alain, Gustavo Cordillo and Elisabeth Sadoulet (1998), *Mexico's Second Agrarian Reform: Household and Community Responses, 1990–1994*, San Diego: Center for US–Mexican Studies.

de Walt, Billie, and Martha Ress (1994), *The End of Agrarian Reform in Mexico: Past Lessons and Future Prospects*, La Jolla, CA: Center for US–Mexican Studies, University of California, San Diego.

Dominguez, J., and A. Lowenthal, eds (1996), Constructing Democratic Governance, Baltimore: Johns Hopkins University Press.

Duncan, Kenneth, Ian Rutledge and Colin Harding, eds (1977), *Land and Labour in Latin America: Essays on the Development of Agrarian Capitalism in the Nineteenth and Twentieth Centuries*, New York: Cambridge University Press.

Dunkerley, James (1984), *Rebellion in the Veins: Political Struggle in Bolivia 1952–82*, London: Verso.

Dunkerley, James (1992), *Political Suicide in Latin America*, New York: Verso.

ECLAC (Economic Commission for Latin America and the Caribbean) (1998), *Economic Survey of Latin America and the Caribbean, 1997–1998*, Santiago: ECLAC.

Escobar, Ernesto (1995), *Encountering Development: The Making and Unmaking of the Third World*, Princeton, NJ: Princeton University Press.

Escobar, Arturo, and Sonia Alvarez, eds (1992), *The Making of Social Movements in Latin America: Identity, Strategy, and Democracy*, Boulder, CO: Westview Press.

Esteva, Gustavo, and Madhu Suri Prakash (1998), *Grassroots Postmodernism*, London: Zed Books.

Feder, Ernest (1971), *The Rape of the Peasantry: Latin America's Landholding System*, New York: Doubleday.

Figueiras, Otto (1999), 'O Campo em Chamas', *Sem Terra*, April–June.

Florescano, Enrique, ed. (1975), *Haciendas, Latifundios y Plantaciones en América Latina*, Mexico DF: Siglo XXI.

Fogel, Ramon Bruno (1986), *Movimientos Campesinos en el Paraguay*, Asunción: Centro Paraguayo de Estudios Sociológicos (CPES).

Foley, Michael W. (1991), 'Agrarian Conflict Reconsidered: Popular Mobilization and Peasant Politics in Mexico and Central America', *Latin American Research Review* 26(1): 216–38.

Ghimire, Krishna B., ed. (2001), *Land Reform and Peasant Livelihoods: The Social Dynamics of Rural Poverty and Agrarian Reform in Developing Countries*, London: ITDG.

Gould, Jeffrey (1983), 'El trabajo forzoso y las comunidades indígenas nicaragüenses', in *El café en la historia de Centroamérica*, ed. Hector Pérez Brignoli and Mario Samper, San José: FLASCO.

Guimarães, Roberto (1997), 'The Environment, Population and Urbanization', in *Understanding Contemporary Latin America*, ed. R. Hillman, Boulder CO: Lynne Rienner.

Gutelman, Michel (1971), *Réforme et mystification agraires en Amérique latine: Le cas du Mexique*, Paris: François Maspero.

Gwynne, Robert, and Cristóbal Kay, eds (1999), *Latin America Transformed*, New York: Oxford University Press.

Hardoy, Jorge Enrique, and David Satterthwaite (1981), *Shelter, Need and Response: Housing, Land, and Settlement Policies in Seventeen Third World Nations*, New York: Wiley.

Harris, Richard L., Anthony Winson, Florencia Mallon, Rosemary Galli, Alain de Janvry, Lynn Ground and Roderigo Montoya (1978), 'Peasants, Capitalism, and the Class Struggle in Rural Latin America (Part II)', *Latin American Perspectives* 5(4): 71–89.

Heath, Dwight B. (1969), *Land Reform and Social Revolution in Bolivia*, New York: F.A. Praeger.

Helmore, Kristen, and Naresh Singh (2001), *Sustainable Livelihoods: Building on the Wealth of the Poor*, West Hartford, CT: Kumarian Press.

Hobsbawm, Eric (1984), *The Age of Extremes: The Short Twentieth Century, 1914–19*, London: Weidenfeld & Nicolson.

Horton, Lynn (1998), *Peasants in Arms: War and Peace in the Mountains of Nicaragua, 1979–1994*, Athens, OH: Ohio University Center for International Studies.

Huizer, Geritt (1973), *Peasant Rebellion in Latin America*, Harmondsworth: Penguin.

Huizer, Geritt (1999), *Peasant Mobilization for Land Reform: Historical Case Studies and Theoretical Considerations*, Discussion Paper 103, Geneva: UNRISD.

Hunter, Allan (1989), 'Post-Marxism and the New Social Movements', *Theory and Society* 17(6): 885–900.

Jacobi, Pedro (1985), *Movimentos Sociais Urbanos e a Crise: Da Explosão a Participação Popular Autonoma,* São Paulo: FESP.

Jacobsen, Nils (1993), *Mirages of Transition: The Peruvian Altiplano, 1780–1930*, Berkley, CA: University of California Press.

INCRA (Instituto Nacional de Colonização e Reforma Agrária) (1999), *Balanço da Reforma Agraria e da Agricultura Familiar 1995–99*, Brasília: Ministério do Desenvolvimento Agrário.

Katz, Friedrich (1988), *Riot, Rebellion, and Revolution: Rural Social Conflict in México*. Princeton, NJ: Princeton University Press.

Kay, Cristóbal (1981), 'Political Economy, Class Alliances and Agrarian Change in Chile', *Journal of Peasant Studies* 8(4): 485–513.

Kay, Cristóbal (1982), 'Achievements and Contradictions of the Peruvian Agrarian Reform', *Journal of Development Studies* 18(2): 141–70.

Kay, Cristóbal (1999), 'Rural Development: From Agrarian Reform to Neo-liberalism and Beyond', in *Latin America Transformed*, ed. Robert Gwynne and Cristóbal Kay, New York: Oxford University Press.

Kay, Cristóbal (2000), 'Latin America's Agrarian Transformation: Peasantisation and Poletarianisation', in *Disappearing Peasantries? Rural Labour in Africa, Asia and Latin America*, ed. D.F. Bryceson, Cristóbal Kay and Jos Mooij, London: Intermediate Technology Publications.

Kearney, Michael (1996), *Reconceptualizing the Peasantry*, Boulder, CO: Westview Press.

Landsberger, Henry A., ed. (1969), *Latin American Peasant Movements*, London and Ithaca: Cornell University Press.

Landsberger, Henry A., ed. (1974), *Rural Protest: Peasant Movements and Social Change*, London: Macmillan.

LeGrand, Catherine Carlisle (1983), *From Public Lands into Private Properties: Landholding and Rural Conflict in Colombia, 1870–1936*, Ann Arbor, MI: Michigan University Microfilms.

Lehmann, David (1978), 'The Death of Land Reform: A Polemic', *World Development* 6(3): 39–345.

Lindqvist, Sven (1979), *Land and Power in South America*, Harmondsworth: Penguin.

Lora, Guillermo (1964), *La Revolución Boliviana*, La Paz: Difusión SRL.

Lora, Guillermo (1970), *Documentos Políticos de Bolivia*, La Paz: Editorial Los Amigos del Libro.

Loveman, Brian (1976), *Struggle in the Countryside: Politics and Rural Labor in Chile, 1919–1973*, Bloomington, IN: Indiana University Press.

McEwan, Arthur (1981), *Revolution and Economic Development in Cuba: Moving Towards Socialism*, New York: St. Martin's Press.

Mahoney, James (2001), *The Legacies of Liberalism: Path Dependence and Political Regimes in Central America*, Baltimore: Johns Hopkins University Press.

Malloy, James M., and Richard S. Thorn, eds (1971), *Beyond the Revolution: Bolivia Since 1952*, Pittsburgh, PA: Pittsburgh University Press.

Meyer, Carrie A. (1989), *Land Reform in Latin America: The Dominican Case*, New York: Praeger.

Midlarsky, Manus, and Kenneth Roberts (1995), 'Class, State and Revolution in Central America: Nicaragua and El Salvador Compared', *Journal of Conflict Revolution* 29 (June).

MST, Setor de Documentação do SN da CPT Nacional (2002), São Paulo.

Orlove, Benjamin S., and Glynn Custred, eds (1980), *Land and Power in Latin America: Agrarian Economies and Social Processes in the Andes*, New York: Holmes & Meier.

Paige, Jeffery M. (1975), *Agrarian Revolution: Social Movements and Export Agriculture in the Underdeveloped World*, New York: The Free Press.

Pearse, Andrew (1975), *The Latin American Peasant*, London: Frank Cass.

Petras, James (1997a), 'MST and Latin America: The Revival of the Peasantry as a Revolutionary Force', *Canadian Dimension* 31(3): 53–4.

Petras, James (1997b), 'The Resurgence of the Left', *New Left Review* 223: 17–47.

Petras, James, and Henry Veltmeyer (2001a), *Brasil de Cardoso: Expropriação de um País*, Petrópolis: Editorial Vozes.

Petras, James, and Henry Veltmeyer (2001b), 'Are Latin American Peasant Movements Still a Force for Change? Some New Paradigms Revisited', *Journal of Peasant Studies* 28(2): 83–118.

Petras, James, and Henry Veltmeyer (2002), 'The Peasantry and the State in Latin America', in *Latin American Peasants*, ed. Tom Brass, London: Frank Cass.

Portes, Alejandro, Manuel Castells and Lauren Benton, eds (1989), *The Informal Economy: Studies in Advanced and Less Developed Countries,* Baltimore, MD: Johns Hopkins University Press.

PREALC (Programa Regional de Empleo de America Latina y el Caríbe) (1993), *PREALC Informe*, Santiago: ILO–PREALC.

PRONASOL, Advisory Council (1992), *El Combate a la Pobreza*, Mexico: PRONASOL.

Roseberry, William, Lowell Gudmundson, and Mario Samper Kutschbach, eds (1995), *Coffee, Society, and Power in Latin America*, Baltimore, MD: Johns Hopkins University Press.

Rosset, Peter (1999), 'On the Benefits of Small Farmers', Food First (Institute for Food and Development Policy), *Back Grounder* 6(4), www.foodfirst.org//pubs/backgrdrs/1999/w99v6n4.html.

Sachs, Wolfgang, ed. (1992), *The Development Dictionary: A Guide to Knowledge and Power*, London: Zed Books.

Sanderson, Steven E. (1981), *Agrarian Populism and the Mexican State: The Struggle for Land in Sonora*, Berkeley, CA: University of California Press.

Schneider, Cathy (1988), *The Mobilization at the Grassroots: Shantytowns and Resistance in Authoritarian Chile*, New York: Institute for Latin American and Iberian Studies, Columbia University.

Silva, Patricio (1990), 'Agrarian Change Under the Chilean Military Government', *Latin American Research Review* 25(1): 193–205.

Simpson, Eyler N. (1937), *The Ejido: Mexico's Way Out*, Chapel Hill, NC: University of North Carolina Press.

Slater, David (1994), 'Power and Social Movements in the Other Occident: Latin America in an International Context', *Latin American Perspectives* 21(2): 11–37.

Slater, David (1985), *New Social Movements and the State in Latin America*. Amsterdam: CEDLA.

Stavenhagen, Rodolfo (1970), *Agrarian Problems and Peasant Movements in Latin America*, New York: Anchor Books.

Stédile, João Pedro (2000), Interview with James Petras and Henry Veltmeyer, 14 May.

Steenland, Kyle (1977), *Agrarian Reform under Allende: Peasant Revolt in the South*, Albuquerque, NM: University of New Mexico Press.

Tannenbaum, Frank ([1929]1968), *The Mexican Agrarian Revolution*, New York: Archon Books.

Thiesenhusen, William (1995), *Broken Promises: Agrarian Reform and the Latin American Campesino*, Boulder, CO: Westview Press.

Thiesenhusen, William, ed. (1989), *Searching for Agrarian Reform in Latin America*, Winchester, MA: Unwin Hyman.

UNRISD (2000), 'Civil Society Strategies and Movements for Rural Asset Redistribution and Improved Livelihoods', UNRISD, Civil Society and Social Movements Programme, Geneva: UNRISD.

Veltmeyer, Henry (1997), 'New Social Movements in Latin America: The Dynamics of Class and Identity', *Journal of Peasant Studies* 25(1): 139–69.

Veltmeyer, Henry (2002), 'The Politics of Language: Deconstructing Postdevelopment Discourse', *Canadian Journal of Development Studies* 22(3): 597–620.

Veltmeyer, Henry (2003), 'Social Exclusion and Rural Development in Latin America', *Canadian Journal of Latin American and Caribbean Studies* 27(54): 251–80.

Veltmeyer, Henry, and James Petras (1997), *Economic Liberalism and Class Conflict in Latin America*, London: Macmillan.

Veltmeyer, Henry, and James Petras (2000), *The Dynamics of Social Change in Latin America*, London: Macmillan.

Vilas, Carlos (1995), *Between Earthquakes and Volcanoes: Market, State and Revolutions in Central America*, New York: Monthly Review Press.

Walker, Thomas, ed. (1997), *Nicaragua without Illusions: Regime Transition and Structural Adjustment in the 1990s*, Wilmington, DE: Scholarly Resources Press.

Wheelock Román, Jaime (1975), *Imperialismo y Dictadura: Crisis de una Formación Social*, Mexico City: Siglo XXI Editores.

Whetten, Nathan (1948), *Rural Mexico*, Chicago, IL: University of Chicago Press.

Wolf, Eric R. (1969), *Peasant Wars of the Twentieth Century*, London: Faber & Faber.

Weller, Robert P., and Scott E. Guggenheim (1982), *Power and Protest in the Countryside: Studies of Rural Unrest in Asia, Europe, and Latin America*, Durham, NC: Duke University Press.

Wheelock Román, Jaime (1975), *Imperialismo y Dictadura: Crisis de una Formación Social*, Mexico City: Siglo Veintiuno Editores.

Whetten, Nathan (1948), *Rural Mexico*, Chicago, IL: University of Chicago Press.

Woolcock, M., and D. Narayan (2000), 'Social Capital: Implications for Development Theory, Research and Policy', *World Bank Research Observer* 15(2): 225–49.

World Bank (1996), *World Development Report 1996*, Washington, DC: World Bank.

World Bank (1997), *World Development Report 1997*, Washington, DC: World Bank.

II

The Occupation as a Form of Access to Land in Brazil: A Theoretical and Methodological Contribution

Bernardo Mançano Fernandes

The land occupation has become the principal form of struggle against the *latifúndio* and an important form of access to land in Brazil. It is by means of the land occupation that the landless have spatialized the struggle, conquered land and territorialized the Movimento dos Trabalhadores Rurais Sem Terra (MST, or Landless Rural Workers' Movement). The objective of this chapter is to reflect upon this extraordinary form of popular struggle developed by the MST and other social movements, to offer an analytical construction of the process of (re)creation of the peasantry through this form of struggle, and to interpret its significance vis-à-vis the resettlement policy of the government.

The struggle for land is a central dimension of the agrarian question. As a form of access to land, it is an action of resistance inherent to the formation of the peasantry within the contradictory process of capitalist development. As Ariovaldo Umbelino de Oliveira (1991: 20) observes,

> capital does not expand wage work, its typical labour relationship, everywhere in an absolute manner, destroying totally and absolutely peasant family labour. To the contrary, capital creates and re-creates it, so that its production is possible and with it there may be as well the creation of new capitalists.

Within this process of its creation and re-creation, exclusion occurs through the differentiation of the peasantry. This process does not necessarily lead to the so-called disintegration of the peasantry – that is, proletarianization or the transformation of the peasant into a capitalist (Lenin 1985: 35; Kautsky 1986: 149). It leads also to the re-creation of the peasantry in different forms. One form, as de Oliveira (1991: 11) has noted, is by

> [the] subjection of income from land to capital that occurs with the subordination of peasant production to capital that dominates and expropriates income from the land and, in addition, expropriates practically all of the surplus produced, reducing the income of the peasant to the minimum necessary for his/her physical reproduction.

Thus the movement of the formation of the peasantry occurs simultaneously through the exclusion and generation of the conditions for the realization of family labour in the creation, destruction and re-creation of social relations, such as peasant ownership of land, squatting, rental, sharecropping and contract farming.

Another form of re-creation of the peasantry is through land occupation. In its amplified reproduction, capital cannot contract everyone, and it always excludes a large proportion of the workers. In the same way, within the Brazilian reality, capital, in its contradictory process of reproduction of non-capitalist relations, does not re-create the peasantry with the same intensity as it excludes it. Thus, by means of the land occupation, the workers re-socialize themselves, struggling against capital as well as subordinating themselves to it, because, upon occupying and conquering land, they reinsert themselves into the capitalist production of non-capitalist relations of production (Martins 1981).

In its unequal development, the capitalist mode of production inevitably generates expropriation and exploitation. The expropriated make use of the land occupation as a form of reproduction of family labour. Thus, in the resistance against the process of exclusion, the workers create a political form – the land occupation – in order to re-socialize themselves, struggling for land and against proletarianization. In this sense, the struggle for land is a constant struggle against capital. It is the struggle against expropriation and against exploitation. The occupation is a form of materialization of class conflict.

The territorialization of capital means the deterritorialization of the peasantry and vice versa. It is evident that these processes are not linear, nor separate, and they contain a contradiction, because in the territorialization of one is contained the production and reproduction of the other. Within the process of territorialization of capital, there is the creation, destruction and re-creation of family labour. Through the territorialization of the peasantry, wage labour and the capitalist are produced. The advances and retreats of these processes within a territory are determined by a set of political and economic factors. Thus, I will highlight a number of those factors that have been determinants for the formation of the current agrarian question in Brazil.

The model of agricultural development implemented since the 1960s has intensified the concentration of land ownership, entailing the expropriation and the expulsion of millions of families. In this historical process, agrarian reform policies have been elaborated, such as the Land Statute (1964) and the National Agrarian Reform Plan (1986), but have not been implemented – itself a reflection of the correlation of forces around the agrarian question.

It is within this process of exclusion that the workers have intensified the struggle for land. The occupation is knowledge built upon the experiences of popular struggle against the hegemonic power of capital. It is a complex socio-spatial and political process in which the experiences of resistance of the landless are created and re-created.

Mobilization, Spatialization and Negotiation

The occupation is to be understood as an action that results from the needs and expectations of workers, and that introduces questions, creates facts, and reveals situations. As such, it modifies reality, increasing the flux of social relations. The occupation is part of a movement of resistance in defence of the interests of workers, including the expropriation of the *latifúndio*, the settlement of families, the production and reproduction of family labour, the creation of agricultural policies directed at the development of peasant agriculture, and the generation of public policies to guarantee the basic rights of citizenship. Workers thus challenge the state, which has always represented the interests of the agrarian bourgeoisie and capital in general, and which has thus pursued policies under pressure from workers aiming only to attenuate the processes of expulsion and exploitation.

The organization of a land occupation results from the needs of survival. It results from the consciousness constructed within the lived reality. It is, therefore, an apprenticeship in a historical process of construction of experiences of resistance. When a group of families begins to organize with the objective of occupying land, it develops a set of procedures that defines a methodology of popular struggle. This experience has its logic constructed in praxis. This logic has as its constitutive components indignation and revolt, necessity and interests, consciousness and identity, experience and resistance, a concept of land for work rather than for commerce and exploitation, and movement and overcoming.

In the formation of the MST, the landless have created distinct methodologies of resistance, developed in the trajectory of the struggle. These actions are differentiated throughout Brazil. In the spatialization of the struggle for land, each of the spaces of political socialization has its own temporality. The encampments are of diverse types, whether permanent or determined by one group of families. The forms of pressure are distinct, according to the political circumstances as well as negotiations. These practices are the result of the knowledge of experiences, of exchanges and reflection upon them, as well as the political landscape and the situations in which the fractions of territories are located in different regions of Brazil. The elements that compose the methodologies are the formation, organization and tactics of struggle, including negotiations with the state and landowners, all with their starting point in grassroots work. The Ecclesial Base Communities (CEBs), rural workers' unions, schools, and even homes are some of the principal social places where grassroots organizational meetings take place.

The grassroots efforts may be the result of the 'spatialization' or 'spatiality' of the struggle for land. Spatialization is a process of concrete movement of the action in its reproduction in space and territory. In this manner, the grassroots efforts may be organized by people who came from elsewhere, where they constituted their experiences. For example, one or more landless from one state may move to other regions of the country to organize landless families. And in this manner they create the movement in its territorialization. Spatiality is a continuous process of an action, the dimensioning of the meaning of an action. Thus the workers in one place begin the grassroots work because they heard, saw or read about land occupations; that is, they became aware through a variety of means of communication, spoken, written or televised. And so they begin the struggle for land, constructing their experiences.

Grassroots efforts, carried out in different places and under distinct conditions, construct the space of political socialization. This space involves three dimensions: communicative space, interactive space, and the space of struggle and resistance. Communicative space is constructed from the first meetings. It is the first moment of meeting and learning about each other and defining the objectives. Participants know why they are in that place. Their motives are necessity and interest, which, together with revolt and indignation, represent attitudes and feelings that will determine when the land is occupied. It is the initiation of an experience of transformation of their realities.

The second dimension is the interactive space. This, depending on the methodology, is realized before, during or after the land occupation. The interactive space is a continuous process of apprenticeship. The meaning of the interaction is located in the exchange of experiences, in the knowledge of life histories, in the conscientization in the condition of expropriation and exploitation, in the construction of landless identity. The content of the grassroots meetings is the recuperation of life histories associated with the development of the agrarian question. Thus, life is experienced through interactions. Participants, by analysing the situation, the relationships of political forces, the formation of articulations and alliances for political and economic support, transform the subjective conditions by means of interests and will, recognizing their rights and participating in the construction of their destinies. They come face to face with the objective conditions of the struggle against landlords and their hired gunmen, of the confrontation with the police and the state.

This is a process of political formation, generator of the militancy that strengthens the social organization. All of these processes, practices and procedures galvanize the people, in the construction of the consciousness of their rights, in an effort to overcome the condition of expropriation and exploitation. The overcoming of their realities begins with deliberation regarding participation in the land occupation. This decision has its basis in the knowledge that only with this action will the people be able to find a solution to the state of misery in which they live. They must then decide which land to occupy. The *latifúndios* are numerous and it is not difficult to locate them. There exist various information sources on the location of lands that are not fulfilling their social function,[1] from the knowledge that the communities themselves possess regarding

the many *latifúndios* by which they are often surrounded to knowledge obtained through diverse governmental and non-governmental
organizations working on the agrarian question. Once the land is
identified, the only decision remaining is when to occupy. It is
through the occupation that the landless present themselves to the
public and dimension the space of political socialization.

Participation in an occupation is not a simple decision. After all,
in addition to the experience, it means the transformation of one's
own life. For this reason, there is often indecision and fear among
families. In order to overcome fear it is necessary to trust the people
who constitute and coordinate the movement. Thus, while defending
an occupation, a leader has the responsibility to present ideas and
references that will enable doubt to be overcome. These arguments
are developed in the grassroots meetings, in the definition of the
space of political socialization. In this way, the coordinators, the
priests, the union leaders become important references for indecisive
workers. Visits to encampments and settlements, or testimonies of
struggles by settled families, serve as reassurance. Still, many remain
on the sidelines, as observers, and only go to the encampment after
the occupation has been realized. These attitudes inevitably generate
internal debate, as many families complain that they feel like 'cannon
fodder'. There are also those known as 'swallows', who appear once in
a while at the encampment; they are an expression of indecision or
opportunism. Finally, there are also those who participate in groups
of families, assisting with the realization of various occupations, until
they themselves decide to occupy.

The grassroots meetings are generative spaces wherein subjects
construct their own existences. These meetings may last from one to
many months or even years, depending on the circumstances. They
may involve a municipality, various municipalities of a region, various
municipalities of various regions, or even more than one state in
border areas. During the military dictatorship, these meetings had to
be organized with a great deal of secrecy, due to repression. Since
then, with the territorialization of the struggle and the growth of
the participation of families, these meetings have multiplied and
expanded in size, no longer consisting of dozens of families but of
hundreds.

This growth also brought problems. Police and gunmen began to
infiltrate meetings to spy on their development and interrupt the
struggle. These spies often are never discovered, and the occupation

ends up being frustrated. In order to avoid this, the leaders inform the coordinators of groups of families of the day and place of the occupations only hours before they are due to take place. On the other hand, the growth of the occupations results not only from the organization of the landless but also from the growth of forms of support. Increasingly, the families that participate in these meetings receive support from urban communities and rural settlements, as well as from prefects who offer transportation, even for participation in the occupation.

During this process, the landless attempt to negotiate with the state the settlement of the families. Promises and compromises, which for the most part never materialize, are always the response they receive. With the benefit of experience, they learn that they must construct the conditions necessary to persevere, through the creation of commissions, nuclei, sectors and coordinations. They are part of the form of organization of the movement. Each one is composed of groups of people responsible for the diverse needs of the families, beginning with food, health and the provision of education for children, teenagers and adults. Moreover, they create commissions for negotiation in order to follow the progress of the issue, together with the other institutions, and to inform the society of their actions; and they create nuclei and coordinations in order to keep the encampment informed and organized. In the MST, diverse sectors work together to achieve these tasks, with the 'Front of the Masses' responsible for grassroots work and the development of actions. The landless workers are the principal subjects of this process.

From the beginning of the struggle, the landless have received support from different institutions, through the alliances that form a political articulation. The institutions involved defend the occupation as a form of access to land. During the twenty-plus years of existence of the MST, in different circumstances, it has received support from the Pastoral Land Commission (CPT), the Workers' Party (PT) and other political parties, and a diversity of other organizations. Still, the relationships within the articulation have always generated political clashes, due to the different conceptions of the roles that the parts of the alliances have in the development of the struggle for land. Some of these clashes relate to the autonomy of the workers. Often the organizations attempt to interfere in the decisions of the workers, not recognizing their respective competencies. This happens, for example, when they attempt to coordinate the struggles, trying to represent the workers, and arguing that the MST should only support the landless, when in fact the landless are those who make up the movement.

Clashes also occur due to different conceptions of struggle. These are extremely differentiated throughout the country. There are conceptions favourable to defensive postures and others to offensive ones, understood as different forms of resistance to the actions of police and gunmen. The more defensive postures privilege non-confrontation, opting only for negotiation, while the offensive postures privilege both confrontation and negotiation. The overcoming of the disagreement occurs through the recognition of the autonomy of the workers and the competencies of each institution. In the formation of the MST, this was possible only after the rupture and re-establishment of relations, through the lessons constructed in the struggles. In different forms, there has always persisted the idea that occupation is the solution. This was, for all organizations involved in the struggle, a learning process.

Until the mid-1990s, the landless confronted this issue. After years of tension, the institutions recognized the experiences and autonomy of the landless. Thus, these landless peasants speak with their own voices, winning the respect and admiration of some and the aversion of others. It was this incessant struggle for political autonomy that greatly contributed to the spatialization and territorialization of the MST throughout Brazil. In this sense, the MST is not the result of a proposal of a political party, nor the fruit of a proposal or policy of the Church, nor is it a labour movement, although it has received support from a conjunction of these political forces. The MST is the fruit of this reality, not of these institutions.

Processes of Occupation: Types and Forms

The occupation, as a form of struggle and access to land, is a constant in the history of the Brazilian peasantry. Over the past four decades, the settlers (*posseiros*)[2] and the landless have been the principal subjects of this struggle. The settlers occupy lands predominantly at the edges or fronts of expansion, in frontier areas. With the advance of the frontier, there occur processes of expropriation of these peasants, developed primarily by the land-grabbing of large landowners and businesspeople. The landless, on the other hand, occupy lands predominantly in regions where capital has already territorialized. They occupy *latifúndios* as well as lands of commerce and exploitation (lands forfeited or grabbed with no legal claim).[3] The important difference between the struggles of the *posseiros* and the landless is that in the former case the landgrabber, landlord and businessperson arrives at and expropriates land that is already settled by *posseiros*, while in the latter case the landless arrive at and occupy the land of the established landgrabber, landlord and businessperson.

Since the mid-1980s, when the MST territorialized throughout Brazil, the landless workers, along with settlers, small farm owners, sharecroppers, renters and contract farmers, intensified the process of the formation of the Brazilian peasantry. The intensification of the land occupations had great political impact, such that the landless became the principal interlocutors in their confrontation with the state in the struggle for land and agrarian reform. These rural and urban workers have been struggling for land in all regions of the country.

In order to understand this process better, it is necessary to analyse the different types and forms of occupations. A useful starting point is the analytical approach developed by Eric Hobsbawm (1998: 241–76), in his *Peasant Land Occupations*. Here Hobsbawm employs only the component of *land*, while in this chapter other components are also utilized, such as *family* and *experience*. In this manner, the types of occupation are related not only to the ownership of land – public, capitalist, held by non-governmental organizations – but also to the forms of organization of the families and the types of experience they construct.

Hobsbawm points to three types of occupation: (a) *recuperation*, or reconquering of land for work, referring to lands that were occupied for decades by peasants but became contested due to the territorialization of capital in the expropriation of peasant families; (b) *forfeited* lands, or lands belonging to the state in frontier areas but grabbed by landlords; and (c) *occupation* of *latifúndios*. Hobsbawm is primarily concerned with occupations of the first type, which are also relevant in Brazil, especially in the Amazon region. Nevertheless, in Brazil the occupations that predominate are those pertaining to forfeited and/or public lands and *latifúndios*.

With respect to the form of organization of the groups of families, there are two types: *territorialized movements* and *isolated movements*. The distinction between the two relates to the social organization and geographical space. Territorialized movements are those that are organized and act in different places at the same time, made possible by their form of organization, which permits the spatialization of the struggle for land. The MST is an example of this. Territorialized movements have structures that may take two forms, social movement or labour movement.[4] These movements, together or separately, receive support from different institutions. The forms of support are political and economic, and result through articulations or alliances. They may receive support and/or be linked to a pastoral of the Catholic Church (Pastoral Land Commission or the Rural Pastoral). Similarly, they may receive support from trade unions, political parties or non-governmental organizations. These are the institutions that have supported the struggle for land, principally the occupations.

An isolated movement is a social organization that is realized in a delimited territory, in a municipality or a small group of municipalities. It is defined by circumstances inherent to the movements; that is, they are born in different points of geographic space, in different struggles of resistance. These movements may receive support from one or more parishes, through pastorals, as well as from unions, parties, politicians and prefects, among others. They also may be the result of dissent within the socio-territorial movements. However, their territorial base of action is limited by the action of the movement. In the case in which this condition is overcome, the isolated movement may become territorialized, organizing actions beyond its original territorial base, or it may attach itself to an existing territorialized movement. It is in this way that recent land movements have developed.

Failing to overcome these circumstances, isolated movements are extinguished. The vision of territorialization is related to its form of socio-political organization. When the movements are the result of immediate community interests, defended by personalized leaders and populist practices that create relationships of dependency, the tendency is the exhaustion of the movement. When movements contemplate broader objectives that aim not only to resolve their own problems but to insert themselves in the broader process of struggle, and the leaders promote spaces of political socialization for the formation of new leaderships and experiences, the tendency is the development of the form of organization, spatialization and territorialization. In this manner, frequently, they work not only on their own problems but also carry forward the dimension of the struggle for land, organizing new groups of families, inaugurating new places, spatializing and territorializing the movement and the struggle. Every socio-territorial movement is born of one or more isolated social movements.

In this sense, it can be affirmed that the territorialized movements possess a political dimension that overcomes the limits of daily problems and issues of place. For a movement to territorialize, it must understand the logic of capitalist society, its inequalities and contradictions. Territorialization, in this case, means moving beyond, as much in terms of space as in terms of time, always with the perspective of the construction of a new reality.

The occupations realized by these movements may be developed by means of the following types of experience: spontaneous and isolated; organized and isolated; organized and spatialized. The experiences are always forms of struggle and resistance because they inaugurate a space in the struggle for land that is the encampment. In respect of the number of families involved, they may be in small or large groups.

The spontaneous and isolated occupations are conducted primarily by small groups in a singular action of survival when some families occupy an area without configuring a form of social organization. They enter the land in groups and then, of necessity, begin to constitute a social movement. The characteristic of spontaneity is located in the fact of not having a prior concern with the construction of a form of organization, which may occur in the process of occupation. These occupations may result in an isolated social movement.

The organized and isolated occupations are carried out by isolated social movements from one or more municipalities. The formation of small groups predominates, but massive occupations have also occurred. The families form the movement before occupying the land. They organize at the grassroots level, conducting various meetings until the action has been taken. These movements either end after the conquest of the land or transform themselves into territorialized movements. These two types of occupation are the product of the spatiality and territoriality of the land struggle.

These types differ from ocupations realized by territorialized movements that execute organized and spatialized occupations. These are experiences of struggle that result from experiences brought from other places. They are contained within a broader political project and can constitute part of the agenda of the struggle.

Spatialization implies the participation of workers who have already lived the experience of occupation in diverse places and regions, and as militants they spatialize these experiences, working with the organization of new occupations, territorializing the struggle and the movement in the conquest of new areas of territory. It is within this process that they are educated, in a constant remaking – what E.P. Thompson (1963) referred to as *making oneself* into a social movement – that is, constructing their spaces and their times, transforming their realities.

The experience of the occupation in the process of territorialization is an apprenticeship. It is in the construction of knowledge of the realities of the groups of families and referential struggles that they learn to make their own struggle. *Referential struggles* are those that they have been told about or that they have known. The socio-territorial movements, in their processes of formation, multiply their actions and begin to undertake various occupations in short intervals or simultaneously. In the meantime, during the negotiation process to establish settlements, they undertake new occupations, in a continuous spatialization and territorialization. Because of this, the interval, during which another struggle is born, is a very important period, intensifying the number of occupations, mobilizing and organizing more and more families.

In the development of direct action on the land, it is possible to define two types of occupation: *occupation of a delimited area* and *mass occupation*. The principal difference between the two is that the former consists in an occupation by small groups, or even larger ones, in a specified area of occupation, while in the latter, mobilization and organization have as a goal the settlement of all the landless families, occupying as many areas as necessary. In the first type, the occupation is realized with the objective of acquiring only the occupied land. Thus, the families are mobilized and organized to demand the occupied land. If there are more families than can be settled in that area, they begin a new action to gain access to another area. Each occupation results in the establishment of a settlement. The logic of the organization of the families is to mobilize according to the areas demanded. In the case of mass occupations, this logic changes. The landless overcome the constraints of a specific area, such that the meaning of the occupation is no longer merely the conquest of the area in question but the settlement of all families, possibly resulting in the establishment of various settlements. The principal criterion for the settlement of families is no longer the territorial limit, but instead the time and forms of struggle in which the families participate. Thus, as segments of territory are conquered, more families join with the groups of remaining families.

An occupation of a delimited area may transform into a mass occupation, not only as a result of the number of families that participate, but also by the unfolding of the struggle. This happens when, after winning access to the demanded land, they become aware of other groups of areas that can be demanded and also consider the possibility of joining diverse groups of families in the same occupation. Thus, it is important to point out that massification involves not only quantity but also quality. This is determined by the definition of the space of political socialization, principally by the strengthening of interactive space that occurs by means of diffusion of nuclei, sectors and commissions, as a way of strengthening the movement. In these spaces, the families begin to work more intensely on their needs and perspectives, such as food, health care, education and negotiation, among others.

With these practices, the landless meet with each other in movement. They overcome territorial bases and official borders. In the organization of mass occupations, families from various municipalities and from more than one state in border areas join together. In this manner, they break with parochialisms and other strategies based in interests that they see as impeding or making more difficult the development of the workers' struggle.[5] Thus, the criteria for selection of the families to be settled cannot remain restricted to the origins of the families. The people who make up the selection commissions need to consider among their criteria, in addition to those determined by the government,[6] the history of the struggle.

In the execution of the occupations, the landless may pursue different tactics on the land. There are cases in which they occupy a strip of land and begin negotiating, demanding the expropriation of the area. In other instances, they occupy the land, divide it into lots and begin to work. In yet others, they demarcate a single area and plant collectively. These practices are the result of the development of the organization of the landless. They are forms of resistance that assert the notion of land for work as opposed to land for exploitation.

The processes of spatialization and territorialization diminish and may end when the landless families conquer all of the *latifúndios* of one or more municipalities.[7] Thus is brought to a close what we call the cycle of occupations. This cycle begins with the first occupations and lasts as long as there exists land to be conquered.

Finally, it is important to note that, in the course of mobilization and spatialization, the landless combine other forms of struggle with that of the occupation, and pursue these separately or simultaneously. They include marches or demonstrations, occupations of public buildings, and protests in front of credit agencies. In this manner, the landless transform land and public spaces into political spaces from which to denounce exploitation and expropriation; these acts intensify the struggles and the relations with different government organs, and, equally, they expose the realities of the landless, receiving support and criticisms from the public and diverse sectors of society. The marches are especially important, in so far as they become pilgrimages with world-historical referents. Indeed, some of the referents incorporated into the *mística* (collective acts or rituals of meaning and identity production) of the movement include the migration of the Jewish people to the Promised Land, in the struggle against slavery in Egypt; the march of Gandhi and the Hindus to the sea, in the struggle against British imperialism; and the marches of the Mexican and Chinese revolutions, among others (Stédile and Fernandes 1999: 149–55).

The Encampments:
Spaces of Struggle and Resistance

To be encamped is to be landless. To be in an encampment is the result of decisions based upon desires and interests, objectifying the transformation of reality. The encamped are the landless who have as their objective becoming settled. These are two categories of an identity in formation.

The encampments are spaces and times of transition in the struggle for land. They are, consequently, realities in transformation. They are forms of materialization of the organization of the landless, and they embody the principal organizational elements of the movement. They are predominately the result of occupations, hence spaces of struggle and resistance, demarcating within the *latifúndios* the first moment of the process of territorialization of the struggle. The actions of occupation and encampment integrate processes of spatialization and territorialization. They may be located within a *latifúndio* or on the margins of a highway, according to the combination and correlation of political forces. They may be the first actions of the families, or they may be the repetition of this action. The encampment is the place of mobilization to pressure the government in the expropriation of lands, while it is also understood that encampment without occupying will only rarely result in the conquest of land. The occupation of the land is the trump card in the negotiations. Many of the encamped remain for years on the margins of highways without ever being settled. Only with the occupation have they achieved success in the struggle.

At first glance, the encampments appear to be disorganized groupings of shacks. However, they reveal certain arrangements according to the topography of the site, the conditions of the resistance to expulsion, and the prospect of confrontation with gunmen. They may be located in the bottom of valleys or on ridges. The arrangements of the encampments are predominantly circular or linear. There exist spaces where, often, the landless plant their gardens, establish a makeshift school and pharmacy, as well as a location for assemblies.

Upon organizing an encampment, the landless create a number of commissions or teams that give form to the organization. Either entire families or just some of their members participate, creating the basic conditions for meeting their necessities: health care, education, security, negotiation and work. In this manner, the encampments frequently have schools – that is, tarpaulin-covered shacks in which classes are held, principally for the first four years of primary education; they have a tent or shack that functions as an improvised pharmacy, and, when located in a *latifúndio*, they plant collectively in order to guarantee part of the foods they need. When on the side of a highway, they plant between the road and the fence. When next to settlements, the encamped work on the lots of the already settled, as daily wage labourers or in different forms of sharecropping. They also sell their labour as migrant workers to sugar or alcohol plants, or to ranchers, or to other capitalist enterprises.

During the 1980s, the encamped received food, clothing and medicine, principally from the communities and institutions supporting the struggle. At the end of the 1980s and the beginning of the 1990s, with the growth in activity, the settlements also began to contribute to the struggle in various ways. Many loaned trucks to aid the occupations, tractors for the preparation of the land, and food for the encamped population. This support is more significant when the settled families are working as a cooperative. This gives an indication of the organizational capacity of the MST. With the growth in support from communities, institutions and settlements, and with the consolidation of the MST, the landless have been able to intensify the number of occupations and develop the resistance so as to be able to carry out dozens of simultaneous occupations.

In the second half of the 1990s, in some states the MST began to experience what it called the 'permanent' or 'open' encampment. This encampment is established in a region where many *latifúndios* exist. It is a space of struggle and resistance where many families from diverse municipalities are directed and organized. From this permanent encampment, the landless leave for various occupations, where they may be able to settle, or from which they can return to the encampment, in the case of expulsion. Also, as they continue to gain title to land, they continue to mobilize and organize new families, which then make up the encampment.

The encampment is a place of constant mobilization. Apart from being a space of struggle and resistance, it is an interactive and communicative space. These three dimensions of the space of political socialization are developed differently in the encampments depending on the situation. At the beginning of the process of formation of the MST, in the 1980s, families would leave for an occupation only after months of grassroots preparation. During this period, the landless visited communities, related their experiences, provoked debate, and developed the space of political socialization in its communicative and interactive dimensions. This procedure made possible the establishment of a better organized space of struggle and resistance, since the families would become aware of the types of confrontation to be faced. Thus, in the process of formation, through the very demands of the struggle, the MST would construct other experiences and build foundations for further struggles.

In the encampment, the landless periodically analyse the political circumstances of the struggle. This political analysis is facilitated by the permanent contact of these territorialized movements with their coordinating offices, so that they are able to make analyses from the broader political situation, such as the negotiations taking place in the state capitals and in Brasília, or other organized protests including marches to cities and occupations of public buildings. Thus, they associate forms of local struggle with struggles in the capitals.

Through the correspondence between these spaces of activism in the countryside and the city, there is always a determination of one over the other. The local realities are very diverse, and the priorities of the families engaged in the struggle tend to predominate in the final decisions. Thus, the political lines of action are constructed from within these parameters. And the representative moments of the MST carry this spatiality and this logic, since members of the coordination or national directorate live this process from the encampment to the broader regional, state and national levels.

With these actions, which count on the support of political articulations, the landless seek to change circumstances in order to stimulate the process of negotiation. Nevertheless, they are not always able to change the situation. When negotiations reach an impasse, violent confrontations can take place, such as that which occurred in the Praça da Matriz in Porto Alegre and the massacre at Eldorado dos Carajás, in the state of Pará.[8]

All of the encampments have their history in the struggles of the landless families. It is worth highlighting at least two of the MST's historic encampments in the process of formation and territorialization: Encruzilhada Natalino, in Ronda Alta, Rio Grande do Sul; and the Capuchins, in Itamaraju, Bahia. These encampments suffered the most diverse forms of pressure from the government and the landlords, but persisted and succeeded in conquering the land. The value of resistance and perseverance is the main lesson learned in these two struggles. Today, they serve as reference points and examples of successful resistance. Guaranteeing the existence of the encampment by means of resistance, and impeding dispersal in the face of various forms of violence, are fundamental for the success of the struggle for land reform.

Saving the occupation, under threat of dispersal, is part of the logic of resistance. When an expulsion (*despejo*) takes place, the families transfer the encampment to other areas, such as the margins of highways to lands ceded by city governments or other institutions.[9] When they are expelled from the edges of highways, they set up encampments within nearby settlements. Saving the occupation entails guaranteeing a place for the encampment.

Sustaining the encampment is a form of pressure to demand the settlement. And this is a practice of the MST, to guarantee the encampment until all of the families are settled. For the other movements, this practice is not as permanent. Often the families negotiate a settlement with the government and, believing in its promises, return to their municipalities; consequently, the majority of settlements are not consolidated. Nor is it uncommon for many families that remain encamped to succumb eventually, for a number of reasons, but principally due to a lack of political direction and the violence of the expulsions and the gunmen.

The Occupation as a Form of Access to Land

In little more than two decades of struggle, the occupation has become an important form of access to land. Approximately 77 per cent of all settlements created between 1986 and 1997 in thirteen states across the Northeast, Central West, Southeast and South have their origins in land occupations (see Table 11.1).

The federal government claims to have settled hundreds of thousands of families, but the truth is that this resulted primarily from the pressure of land occupations. Between 1995 and 1999 specifically, 2,750 land reform settlements with 299,323 families were created, following 1,853 occupations with 256,467 families participating, amounting to 85 per cent of the total settled (Fernandes 2000). It is important to realize that part of what the government calls 'land reform settlements' consists, in fact, in the formal titling of the lands of the *posseiros*.

For the Northeast and Central West, the number of occupying families represents proportionally 84 per cent of the settled families. For the South and Southeast regions, they represent, respectively, 273 per cent and 175 per cent. That is, 45,845 families struggled for land in the South as the government settled 12,272. Of the 44,225 families that struggled for land in the Southeast, the settlements created benefited only 16,068 families. The greatest activity by the government occurred in the North, where it settled or regularized ownership of 98,657 families (Fernandes 2000).

According to Table 11.1, the state of Ceará is where the greatest number of government-created settlements are located. This is the result, in large part, of the policies of the state government and of the implementation of the Land Registration and Land Bank programmes. Yet these data do not have the same correspondence in the states of Pernambuco and Minas Gerais, where such projects have also been implemented. It is notable, moreover, that in the states of

Table 11.1 Number of settlements according to origin, 1986–97

State[*]	Land occupation	Government project	Unknown
Alagoas	21	7	6
Ceará	92	89	4
Espírito Santo	32	3	0
Goiás	63	23	31
Mato Grosso do Sul	22	25	7
Minas Gerais	80	16	0
Paraná	158	22	4
Pernambuco	106	22	0
Rio de Janeiro	45	3	0
Rio Grande do Sul	159	0	0
Santa Catarina	94	6	2
São Paulo	79	4	0
Sergipe	28	12	0

[*] The main states in which the MST is organized.

Source: Dataluta 1998.

the South and Southeast, where 24 per cent of the total settlements created up to June 1999 are located, approximately 92 per cent of the settlements originated in land occupations.

It has been the struggle for land that has stimulated the rural settlement policies of the federal government. And it is for this reason that we ask, what agrarian reform? To call this reality 'agrarian reform' is to interpret it in the language of the state and the dominant classes that it serves (Fernandes 1998).

As demonstrated, the agrarian question in Brazil will remain unresolved as long as it is treated with compensatory policies. The struggle for democratization of access to land has been growing, while the land tenure structure has remained concentrated and the number of landless has increased, mainly due to the growth of unemployment. According to recent studies (Gasques and Conceição 1999), based on the 1995/1996 Agricultural Census, the potential public for agrarian reform – including small farmers (on sub-family plots), renters, contract farmers, occupants and wage workers – amounts to as much as 4.5 million families. From these data, it is estimated that the area needed for settlement, based on a family-sized landholding, is approximately 160 million hectares. From 1979 to June 1999, 475,801 families were settled. This is the equivalent of 10.5 per cent of the potential constituency and 14 per cent of the area. Without the implementation of a policy of agrarian reform that speeds up this process, the struggle for land will continue to develop through the actions of landless families.

The Reaction of the Cardoso Government

Government policies have been tied to the actions of peasant movements. Although the Cardoso government implemented a policy of rural settlements, in fact it has not been able to stem the increase in land occupations. In terms of confrontation, the government understood that it would not be able to overcome the conditions of conflict constructed by the processes of spatialization and territorialization of the struggle, and thus concluded that it was necessary to formulate policies that would impede the expansion of these processes.

Yet, during the 1990s, with the advancement of neoliberal policies and, consequently, structural unemployment, the land occupations have intensified, rising from 11,000 families in 1991 to 79,000 families in 1999. Thus the struggle for land has grown, and unemployed urban workers have begun to participate as well. They are, in large part, families that were expelled from the land in recent decades and are now without prospects of employment in the city. They see in the rural settlements the conditions for a dignified life.

The government has always treated the agrarian question with compensatory policies, creating settlements on the heels of land occupations of *latifúndios*. Since 1997, through agreements with the World Bank, the government has created policies, known as Land Registration and the Land Bank, intended to establish a market-based land reform framework (see Mattei, Chapter 12 this volume). It has also created 'agrarian reform through the post office' – whereby the landless register at the post office and wait for a response from the government – in an effort to demobilize social movements and end their grassroots organization and occupations. Nevertheless, these policies have not been sufficient to deconcentrate the land tenure structure. In reality, what we are witnessing is a process of creation of rural settlements coterminous with the intensification of land tenure concentration, as can be observed in the agricultural census (IBGE 2000). In an attempt to impede further the growth of land occupations, the government has also created provisional decrees to criminalize the landless, refusing to acquire occupied lands for a period of two years, and denying settlement to families that participate in occupations.

This policy has made the landowning and capitalist classes stronger since it attempts to end occupations by means of criminalization, with the struggle for agrarian reform being pushed further into the judicial branch of government (Fernandes 1997). Also, in part, the government has moved to relieve itself of its responsibility for land reform by commercializing the land question, via the Land Bank, to the benefit of landlords, who gain greater bargaining power over workers, and who now receive money up front. In this sense, the government has created an enormous inequity in political negotiations, since the market becomes the formal condition for access to land instead of the actions of workers and the intervention of the state. This process of settlement – whose basic features are land occupations, the formalization of tenure on the settlers' lands, and the purchase of land through the Land Bank – is called 'agrarian reform' by the government and the scientists that constitute part of its intelligentsia.

Just as the government appropriates concepts for itself and attempts to transfigure them, it also tries to dominate political spaces, such as in the process of public policymaking. In this space, many confrontations take place between the government and the MST. Logically, the landless seek to participate in the entire process of policymaking. Thus the policies generated by the government in any aspect of the development of the settlements are important spaces to be occupied. This means working to advance principles, to struggle and to construct new experiences. The challenge to the government is to impede the landless from participating in this way. Its objective is to ensure that its programme is not politically appropriated by the MST. For this reason, the government ended PROCERA (Programa Especial de Crédito para a Reforma Agrária), a special credit programme for agrarian reform, and Lumiar (Programa de Assistência Técnica), a technical assistance programme, which were strengthening the cause of the workers. In the absence of any alternative proposal, millions of farmers were left without technical assistance.

The objective of the government is to control the struggle of rural workers, confining it to a determined political space, *the space of capital*. The strategic action of the government is to destroy the values of the historical institution that is the peasantry. The theses developed by the government intelligentsia, which propose the sub-servient integration of the peasantry into capital, contribute to this destruction. Thus the expropriation of rural workers is a consequence not only of the unequal logic of capital but also of the theories that enable the elaboration of policies to activitate this process. With these policies, the government becomes the main adversary of the MST.

In this confrontation between the government and the MST, rural conflicts have intensified. This conflict takes a particular form. In 2000 alone, the MST was involved in approximately 180 trials, and ten of its organizers were killed. In terms of qualitative analysis, it is evident that violence in the Brazilian countryside is centred on those who struggle for land and challenge the project of the government. This effectively reduced the number of occupations, a situation of which the government has been proud. But it is important to point out that the reduction in occupations is related to the intensification of different forms of violence and the criminalization of the landless within the closing circle of judicialization.

The struggle against capital by means of land occupation is a form of resistance for the peasantry. In order to break this resistence, the government attempts to resolve the agrarian question exactly on the terrain of the enemy: the territory of capital. It thus attempts to destroy the forms of struggle waged by the landless by engaging in the political dimension of the struggle for land. This involves a political exclusion that may result in the intensification of the struggle, or the suppression of social movements in the countryside, which may weaken or eliminate the organization of rural workers. This places in question, once again, the resistance of the peasant move-ments. At various moments in Brazil's history, the government and the elite have pursued strategies to destroy the peasant movement. This is what happened at Canudos and with the Peasant Leagues (da Cunha 2002), and it is what is happening at the present time. The peasantry is accepted so long as it remains subservient.

These new elements of the agrarian question place challenges before us. There is still a lack of adequate research and analysis of the problems and impasses that have been recently generated. It is now twenty years since the Encruzilhada do Natalino occupation, when the MST was still in gestation (Fernandes 2000). In the resistance that resulted in the breaching of the fence of Coronel Curió, accomplice to General Figueiredo, is to be found the meaning of the peasant struggle. From this resistance, experiences and lessons will be harvested that will allow the breaching of the new fences that are being built today.

Translated by Malcolm K. McNee

Notes

1. The Brazilian Constitution defines 'social function' through a group of criteria that the rural properties need to meet: rational use, environmental preservation, respect for labour laws, and production and employment.

2. A *posseiro* is a peasant who possesses land but does not own it. In order to be a landowner, it is necessary to have possession and dominion, through a property title known in Brazil as *escritura*.

3. Lands forfeited or grabbed with no legal claim: large areas of land owned by the state which have been appropriated by businesspeople by means of false documents.

4. By labour movement here is meant an institution that is recognized officially by the state and conforms to the state laws and criteria pertaining to registered organizations. Social movements are popular organizations that have a structure independent of the state.

5. One such impediment, for example, is Decree 35.852 of the Government of the State of São Paulo: Article 1 determines that families not residing at least two years in the region cannot be settled.

6. The criteria determined by the government are: to be a rural worker, not be a landowner or a public functionary.

7. Rare examples are the municipalities of Mirante do Paranapanema (SP), Ronda Alta (RS), and Pontão (RS), where the landless conquered the majority of the *latifúndios*.

8. In Praça da Matriz, a police officer was killed in confrontation with the landless; in the massacre of Eldorado dos Carajás, nineteen landless were murdered in a confrontation with the police.

9. *Despejo* also means to free oneself from impediments, such as the treatment of people as objects, rather victims of violence, and the relegation of the struggle for land to the power of the judiciary and the 'rule of law' (Fernandes 1997; Moreyra 1998).

References

Constituição da República Federativa do Brasil (1990), Brasília: Senado Federal.

da Cunha, Euclides (2002), *Os Sertões*, São Paulo: Abril Cultural.

de Oliveira, Ariovaldo Umbelino (1991), *A agricultura camponesa no Brasil*, São Paulo: Contexto.

Dataluta (1998), *Banco de Dados da Luta pela Terra: Relatório das Ocupações de Terra, 1998*, Presidente Prudente: Dataluta.

Fernandes, Bernardo Mançano (1996), *MST: Formação e Territorialização*, São Paulo: Hucitec.

Fernandes, Bernardo Mançano (1997), 'A Judiciarização da Luta pela Reforma Agrária', in *GEOUSP–Revista de Pós-graduação em Geografia*, São Paulo: Departamento de Geografia da FFLCH-USP.

Fernandes, Bernardo Mançano (1998), 'Que Reforma Agrária?', in *A Questão Agrária na Virada do Século*, Volume II, *Mesas Redondas*, XIV Encontro Nacional de Geografia Agrária, Presidente Prudente.

Fernandes, Bernardo Mançano (2000), *A Formação do MST no Brasil*, Petrópolis: Vozes.

Gasques, José Garcia, and Júnia Cristina P.R. da Conceição (1999), *A Demanda de Terra para Reforma Agrária no Brasil*, Rio de Janeiro: www.dataterra.org.br.

Hobsbawm, Eric (1998), *Pessoas Extraordinárias*, São Paulo: Paz e Terra.

IBGE, Instituto Brasileiro de Geografia e Estatística (2000), *Censo Agropecuário, 1995–96*, Rio de Janeiro: IBGE.

Kautsky, Karl (1986), *A Questão Agrária*, São Paulo: Nova Cultural.

Lenin, Vladimir Ilyich (1985), *O Desenvolvimento do Capitalismo na Rússia*, São Paulo: Nova Cultural.

Martins, José de Souza (1981), *Os Camponeses e a Política no Brasil*, Petrópolis: Vozes.

Moreyra, Sérgio Paulo (1998), 'As Novas Caras da Violência no Campo Brasileiro', in *Conflitos no campo–Brasil 97*, Goiânia: CPT.

Stédile, João Pedro and Bernardo Mançano Fernandes (1999), *Brava Gente: a Trajetória do MST e a Luta pela Terra no Brasil*, São Paulo: Fundação Perseu Abramo.

Thompson, Edward P. (1963), *The Making of the English Working Class*, London: Penguin.

12

Agrarian Reform in Brazil under Neoliberalism: Evaluation and Perspectives

Lauro Mattei

The issue of land ownership in Brazil has animated the national political debate from the beginning of the colonization process, through the several economic cycles (mining, rubber, sugar and coffee) to the present. However, the question became more urgent in the postwar period with the implementation of agricultural 'modernization', based on two pillars: the concentration of land and the social exclusion of peasants. This process has caused deep transformations in the agricultural sector and brought with it adverse environmental and social consequences, primarily due to the enormous population displacement that it set into motion. Contemporary social conflicts are directly related to the Brazilian model of agricultural development.

This chapter assesses agrarian reform experience under neoliberalism, and specifically under the two-term government of F.H. Cardoso, from 1995 to 2002. It begins with a brief historical overview before proceeding to address the contemporary debates on the agrarian question and to evaluate the recent period of reforms.

Historical Overview of Land Policies and Reforms

There have been three historical moments in which the role of land has been decisive in the formation of the political economy of Brazil. The first was 1850, when private ownership of land was established through the Land Law (Lei das Terras), thus preventing a large part of the rural population from having access to land. The second moment ran through the second and third decades of the last century, when the Tenants' Movement (Movimento Tenentista) challenged the existence of large and unproductive tracts of land (*latifúndios*) and introduced the first debates about the need to reform the agrarian structure of the country. The third phase began in the postwar years with the emergence of the Peasant Leagues (Ligas Camponesas) and has continued, more recently, with the rise of the Landless Workers' Movement, or MST (Movimento dos Trabalhadores Rurais Sem Terra). Such movements have elevated the status of the peasantry as one of the most important social actors in the country and affirmed agrarian reform as a crucial means of transforming Brazilian society.

In the early postwar period, demands for agrarian reform were routinely repressed, while the land reform wave that swept through Latin America in the 1960s did not impact on Brazil. With the installation of military rule in 1964, the several military governments that followed until 1985 did not implement significant land distribution programmes. Their only plan was to establish the unsuccessful Agricultural Colonization Project (Colonização Agrícola), whose strategy – to settle all the borders of the country – was more concerned with national security than with transformation of Brazil's agrarian structure.

The 're-democratization' period, beginning in 1985, established a new constitution with commitments to agrarian reform; this created strong expectations and invigorated the rural segments of society. The New Republic government (1985–89) promulgated the First National Plan of Agrarian Reform, setting an initial goal to settle 1.4 million families in a five-year period. But at the end of that period only 85,000 families of rural workers had been settled, while the rural exodus had increased significantly. With the election of Collor de Mello's government in 1990, the stated target of resettlement was reduced to 500,000 families. Moreover, it abolished the Ministry of Agrarian Reform and soon committed the Brazilian economy to a neoliberal political agenda. As a result, up to the moment of Collor de Mello's impeachment in 1992, the programme to settle rural families remained untouched. For this reason there was neither expropriation of land for agrarian reform nor the settlement of rural families. De Mello's actions in this area were actually limited to the regularization of old settlements. Thereafter, Itamar Franco, de Mello's vice-president, assumed the presidency to complete the mandate term (1993–94). In this period, an emergency programme of agrarian reform was formulated. This programme planned to settle 80,000 rural families, but by the end of 1994 only some 150 settlement projects had been undertaken, which benefited no more than 23,000 families.

Fernando Henrique Cardoso was elected to the presidency at the end of 1994 for a period of four years and was re-elected in 1998 for a second term, having amended the constitution to allow for the possibility of re-election. Cardoso's government proceeded to define the agrarian question not only in economic but also in social and moral terms. Thus its resolution would depend on the integration of efforts between government and civil society, and reforms would be accompanied by other social programmes, such as professional development and income generation. Moreover, agrarian reform was to be complemented by several other types of action, including revision of the legislation for land expropriation, redefinition of the taxes on property, urbanization of rural areas, an increase in technical support programmes, and improvement of the rural infrastructure network. Hence, in Cardoso's first term agrarian reform policy was a matter of substituting the old agrarian question with a more modern and articulated set of public policies. The commitments assumed by Cardoso's government regarding land distribution took the form of annual goals: 40,000 families in 1995, 60,000 in 1996, 80,000 in 1997, and 100,000 in 1998. Thus, during his first four-year mandate, 280,000 rural families should have been settled, although this was an extremely modest goal if we take into consideration the state of the country's agrarian situation. In Cardoso's second mandate (1998–2002), the exercise of goal-setting was replaced by loose statements on a 'new' agrarian reform. In essence, this meant the continuation of the programme of the previous mandate, plus the signalling of market-based reform, which was to coexist with the constitutionally established principle of land expropriation. The Land Bill (Cédula da Terra) and the Land Bank (Banco da Terra) were thereby set into motion.

Before we assess the agrarian reform under Cardoso's eight-year government, we turn to the question of whether agrarian reform is still relevant in Brazil, given the extent of urbanization and the development of the agro-industrial sector.

Is There Still an Agrarian Question in Brazil?

In the early postwar decades an intense debate took place on the role of agriculture in the country's economic development, in which the issue of agrarian reform assumed a special place. The debate was led by national figures, including Celso Furtado, Caio Prado Júnior, Ignácio Rangel, and Alberto Passos Guimarães, who conceptually connected agrarian modernization with rural poverty and population dynamics.

Specifically, Furtado (1972) connected the concentration of land in the countryside with the maintenance of low wages and, moreover, argued that low wages were a barrier to technical progress and also that they perpetuated an agricultural model with high social costs, which in turn demanded high expenditures of the country's resources. Furtado affirmed that the redistribution of uncultivated estates in Brazil were above all a political problem, since their main function was to obstruct rural workers from having access to land. Prado Júnior (1979) made similar connections, demonstrating that the miserable living and working conditions of the rural population derived from low wages, as well as from the absence of labour legislation to benefit rural workers. He recommended a dual agrarian reform policy of deconcentrating land ownership and regulating labour relations in the large farming areas. Guimarães (1982), in turn, argued that the monopoly of land was responsible for the late industrialization of the country and recommended a land reform that abolished non-productive farming. Finally, Rangel (2000) pointed out that the disentanglement of the traditional rural complex in Brazil had entailed an industrialization process that could not absorb the reallocated labour force. Together these authors agreed that agrarian reform should have two goals: to dismantle the ownership of large uncultivated estates and to regulate work relationships in the large farming areas. They also agreed that the obstacle to industrialization was the absence of agrarian reform, which prevented the development of the internal market for wage goods, including food.

After the onset of the deep economic, social and political changes associated with modernization, new issues appeared regarding the role of agrarian reform in contemporary society. The workers, both rural and urban, broke with past traditions and incorporated new values into their historical struggles. At the same time, agriculture lost its artisanal character, giving way to a progressive technical specialization in production, which radically altered the traditional production methods, as well as labour relations. This passage was marked by the concentration of land ownership, the alienation of land from the peasantry (which lacked the resources for technological improvements on its own land), and its migration to urban centres in search of economic alternatives.

As is widely known, agricultural modernization did not become a hindrance to Brazil's industrialization, either in terms of food production or in the primary goods sector. In fact, agriculture was central to the consolidation of a set of inter-sectoral economic relations which were capable of connecting the country into the global production circuit. According to Graziano da Silva (1990), this was possible because market expansion in the developing capitalist economies did not occur exclusively due to the rise in consumption of final goods, but through the growth of the intermediate goods market, which was necessary to sustain the industrialization process. On the other hand, the non-consolidation of a mass consumption market internally had severe social consequences, characterized by high levels of social exclusion. In this regard, the classic agrarian reform proposals might have changed not only the course of Brazilian history but also the history of all Latin America, by means of democratizing the ownership of land, opening up the means of income, and reducing the gap between the social classes. More recently, though, the economic policies and crises of the 1980s and 1990s seemed only to have deepened the social gap, with direct repercussions on the least capitalized segments of Brazilian agriculture and an acceleration in rural displacement to the burgeoning urban centres.

Thus the agrarian question reappears in the national debate at a critical moment, and with strongly polarized protagonists. In 1988 a new federal constitution was established, marking the post-dictatorship transition. This retained a conservative order, and even reversed elements of the Land Law of 1964 by placing limits on the land acquisition process. This resulted from a fierce dispute and misunderstanding in the course of the constitution-making process, during which the landed oligarchy prevailed. At that moment, the Rural Democratic Union (UDR) constituted itself, with the objective of defending the interests of large-scale farmers and preventing the realization of agrarian reform. The UDR constituted itself into a bloc with enormous economic and political power, counting among its members almost half of the national congress, a situation that pertained until the end of the 1990s. Once again the country missed an opportunity to set in motion a lasting solution to the agrarian problem.

Set against these landed interests, the MST emerged with the purpose of mobilizing rural workers and reigniting the agrarian reform struggle. In less than twenty years, the MST transformed itself into one of the major social movements in the country, owing to its organizational capacity and its commitment to the less privileged layers of the population, acting in rural areas as well as urban centres. The social power of the MST lies in the hope it provides to millions of excluded for a change in their living conditions. This is articulated through systematic advocacy of agrarian reform, combined with other social demands, and is expressed most symbolically by the collective occupation of unproductive farmlands. Through occupations, the MST has intensified the resistance of landless rural workers and ensured that the agrarian question has remained on the political agenda.

The question that is debated today is fundamentally provocative due to the way in which it is framed. Does Brazil still need to institute agrarian reform? Is agrarian reform still a pertinent issue for Brazilian society at the beginning of the twenty-first century? It is obvious that if we accept the existence of 'the agrarian problem', then the answer is affirmative: agrarian reform is a decisive and effective factor in changing rural political power, which imposes itself through land proprietorship. To admit there is an agrarian problem is to believe in only one way of solving it: alter the agrarian structure through an extended agrarian reform programme, which consists mainly of destroying the power of the traditional agrarian oligarchies, as well as reordering the production model controlled by the large agro-industrial corporate network. For the rural workers' organizations, the answer to the question as to whether an 'agrarian problem' exists is demonstrated in their different forms of struggle, land occupations, organization of settlements, and the redefinition of production systems. Nevertheless, it must be recognized that even among the rural workers agrarian reform is no longer their exclusive demand, as it was it in previous decades.

The controversy over this question is no less heated in the academy, where several groups of social scientists claim that agrarian reform has ceased to be a national demand and a decisive instrument capable of changing the historical destiny of Brazil (Navarro 2002). Thus, they argue, the 'agrarian question' has lost its central position in the national development debate. To a large extent, these arguments are based on the diagnosis that: (a) there is a wide regional productive differentiation; (b) there has been a reduction in the role of agriculture in the national economy; (c) the current agricultural model is able to satisfy the demands for food and raw materials; and (d) there is an onging urbanization of rural life. The conclusion is that support should be given to a regional agrarian reform (in areas with agrarian conflict) that is capable of responding immediately to local land problems.

Another group of researchers has recently begun to promote an agrarian reform of a 'social' rather than 'economic' nature (Graziano da Silva 2001). They believe reform should create jobs and reduce migratory flows from rural to urban areas. In this case, the role of agrarian reform would be to help equalize the country's population problem until the demographic transition that began in the last decade is completed. In order for this to happen, the policies of an agrarian programme should be oriented less towards production and more towards alleviating the poverty of those rural people who are not involved exclusively in agricultural activities.

The argument defended in this chapter maintains that so long as Brazil has more than 90 million hectares of unproductive land and more than 4 million landless rural families, together with the fact that it has alarming indices of economic and social inequality, we cannot withdraw the instrument of agrarian reform, precisely the instrument which has been so effectively used historically in many of the countries that today are considered 'developed'. Therefore, the character of agrarian reform – whether large-scale, social or economic – as well as the necessary instruments to carry it out must continue to be widely discussed. However, we must keep in mind that agrarian reform is fundamentally of a political nature. While the landed property bloc persists, the poverty levels of the rural population will be kept high, the rural job market will continue to be extremely scant, and rural social conflicts will continue to intensify. These problems, in turn, will continue to find urban expression, aggravating the urban social panorama of misery and poverty. The main challenge consists in building the social, economic and political conditions such that all the segments of rural workers are able to benefit from agrarian reform; it also consists in building an alliance with urban forces against the powerful interest groups which do not admit to the need for changes to the status quo.

Agrarian Reform under Cardoso's Government

The controversy over Cardoso's agrarian reform figures

Cardoso's government, in its first four-year mandate, committed itself to land distribution through the setting of annual goals, amounting to a total of 280,000 families between 1995 and 1998. This was an extremely modest goal, taking into account the extent of landlessness in the country. In the second four-year term, Cardoso's government did not present goals for settling families, but instead proclaimed a vague 'new' agrarian reform programme.

Over these eight years, Brazilians became accustomed to an extremely positive daily discourse from the government in relation to its record on agrarian reform. Let us consider two classic examples:

> Brazil is accomplishing the world's largest agrarian reform in progress. In less than four years, FHC's administration distributed more than 8 million hectares of land and settled about 300,000 peasant families.[1]

> Which administration has done more than ours for agrarian reform? Three hundred thousand settled families. If you add everything – I repeat – if you add everything that was done in Brazil, you do not reach this figure. In four years we have done more than has been done in the whole history of our country.[2]

The official data released by the government throughout the eight years are displayed in Table 12.1. We observe that, during the second mandate, a reduction occurred in the official numbers, in terms of both settled families and the land area aquired.

Not all that glitters is gold. In the last months of Cardoso's government, the Brazilian people became aware of a big controversy regarding the veracity of the government's agrarian policy. According to a series of articles in *Folha de São Paulo* (the highest selling newspaper in the country), 'the federal government is increasing the agrarian reform's numbers by using settlement projects that have never occurred, in addition to empty land and areas where there are no houses and not even basic infrastructure for the rural workers such as water, electricity and the sewerage system' (*FSP*, 21 April 2002).

Besides the press, the Institute of Applied Economic Research (IPEA, the government organ responsible for planning) carried out an evaluation study of resettlement for the years 1999 and 2000 (IPEA 2001). The conclusion was much more emphatic, since it was able to prove the fraud technically. In 1999, only 53,197 families

Table 12.1 Families settled by Cardoso's government (official figure)

Year	Government goal	Settled families	Area (1,000 ha)
1995	40,000	42,912	1,313
1996	60,000	62,044	4,451
1997	80,000	81,944	4,394
1998	100,000	101,094	2,540
Subtotal	**280,000**	**287,994**	**12,698**
1999	–	85,226	1,478
2000	–	108,986	3,861
2001	–	63,477	1,336
Total		**545,683**	**19,373**

Sources: MDA (Ministry of Agrarian Development) and INCRA (National Institute of Agrarian Reform).

were settled, which means a figure 38 per cent lower than the one published by the government. In 2000, the difference was still larger since only 36,061 families were settled. These differences led the study to conclude that the data of Cardoso's administration concerning the agrarian reform programme possess little reliability.

New studies subsequently emerged to corroborate the fraud. Table 12.2 compares the data published by government with the information that circulates among the representative entities of civil society, including social movements, non-governmental agencies, academic study centres, and even some government organs. The data relate to the number of families effectively settled, and corroborate that there has indeed been an extensive embellishment in the information published by the Ministry of Agrarian Development.

The data released by INCRA, the government organ responsible for the execution of agrarian reform, was produced by the National Commission of Control and Monitoring of agrarian reform, which was created to control government actions in all states of the federation. The first results of the commission showed that the data that were regularly being published by the Ministry and by the president himself were not reliable. After a meticulous analysis of the agrarian

Table 12.2   Comparison of data on total number of families settled, 1995–2001

Year	Government	INCRA	ABRA
1995	42,912	33,312	40,993
1996	62,044	19,800	18,558
1997	81,944	60,425	59,501
1998	101,094	76,027	76,027
1999	85,226	56,000	14,218
2000	108,986	39,000	24,735
2001	63,477	33,269	32,966
Total	545,683	317,833	266,998

Sources: Government data: Ministry of Agrarian Development (MDA); INCRA data: INCRA's National Commission of Control and Monitoring; ABRA data: Brazilian Association of Agrarian Reform.

reform projects carried out since 1995, the Commission concluded that the 'settlement capacity' for the period 1995–2001 was about 317,000 families, which indicates a difference of almost 228,000 families from the official numbers.

The results obtained in a study by ABRA (Brazilian Association of Agrarian Reform), which carried out a rigorous analysis of INCRA's annual reports, are even more damning.[3] In determining the exact resettlement numbers, ABRA excluded from the official numbers (a) those families that had already been settled and whose projects had only been recently regularized; (b) the families of the old projects that benefited from some type of governmental action in the relevant period; and (c) the families that were in the government's plan but were never actually settled. The analysis revealed that the larger part of what the government calculated as 'settled' families actually referred to: actions by government to regularize properties; the regularization of constructions and services provided by the government for old settlements; and the regularization of properties that might have been used in the future to settle rural workers. The conclusion is that Cardoso's agrarian reform did not reach even 50 per cent of the published numbers.

The same disparity appears also when one analyses the total physical area that was acquired by the government for agrarian reform, according to ABRA (2002). In this case, the discrepancies become even larger with the onset (after 1998) of market mechanisms for land. We observe an approximately 60 per cent difference between the official propaganda and the real numbers. The explanation for this massive difference lies in the fact that the government included in its data the estates – especially in the Amazon area – that already belonged to the federal government but that were reallocated for agrarian reform programmes.

Agrarian reform through market mechanisms

The World Bank began to support pilot projects financially to demonstrate the efficiency of market mechanisms in land reform. In the 1990s, several countries from Latin America and Africa received a considerable amount of resources towards the financing of these market mechanisms. In promoting market-assisted reform, the World Bank claimed that the main advantages would be as follows: the land market would be stimulated and strengthened; the state bureaucracy would be replaced by more nimble mechanisms; agrarian reform would be decentralized; the costs of reform would be reduced; and agrarian conflicts would themselves decline. These points still require comparative analysis among all those countries that have adopted the programmes. The first results from the specific case of Brazil seem not to confirm the optimistic projections of the Bank.

In Brazil, the first steps towards market-based reform began in 1996, when Cardoso's government established a partnership with the World Bank to implement a pilot called 'The Land Reform and Poverty Alleviation Pilot Project'. This project, which became known as the 'Land Bill' (Cédula da Terra), was implemented from 1997 in five federal states (Ceará, Maranhão, Pernambuco, Bahia and Minas Gerais). Its operational method was to extend a credit line to the agriculturist who had little or no land and who wanted to acquire plots of land in an associative form. In terms of goals, the idea was to settle 15,000 families in a four-year period, at a cost of US$150 million. Of this amount, the World Bank extended US$90 million and the Brazilian government the remainder. The financing terms included a three-year interest-free period and thereafter a twenty-year repayment period at an interest rate of 4 per cent per annum.

At the end of 2000, the World Bank approved a new loan of US$200 million to expand the project to another fifteen states, under the so-called 'Land-based Poverty Alleviation Project I'. On the basis of this new loan, the government created two new sets of 'agrarian' policies to operate in parallel with the Land Bill: the Land Bank (Banco da Terra) in 2000, consisting of the same characteristics as the previous programme but now extending operations to the whole country; and the Credit Fund (Crédito Fundiário) in 2001, a programme of rural credit for settled families with the express purpose of combating rural poverty. The government justified these programmes as a means to accelerate the agrarian reform process and make it less onerous on the fiscal resources of the state. Moreover, these market mechanisms were presented as capable of delivering land without social conflicts and judicial disputes, and as auxiliary instruments in the reduction of rural poverty.

Given the fact that these are recent programmes and that they are still being implemented, there are as yet few evaluations, except in the case of the first phase of the Land Bill. While we do not intend to express a more conclusive opinion about the new programmes, we summarize the recent assessment of the Land Bill, conducted in 2001 by the Fórum Nacional de Reforma Agrária e Justiça no Campo, an entity that encompasses several social movements, political parties and NGOs (Sauer 2001, 2002). This study evaluated sixteen areas covered by the programme in five states, with the objective of establishing whether the goals of that programme were being met, as well as eliciting the opinions of the settled families themselves about their life conditions. Although the families evaluated positively the fact that they possessed a plot of residential land, there was a high level of dissatisfaction with the programme. In general, this dissatisfaction has been related to the non-disbursement of the promised resources for production and for basic infrastructure (water, highways, schools, health centres, and electric power), as well as to the lack of technical support for the implementation of agricultural activities. To a certain extent, one can say that these factors are influencing the families to leave. In some cases, the study verified that about 60 per cent of the families had abandoned the settlement areas.

In addition, the study concluded that due to the scarce availability of resources for each family – the total for each being US$11,000 for the purchase of land and the construction of all necessary in-frastructure, including home construction, machinery acquisition, etc. – the areas acquired by them have usually been of low quality and with serious limitations for the development of agricultural activities. These aspects will certainly have a negative impact on the capacity of the newly settled families to pay their debts. In addition to that, the research verified that the families exercise little influence on land choice, since the government organs responsible for the programme usually do the choosing. To a considerable extent, this happens because the rural workers are unaware of the rules of the project, namely the interest rate and the annual interest that they need to pay (which should have started to be paid in the period that the study was conducted).

Finally, the study observed that the productive activities of the families do not generate enough income to guarantee their survival. Many of them, therefore, are forced to work outside the settlement area (e.g. housekeeping, stonemasonry, etc.). For this reason the interviewees affirmed that it would be difficult for them to honour their commitments, despite their willingness to pay their debts. These facts, combined with the weak contribution of market-based land acquisitions to total land acquisitions, lead to the early conclusion that the attempt to carry out a 'new agrarian reform' is failing.

Neoliberalism versus Agrarian Reform

The liberalization process of the last two decades has disarticulated the economic basis that had sustained import-substitution industrialization over the earlier decades, placing the country in a regressive economic path. The indiscriminate commercial opening up to international competition affected hundreds of sectors, with negative impacts on employment levels and general income. Indeed, the 1990s evinced the highest unemployment rates in the history of the country. The impact of liberalization was immediately felt on the agrarian sector as well, where expenditures were cut and the sector was restructured to improve productivity and competitiveness in external markets. Besides the negative consequences intrinsic to this process, as we will see, this market opening up occurred in an extremely protectionist global agricultural market, which in turn had further negative consequences for several Brazilian products, including wheat, cotton, corn and rice. Meanwhile, the ability of the sector to respond to these challenges was diminished by the withdrawal of state support in the 1990s.

The withdrawal of state support has been evident in many facets of the economy, including in the total volume of rural credit resources. In the past decade, a strong reduction in the provision of public money has occurred, as the state has left the task of motivating and financing agricultural production to the market. At the same time, the prices of agricultural products that are paid to agriculturalists have ranged at very low levels compared to the cost of the products used in the production process. These facts have contributed to the reduction of the income of the agricultural sector. The restructuring of priorities has been no less evident in the proportion of resources expended on debt servicing (internal and external). In 1999, for example, the government spent around R$80 billion on the payment of interest, which amounted to seventy times the resources destined for agrarian programmes. The outcome of this policy is reflected in the worsening of some indicators, as we see below.

In agrarian societies like Brazil, the distribution of land is one of the fundamental indicators measuring whether a society has a democratic character or not. Thus, in Brazil, we note that the concentration of land ownership increased sharply during the agricultural modernization process and continues to be extremely unequal today. According to official statistical data, the Gini coefficient[4] reached its highest value in 1975, with a level of 0.87. At the beginning of 1980, this value had retreated to 0.82 and by 1995 it was about 0.81. These indicators give Brazil another world title: a country with one of the biggest land concentration indexes in the world.

Several analysis have indicated the same problem. The work of Hoffmann (1998), which is based on INCRA's cadastral data, shows that since the 1990s Brazil's land concentration problem has become worse, as we can see in Table 12.3. The data indicate that during the 1990s the land concentration process continued to grow in Brazil. Only in one area (centre-east) has the Gini index remained more or less stable. In all the other areas there were substantial increases, thus indicating that the effects of neoliberalism on agrarian reform have been negative. Further evidence shows that the number of farmers who possessed more than 2,000 hectares of land increased from about 19,000 in 1992 to more than 27,000 in 1998. This sector now holds approximately 43 per cent of all the land in Brazil, while the other group, which is constituted by more than 1 million small farming families, with land of less than 10 hectares, owns about 2 per cent of the land (IBGE 1998). Perhaps the most damning evidence of

Table 12.3 Agricultural land distribution, 1992–98

Region	Gini coefficient	
	1992	1998
South	0.705	0.712
Southeast	0.749	0.757
Northeast	0.792	0.811
North	0.849	0.851
Centre-east	0.811	0.810
Brazil	0.831	0.843

Source: Hoffmann 1998.

all, provided by the Brazilian Geographical and Statistical Institute (IBGE), is that between 1995 and 1998, 450,000 rural properties disappeared. If we compare this with the approximately 200,000 families resettled in those four years, we arrive at the conclusion that more than twice as many families lost land as gained land through resettlement. The IBGE also observes that in the same period as many as 1 million agricultural jobs were cut, as the structural transformation of the agricultural sector continued to shed labour.

This is the paradox of the Brazilian agrarian question today. On the one hand, the government has been implementing an inadequate land reform programme – and grossly inflating its official data. On the other hand, the neoliberal macroeconomic policies that have been pursued have cancelled out the agrarian reforms, by encouraging land alienation and concentration and aggravating the unemployment situation.

Several authors agree that the mechanization of the productive cycle results in the reduction of the total level of agrarian labour, creating a decline in the absolute number of agricultural jobs. This highlights the fact that the restructured agrarian sector is incapable of sustaining a high employment level, a fact which is not unique to Brazil but has been evident in other countries that have been restructuring and enhancing agricultural productivity and competitiveness. These are transformations with adverse implications for the rural workers who enter an urban job market that is even more restricted. In the case of Brazil, industrial employment levels have remained insufficient, and, indeed, in recent years the job market has tended to absorb the qualified workforce, not the rural workers dispensed by neoliberalism.

Conclusion

Agrarian reform entails a deep transformation in a country's agrarian structure in order to allow for democratic access to land and the improvement of the distribution of wealth among the rural population. This has not happened in Brazil. Despite the claims by the Cardoso government that Brazil has been undergoing 'the largest agrarian reform in the world', the neoliberal macroeconomic policies implemented have facilitated the concentration of land and produced a rise in unemployment. Moreover, the resettlement claims themselves have been grossly inflated.

Under the Cardoso government, the interests of the owners of huge estates were thoroughly attended to, either through specific policies targeted at this sector or through the new market mechanisms of agrarian reform. Indeed, if we take into further account that the settlements created have been largely the result of the direct action of the landless themselves (see Fernandes, Chapter 11 in this volume), then it is indeed very difficult to say that there has been an agrarian reform programme at all in Brazil. The more recent idea of a market-assisted agrarian reform is even less likely to deliver land to the 4.5 million rural families that are landless or near landless, as it has displaced responsibility for land reform onto society, and specifically onto the farmers which dominate it.

We must thus return to our earlier political assessment to affirm that the precondition for transformation is the convergence of rural and urban social forces. The rural struggles for agrarian reform must combine with the urban social struggles (for urban reform, employment, wages and shelter) with enough social strength to destroy the economic and political power of the antiquated Brazilian rural oligarchies, which prevent the opening up of a new horizon of national development. In this light, the current struggle of the MST is a struggle for all oppressed Brazilians for the construction of a democratic and autonomous country.

Notes

1. From the website of INCRA, the government organ responsible for the execution of the agrarian programme; www.incra.gov.br.
2. Declaration of President Cardoso to the daily newspaper *Folha de São Paulo*, 2 July 1998.
3. ABRA (Associação Brasileira de Reforma Agrária) is a non-governmental organization that works with agrarian problems. Its long historical trajectory in the struggle for agrarian reform has guaranteed its credibility in questioning the official published data.
4. The Gini coefficient measures the inequality of income distribution or other resources. It varies from 0 to 1: the closer it is to 0, the more equal the distribution of a resource; the closer to 1, the bigger the inequality.

References

ABRA (2002), *A Realidade das Metas e o Fracasso da Estratégia Política do Programa de Reforma Agrária do Governo FHC*, Brasília: Associação Brasileira de Reforma Agrária.

Furtado, Celso (1972), *Análise do Modelo Brasileiro*, Rio de Janeiro: Civilização Brasileira.

Gadelha, R.M.F. (1997), 'O Problema Agrário no Brasil: Evolução e Atualidade', *Pesquisa & Debate* 8(1): 87–125.

Graziano da Silva, J. (1990), *O que é a Questão Agrária*, São Paulo: Editora Brasiliense.

Graziano da Silva, J. (2001), 'Ainda precisamos de Reforma Agrária no Brasil?', *Ciência Hoje* 27(170): 81–3.

Guimarães, Alberto Passos (1982), *A Crise Agrária*, Rio de Janeiro: Editora Paz e Terra.

Hoffmann, R. (1998), *A Estrutura Fundiária no Brasil de Acordo com o Cadastro do INCRA: 1967–1998*, Campinas: Convênio INCRA/UNICAMP.

IBGE (Instituto Brasileiro de Geografia e Estatística) (1998), *Censo Agropecuário 1995–1996*, Rio de Janeiro: IBGE, Departamento de Geografia e Estatística.

IPEA (2001), *Transformações da Agricultura e Políticas Publicas*, Brasília: IPEA.

Medeiros, L. (1994), *Reforma Agrária: Concepções, Controvérsias e Questões*, Cadernos Temáticos, No. 1, Rio de Janeiro: RIAD.

Navarro, Zander (2002), 'O Brasil Precisa da Reforma Agrária?', *Muito Mais*, January.

Prado Júnior, Caio (1979), *A Questão Agrária no Brasil*, 2nd edn, São Paulo: Editora Brasiliense.

Rangel, Ignácio (2000), *Questão Agrária, Industrialização e Crise Urbana*, Porto Alegre: Editora Universidade/UFRGS.

Sampaio, P.A. (2001), 'A Questão Agrária Brasileira e a Luta pelo Socialismo', unpublished MS.

Sandroni, P. (1980), *Questão Agrária e Canmpesinato*, São Paulo: Editora Polis.

Sauer, Sergio (2001), *A Proposta de Reforma Agrária de Mercado do Banco Mundial no Brasil*, Brasília: Senado Federal.

Sauer, Sergio (2002), *Projeto Cédula da Terra: a Reforma Agrária de Mercado no Brasil*, Brasília: Senado Federal.

Stédile, João Pedro, ed. (1994), *A Questão Agrária Hoje*, Porto Alegre: Editora da UFRGS.

Teixeira, G. (2001), *A Problemática Agrária no Brasil Contemporâneo*, Brasília: Câmara Federal.

Teixeira, G. (2002), *A Realidade das Metas e o Fracasso da Estratégia Política da Reforma Agrária do Governo FHC*, Brasília: Câmara Federal.

www.presidência.gov.br/publi.coleção/refagri.htm, August 2002.

www.incra.gov.br/dados/refagrária, August 2002.

www.ipea.gov.br, August 2002.

www.mda.gov.br, August 2002.

13

The Agrarian Question and Armed Struggle in Colombia

Igor Ampuero and James J. Brittain

Colombia is a country with periodic economic crises and persisting social and political conflict.[1] Spanning well over half a century, this state of affairs has traversed the Cold War, from the US-led Alliance for Progress in the early 1960s to the present period marked by neoliberalism and Plan Colombia. It has become glaringly evident that throughout this period the Colombian state has remained partial and localized in its functioning, incapable of promoting sustainable and equitable development and guaranteeing the human rights of its population. This failure, in turn, has fuelled an internal conflict and 'dirty war', drawing in the sectors of the population that have borne the brunt of underdevelopment. The recent neoliberal offensive and proliferation of the drug trade have compounded and aggravated a pre-existing problem.

Despite these weaknesses and failures, however, the Colombian state is not to be seen as a 'failed state'. The Colombian state has been successful in imposing the imperatives of international capital through its local surrogate, the national oligarchy that continues to dominate the state. As such, the Colombian state is to be seen as a powerful instrument of imperialism. This has been reaffirmed since the 1980s by the imposition of the neoliberal model of development on Colombia. In the name of improving market competition and efficiency, the state has divested itself of strategic areas of production by privatizing basic industries including petroleum, energy, mining and communication, while at the same time it has abandoned its obligations in areas such as education and health. More than ever before, profits have been privatized, while losses have been socialized.

The current phase of internal violence in Colombia is intimately connected with the processes of economic expansion induced through the liberalization of the national economy. The extreme efforts of the Colombian state to attract and secure foreign investment have further embedded the structural conditions of social, political and economic exclusion of the majority. This exclusion demands that we focus our analysis on the agrarian question and the broader framework of rural-based struggle for inclusion in national development processes.

The Political Economy of Colombia

Colombia has a long history of social and political conflict, the latter culminating in *La Violencia* (1948–58). This period left well over 200,000 dead and an even greater number dispossessed of their land and traditional livelihoods in agricultural production to the benefit of the large landowners (Petras and Zeitlin 1968; Wickham-Crowley 1991; Chaliand 1977). What emerged at the 'end' of *La Violencia* was a national formula of political exclusion in the form of the National Front Agreement (1958–74). The National Front, in order to maintain political and economic control over the majority of the Colombian populace, established a 'power sharing agreement' in which the Liberal and Conservative parties alternated 'four-year terms in the presidency and divided all government positions evenly between themselves' (Leech 2002: 13). Through this political arrangement,

> the state under the National Front inhibited any expression of social conflict and excluded the subordinate classes from politics … the National Front eliminated the possibility by limiting government succession and alternation only to its handpicked members, thus becoming the institution through which the dominant class negotiated and resolved its differences. (Richani 2002: 25)

At the present time, Colombia is a republic with elected presidents serving four-year terms without the possibility of re-election, as stipulated in the 1991 Constitution. Yet this political structure continues to be accompanied by extreme oppression and violence, which has resulted in the displacement of over 2 million Colombians at the hands of state/paramilitary forces (Petras and Veltmeyer 2003). The monopolization of political life by the Liberal and Conservative parties, coupled with the destructive implications of displacement, in terms of socio-economic development, remains a key barrier to negotiating a political solution to the violence that continues to plague the country. It is in this hegemonic and indirect omission that many within Colombia's borders are negated from the political process and their voices, while crying, remain silent.

Colombia is a country of 41 million people. Historically, agriculture employed the vast majority of Colombians, while during the postwar era there was a steady movement of people from the rural to urban areas (Chasteen 2001). In this process of migration, several urban centres have developed in the country: Bogotá with a population of 7 million, Medellín with 2.1 million, Cali with 1.9 million, and Barranquilla with 1.2 million. Large portions of the population are being forced to leave the rural and town-based societies for the foreign metropolis in the quest for security, employment and income. Urban life is itself highly polarized, with only a small proportion of the population considered 'upper class'. This is due to the fact that many people have migrated from the rural areas out of economic necessity, only to be greeted with equally grim employment prospects in the cities. For example, in Bogotá, the country's capital and the most wealthy city in the country, over half of the population live in poverty (Caballero 2004).

Peasants have been seen as a deterrent to progress. Hence, as Ellen Meiksins Wood (2003: 76–7) has argued, there has been

> increased pressure to concentrate land in the hands of landlords and more successful farmers, who would have the capital and the flexibility to make the most profitable use of land. With that pressure, the enclosure of common land or open fields by communal agreement, or by exchanges among smallholders, gave way to a more coercive process of extinguishing customary rights, driving small producers off the land and excluding the community from regulation and production.

This notion of economic development has been supported within Colombia for decades through theories like Lauchlin Currie's 'accelerated development' (Currie 1966). In 2002 alone, over 412,000 people were displaced within Colombia (LAWG 2003). The vast majority of these live in the rural regions of the country, and are mostly peasants. In the post-World War II period, many peasants have tried to earn an income through the sale of their labour-power within the rural regions, but have been the victims of 'accelerated development programmes' or direct violence, which has forced them to leave their land and structures of cooperation and ownership. Historically this model of primitive accumulation and displacement was conducted through hired agents of large landowners and/or by the domestic military, while today it has been placed in the hands of far-right state/paramilitary groups (Leech 1999). While much of the Colombian population now surrounds urban areas, most Colombians lived and worked in rural regions prior to the displacement that began in the 1980s. Studies conducted during the 1960s and 1970s showed that 50 per cent of the country's economic activity and production was rural-based (Weil et al. 1970; Gilbert 1974).

Even in the late 1980s and 1990s, agriculture continued to be the primary economic sector, despite decline over the previous decades; in 2000, agriculture accounted for 19 per cent of GDP and provided employment for 30 per cent of workers (EIU 2003), including agricultural labour and peasant crop production. Today, within the central regions of the country, many peasants work in a cooperative method to provide internal subsistence goods, as well as to construct a unified front against repressive agents (Brittain 2004). Many peasants within these rural regions maintain a system that is quite similar to what Marx described, where they 'produce almost all their requirements in their own holdings, with the aid of their families, and obtain only a small portion of the items they need from outside, in exchange for their own surplus product', thus establishing that 'the family or family group is basically self-sufficient' (1991: 1034). This is not to say that peasants are not dependent on or involved in the market, but that some peasants are mutually supportive of each other, and against the compulsions of the market.

Coffee has historically been, in the words of Timothy Wickham-Crowley, a 'critical crop' to Colombia's existence (1992: 125). It has been one of the most important agricultural export crops, at times representing over half of the total export earnings. However, with trade liberalization and falling world market prices, there has been a sharp decline in coffee exports, down to a mere 8.2 per cent of total exports. This has precipitated major socio-economic upheaval in the countryside, as plantations owners and rural workers have scrambled to replace coffee with a more viable and lucrative crop (Agriculture and Agri-Food Canada 2002; Mondragon 2001). Agricultural products other than coffee have also experienced difficulty due to falling producer prices and increased marketing costs (Richani 2002), to the point of making peasant production unsustainable. This has resulted in two outcomes: the first is migration to urban zones; the second is increased resentment towards the state, specifically its implementation of neoliberal reforms as against the provision of social and economic security and sovereignty.

A major change in the economy of Colombia has been the shift away from agriculture to natural resource extraction. In the last two decades, oil reserves and production have greatly increased. The country's natural resource sector has established itself as the backbone of the national export economy and is currently a major source of foreign exchange earnings and domestic employment: in 2000, oil and coal accounted for 41.5 per cent of total exports (Agriculture and Agri-Food Canada 2002). Within the past fifteen years, since the US-launched Andean initiative in 1989, Colombian oil production has risen almost 80 per cent. Most of the exports have gone to the United States, making Colombia the eighth largest supplier of foreign crude oil to the United States (Scott 2003). This increase in oil production has been supported economically and militarily by the past three political administrations of the United States.

In the period 1970–95, Colombia had the lowest macroeconomic volatility rates and the second highest economic growth rate in Latin America (EIU 2003). The economic crisis within Latin America during the 1980s, known as 'the lost decade', did not seem to have a great effect on Colombia (Chasteen 2001). Economic liberalization in Colombia began in the early 1990s, under the direction of international financial institutions (IFIs), in an effort to boost economic growth. The IFIs expressed the need for the Colombian government to liberalize the economy, by implementing economic and social reforms, reducing import tariffs, deregulating finance and implementing a more 'market-friendly' foreign exchange rate. More recently, telecommunications, energy, tourism, financial services, and the accounting/auditing sectors have been, or are on their way to becoming, the primary areas of liberalization. In 1998–99, the Colombian economy entered a period of recession, primarily attributed to external shocks, followed by monetary tightening efforts aimed at curbing the rate of inflation that had been fuelled by the devaluation of the currency and the overall deterioration of public finances (EIU 2003). However, beginning in 2000, the Colombian economy began to show signs of recovery, assisted greatly by exports, and in particular the rise of the oil sector, which is the primary destination of foreign direct investment.

Liberalization and the growth of the oil sector have been accompanied by economic, political and military support from the
United States, within the framework of 'Plan Colombia' launched
by the Clinton administration in the late 1990s. Plan Colombia was
a $1.3 billion package intended, in the words of the US Embassy
in Bogotá (2000),

> to meet the needs that the other sources cannot. It is based on the shared
> hope of achieving peace and prosperity in Colombia through the overall
> reduction of illicit drug production and trafficking, thereby allowing
> the Colombian government to establish democratic control and provide
> services and infrastructure throughout its national territory.

In fact, Plan Colombia has been the heir of the Kennedy-led 'Alliance
for Progress', combining economic and military aid within a highly
militarized geo-strategy of control and accumulation. In its present
reincarnation, this imperialist strategy has deployed the language of
a 'war on drugs and terror'.

Colombia's principal trading partner remains the United States. In
1999, Colombia's exports to the United States amounted to 48.5 per
cent of total exports and its imports from the United States amounted
to 42.5 per cent of the total. The strong economic relationship has
been reinforced by the rise of oil production in Colombia, of which
80 per cent is directly shipped to the United States, and by an
increasingly favourable climate for attracting FDI (Scott 2003). The
United States alone accounts for over a quarter of Colombia's total
FDI and the vast majority of this is being channelled into the growing oil sector. Other important economic partners, though to a lesser
extent, include the European Union and the Andean Community of
Nations (Banco de la Republica Colombia 2003a, 2003b).

The Agrarian Political Economy

While the agricultural sector in Colombia has historically played a
key role in the country's economic development, it has also been
the source of extensive social disintegration, due to the structural
inequalities that characterize its functioning. The result has been the
persistence of conflict over land ownership and access rights among
rural dwellers for over eight decades. The Colombian state has been,
and continues to be, a key agent in maintaining the structural in-

equality, specifically by protecting and securing the economic interests of large landowners and foreign businesses, to the exclusion of rural workers and small landholders throughout the country.

It was following *La Violencia* that the state realized that a growing opposition was starting to emerge throughout the rural regions of the country, with the potential to destabilize the post-*Violencia* political system. Land reform was one means of disarming opposition. As observed by David Bushnell (1993: 232),

> the *Violencia* had amply revealed the pathology of much of rural life in Colombia, including the conflicts over land in certain rural areas and the general state of deprivation and lack of education of the rural masses, which had made them susceptible to murderous political manipulation. Hence, agrarian reform seemed to offer a means of repairing some of the damage done in recent years and creating a sturdy, prosperous peasant class that would resist future calls to partisan insanity.

Thus, in 1961, the state decided to enact Law 135 (The Agrarian Social Reform Law), accompanied by the formation of the Colombian Institute of Agrarian Reform (INCORA). INCORA was a politically organized and formed body that authorized 'the outright expropriation of privately owned estates, if necessary, for the redistribution to those who had insufficient land or no land' (Bushnell 1993: 232). However, the state remained largely ineffective in implementing socially beneficial change through the land reform programme (Lindqvist 1979). Thus, 'by 1971, less than 1 per cent of the lands subject to expropriation were distributed, and most of that was public land'; moreover, 'institutional failure exacerbated land conflicts', as the state and Law 135 'did not provide an efficient mechanism to redistribute land', and as 'INCORA [was unable] to cope with the increasing demand for land' (Richani 2002: 28–31). It is from this failure that organized peasant movements emerged (FARC–EP 1999; Molano 2000).

As a result of these token reform programmes, coupled with the effects of displacement, the agrarian and land situation today is vastly unequal. In a country where 14 million hectares of land are considered suitable for agricultural purposes (comprising close to 13 per cent of the country's total area), 45 per cent of this productive land is owned by 0.3 per cent of the population, with a further 20 per cent of the land being owned by 2 per cent of the population. This leaves the remaining 97 per cent of the Colombian population with access to 35 per cent of the agricultural land (Cortez 2002). These are recent statistics and appear not to reflect the waging of a half-century struggle for, among other things, agrarian reform in Colombia.

Nonetheless, a significant amount of the population maintain a livelihood through agricultural production, for the market and/or subsistence. While displacements and neoliberal reforms have been weakening traditional products such as yucca, coffee and maize (Clawson and Lee III 1998; Richani 2002), many peasants and smallholders have also taken up coca cultivation to maintain some level of subsistence. Illicit agricultural production has been ongoing in many regions of Colombia for three decades, but since the 1990s smallholder production of the coca plant has proliferated. Some of these growers, who are very poor and primarily peasant subsistence farmers, establish a small plot of land to grow coca along with their family crops (yucca, lemons, maize) and after a year are able to make more than they would have with an alternative crop in the legal market. A portion of these farmers live in regions where the FARC–EP operate, and in these regions the insurgency is able to protect the smallholders and peasants from paramilitary forces who finance themselves through the production, processing and trafficking of cocaine, heroin and marijuana (Richani 2002; Scott 2003). However, this is not what is commonly reported by news sources, which claim that the FARC–EP is involved in drug production (hence the terms 'narco-guerrilla' or 'narco-terrorism'). On the contrary, the FARC–EP, for all its size and geographical spread, only involves itself in 2.5 per cent of peasant drug production (Scott 2003). This involvement is not in trafficking or smuggling, but in measures to ensure that the peasantry is paid fairly and not deprived of an income by purchasers of the leaves. In this process of equity and protection, the FARC–EP receives a tax from the peasant's earnings (although the poorest peasants are relieved of the tax) in the form of money, animals or fruit (Richani 2002; Clawson and Lee III 1998; Galvis 2000).

Gender relations in the rural political economy of Colombia are another important aspect to be addressed. In Colombia, as elsewhere, women are largely responsible for the reproduction of the household. This responsibility has many dimensions, which have previously been explored and analysed in feminist and development literature (Pearson 1992; Sachs 1996; Parpart 2000). In Colombia *machismo*, in particular the marginalization of women from access to productive and reproductive resources, has been systematically reinforced by state policies and economic liberalization. Women in Colombia head over 30 per cent of households and comprise the poorest sector of peasants and workers; however, the state has systematically denied women the title to land and access to credit, on the assumption that the head of household is typically male. Moreover, the combined processes of liberalization and armed conflict have increased enormously the burden of social reproduction, and consequently women's unwaged labour. Specifically, liberalization has undermined smallholder incomes, off-farm employment, and wages, while armed conflict has involved the loss of livelihoods in a more outright way, by the forced displacement of thousands of families, particularly in the southern coca-growing regions, and the aerial spraying of coca crops. Again the outcome of such processes is increased dislocation and outrage against the state.

Forced displacement and the 'drug war' have left whole families economically and socially destitute, with the severest effects on women. The immediate economic reasons have to do with obvious problems of food security and housing; these are accompanied by psychosocial distress related to the loss of stability, severe familial upheaval, and long-term and relentless fear of loss of spouse and/ or other family members (Galvis 2002). Redressing the problem demands gender-inclusive agrarian reform programmes, as well as the redirection of public funds towards the strengthening of the delivery of social services on the part of the Colombian state, including education, health care and unemployment insurance.

The Social and Political Structure of the FARC–EP

The political monopoly established by the national coalition between the Liberal and Conservative parties in the aftermath of *La Violencia* has left a legacy of repression, violence and systemic mistrust between the rulers and the ruled. It is within this context that land struggles in Colombia must be understood. This section discusses the emergence of the Revolutionary Armed Forces of Colombia–People's Army (FARC–EP) and its social basis, while the next section turns to its political strategy and tactics.

The FARC–EP represents a large-scale, rural-based and peasant-led armed struggle that has emerged within a broad-based struggle for access to productive land and socio-political transformation. Founded in 1964, the FARC–EP is a mobile guerrilla movement that has consistently pursued direct-action tactics, making it the most persistent of anti-imperialist movements in Latin America, and arguably the most potent of all insurgencies on the continent (Rochlin 2003; Veltmeyer and Petras 2002; Fisher and Ponniah 2003; Carr and Ellner 1993; FARC–EP 1999). The FARC–EP occupies close to two-thirds of Colombia's municipalities (Leech 2002), and continues to develop extensive ties throughout the rural and urban regions of the country (Richani 2002). Central to the mandate of the FARC–EP is the protection and defence of the peasant settlements from large landowners and paramilitaries. The latter forces function in collusion with the national government and the armed forces, many of whom have been trained in the School of the Americas in Fort Benning, Georgia (renamed the Western Hemisphere Institute for Security Cooperation).

The predecessor of the FARC–EP was an important and progressive peasant movement, which saw *campesinos* and other conscious Colombians organize themselves into communities to establish communal structures of cooperation and security (Petras and Zeitlin 1968). The communities advanced and expanded throughout Colombia in the late 1950s and early 1960s, establishing over sixteen communities, until a direct military intervention in 1964 (Petras and Morley 1990; Osterling 1989). From the beginning, therefore, the FARC–EP was organized around a peasant agrarian platform in the face of extreme political oppression.

At its inception in 1964, the FARC was primarily a peasant-based movement, largely consisting of subsistence agriculturalists living in Marquetalia, a relatively underdeveloped region in Colombia (Osterling 1989). The objective of the FARC–EP was to 'establish a stable society, uncorrupted and based on local control, and a new approach to counter the repressive central government by extending the region into other areas' (Petras and Zeitlin 1968: 335; see also Gott 1970). However, throughout the four decades since its inception, the FARC–EP has developed a complex platform intended to address a plethora of critical political, social and economic issues. These issues exist as threads that have become increasingly tangled in a knot of class conflict, state repression, brutal violence and extreme socio-economic inequality and poverty. The current constituency of the organization continues to include subsistence farmers, but has grown to include displaced peasants and landless rural labourers, as well as a section of urban workers (FARC–EP 2003b).

The FARC–EP, as a 'people's army', necessarily includes women and men, and on increasingly equal terms. While the majority of the mobile guerrilla force consists of men, women play a substantial role within the insurgency. At the time of the initial attack on Marquetalia which prompted the formation of the FARC–EP, among the forty-eight guerrillas were two women (FARC–EP: 1999, 2000/2001; Richani 2002). Since the 1960s the FARC–EP has continued to build gender equality within the organization. During the 1970s, the number of women involved in the movement grew to 20 per cent (Richani 2002). It is estimated that through the 1990s the number of women within the organization was well over 30 per cent; it now stands at 40 per cent (Roman 2000; Leech 2003; FARC–EP 2001). By way of comparison, the proportion of women in the Colombian government (House of Representatives) stands at 12.6 per cent (Cordoba Ruiz 2002), while the national army only maintains a women's contingent of 2 per cent (Penhaul 2001). In the insurgency women play a key role in efforts to politicize the movement through the performance of communication and education responsibilities. Also, women, alongside men, make up 'accountants, cooks, fundraisers, logistics specialists, medical doctors, or recruiters who may play only a passive role' (Hudson 2002: 18–19). We may conclude, therefore, that while the dynamics of poverty and violence affect women and men differently, women and men have joined together in the FARC–EP in a spirit of solidarity towards the defence of agrarian reform and socio-political transformation, against the hegemony of the national and international elite and business classes.

In the areas under its control, the FARC–EP has been actively promoting a different socio-economic and political model. In the realm of economic and social development, the organization has established an economically beneficial and democratic arrangement to reinvest in the communities in which it is involved by establishing agrarian credit systems so that farmers can have the ability to establish a product that can then provide sustenance for the community (Rochlin 2003). In effect, the FARC–EP, while not supportive of coca production, has allowed peasants to benefit financially both domestically (through fair prices for goods) and in the international market.

In the area of health, the FARC–EP (with the support of hospitals and pharmacies) has carried out massive vaccination campaigns from which 20,000 children and adults have benefited (FARC–EP 2001). The FARC–EP has built roads and infrastructure to facilitate the delivery of services to the public while also providing an avenue for goods and products from the region to leave for sale and trade.

In the realm of local government, the FARC–EP has removed top-down judicial models of justice and established community-organized gatherings to try persons who have been accused of misconduct. As Richani (2002: 89) has shown, the FARC–EP, with the help of the community, has implemented Reglas de Convivencia (Rules of Cohabitation), which are the 'laws and sanctions' regarding issues such as domestic violence, drug use and environment depletion. In many regions of the country, as Nazih Richani (2002: 89) has indicated,

> the guerrillas' power is exercised through the election of local municipal councils and mayors and the disbursement of public funds. According to some testimonies, the FARC does not impose candidates but rather as in the cases of the 1998 municipal elections in Yondo, Cantagallo, and San Pablo (all in the Middle Magdalena), town meetings were organized where candidates were chosen freely and then a general election was held.

Today over 93 per cent of all 'regions of recent settlement' in Colombia have a guerrilla presence, thus ensuring their continued growth (Bergquist et al. 2003: 15). The insurgency is presently located in over 622 municipalities, out of a total 1,071 (Leech 2002). Since 1999, the FARC–EP has had a presence in more than 60 per cent of the country (Vanden and Prevost 2002), and this is steadily expanding. Also, for the past several years many people have been migrating to FARC–EP regions, in the knowledge that they will be protected and will be able to grow subsistence and export crops freely (Wilson 2003). In one year alone (2000) more than 20,000 people migrated to the FARC–EP-held Villa Nueva Colombia (FARC–EP 2000/2001).

Militarily, the FARC–EP is organized in a chain of command. The Secretariat of the Central General Staff consists of seven members (Manual Marulanda Vélez, Raúl Reyes, Iván Márquez, Jorge Briceño, Timoleón Jiménez, Alfonso Cano and Ivan Rios). The Central General Staff itself has twenty-five members throughout the country, which are organized in seven blocks (East, West, South, Centre, Middle Magdalena, Caribbean and Cesar) (Richani 2002;

FARC–EP 2001). Within these blocks there are over 100 *frentes*, or fronts, numbering an average of 300 to 600 soldiers per front. In 2002, it was estimated that there were over 105 fronts throughout Colombia (Crandall 2002: 62; Bergquist et al. 2003: 15); further data collected (by the author) in December 2003 suggest that there are possibly several dozen more fronts (bringing the total number to as high as 165).

External support for the FARC–EP (outside combatant forces) has become quite extensive. While it is very difficult to reference an exact number, for many Colombians live in fear that their communities will be targeted by paramilitaries, some figures estimate that close to a million Colombians (rural and urban) are in direct support of the FARC–EP, while others state numbers in the multiple millions (Petras and Veltmeyer 2001; FARC–EP 2001).

The Strategic Objectives of Armed Struggle

The struggle for land in Colombia confronts and seeks to address entrenched social, political and economic problems. These problems are largely attributable to the socio-political marginalization of the rural populace, rampant and growing rural poverty, loss of livelihood, and state sanctioned/sponsored acts of terrorism against the rural citizenry engaging in (or suspected of supporting) the armed struggle of the FARC–EP (Leech 2002; Scott 2003; FARC–EP 1999).

The emancipatory objectives of the FARC–EP have always been born out of the imperatives associated with achieving a political solution to the social and economic problems of the country (Pearce 1990). In this way, the objectives of the people's struggle have been and continue to be guided by the belief that anti-systemic structural transformation of a revolutionary nature is the only way effectively to improve the living conditions of the vast majority of the Colombian citizenry (FARC–EP 2000). In this context, then, dismantling the opposing entrenched power structures and institutions that protect the interests of the domestic elite is perceived to be one element, and a crucial one, of the radical transformation that is being called for by the FARC–EP.

Indeed, what began as a largely peasant-led, rural-based land struggle in the 1950s has since become a national political movement possessing an alternative vision of how to facilitate the achievement of modern development objectives (Ortiz 2002; FARC–EP 2000; Pearce 1990; Brittain 2004). However, it must also be recognized that throughout the evolution of the FARC–EP movement, the organization's commitment to agrarian reform has been unwavering. Intricately connected to the FARC–EP's socio-political objectives, genuine land reform is perceived to be dependent upon the abolition of the Colombian oligarchy that has for centuries dominated political, social and economic life in the country.

Three important documents outline the strategic struggles of the FARC–EP. These documents are (a) the Agrarian Programme, (b) the Uribe Accords, and (c) the Platform for a Government of National Reconciliation and Reconstruction.

The Agrarian Programme

The Agrarian Programme of the FARC–EP was proclaimed on 20 July 1964, amidst the armed struggle of Marquetalia, and was subsequently revised and broadened during the Seventh National Conference of the organization in April of 1993. These programmes have become 'the banner of struggle for the revolutionary movement and especially the revolutionary guerrillas' (FARC–EP 1999: 18). The overall objective of this programme is to raise the standard of material and cultural life of the whole peasantry. The imperatives of achieving this objective include the elimination of unemployment, hunger and illiteracy. Within this vision, the freeing of the peasantry from the fetters of the *latifúndio* system remains a central goal, alongside the promotion of agricultural development and industrial production. Overall, the FARC–EP is calling for the confiscation of the large landholdings for the benefit of all working people (FARC–EP 1993).

The second feature of the Agrarian Programme is that all tenant farmers, occupants, renters, sharecroppers, lessees and farmhands on the large landholdings (*latifúndios*) and state lands are to receive property titles for the lands they exploit. Furthermore, systems of sharecropping, unsustainable and destructive forms of land use, and rent (in kind or in money) are to be eliminated. All of the debts of the peasants owed to usurers, speculators, and official and semi-official institutions of credit are to be written off. New systems of credit are to be established by the insurgency with facilities for payment, provision of technical assistance, agricultural resources, such as seeds, tools, and equipment and irrigation systems, all of which have already been issued to peasants by the FARC–EP (Rochlin 2003; Richani 2002). These services are to be offered to individual peasants as well as to co-operatives that may arise during the process of agrarian reform.

The Agrarian Programme also calls for special provisions to be made for the establishment and maintenance of adequate health-care and educational services for the peasantry. The problems of poor health-care facilities and rural illiteracy are viewed as priority areas in need of improvement. The FARC–EP also call for the total eradication of illiteracy and the implementation of a system of scholarships based on merit and need for the children of those who work the land. A large-scale housing scheme for the peasantry is also included in the Programme, aiming to ensure the right of all people to adequate shelter. Finally, massive improvements in communications systems in the rural areas are also called for, with technical educa-tion to be administered to all persons so as to raise the standards of the rural areas and the poor to those of the upper class and the urban regions. Presently, one out of eight Colombians has access to a telephone (and one in forty has access to a computer), and this access is obviously concentrated in the more wealthy economic bracket of society, located in the larger urban centres.

All the changes presented in the above programme have been discussed or implemented within the FARC–EP's own limited means and resources. Through the income that the organization collects, 'most of the moneys end up in investments in public projects such as vocational schools, road paving, public health, and environmental protection' (Richani 2002: 80). Following these activities another portion of the remaining income is then distributed for the con-struction and extension of infrastructure (the building of modern transportation routes, alternative methods for trade, etc.).

Regarding the unique conditions and demands of indigenous communities in the Colombian countryside, the Agrarian Programme explicitly states that some groups will also be provided with suf-ficient land for development. While indigenous communities are to enjoy all the benefits of the revolutionary agrarian policy, the establishment of autonomous indigenous organizations within these communities will be supported by the FARC–EP out of a genuine respect for their community councils, way of life, culture, languages and internal organization (FARC–EP 1999). In this policy, FARC–EP aims to advance its relationship with the many indigenous communities within Colombia and start a healthy peaceful commitment to cultural recognition, which has been denied by armed and political movements in the past.

Finally, the Agrarian Programme requires that solid peasant organizations – unions, committees of land users, and neighbourhoods – be formed. It is viewed as essential that the struggle should represent the broadest united front of all the democratic, progressive and revolutionary forces of the country to carry out a permanent process of transformation against the national oligarchy and their imperial patrons.

The Uribe Accords

The negotiations between the FARC–EP and the government of President Belisario Betancur (1982–86) have expressed the desire on the part of the FARC–EP to find a peaceful and socially beneficial solution to the problems of Colombia. During President Betancur's second year in office, discussions began between the government and the FARC–EP towards this end, and in the spring of 1984 the two parties concluded their talks with the Uribe Accords (FARC–EP 1999; Dudley 2004).

The Uribe Accords represent the FARC–EP's eleven-point strategy for strengthening the national peace-building process and facilitating a process of sustainable social and economic development based on a solid foundation of freedom and justice for all Colombian peoples (Arenas 1985). Essentially, these accords outline the conditions that must be in place in order to ensure a genuine ceasefire on the part of *both* the guerrilla movement and those groups (National Army and other paramilitary organizations) that remain within the jurisdiction of the Colombian state. The FARC–EP agreed that a ceasefire was a positive means to open discussions between the two opposing forces, under the understanding that the government would implement, by means of legislative acts, a series of economic, social and political reforms, and that the FARC–EP, for its part, would allow a time period for implementation of the reforms and for a search for lasting political solutions (FARC–EP 1999). The Accords foresaw the creation of political space for the establishment of a Peace Commission to ensure the fulfilment of government obligations under the Accords. These obligations included the modernization of the political institutions, the prompt implementation of political reforms, and the implementation of agrarian reform. As such, Betancur and the government 'recognized that guerrilla violence was the product of real social conditions and he understood the relationship between those conditions and the demands of the insurgents' (Meza 1998: 24). The government was also called upon to acknowledge the necessity of involving multiple agencies of the state in processes aimed at permanently expanding services to the peasantry in order to improve its quality of life and the normal production of food and raw materials for industry.

The outcome of the Uribe Accords was contrary to the original proclamations. In November 1985, a process of reversal began. The FARC–EP started to receive strong support for their policies under the Accords (Osterling 1989), broadened their alliances to include unionists, peasant organizers and other Colombians, and decided to facilitate the formation of the Patriotic Union (UP) (Dudley 2004; Aldana 2002). This, in turn, threatened to become a viable instrument for political reform within the country. In 1986, the UP participated in the elections at various levels of government and elected more than 350 municipal councillors, 23 deputies, 13 mayors, 9 members of parliament, and 6 senators to the Congress of the Republic, thus demonstrating the potential of an effective and broad alliance. The UP also participated in the presidential elections, obtaining 350,000 votes, something unheard of in the history of the Colombian left. In its first seven months, this young political movement surpassed by 300 per cent the efforts of the entire left of Colombia, and established itself as the nucleus of a political alternative opposing the Liberal–Conservative party monopoly (FARC–EP 1999; Dudley 2004).

The oligarchy was gravely concerned. Indeed, despite the Uribe Accords, large landowners enhanced the process of militarization, through the employment of paramilitary organizations (Bergquist et al. 2003). During this same period, the military itself was concerned that the government was allowing too much leeway to the FARC–EP's ideology and alliances. It was in this context of fear and mistrust that the paramilitary groups turned on 'the easiest targets – Colombians who had joined the Patriotic Union' (Kirk 2003: 117). The 'paramilitary organizations were undermining Betancur's peace process by intensifying their "dirty war" against suspected leftists, especially against members of the Patriotic Union' (Leech 2002: 20). The result was that numerous senators, deputies, councillors, mayors, and 5,000 of its militants and supporters were killed, and the peace process abandoned (Galvis 2000; FARC–EP 2000; Aldana 2002).

It is important to note that the Reagan administration, which was in office at the time of these killings, was strongly opposed to the Betancur government and its methods of ceasefire negotiations with the FARC–EP (Scott 2003). Although the US government was never identified as having had any involvement in the murders, later accounts would reveal that, after 1984, the United States School of the Americas, based in the state of Georgia, had been training Colombian soldiers in counter-insurgency operations (Weeks and Gunson 1991), of which over 150 have been linked to major human rights abuses (Leech 2002).

The Platform for a Government of National Reconciliation and Reconstruction

Since the abandonment of the Uribe Accords, the FARC–EP has developed a comprehensive strategy intended to facilitate the establishment of a Colombian state dedicated to and founded upon the principles of pluralism, democracy and justice. This strategy is referred to as the Platform for a Government of National Reconciliation and Reconstruction (1993), and continues to constitute a key dimension of the politico-military efforts of the FARC–EP today. The Platform understands that until there is a political solution to the Colombian crisis, in all its manifestations, peace, social stability and economic prosperity will remain elusive.

Specifically, the Platform calls for a government of national reconciliation with specific tasks. First, the FARC–EP calls for the reorientation of the mandate of the National Armed Forces around the goals of ensuring national sovereignty and protection of human rights (FARC–EP 1999). The elimination of paramilitary organizations, which operate in a manner inimical to the objectives of achieving peace, is further viewed as a precondition for the achievement of a political solution. Second, freedom of the press and the strengthening of public accountability processes are perceived as critical conditions for national socio-political stability. Third, a government of national reconciliation and reconstruction must implement reforms aimed at redistributing national wealth in a more equitable and just manner. The Platform specifically proposes that the state commits to the redirection of 50 per cent of the national budget to social services and 10 per cent towards scientific research (FARC–EP 1999). Reminiscent of past discussion, the FARC–EP calls on the state to ensure that all citizens have fair access to adequate health and education facilities.

Finally, the platform calls for economic modernization and development with social justice. In opposition to neoliberal policies favouring the privatization of state-owned enterprises, the platform calls on the state to become the principal owner and administrator of the strategic sectors, including energy, communications, public services, roads, ports and natural resources. Indeed, it is proposed that the emphasis of economic development policy must be on strengthening and expanding the domestic market, food self-sufficiency, and active support for industrial production at all levels. Also identified are the imperatives associated with promoting national economic solidarity, self-management and micro-enterprise. The FARC–EP presented this agenda over a decade ago, yet none of the measures has yet been implemented.

The FARC–EP has expanded its political action internationally and launched a wider dialogue through which it seeks to inform non-Colombians about the FARC–EP's programme for change within Colombia. This dialogue has provided an open and democratic avenue for the FARC–EP to be criticized, questioned and respected – in contrast to the stance of the Colombian government (of President Alvaro Uribe and then Interior Minister Fernando Londono), which has sought to silence and exclude non-governmental organizations and outside 'interference' on such issues as human rights and political development. In the past, several countries, including France, Norway, Sweden, Canada and Brazil, have been in direct contact with the FARC–EP to negotiate and discuss peace, security, inclusion and trade. Even the World Social Forum (WSF) has invited the FARC–EP as representatives and discussants that received a great deal of attention, applause and respect at the 2001 meetings (Nichols 2001). However, following the US-launched 'war on terror' in 2001, the WSF has, on paper, not allowed any armed group openly to attend the meetings, including the FARC–EP, as well as state leaders such as Fidel Castro. In reality the FARC–EP has remained involved, and the WSF has been under pressure to encourage openly the attendance of the FARC–EP (Research Unit for Political Economy 2003); however, as the 'war on terror' continues, such encouragement would be difficult.

The FARC–EP has been able to make more inroads domestically, with the support of, and military alignment with, the National
Liberation Army (ELN), another strong national guerrilla movement
(FARC–EP 2003a). It was once said that if these guerrilla armies
united they would never pose a real threat to the government
(Bushnell 1993), yet in recent years the two have been organizing
and initiating united attacks against state forces, dealing devastating
blows against the paramilitary/state counterinsurgency forces. This has
been accompanied by an ideological convergence between the two
movements and the overcoming of their historical disputes.

Conclusion

The insurgency within Colombia has shown much greater vigor and
strength than the state within specific geographical spaces. Indeed,
over four decades the political map of Colombia has been steadily redrawn by the expansion of the insurgency and the retreat of
the state. This process is expected to continue, as long as the state
continues to impose an imperialist agenda and social opposition
proliferates. The FARC–EP's influence is expected to increase and
extend throughout the remaining regions of the country.

Under the circumstances, the state has two options: either to
address the urgent development needs in the areas of agriculture,
education and health, as outlined by the FARC–EP; or to persist
with its policy of direct social, economic, political, and cultural violence through state and paramilitary forces. These forces, as history
has shown, fuel a vicious cycle of oppression and resentment, and
generate more violence. The key variable that the state has consistently tried to leave out of the equation is the social basis of the
insurgency. The FARC–EP is not just an armed opposition to the
state, but a tangible social force with a different model of socio-
economic and political development.

Note

1. We wish to express our thanks to Carly Manion for research assistance.

References

Agriculture and Agri-Food Canada (2002), *Colombia: Agri-Food Country Profile Statistical Overview*, http://ats.agr.ca/latin/e3007.htm.

Aldana, Luis Alberto Matta (2002), *Poder Capitalista y Violencia Política en Colombia: Terrorismo de Estado y Genocidio contra la Unión Patriótica*, Bogotá: Ideas y Soluciones Graficas.

Arenas, Jacobo (1985), *Cese El Fuego: Una Historia Politica de Las FARC*, Bogota: Editorial La Oveja Negra.

Banco de la Republica Colombia (2003a), *Foreign Trade: Exports*, www.banrep. gov.co/estad/ingles/pg6994.htm#6.

Banco de la Republica Colombia (2003b), *Foreign Trade: Imports*, www.banrep. gov.co/estad/ingles/pg7994.htm#7.

Bergquist, Charles, Ricardo Penaranda and Gonzalo Sanchez (2003), *Violence in Colombia 1990–2000: Waging War and Negotiating Peace*, Wilmington: Scholarly Resources.

Betancourt, Ingrid (2002), *Until Death Do Us Part: My Struggle to Reclaim Colombia*, New York: HarperCollins.

Bowden, Mark (2001), *Killing Pablo: The Hunt for the World's Greatest Outlaw*, New York: Atlantic Monthly Press.

Brittain, James J. (2004), 'The Revolutionary Armed Forces of Colombia – People's Army: A Marxist Insurgency for Revolution?', M.A. thesis, Acadia University.

Bushnell, David (1993), *The Making of Modern Colombia: A Nation in Spite of Itself*, Berkley, CA: University of California Press.

Caballero, Maria Cristina (2004), 'A Lefty Takes Bogotá: Mayor Luis Eduardo Garzon Will Complicate Uribe's Agenda', http://msnbc.msn.com/id/3989953/.

Carr, Barry, and Steve Ellner (1993), *The Latin American Left: From the Fall of Allende to Perestroika*, London: Westview Press.

Chaliand, Gerard (1977), *Revolution in the Third World: Myths and Perspectives*, New York: Viking.

Chasteen, John Charles (2001), *Born in Blood and Fire: A Concise History of Latin America*, New York: W.W. Norton.

Clawson, Patrick L., and Rensselaer W. Lee III (1998), *The Andean Cocaine Industry*, New York: St. Martin's/Griffin.

Cordoba Ruiz, Piedad (2002), *Women in the Colombian Congress*, Stockholm: International Idea.

Cortez, Hernan (2002), *Colombia Country Guide*, www.oneworld.net.

Crandall, Russell (2002), *Driven by Drugs: US Policy toward Colombia*, London: Lynne Rienner.

Currie, Lauchlin (1966), *Accelerating Development: The Necessity of the Means*, New York: McGraw-Hill.

Dudley, Steven (2004), *Walking Ghosts: Murder and Guerrilla Politics in Colombia*. London: Routledge.

EIU (Economist Intelligence Unit) (2003), *Country Report: Colombia*, www. economist. com/countries/Colombia/profile.cfm?folder=Profile-Fact.

Fals-Borda, Orlando (1976), *Peasant Societies in the Colombian Andes: A Sociological Study of Saucío*, Westport: Greenwood Press.

FARC–EP (1993), *The Agrarian Programme of the Guerrillas of the FARC–EP*, FARC–EP International Commission.

FARC–EP (1999), *FARC–EP Historical Outline*, FARC–EP International Commission.

FARC–EP (2000), *Resistencia 24*.

FARC–EP (2000/2001), *Resistencia 25*.

FARC–EP (2001), *Resistencia 26*.

FARC–EP (2003a), *Joint Communique of the FARC–EP and the ELN, July 13, 2003*, Secretariat of the Central General Staff of the FARC–EP and the ELN General Command.

FARC–EP (2003b), *Solidarity Communique from the FARC–EP, 22 June 2003*, Secretariat of the Central General Staff of the FARC–EP.

Fisher, William F., and Thomas Ponniah (2003), *Another World is Possible: Popular Alternatives to Globalization at the World Social Forum*, Halifax, NS: Fernwood.

Galvis, Constanza Ardila (2000), *The Heart of the War in Colombia*, London: Latin American Bureau.

Gilbert, Alan (1974), *Latin American Development: A Geographical Perspective*, Harmondsworth: Penguin.

Gott, Richard (1970), *Rural Guerrillas in Latin America*, London: Pelican Latin American Library.

Eric J. Hobsbawm (1973), *Revolutionaries: Contemporary Essays*, New York: Pantheon Books.

Hudson, Rex A. (2002), *Who Becomes a Terrorist and Why: The 1999 Government Report on Profiling Terrorists*, Guilford, CT: Lyons Press.

Kirk, Robin (2003), *More Terrible than Death: Massacres, Drugs, and America's War in Colombia*, New York: Public Affairs.

LAWG (Latin American Working Group, Colombia Steering Committee, Working Group on Displacement) (2003), *Colombians Displaced by Violence Need Protection and Assistance*, Washington DC: Latin American Working Group.

Leech, Garry M. (1999), 'Fifty Years of Violence', *Colombia Journal Online*, www.colombiajournal.org/fiftyyearsofviolence.htm#three.

Leech, Garry M. (2002), *Killing Peace: Colombia's Conflict and the Failure of US Intervention*, New York: Information Network of the Americas.

Leech, Garry M. (2003), 'Photo Gallery: FARC Guerrillas', *Colombia Journal Online*, www.colombiajournal.org/farcphotos.htm.

Lindqvist, Sven (1979), *Land and Power in South America*, Harmondsworth: Penguin.

Marx, Karl (1991), *Capital: A Critique of Political Economy*, Volume 3, Harmondsworth: Penguin.

Meza, Ricardo Vargas (1998), 'The FARC, the War and the Crisis of State', *NACLA Report on the Americas* 31(5): 22–8.

Molano, Alfredo (2000), 'The Evolution of the FARC', *NACLA Report on the Americas* 34(2): 23–32.

Mondragon, Hector (2001), 'Towards "Humanitrian Intervention" in Colombia?', www.zmag.org/crisescurevts/colombia/hemon.htm.

Nichols, Dick (2001), 'Thousands Attend World Social Forum in Brazil', *LINKS: International Journal for Social Renewal*, www.dsp.org.au/links/back/issue18/Nichols.htm.

Ortiz, Roman D. (2002), 'Insurgent Strategies in the Post-Cold War: The Case of the Revolutionary Armed Forces of Colombia', *Studies in Conflict and Terrorism* 25: 127–43.

Osterling, Jorge P. (1989), *Democracy in Colombia: Clientelist Politics and Guerrilla Warfare*, Oxford: Transaction.

Parpart, Jane (2000), 'Rethinking Participation, Empowerment, and Development from a Gender Perspective', in *Transforming Development: Foreign Aid for a Changing World*, ed. J. Freeman, Toronto: University of Toronto Press.

Pearce, Jenny (1990), *Colombia: Inside the Labyrinth*, London: Latin America Bureau.

Pearce, Scott (2002), 'Fuelling War: The Impact of Canadian Oil Investment on the Conflict in Colombia', *Centre for Research on Latin America and the Caribbean (CERLAC)*, Working Paper Series.

Pearson, Ruth (1992), *Poverty and Development in the 1990s*, Oxford: Oxford University Press.

Penhaul, Karl (2001), 'Colombia's Communist Guerrillas Take On a Feminine Face', *Global Correspondent*, 1 January.

Petras, James, and Morris Morley (1990), *US Hegemony under Siege: Class, Politics and Development in Latin America*, London: Verso.

Petras, James, and Henry Veltmeyer (2001), *Globalization Unmasked: Imperialism in the 21st Century*, London: Zed Books.

Petras, James, and Henry Veltmeyer (2003), *System in Crisis: The Dynamics of Free Market Capitalism*, London: Zed Books.

Petras, James, and Maurice Zeitlin (1968), *Latin America: Reform or Revolution? A Reader*, Greenwich, CT: Fawcett Publications.

Randall, Stephen J. (1992), *Colombia and the United States: Hegemony and Interdependence*, Athens, GA, and London: University of Georgia Press.

Research Unit for Political Economy (2003), 'How and Why the World Social Forum Emerged', *The Economics and Politics of the World Social Forum*, www.rupe-india.org/35/howandwhy.html.

Richani, Nazih (2002), *Systems of Violence: The Political Economy of War and Peace in Colombia*, New York: SUNY Press.

Rochlin, James F. (2003), *Vanguard Revolutionaries in Latin America: Peru, Colombia, México*, Boulder, CO: Lynne Rienner.

Roman, Fernando (2000), 'Plan Colombia Means War', *Buenos Aires Daily*, 2 October.

Sachs, Carolyn (1996), *Gendered Fields: Rural Women, Agriculture, and Environment*, Boulder, CO: Westview Press.

Scott, Peter Dale (2003), *Drugs, Oil, and War: The United States in Afghanistan, Colombia and Indochina*, New York: Rowman & Littlefield Publishing.

United States Embassy in Bogotá (2000), *Statement of Rand Beers Assistant Sectary of State Bureau for International Narcotics and Law Enforcement Affairs before the Subcommittee on Foreign Operations, Export Financing, and Related Programs of the*

House Appropriations Committee, 29 February, Washington: Bureau for International Narcotics and Law Enforcement Affairs.

Vanden, Harry E., and Gary Prevost (2002), *The Politics of Latin America: The Power Game*, New York: Oxford University Press.

Veltmeyer, Henry, and James Petras (2002), 'The Social Dynamics of Brazil's Rural Landless Workers' Movement: Ten Hypotheses on Successful Leadership', *Canadian Review of Sociology and Anthropology* 39(1): 79–96.

Weeks, John, and Phil Gunson (1991), *Panama: Made in the USA*, London: Latin American Bureau.

Weil, Thomas A., et al. (1970), *Area Handbook for Colombia*, Washington, DC: Foreign Area Studies of the American University.

Wickham-Crowley, Timothy (1992), *Guerrillas & Revolution in Latin America: A Comparative Study of Insurgents and Regimes since 1956*, Princeton, NJ: Princeton University Press.

Wickham-Crowley, Timothy (1991), *Exploring Revolution: Essays on Latin America Insurgency and Revolutionary Theory*, New York: M.E. Sharpe.

Wilson, Scott (2003), 'Colombia's Rebel Zone: World Apart', *Washington Post Foreign Service*, 18 October.

Wood, Ellen Meiksins (2003), *Empire of Capital*, London: Verso.

14

Indian Peasant Movements in Mexico: The Struggle for Land, Autonomy and Democracy

Armando Bartra and Gerardo Otero

> In spite of it all, Indians knew that the land was theirs, due to their history, right and also labour, which ... is what made it blossom. (Warman 1974)

The purpose of this chapter is to assess the emergence of the Indian peasant movement in Mexico at the turn of the twenty-first century. Just as indigenous peasants were the most radical group in the Revolution of 1910–20, the 1 January 1994 uprising led by the Zapatista National Liberation Army (EZLN) has also represented a watershed in Mexico's political history. Most analysts of indigenous peasant movements in Latin America tend to emphasize either the class basis of rural movements (Petras and Veltmeyer 2001) or the identity politics involved in their mobilization (Esteva 1999; Alvarez et al. 1998). By contrast, we argue that in most social movements, but particularly so in the case of indigenous peasant struggles, material (land) and identity (culture) demands are inseparable.

Indigenous ethnicity and culture are simply the anchoring points of the struggle for land. Indigenous ethnicities have been reproduced for centuries in a subordinate interaction with ruling and middle groups and classes, and its reproduction has depended primarily on having access to land (Otero 2004a). When the linkage with land as the means of livelihood was severed permanently, former indigenous peoples had no choice but to assimilate to *mestizo* society after only a couple or so generations. Although assimilation has resulted in lost languages and cultural practices, Mexico has witnessed since the 1970s, and most forcefully in the 1990s, a strong resurgence of the struggle by Indian peoples for land and autonomy to reproduce their culture. Part of this resurgence is explained by the duplicity of the Mexican government: on the one hand, new agrarian legislation in 1992 cancelled the possibility of further agrarian reform, by changing Article 27 of the 1917 Constitution, which had emerged from the Revolution (Bartra 1992, 2003a); on the other hand, the government signed the 1989 ILO Convention No. 169 on Indigenous Peoples (Hernández Navarro 1994). The latter has given legitimacy to the continued struggle for land and territory, now with the added central demand for autonomy in culture and self-governance. In a country that has been guided by liberal ideology since the nineteenth century, and that has fervently tried to establish a homogeneous, monolithic, *mestizo* (mixed-blood) national identity, indigenous struggles represent a major challenge (Hernández Navarro 1997).

This chapter traces the rise of the indigenous peasant movement in Mexico, with emphasis on the last three decades of the twentieth century. The first section offers background information on indigenous struggles for land and autonomy and the conceptual framework used to interpret them. The second section discusses the relations between the Mexican state and Indian peoples throughout the twentieth century, with emphasis on the 1970s–1980s. The third section offers an analysis of the EZLN uprising in 1994, with attention paid to how the EZLN and the broader indigenous movement in Mexico have impacted on each other. Finally, our conclusion addresses the dilemma of the indigenous movement today: will it consolidate itself as a strictly indigenous movement, or go beyond its ethnic boundaries to found its class identity as part of the peasantry, and thus establish alliances with the rest of the peasantry and other subordinate classes in Mexico?

History and Concepts

Indigenous peoples in postcolonial Mexico

If the colonial state dispossessed Indian communities and subjected most of their members to slavery and harsh working conditions, the postcolonial Mexican state attempted to eliminate Indians as a social category altogether. Upon Mexico's political independence from Spain in 1821, the ruling classes, which descended from Spaniards and propagated a white supremacism, sought to constitute a national identity that excluded the Indian. While this white supremacism was established in the initial legislation of independent Mexico, the state moved most vigorously to deprive Indian communities of their means of livelihood several decades later, during the *Porfiriato* of 1876–1910, the period prior to the revolution. The liberal dictator Porfirio Díaz set out to unify the nation, extend the railroad network, and impose military rule from the centre. Capitalism was in full expansion at this time, but because vast tracts of land remained in the hands of indigenous communities the Díaz government changed the law to allow the process of primitive accumulation to proceed freely.

Primitive accumulation consisted in a double 'liberation' of direct producers from the means to produce their livelihood (i.e., expropriation of indigenous lands) and from any dependency relations which may have prevented them from selling their labour-power, thus creating a free proletariat for capitalist development. Importantly, at the centre of this process were the landholdings of the Roman Catholic Church, which by the mid-nineteenth century was the largest landowner, under a type of feudal ownership. This contrasted markedly with the emerging liberal ideology and represented a major fetter to capitalist development. Thus the liberal reforms in the 1857 Constitution provided the legal instruments to expropriate the Church's landholdings. And the same law, aided by further legislation in 1883 and 1884, went on to be applied to indigenous community land. Thus, after the liberal reform laws and during the *Porfiriato*, the Indian communities were deprived of 90 per cent of their land.

The immediate outcome of the liberal reforms was a transfer in land ownership from the Church and the Indian communities to existing and new *latifundistas*, large landholders in the private sector of Mexican agriculture. In the decades that followed, they satisfied their voracious appetites for land by fencing off large portions of Indian communal land, while also bonding dispossessed Indian peasants to the land through various debts that they would incur as workers to the landowner (credits for wedding feasts, goods advanced at *tiendas de raya* or hacienda stores, and so on). These debts were inherited by the peons' children, who were not able to leave their 'jobs' until all outstanding debts to the landlord were settled (López Cámara 1967; Hansen 1974).

The 1910 revolutionary movement coalesced in different ways in the various regions of Mexico. In the North, revolution was led

by the *hacendados*, large landowners who were excluded from political power during the *Porfiriato*. They formed a broad and unlikely
alliance with their own peons, small farmers, ranchers and urban
middle classes. In central Mexico, by contrast, the main social rift
was between the expropriated indigenous communities and the
hacendados. Specifically, in the state of Morelos, indigenous peasants had been organized to oppose the *Porfiriato* since 1908, before
northern *hacendado* Francisco I. Madero had even called for the
revolution's first shot (Womack 1969). Unlike the broad alliance
in the north, which was led by *hacendados*, the Morelos peasantry
named their leader from among their own community: Emiliano
Zapata. Strictly speaking, Zapata was not a peasant since he earned
his livelihood from working on a hacienda for wages, yet he was a
respected member of the community. Followers of Zapata decided
to ally themselves with Madero's *hacendados* because an effort to air
their grievances had been repulsed at the state level.

The Zapatista alliance with Madero was short-lived. Soon after
the dictator was deposed it became obvious that Madero was surrounded by similarly conservative forces, which prevented him from
fulfilling his promises of land reform. Hence Zapata launched his own
revolutionary call, the Plan de Ayala, in 1911. In 1912, Madero was
overthrown and killed by his right-wing forces of restoration, detonat-
ing Mexico's civil war. By December 1914, the peasant armies led by
Emiliano Zapata in the south and Francisco Villa in the north had
the upper hand militarily, with radical agrarian reform as their main
political banner. But the northern *hacendados* reconstituted their armies
and eventually defeated the radical peasant armies. Politically, they
co-opted the peasant banner of agrarian reform by including Article
27 in the 1917 Constitution, a paper promise of agrarian reform that
was implemented only timidly until the 1930s, when more significant
land redistribution was carried out by the administration of Lázaro
Cárdenas (1934–40). After this, the revolution became institutionalized, with the so-called 'great revolutionary family' at the helm. At
least with regard to the peasantry and agrarian reform, the revolution
was basically over: land distribution slowed down considerably, most
of the land granted to peasants thereafter was either not suitable for
agriculture or if it was the state directed their productive processes,
and peasants now had to deal with a whole set of state institutions
that tended to co-opt their class organizations. For the rest of the
twentieth century, one of the greatest challenges for rural peoples

of Mexico was to gain organizational independence from the state and autonomy from other political organizations. We now turn to a brief outline of our conceptualization of this quest.

The political-cultural theory of class formation

The central question for the theory of political-class formation may be phrased as follows: how can subordinate groups, communities or classes become hegemonic or dominant, or at least gain the ability · to push for state interventions in their favour, while remaining independent? Political-class formation may be defined as the process through which direct producers and other exploited and/or oppressed social groups shape demands, form organizations to pursue them, and generate a leadership to represent them before the state and other organizations with which alliances are built. The question of how indigenous peasants are constituted into a political class could conceivably be answered from a strictly economic-class perspective or from an identity-based point of view. Nevertheless, the distinctiveness of the theory of political-class formation used here is, precisely, that both economic and cultural issues are integral parts of what constitutes classes *politically*. A politically formed class involves both material interests and cultural aspects of identity, which result from the relations of production (between exploiters and exploited) and the relations of reproduction (among the exploited), respectively.

For Indian peasants, a key component of the relations of production comprises their relations with other ethnic groups, namely with the dominant groups of *mestizos, ladinos, cholos* or whites (the names vary by country and ethnic social construction). Now, for predominantly subsistence peasants, it may well be that the key relation with the dominant groups takes place through the market, and not through production. In either case, ethnic relations within asymmetrical production or market relations will tend either to reinforce ethnic identities or to force the subordinate ethnic group into assimilation. In Laclau and Mouffe's terms (1985), the antagonism between the two subject positions constitutes their respective identities. The remarkable fact about many Indian ethnicities in Latin America is that they have resisted assimilation for about half a millennium, despite the fact that they have always occupied a subordinate position.

Political-class formation theory is clearly located in a post-Cold War era, one in which the struggle for socialism through violent revolutionary means is essentially over, at least in the Americas. The struggle for democratic socialism must now be waged by expanding liberal-democratic structures and building a new, popular-democratic hegemonic bloc around human needs and environmental sustainability.

Political-class formation theory proposes regional cultures, state intervention and leadership types as the mediating determinations between class structural processes and political-formation outcomes. Regional cultures, in which relations among the exploited (e.g. kinship and community relations) are critical, form the basis on which direct producers articulate their demands. State intervention shapes the initial contours of the resulting character of a class organization: the state always tries to co-opt organizations, while the latter fight for their independence. Finally, leadership types and grassroots modes of participation determine both the organization's chances of remaining independent from the state and autonomous from other political organizations and the character of its alliances with other movements and organizations (Otero 1999; Otero and Jugenitz 2003). We now turn to how the 'great revolutionary family' constructed the Mexican state from 1929 until 2000, when its ruling Institutional Revolutionary Party (PRI) lost the presidential election. The following sections discuss how indigenous peasants fought cooptation and became increasingly constituted into a politically formed class.

Indian Peoples and the Mexican State

The wars of the state, or the 'philanthropic ogre'

If Mexican peasants invented themselves during the revolution, they were eventually oppressed by the state during the twentieth century. But peasants also received a series of concessions from the state, which in most cases resulted in their political co-optation. Hence the Mexican Nobel laureate Octavio Paz characterized the state as the 'philanthropic ogre': it oppresses and represses those who dissent, while rewarding loyalty. For peasants, then, the tension between co-optation and rebellion has marked their history (Bartra 1985, 2003b). The rural insurgency of the past century was made up of the wars of the ogre: attempts to break with the material and hegemonic knots of state power. In Mexico, Nietzsche's view of the state became materialized when the revolution became the state: 'A state, is called the coldest of all cold monsters. Coldly lieth it also; and this lie creepeth from its mouth: "I, the state, am the people"' (1962: 44).

Few police states of the twentieth century had the social control that the Mexican state did. This was a benevolent autocrat that restructured workers, peasants, middle classes and entrepreneurs from top to bottom. It was achieved by an implacable corporatist system articulated to the state and the PRI, the latter in charge of the system's electoral rituals. The 'civil society' organizations created from the top amounted, in fact, to a realm of politics confiscated by the state, the result being loyalty, co-optation and the assurance of electoral triumph for the ruling party. The 'sectors' of this quasi-single-party state were the political and union supports of the 'revolution made government': the workers' sector, made up of the Mexican Workers' Confederation (Confederación de Trabajadores de México) and the other large national unions (oil, electricity, railroad, phone, mining, etc.); the peasant sector, made up mainly of the National Peasant Confederation (Confederación Nacional Campesina, CNC) and the Agrarian Communities Leagues; and the popular sector, constituted by state employees, teachers, and other middle strata, organized in the Popular Organizations National Confederation (Confederación Nacional de Organizaciones Populares, CNOP). For their part, entrepreneurs, without being formally a sector inside the ruling party, were organized into associations, confederations and chambers, and were lined up in a corporatist relation *vis-à-vis* the state.

In twentieth-century Mexico, the Leviathan was a cold monster commanded by all-powerful princes whose power lasted only six years, until the next election. The command of the president, however, was as absolute in space as it was limited in time. Philanthropic ogres, as Octavio Paz would call them, were at times prodigal or petty, but they were always providers.

Mexicans now need to liberate themselves by killing the Leviathan, even if the old patriarch is no longer scary. Despite the fact that it is surrounded by a warrior empire, multilateral organizations, draconian trade agreements, and planetary corporations, and is increasingly capable of doing less, it should be killed. Without a symbolic parricide we will never exorcize the intimate and cold monster, to put in its place a state with a human face. Notwithstanding neoliberal globalization, it is time for civil societies to construct good governments: public powers that are limited by civil society but that are also willing to confront the large national problems, asserting what remains of sovereignty. Therefore, we need to kill the autocratic state to reconcile ourselves with a new, popular–democratic state that responds to civil society (Otero 2004b).

In a country in which civil society was created by the bureaucratic ogre in its own image, the citizen struggle for self-governance at the community and regional levels becomes an issue of the first order. If the radical state reformism under the presidency of Lázaro Cárdenas in the late 1930s conferred temporary legitimacy to the unions fighting for social justice, these were always anti-democratic and corporatist. But in the second half of the century, the relentless proliferation of struggles for autonomy converged, first, with the progressive loss of legitimacy of the political system, which started symbolically with the 1968 student movement, which was violently repressed; and, second, with the wearing down of union discipline, exposed by the worker, peasant and popular insurgencies of the 1960s. This new political mobilization was followed by the failings of the import-substitution, protectionist and state-centred economic model, which were dramatized by the debt and financial crises of the 1980s and 1990s. Lastly, the rupture of the PRI's 'democratic current', in 1988, signalled the definitive sclerosis of the political system's informal reproduction mechanisms, and the beginning of the end of the 'great revolutionary family'.

The war against the ogre has gone through various phases. During the 1960s and 1970s the word 'independent' became the symbol of democratic opposition: 'independent' peasant unions and confederations, 'independent' conferences of indigenous organizations, fronts for union 'independence', political parties 'independent' from the state, 'independent' magazines and journals that did not accept funding from the government; even 'independent' picture exhibitions, 'independent' films, and an 'independent' dance company. In those years, 'independence' meant simply not belonging to the PRI, marking a distance from the omnipresent Mexican state. Thus, a federation of democratic students or a peasant confederation may have proclaimed themselves 'independent', but they could still be politically subordinated to an opposition organization like the Mexican Communist Party (Partido Comunista Mexicano, PCM) – that is, lacking 'autonomy'.

Hence, in the last quarter of the century, 'autonomy' became the rallying cry among oppositional and popular-democratic organizations.

This concept began to become generalized after 1984, when about fifty rural organizations constituted themselves into the National Union of Autonomous Regional Peasant Organizations (Unión Nacional de Organizaciones Regionales Campesinas Autónomas, UNORCA). Although initially this coordinating organization rejected the term 'independent' for the questionable reason of avoiding direct confrontation with the state – the two being virtually synonymous (Gordillo 1988) – in the coming years 'autonomy' came to be associated, as 'independence' had, with the rejection of political subservience, but more than this, with social and economic self-management of peasant and cooperative production. Thus, 'autonomous' peasants rejected the guardianship of the state and set out to 'appropriate the productive process' – self-management – while neighbourhoods and communities organized around the self-managing provision of basic services like schooling and security.

Indigenous struggles for autonomy, in the 1980s and 1990s, supplemented and further radicalized the peasant movement. First, the meaning of 'autonomy' for indigenous peoples went beyond organizational independence and socio-economic self-management to mean free self-determination; that is, self-government at the community level, according to their own norms, practices and customs (*usos y costumbres*). Second, demands for 'autonomy' invoked an autochthonous peoples' history, founding the demand in a right that precedes the current national state. In a sense, this claim is external to the hegemonic social system.

In the transition from political independence to socio-economic self-management and then to self-government, the underlying concept of autonomy sharpened its connotation of otherness, of an alternative, popular-democratic and multicultural hegemonic project. Initially, the demand for autonomy may be a non-submissive way of becoming inserted into the existing order; in its higher form, however, autonomy becomes an anti-systemic practice by which the oppressed resist by constructing alternative organizational orders. But the progression from repealing unanimous and monolithic politics towards a form of depoliticized self-management and then towards the demand for a multicultural 'world where all the worlds fit' is a process of overcoming-and-conservation of stages, so that each new stage contains and retains all the previous ones.

The fact is that the most radical autonomous experiences are not islands, and they will not survive without independent organizations that fight here and now for the basic demands for their constituencies. Autonomous organizations also require collective self-managing operators of popular production and services in perpetual tension with the state and the market. They also need institutional parties that are capable of promoting alternative reforms and projects from an oppositional position or within the state. The peoples' struggle for autonomy is symbolic of Max Weber's view: 'Certainly all historical experience confirms the truth – that man would not have attained the possible unless time and again he had reached out for the impossible' (1958: 128).

First peoples: from cooptation to the struggle for autonomy

State policy of nineteenth-century Mexico attempted to exterminate Indians, statistically or physically, so as to construct a homogeneously white nation-state. In contrast, the post-revolutionary state of the twentieth century engaged in a concerted policy of integration, which assumed the abandonment of indigenous cultures in favour of adopting the dominant, *mestizo* culture. Throughout most of the twentieth century, therefore, the social and political presence of First Peoples was diluted. But they reappeared forcefully in the last decade of the century, organized around their demands for autonomy, self-governance and democracy. These demands presume that Indian peoples will have control over land and territory, while remaining an integral – and dignified – part of the Mexican nation-state.

Essentially, indigenous participation during the violent stage of the 1910–20 revolution adopted three modalities: first, in a kind of armed extension of servile labour, some Mayan Indians signed up with the landlord forces that resisted the revolution. Second, in the north, certain ethnic groups took advantage of the war conjuncture to exchange their armed support for national revolutionary forces for the promise of a solution to their ancestral local problems. Third, the Zapatistas of the central part of Mexico developed autonomous policies and a peasant programme in which their Nahuatl ethnic and linguistic condition in fact was not expressed.[1] All of these ethnicities were doubtless indigenous, but racism was too prevalent and strong for indigenous ethnicity to become a rallying point of organizing at the time.

The first revolutionary Indianism (a term to distinguish the Indian-initiated efforts in identity construction from 'Indigenism', the state's policy of integration that pursues acculturation and assimilation) emerged at the end of the second decade of the twentieth century, when Carrillo Puerto, leader of the Socialist Party of the Southeast, introduced agrarian reform similar to the Zapatismo of Morelos, in central Mexico. He provided the former, semi-slave hacienda peons with the territorial basis for autonomy, an agricultural development based on the return to maize, dissolving their food dependency on the hacienda. Red Sundays and other cultural and educational activities promoted the recovery of the indigenous language, culture and self-esteem. Land, liberty and dignity became integrated in a sort of indigenous socialism, a Mayan utopia. This was frustrated in 1923 by the uprising of the 'Divine Caste', the landed ruling class in Yucatan, and the murder of Carrillo Puerto (Paoli and Montalvo 1977).

From the 1940s onwards, autochthonous peoples became the subjects of bureaucratic indigenism, the policy of a paternalistic state implemented through the National Indigenist Institute (Instituto Nacional Indigenista, INI), which sought to integrate them into national society. INI wanted to rescue their culture as folklore and, at best, to address their economic, social and political needs as citizens, but overlooked their demand for identity and the rights that emanate from it. Thus, if the peasantry created by the revolution was firmly contained in the corporatist institutions of the state, twentieth-century Indians were reinvented by INI during peacetime. Their struggle to free themselves from the networks of political power has been more delayed, but in a sense more profound.

The new Indianism began to define its profile during the 1970s and 1980s, when a number of communities in central and western Mexico developed local or regional movements in defence of land, forests and water, and against *caciques* (political and economic strongmen) and municipal government, as in Oaxaca in the south. In these struggles, however, Indians did not put forward their specificity. Land remained the centre of their demands.

The agrarian reform that emerged from the revolution provided for two forms of land tenure: *ejido*, designed for land to be redistributed to *mestizo* peasants, with usufruct rights over the land but with ownership vested in the state; and agrarian communities, designed for collective use by indigenous communities that could prove a claim to land on the basis of colonial documents. In practice, however, Indian communities pushed their demands for land not so much by the historical roots of their rights, but by what was more feasible according to the new agrarian legal structure: there were Indians who sought *ejido* land grants and *mestizos* that found some colonial archive to claim the restitution of communal lands. Thus, the first explicit neo-Zapatismo in the post-revolutionary era was organically expressed in the 'Plan de Ayala National Coordinator' (Coordinadora Nacional Plan de Ayala, CNPA), which held its first National Meeting of Independent Indigenous Organizations in the Nahuatl community of Milpa Alta. CNPA's majority membership is indigenous: of the 21 regional organizations that comprised its founding in 1982, 7 were mestizo and 14 were integrated by 12 different indigenous ethnicities: Nahuatl, Purhépecha, Otomí, Huasteca, Mazahua, Zapoteca, Chinanteca, Triqui, Amusga, Chatina, Tzotzil and Tzeltal. Although with less weight, the coordinating organization of regional groups, UNORCA, has an important militancy for the autochthonous peoples. Nevertheless, neither of these two convergent organizations posited the ethnic question with any force.

The first Indigenous Congress held in Chiapas in 1974 was Indianist in form: communication was in the Mayan languages Chol, Tzeltal, Tzotzil and Tojolobal; it produced diagnostic studies and proposals by community and linguistic groups; and papers and conclusions were elaborated by consensus. Yet its agenda and action conclusions were basically peasant, as the major issues were land, trade, health and education.

During the early 1970s, Oaxaca state was the main producer of indigenous regional organizations: the Worker Peasant Student Coalition of the Isthmus (Coalición Obrero Campesino Estudiantil del Istmo, COCEI), constituted by Zapotecs; the Yacaltecos Organization of the Sierra de Juárez, which fought against the regional *cacique*; the Promoters' Coalition of Bilingual Indians, with membership from nearly all ethnicities in the state; the Sierra de Juárez Organization for the Defence of Natural Resources and Social Development (Odrenasij), also Zapotec; the Mixe Natural and Human Resources Defence Committee (Codremi); the Organizing and Consultation Committee for the Union of Peoples of the Northern Sierra of Oaxaca (Codeco).

These organizations started to elaborate a programmatic platform with encouragement by indigenous intellectuals, such as the Zapotec from Guelatao, Jaime Martínez Luna, and the Mixe from Tlahitoltepec, Floriberto Díaz. At the beginning of the 1980s, a joint declaration by Odrenasij, Codeco and Codremi read as follows:

We demand absolute respect for our communitarian self-determination over our lands, over all of our natural resources, and over the forms of organization that we wish to give ourselves.... We demand respect for the expressions of our community life, our language, our spirituality.... We demand respect for and promotion of our forms of community government because it is the only guaranteed way of avoiding the centralization of political and economic power. We are opposed to have our natural resources plundered in the name of a supposed 'national development'.

In order to sharpen its specificity, however, the indigenous movement had to confront the state, which had attempted to appropriate the new ethnicism in formation since the 1970s. It also had to confront the rest of the peasant and popular movement, which was trying to subsume it by inertia or premeditation. Finally, the indigenous movement had to confront the intrusive agenda and practices of NGOs that were present from the 1980s.

Starting with the Chiapas congress of 1974, which was called by the state and Church but was notably self-managed by Indian peoples, the government promoted two organizational initiatives: first, the formation of Supreme Councils by ethnic group, and, second, in 1975, the formation of the Indian Peoples' National Council (Consejo Nacional de Pueblos Indios, CNPI). The Council was supposed to be subordinate to the state, but it soon become restless: in 1976, CNPI demanded the dismantling of INI and, during the López Portillo administration (1976–82), it criticized the Agricultural and Livestock Promotion Law (Ley de Fomento Agropecuario), geared as it was to develop agrarian capitalism via joint ventures between capitalists and *ejidatarios*, using *ejido* land. When the Council called its third congress against the president's will, he tried unsuccessfully to liquidate the emancipated Frankenstein. This task was finally accomplished by his successor, President Miguel de la Madrid (1982–88) in 1985, when CNPI was transformed into the submissive Indigenous Peoples Confederation, which became an affiliate of the ruling PRI.

In a parallel process, however, numerous independent regional organizations emerged during the 1980s and the early 1990s, such as those in Oaxaca: the Northern Isthmus Zone Union of Indigenous Communities (Ucizoni), the Isthmus Region Union of Indigenous Communities (UCIRI), the 100 Years Independent Peasant Union (UCI 100 Años), and the Mixe Authorities Assembly (Asam). Several independent organizations emerged in other states: the Chiapas State Independent Physicians Organization (OMIECH) and the Chiapas

State Indigenous Representatives Organization; in Hidalgo State, the Eastern Mexico 'Emiliano Zapata' Democratic Front (FDOMEZ); and in Guerrero State, the Alto Balsas Nahua Peoples' Council (Bartra 2000, 2001).

Increasing migration, however, first to the irrigated fields of northwestern Mexico and then to the United States, turned many indigenous communities into multi-spatial and discontinuous entities that had to organize outside of their ancestral territories. The forceful struggles of Mixtec and Zapotec in Oregon, Washington and, above all, California during the second half of the 1980s led to several strong organizations, such as the Mixtec Popular Civic Committee, the 'Benito Juárez' Civic Association and the Exploited and Oppressed People's Association. On this basis, in 1991 all of these organizations decided to form the Binational Mixtec–Zapotec Front, which would expand into Baja California and eventually into their native Oaxaca. Because membership was expanded to include Mixes, Triquis and Chololtecas, the organization was renamed the Binational Oaxaqueño Indigenous Front (FIOB) (Kearney 1996, 2000).

With the rise of new organizations came massive meetings and encounters, which strengthened identities, built solidarities and developed leadership: the First Encounter of Independent Indigenous Organizations was held in Puxmecatán, Oaxaca, in 1980; the second in Cherán Atzicurin, Michoacán. This process gained force at the end of the 1980s, in the midst of the commemoration of half a millennium of imposed Indianness, when the First International Forum on Human Rights of the Indian Peoples was held in Matías Romero, Oaxaca, with about 600 participants from 96 organizations, 14 states, and 23 ethnic groups. Also participating were delegates from Guatemala, Honduras, Peru and Bolivia, and representatives from universities and NGOs. This meeting resulted in the 500 Years of Indigenous and Popular Resistance World Campaign. In March of 1990, the Second Forum was held in Xochimilco, Distrito Federal, in the midst of dissent, which did not prevent the constitution of the 500 Years Mexican Council in July, made up of 23 indigenous, peasant and popular grassroots organizations, NGOs and scholars. Finally, the Council called the celebration of the First National Assembly of Indian Peoples and Organizations, which was held in Milpa Alta, in which a new organization emerged: the Indigenous Peoples' National Front (Frente Nacional de Pueblos Indios, Frenapi).

By this time the indigenous agenda had been clearly defined:

the right to autonomy and self-determination ... the right to cultural identity ... the right to land and natural resources ... the right to freely determine the internal political condition of communities, in agreement with traditional forms of organization ... the prevalence of traditional customary Indian right.

It is noteworthy that, in contrast with the trend of differentiation at the end of the 1980s, which caused the rupture of several indigenous organizations with the more peasant-biased CNPA, the 500 Years Mexican Council became more oriented towards a broad convergence. It also called for 'encouraging the unity of ... Indian peoples with the peasant, workers and popular sectors' (Consejo Mexicano 500 Años 1991).

This convergence process coincided with the first few years of the administration of President Carlos Salinas (1988–94), which was trying to bring the independent rural movements to the corporatist fold. The executive's operators had formed the Permanent Agrarian Congress (Congreso Agrario Permanente, CAP) in 1989 to pre-empt the independent Unitary Action Agreement (Convenio de Acción Unitaria, CAU), and in 1990 the pro-government CNC called for the formation of an Indigenous Permanent Congress (CIP) on Salinas's orders. This corporatist organization was geared to challenge the independent Frenapi. Some members of Frenapi, such as the Independent Front of Indian Peoples (FIPI), affiliated with the corporatist organization, CIP, along with the Indigenist Action Section of the corporatist CNC, the Indian Peoples' National Coordinator (CNPI) and others. CIP was formally constituted in October of 1991 and, as with the peasants, Salinas offered millions in resources to this organization through the Indian Fund. This co-optation manoeuvre worked, for just as the peasant independent CAU was not able to survive the emergence of the corporatist CAP, so too Frenapi did not last long as an independent challenger organization.

This organizational co-optation measure was supplemented by a presidential reform of Constitutional Article 4, regarding Indian culture, approved in 1991 (Díaz Polanco 1992). This reform amounted to non-substantive, vague, culturalist changes. In a similarly superficial vein, the Mexican government signed the 1989 ILO Convention No. 169, which was ratified at the end of 1990 and published in January of the following year, but not implemented. A last, top-down symbolic governmental concession to the First Peoples had a mixed content: it amounted to retaining the inalienable character of communal lands in the enabling law of Constitutional Article 27, which fundamentally changed in 1992. Nevertheless, some recourse for privatization was left in the new legislation, as these lands may be lost, for instance, if they make up the indigenous-community share in a corporation constituted in association with private capitalists (Bartra 1992, 2003b).

The significant fact, however, was that lands that had been returned or confirmed to Indian peoples were not excluded from the mechanism by which the government sought to have *ejido* lands adopt the 'free-hold' title, the step before alienation and sale. Prior to the 1992 revision of the agrarian reform law, *ejido* lands were not subject to sale; they could only be transferred to heirs. Because *ejido* and communal lands made up about half of all agricultural, livestock and forestry land in Mexico, they had become a major fetter to capitalist development (Otero 1999: ch. 3).

In order to understand the methodical Indianist bias of a clearly neoliberal government, we must remember that the 1990s started with strong ethnicist winds throughout the world. These were elaborated by multilateral organizations, such as the ILO, and expressed in constitutional reforms that were usually 'light', and limited to multicultural legislation. On occasion, however, Indian territories were acknowledged, and so were customary rights and self-government. Paradoxically, the world trend to counter-agrarian reforms, in which that of Salinas was inserted, was accompanied by a certain degree of ethnic-rights recognition. Thus, for example, the same law that countered the Bolivian agrarian reform laws of the early 1950s established a mechanism to acknowledge the territory of First Peoples. In practice, this resulted in granting title and security to the large landholders, which were now excluded from any threat of expropriation. Ultimately, the 1990s saw a clear paper concession to the 500 years of debt to Indians (Brysk 2000; Van Cott 2000).

The government has not been the only party to intervene in Indian affairs. Since the mid-1980s, the Mexican Indian movement has been the focus of diverse interest groups. First the NGOs became interested, then the 1985 earthquake in Mexico City struck, which together with the economic crisis turned Mexico into a worthy cause for major international cooperation. Church-related organizations also took up the ethnic question. Thus, Indians became the paradigm of 'vulnerable groups' and the object of assistance. In the best of cases they also became the object of solidarity and accompaniment. Projects for education, health, food and housing, and, to a lesser extent, savings, loans and production were multiplied. It is not a coincidence, then, that the Matías Romero International Forum focused on 'human rights', a popular rallying point, and that it was convened by grassroots organizations such as UCIZONI, along with NGOs such as Equipo Pueblo. Internationalism was another decisive factor at this stage, given that the Mexican process is closely linked to that of Latin America at large, dramatized by three meetings of the Continental Encounter of Indian Peoples: the first in Ecuador in 1990, the second in Guatemala a year later, and the third in Nicaragua in 1992.

The events of 12 October 1992, demonstrate both the increasing indigenous activism, as well as the prevailing confusion. Mexico City's Zocalo, or central square, was filled with contingents representing a dispersed plurality of political positions: from ritualist cultural groups to the gathering of the 500 Years Mexican Council, and to religious marchers to the Basílica of the Virgin of Guadalupe, where the Catholic Church was granted pardon for having colonized them. In Morelia, Michoacán, angry Indians brought down the statue of Vasco de Quiroga, a pro-Indian missionary who possibly did not deserve it; and in San Cristóbal, Chiapas, they brought down that of Diego de Mazariegos, a ruthless conqueror who no doubt deserved it.

This was the highest point of the neo-Indianist wave that started in the 1970s. The 500 Years Mexican Council, which in 1991 contained about 350 organizations from 23 states and had coordinating committees in Chiapas, Guerrero, Veracruz, Mexico State and Puebla, became weakened after 12 October 1992. After this critical date, the accompaniment of NGOs also dwindled. The National Encounter of Civil Society and the Indian Peoples held in August of 1993 was unremarkable. The fashion was over. However, if by October of that year there were no more Indians at the Zocalo, by January 1994 they had reappeared with balaclavas on all the television screens, on the occasion of the uprising of the Zapatista National Liberation Army (Ejército Zapatista de Liberación Nacional, EZLN).

The Zapatista Indians:
From Guerrilla to Democratic Fighters

The terrain had no doubt been prepared by almost twenty years of ethnic struggle to gain independence from institutional indigenism, but the Chiapas uprising transformed an assistance-worthy 'vulnerable group' into the emblem of dignity and rebelliousness (Subcomandante Insurgente Marcos 2003; Bartra 2003c). The Zapatista programme is not particularly Indianist (work, land, housing, food, health, education, independence, liberty, democracy, justice and peace), but its constituency is indigenous and so are the strategies that it adopted when national and international mobilization opened the road to peace. In December of 1994, during the Peace with Justice and Dignity campaign that allowed the EZLN to break the army's enclosure, it published the conformation of thirty-eight autonomous 'rebel municipalities'. Months before, on 12 October, during the commemoration of the 502nd anniversary of conquest, the State Council of Indigenous and Peasant Organizations (Consejo Estatal de Organizaciones Indígenas y Campesinas, CEOIC) and the State Assembly of the Chiapas People (Asamblea Estatal del Pueblo Chiapaneco, AEPCH) called for the formation of Multiethnic Autonomous Regions. Meanwhile, several other peasant movements were establishing independent municipalities throughout Mexico: for example, in Ocosingo, Las Margaritas, Chiapas Highlands, and Chalchihuitán (Sarmiento 1994).

To this point we are still witnessing de facto autonomies, which are mixed up with demands for land and other indigenous and peasant demands. But, in 1995, when the first Dialogue Session between the EZLN and the federal government focused on autonomy rights, and, in 1996, when it shaped a proposal for constitutional changes, the indigenous movement entered a dynamic of rearticulation that would define it for the rest of the decade.

The constitutional reform on indigenous rights and culture is usually identified with the 'Ley Cocopa', which adopted the name of the Congressional Commission for Agreement and Peace. This legal initiative synthesized the San Andrés Agreements reached between the EZLN and the government's representatives on 16 February 1996 and defined the objectives and strategies of this new phase of the indigenous movement. It both deepens the organizational segregation between autochthonous peoples and *mestizos*, which was already emerging in the 1980s, and unifies ethnic groups. In spite of the fact that there were different approaches in the gestation of this legal initiative – communalists versus regionalists – it represents a plausible common legal framework, an umbrella of constitutional rights shared by diverse and distant collectivities that could have strong discrepancies around other issues (Hernández Navarro and

Vera Herrera 1998). As two anthropologists have put it, autonomy is not the effect of a unilateral decision from ethnic or national groups, nor from the states. It is a product of a political negotiation (Díaz Polanco and López y Rivas 1994). In contrast with political negotiations between social movements and the state, however, this one does not admit gradualism: substantive constitutional rights for Indian peoples are either acknowledged or they are not.

The definition of a new autonomy platform and strategy also required a renewed articulation, an organizational process that was precipitated by the Chiapas uprising. In the beginning, the ethnic contingents acted within the plural citizen convergence that responded to the EZLN's call in August 1994, the National Democratic Convention, held just two weeks prior to the national elections. The Convention was stimulated by the participation of Cuauhtémoc Cárdenas, the left-of-centre candidate, and resulted in a very broad and multi-class leftist front, articulated first by state conventions and later also within sectoral structures of peasants, workers, Indians, students, women, intellectuals, and artists. With the PRI's triumph in the elections, however, the Convention lost its efficacy for the conjuncture, and the National Liberation Movement (MLN) called by the EZLN in the Third Declaration of the Lacandón Jungle did not prosper. This was the last Zapatista initiative geared to encourage a broad popular and multi-class front, because since the end of 1995 and in 1996 its social calls were primarily Indianist; yet they were not only this, for the Zapatista National Liberation Front (FZLN), the legal and political arm of the EZLN, was organized in 1996.

In April 1995, representatives of about a hundred organizations held a meeting in Mexico City, the First National Indigenous Plural Assembly for Autonomy (Asamblea Nacional Indígena Plural por la Autonomía, ANIPA), which elaborated a project for autonomy legislation. The meeting was prolonged into a second one in Vacum, Sonora, and a third at the end of August in Oaxaca. Each meeting had increasing attendance, and the ANIPA was formalized as an organization that would make a significant contribution to the construction of the San Andrés Accords a few months later. One of the key goals of ANIPA has been to create a fourth level of government, between municipalities and states: the pluri-ethnic autonomous regions (or RAPs, its Spanish acronym). A 'Council of Representatives' would be the highest body of authority in the RAPs: 'All ethnic groups (both Indian and non-Indian) would be represented equally within this body, regardless of the demographic weight of each.' This body would be elected by direct and secret universal vote every three years, 'according to a principle of relative majority rule' (Ruiz Hernández 2000: 25).

The first convergence of autochthonous peoples expressly called by the EZLN was the First National Indigenous Forum. It was held in San Cristóbal, Chiapas, in January 1996, as part of the negotiation process with the federal government that had started a little earlier in San Andrés (Hernández and Herrera 1998; Gilbreth and Otero 2001). This forum was attended by 757 indigenous delegates, 568 observers, 248 guests and 403 journalists. Encouraged by this encounter, there were other meetings, and state and regional forums were constituted. In October of 1996, Comandanta Ramona, terminally ill with cancer, attended the constitution of the National Indigenous Congress (Congreso Nacional Indígena, CNI) in Mexico City. In 1997, when 1,111 Zapatistas left Chiapas en route to Mexico City, the CNI held its second congress. And in March of 2001, the CNI held its third congress, coinciding with the Zapatista Caravan for Indigenous Dignity of 23 comandantes and a subcomandante to Mexico City, where they attended a hearing in the plenary of the national Congress to make their case for the Cocopa legislative proposal, which had been sent to Congress by newly elected president Vicente Fox, the first opposition candidate to win the presidency after seventy-one years of PRI rule. Thus, the CNI sealed its intimate proximity with the course of Chiapas Zapatismo, and the demand for the constitutionality of the right for autonomy was tied to a peaceful solution for Chiapas.

The 'march of the colour of the earth', as the Caravan was also called, was the highest point in the phase of the indigenous movement that started in the mid-1990s, and it was articulated to the constitutional acknowledgement of autonomy. Self-government, by contrast, was an ancestral demand which was expressly pursued for at least a quarter of a century and conceptually formulated as a right during the 1980s. The peculiarity of the EZLN and the CNI movement since 1996, though, is that it has attempted to reach an agreement with the country's political forces that allows constitutional recognition. The novelty is that both Indians and Zapatistas centre their strategy on achieving a reform of the state.

This is no small goal. In a country where demands are fought for in very specific terms in the hope that the government will satisfy them, struggling for the acknowledgement of foundational rights is a big step. This is all the more so when this demand has mobilized the vast majority of indigenous organizations, which have the active support of the progressive social and political forces, with broad sympathy among the general public. Hence the exceptional possibility that a legislative process would be initiated from the bottom up was seen as viable.

The propitious conjuncture was present in two moments: during the San Andrés negotiations, at the start of the Ernesto Zedillo administration (1994–2000), and then after with the Caravan for Indigenous Dignity, at the start of the Fox administration. In both cases, when the negotiations became frustrated – in 1996 by the executive and in 2001 by the legislature, which passed a very watered-down version of the Cocopa initiative – the Indians and Zapatistas were stymied for the balance of the six-year electoral period. Thus the struggle has been markedly discontinuous and prolonged, because in order to develop a new bottom-up campaign they must wait for the 'top' conjuncture to change on its own. Furthermore, this legal route seems to have become exhausted in the eyes of the main protagonists. When Congress severely amputated the Cocopa initiative, and especially after the Supreme Court refused to fix the problem, both CNI and EZLN changed the terrain of struggle: Indians ratified their decision to exercise autonomy in practice, and the Zapatistas announced the suspension of all contact with the government. These are similar responses but with distinct perspectives. While Indian peoples wanted acknowledgement of a right, for the EZLN passage of the San Andrés accords was the major of three 'signals' from the government that they had set as conditions to restart negotiations. Thus Mexicans took steps backward on two terrains: Indian emancipation was halted and peace moved further away. Autochthonous peoples will have to continue fighting along the lines of the more limited protection of ILO Convention No. 169 (Díaz Polánco and Sánchez 2003), and Zapatistas will have to continue doing politics under conditions of exception and within the framework of 'suspended' negotiation with no end in sight. No doubt Indians and Zapatistas will continue to march together, but necessarily with diverse tactics and strategies.

The EZLN has established two key strategies. First, concerning its support bases, subject as they are to a political-military wall that threatens to be extended, the EZLN has substituted the *Aguascalientes* (its former meeting sites with civil society) for the *Caracoles* (self-governing sites for autonomous indigenous communities), creating the Councils of Good Government and a greater autonomy vis-à-vis the political-military command. In this way, the EZLN and its support bases are prepared to resist as long as it takes for a new, more favourable conjuncture to arrive. Second, the EZLN has proclaimed its right to do politics in every realm. Thus, it reanimated the FZLN and its monthly political magazine *Rebeldía*, and during 2003 it increased its public interventions – fighting for peace, protesting against the World Trade Organization in Cancún, holding an international encounter 'in defence of humanity'. The FZLN organized the commemorations of the twentieth anniversary of the EZLN and the tenth of the uprising, which were held in many places around Mexico and in at least sixty-four cities throughout the world, in the five continents.

The most important thing, however, is the lesson that Zapatistas are taking from their recent experience and the national and global circumstances. The EZLN has had several incarnations: a voluntarily pacific army in 1994, it encouraged a democratic transition by democratic means. As Subcomandante Marcos put it: 'the Convention's proposal is to force change through the electoral route.... We are making this effort to convince people to exhaust the electoral route, that it is worth it' (Morquecho 1994). In 1995 and 1996, the EZLN was an insurgent group that sought to negotiate an extensive agenda of reforms with the federal executive power, headed by Zedillo, demanding governmental commitments to favourable public policies for Indian peoples at the San Andrés sessions: 'autonomy does not imply that the state will stop having responsibility with the new levels of organization, which will have the right to public compensation funds and others that are due to Indian peoples' (EZLN 1996). In 2001, the Zapatistas were rebels that organized the Caravan of Indigenous Dignity to demand from legislators the approval of a constitutional reform; in the words of Subcomandante Marcos in an interview with journalists (Bellinghausen 2001), 'The indigenous peoples will win. ... We will convince the deputies [members of the lower chamber of Congress] that it is the hour of Congress.'

Until 2001, the Zapatistas were a group of insurgents that – without laying down their guns – for over eight years had encouraged reforms through elections, negotiation with the executive, and appeals to the legislature. This exceptional paradox from Chiapas has finally reached the conclusion that the institutional system has been exhausted, that all political parties and the bureaucratic elite are a bunch of traitors, that the three main doors – executive, legislature, judiciary – are closed. It realizes that the system is in terminal crisis: 'The art of politics does not work any longer', wrote Subcomandante Marcos (2003).

Some of us may not share this conclusion, although the EZLN has the right to fix its own position and act accordingly. But, except for its decision to advance in de facto autonomy, the bet on the indigenous struggle has not been as clearly established. First, because indigenous mobilization is not an army but a highly pluralistic social movement; second, because for the EZLN the Cocopa legislative change was not merely a 'signal' to restart negotiations but a foundational right, a substantive part of a broader agenda for which Indian peoples have been expressly struggling for over a quarter-century. Therefore the challenge for the indigenous movement is not to take a position as a political actor but to define its strategy as a social movement. This requires taking a position *vis-à-vis* its relation with other popular sectors, its approach before other political forces, and its relation with the state and with the government. But the greatest challenge is to find and develop the mechanisms of unity at a time in which the goal that the EZLN and the Indian movement shared during the past decade – to elevate autonomy to constitutional rank – goes on stand-by. At least for the time being, it is hard for the indigenous movement alone to further a greater mobilization.

Conclusion: Beyond Ethnic Specificity

After some thirty years of Indianist politics, the EZLN uprising and its eventual dialogue with other Indian organizations, we can safely say that the Mexican Indian peasantry has become politically constituted, as defined in the political-cultural theory of class formation. This is so, even if the main demands have not been achieved, to the extent that the EZLN and the CNI have not been co-opted by the state and continue to implement autonomy, in spite of the legislative lag on indigenous rights and culture. But we must remember that this set of negotiations with the state was only one of four major themes that were to be settled; the others are economic and land issues and the reform of the state and women's rights. Clearly, these issues go well beyond the specifically Indian demands that were put forward by the EZLN, once it began its negotiations with the state. Therefore the question is: will the EZLN conduct its future political constitution as merely an Indian organization or as one that also attends to the peasant nature of its constituency? The latter option, which can clearly incorporate the former, may open more doors for Zapatistas to become a broader movement within the general struggle for a popular-democratic and multicultural hegemonic project.

For Alain Touraine, one of the most prominent students of social movements and democracy (see Touraine 1988, 1997), the Zapatistas constitute a diverse movement with at least two currents within it. One of these would like to focus on its indigenous constituency; the other, which includes Subcomandante Marcos and his closest friends, wants to 'visit the world' or open up its spectrum of interpellation towards many other subordinate groups and classes. Touraine makes an explicit analogy between the EZLN's two currents (or factions) and early Christianity: while Peter wanted to remain strictly Jewish, Paul wanted to take the message to the world (cited in Martinez and Mergier 2001: 33).

What has interested Touraine the most about the EZLN is the manner in which it has managed to articulate the material and cultural defence of Mayan collectivities with a will to expand political and economic democracy in Mexico. 'On the one hand, the Zapatistas have supported themselves on these cultures, on the other, they do not allow themselves to become enclosed within these cultures, or in some type of "differencialism"' (cited in Martinez and Mergier 2001: 33). As Touraine puts it, the future challenge is immense: to reject both the possibility of local isolation and the dilution into a great political party, while trying to turn the indigenous movement into the ferment for the renovation of Mexican democracy (cited in Martinez and Mergier 2001: 34).

Thus, practising autonomy is important, yes. But this has as many variants as dimensions. At least with regard to economic self-management, Indians cannot seriously take it on by themselves, for it is a problem shared by millions of *mestizo* peasants and a great task that requires greater alliances and strategic visions (Bartra 2004). In their struggle as corn, vegetable or forestry-goods producers, autochthonous communities are not alone, because for each Indian peasant there are two *mestizos*, almost always as poor. Therefore the rural struggle of Indian peoples is interwoven with that of the peasantry as a class. It has always been so, including the period of the 1970s and the 1980s, when Indians aligned themselves within peasant coordinating organizations in which their specificity was diluted. It was only in the 1990s, when they centred their demands on the constitutionality of their right for autonomy, that the indigenous and peasant roads were split – temporarily.

During the final decade of the twentieth century, the indigenous movement came of age and acquired density to the extent that it identified itself, setting up differences by its demands, campaigns, organizational structure, discourse, imaginary, symbolic systems, and procedures. Thus, Indians who used to be in ruins set up their separate organizational house. This is fine. Except that this change distanced them a little from the peasant, worker and popular family, even though in the process Indians became intimate with 'civil society', an entity that until 1992 was much moved by the 500 Years and eventually infatuated with the EZLN. But in the new home there are also fights, especially because the constitutional issue may not be resolved in the foreseeable future, and de facto autonomies are diverse and introspective, and by themselves do not favour joint mobilization. Therefore, while Indians settle their domestic grievances, they might once again visit the family, now as respectful adults, so that they renew their friendship with their peasant, worker and popular cousins. Perhaps jointly they can make it.

The pertinence of rearticulating with other popular-democratic sectors, in particular with the rural ones, emerges not only from the insufficiency of the indigenous movement and their allied forces to achieve their historical demands, but also from the reappearance of the peasant movement. As of the end of 2002, the peasant movement has been resurrected from the dead, with an imagination, combativeness, capacity for programmatic integration, and breadth of convergence that had not been seen since the early 1990s. Furthermore, Indians are themselves peasants.

Note

1. Nahuatl was the dominant language during the Aztec empire, before arrival of the Spaniards in 1519, and still survives as the indigenous language spoken by the largest number of people, close to three million. There are at least 57 other indigenous languages still spoken in Mexico today.

References

Alvarez, Sonia E., Evelina Dagnino and Arturo Escobar, eds (1998), *Culture of Politics, Politics of Culture: Re-visioning Latin American Social Movements*, Boulder, CO: Westview Press.

Bartra, Armando (1992), 'Las Organizaciones Económicas Campesinas ante la Reforma Rural', *Cuadernos Agrarios*, Nueva Época, 5/6: 126–32.

Bartra, Armando (1985), *Los Herederos de Zapata. Movimientos Campesinos Posrevolucionarios en México*, Mexico City: ERA.

Bartra, Armando (2000), 'Sur Profundo', in *Crónicas del Sur: Utopías Campesinas en Guerrero*, ed. Armando Bartra, Mexico City: Ediciones Era.

Bartra, Armando (2001), 'Sur: Megaplanes y Utopías en la América Equinoccial', in *Mesoamerica: Los Ríos Profundos*, ed. Armando Bartra, Mexico City: El Atajo.

Bartra, Armando (2003a), *Cosechas de Ira: Economía Política de la Contrarreforma Agraria*, Mexico City: Instituto Maya.

Bartra, Armando (2003b), 'Los Ríos Crecidos: Rústicas Revueltas del Tercer Milenio', *Cuadernos Agrarios*, Nueva Época, Special Issue, *¡El Campo no Aguanta Más!*, 13–26.

Bartra, Armando (2003c), '¡Caracoles! Descifrando la Treceava Estela', *Mémoria*, 176: 9–13.

Bartra, Armando (2004), 'Rebellious Cornfields: Toward Food and Labour Self-sufficiency', in *Mexico in Transition: Neoliberal Globalism, the State and Civil Society*, ed. Gerardo Otero, London: Zed Books.

Bellinghausen, Hermann (2001), 'La Caravana Zapatista Hará Visible un México Ignorado: En La Caravana de la Dignidad Indígena: El Otro Jugador', *La Jornada*.

Brysk, Allison (2000), *From Tribal Village to Global Village: Indian Rights and International Relations in Latin America*, Stanford, CA: Stanford University Press.

CNPA (1982), 'La Coordinadora Nacional Plan de Ayala', *Revista de la Universidad Autónoma de Guerrero*, Extra 2: 45–52.

CNPA (2003), *Veinte Años de Lucha por la Tierra*, Mexico City: Instituto Maya.

Cohen, Jeffrey (2004), 'Community, Economy and Social Change in Oaxaca, Mexico: Rural Life and Cooperative Logic in the Global Economy', in *Mexico in Transition: Neoliberal Globalism, the State and Civil Society*, ed. Gerardo Otero, London: Zed Books.

Consejo Mexicano 500 Años de Resistencia India y Popular (1991), 'Declaración de Principios y Objetivos', *Cuadernos Agrarios*, Nueva Época, 2: 127–9.

Convención Nacional Democrática (1995), 'Los Desafíos de la CND, Propuestas de la Presidencia Colectiva a la Segunda Sesión de la CND', *Chiapas* 1(2): 181–6.

Díaz-Polanco, Héctor (1992), 'Autonomía, Territorialidad y Comunidad Indígena: Las Reformas de la Legislación Agraria en México', *Cuadernos Agrarios*, Nueva Época, 5/6: 62–79.

Díaz-Polanco, Héctor, and Gilberto López y Rivas (1994), 'Fundamentos de las Autonomías Regionales', *Cuadernos Agrarios*, Nueva Época, 8/9: 92–9.

Díaz-Polanco, Héctor, and Consuelo Sánchez (2003), *México Diverso: El Debate por la Autonomía*, México: Siglo XXI Editores.

Esteva, Gustavo (1999), 'The Zapatistas and People's Power', *Capital & Class* 68 (Summer): 153–83.

Flores Felix, Joaquín (1992), 'De Aquí para Poder Sacarnos, Primero Tendrán que Matarnos', *Cuadernos Agrarios*, Nueva Época, 5/6: 155–61.

Flores Felix, Joaquín (1998), *La Revuelta por la Democracia: Pueblos Indios, Política y Poder en México*, México: UAM-X y El Atajo.

Flores Felix, Joaquín (1995), 'Los Pueblos Indios en la Búsqueda de Espacios', *Cuadernos Agrarios*, Nueva Época, 11/12: 148–58.

García, María del Carmen, Xóchitl Leyva and Aracely Burguete (1998), 'Las Organizaciones Campesinas e Indigenas de Chiapas Frente a la Reforma del Estado: Una Radiografia', *Cuadernos Agrarios*, Nueva Época, 16: 75–94.

Gilbreth, Chris, and Gerardo Otero (2001), 'Democratization in Mexico: The Zapatista Uprising and Civil Society', *Latin American Perspectives* 119, 28(4): 7–29.

Gordillo, Gustavo (1988), *Campesinos al Asalto del Cielo: De la Expropiación Estatal a la Apropiación Campesina*, Mexico City: Siglo XXI Editores.

Hansen, Roger D. (1974), *La Política de Desarrollo Mexicano*, Mexico City: Siglo XXI Editores.

Hernández Navarro, Luis (1994), 'De Zapata a Zapata: Un Sexenio de Reformas Estatales en el Agro', *Cuadernos Agrarios*, Nueva Época, 8/9: 122–40.

Hernández Navarro, Luis (1997), 'La Autonomía Indígena como Ideal: Notas a *La Rebelión Zapatista y la Autonomía*, de Héctor Díaz-Polanco', *Chiapas* 5: 101–16.

Hernández Navarro, Luis y Ramón Vera Herrera, eds (1998), *Los Acuerdos de San Andrés*, Mexico City: Ediciones Era.

Kearney, Michael (1996), *Reconceptualizing the Peasantry: Anthropology in Global Perspective*, Boulder, CO, and Oxford: Westview Press.

Kearney, Michael (2000), 'La Comunidad Rural Oaxaqueña y la Migración: Más allá de las Políticas Agraria e Indígena', *Cuadernos Agrarios*, Nueva Época, 19/20: 11–23.

Laclau, Ernesto, and Chantal Mouffe (1985), *Hegemony and Socialist Strategy: Towards a Radical Democratic Politics*, London: Verso.

López Cámara, Francisco (1967), *La Estructura Económica y Social de México en la Época, de la Reforma*, México: Siglo XXI Editores.

Martínez, Sanjuana, and Anne Marie Mergier (2001), 'Le Bot, Mitterrand, Saramago, Touraine, Vázquez Montalbán: Ahora Vienen los Verdaderos Desafios de los Zapatistas', *Proceso* 1269 (25 February): 30–34.

Morquecho, Gaspar (1994), 'Tambores de Guerra, Tambores de Paz: Entrevista al Subcomandante Marcos', *Cuadernos Agrarios*, Nueva Época, 10: 164–80.

Nietzsche, Friederich Wilhelm (1962), *Thus Spake Zarathustra*, trans. Thomas Common, New York: Heritage Press.

Otero, Gerardo (1999), *Farewell to the Peasantry? Political Class Formation in Rural Mexico*, Boulder, CO, and London: Westview Press. Revised and expanded Spanish edition: *¿Adiós al Campesinado? Democracia y Formación Política de las Clases en el México Rural*, Mexico City: M.A. Porrúa, UAZ and SFU, 2004.

Otero, Gerardo (2004a), 'Global Economy, Local Politics: Indigenous Struggles, Civil Society and Democracy', *Canadian Journal of Political Science* 37(2).

Otero, Gerardo, ed. (2004b), *Mexico in Transition: Neoliberal Globalism, the State and Civil Society*, London: Zed Books.

Otero, Gerardo, and Heidi Jugenitz (2003), 'Challenging National Borders from Within: The Political-Class Formation of Indigenous Peasants in Latin America', *Canadian Review of Sociology and Anthropology* 40(5): 503–24.

Paoli, Francisco, and Enrique Montalvo (1977), *El Socialismo Olvidado de Yucatán*, Mexico City: Siglo XXI Editores.

Petras, James, and Henry Veltmeyer (2001), 'Are Latin American Peasant Movements Still a Force for Change? Some New Paradigms Revisited', *Journal of Peasant Studies* 28(2): 83–118.

Ruiz Hernández, Margarito (2000), 'The Plural National Indigenous Assembly for Autonomy (ANIPA)', in *Indigenous Autonomy in Mexico*, ed. Aracely Burgete Cal y Mayor, Copenhagen: International Work Group for Indigenous Affairs.

Sarmiento, Sergio (1994), 'El Movimiento Indio y la Irrupción India Chiapaneca', *Cuadernos Agrarios*, Nueva Época, 8/9: 79–91.

Subcomandante Insurgente Marcos (2002), '¿Cuales son las Características de la Cuarta Guerra Mundial?', *Rebeldía* 4: 24–41.

Subcomandante Insurgente Marcos (2003), 'Chiapas: La Treceava Estela', *La Jornada*, 24–26 July 2003.

Touraine, Alain (1988), *Return of the Actor: Social Theory in Postindustrial Society*, trans. Myrna Gozich, Minneapolis, MN: University of Minnesota Press.

Touraine, Alain (1997), *What is Democracy?*, trans. David Macey, Boulder, CO, and Oxford: Westview Press.

UNORCA (1992), 'Declaración de Temporal', *Cuadernos Agrarios*, Nueva Época, 5/6: 211–14.

Van Cott, Donna Lee (2000), *The Friendly Liquidation of the Past: The Politics of Diversity in Latin America*, Pittsburgh: University of Pittsburgh Press.

Warman, Arturo (1974), *Los Campesinos Hijos Predilectos del Régimen*, Mexico City: Nuestro Tiempo.

Warman, Arturo (1976), *Y Venimos a Contradecir: Los Campesinos de Morelos y el Estado Nacional*, México: La Casa Chata.

Weber, Max (1958) 'Politics as a Vocation', in *From Max Weber: Essays in Sociology*, edited and trans. H.H. Gerth and C. Wright Mills, New York: Oxford University Press.

Womack, Jr, John (1969), *Zapata and the Mexican Revolution*, New York: Vintage Books.

Notes on Contributors

Filomeno Aguilar, Jr is Professor in the Department of History and Director of the Institute of Philippine Culture, Ateneo de Manila University. He is the editor of *Philippine Studies*. He works on the constructions of nationhood, global migrations, political culture, and social class relations. He is the author of *Clash of Spirits: The History of Power and Sugar Planter Hegemony on a Visayan Island* (1998).

Kojo Amanor is Associate Professor at the Institute of African Studies, University of Ghana. He has mainly published on land, agricultural, environmental and decentralization issues in Ghana and West Africa.

Igor Ampuero is a Ph.D. candidate in sociology who lives in Canada. Originally from Bolivia, he is a student of Latin American development, with special interest in Colombia. He has examined the socio-economic development of Colombia for two decades and is one of the leading figures in Canada on the country's contemporary political situation. He is currently also conducting research on the affiliations of the Colombian paramilitary with narcotics production and trafficking.

Armando Bartra is Director of the Instituto de Estudios para el Desarrollo Maya, A.C. Originally trained in philosophy, he has authored or co-authored over thirty books in fields ranging from literary essays and poetry to history and social sciences. For the past thirty years his main focus has been the peasant question. His publications include *The Seduction of the Innocents: The First Tumultuous Moments of Mass Literacy in Postrevolutionary Mexico* (1994), *Guerrero Bronco* (1996) and *Cosechas de Ira* (2003).

Henry Bernstein is Professor of Development Studies at the School of Oriental and African Studies, University of London, with long-standing interests in social theory and agrarian political economy. For fifteen years he edited the *Journal of Peasant Studies* and is founding editor of the *Journal of Agrarian Change*, both with T.J. Byres.

James J. Brittain is a Ph.D. candidate and lecturer in sociology at the University of New Brunswick, Canada. His research is centred on analysing the social and political dynamics of the FARC–EP within Colombia and the resurgence of revolutionary/social movements throughout Latin America. He also investigates the contemporary relevance of Marxist theory and its practical applications with respect to the Western Hemisphere.

Salvador Feranil is an independent researcher working on land and agrarian issues in the Philippines. He currently works as Fellow for the Alternate Forum for Research in Mindanao and has been working with rural movements for more than ten years. He obtained his Master's degree in Development Studies from the Institute of Social Studies in The Hague, The Netherlands.

Bernardo Mançano Fernandes is Professor at the Department of Geography, College of Science and Technology, Paulista State University (UNESP), Presidente Prudente Campus, São Paulo, Brazil. He is advisory to the MST and the Pastoral Land Commission.

Fidelis Edge Kanyongolo is Senior Lecturer in the Faculty of Law, Chancellor College, University of Malawi. His main research interest is the relevance of critical and Marxist legal theories to contemporary constitutional and human rights jurisprudence in Malawi.

Lauro Mattei is Professor at the Department of Economics, Federal University of Santa Catarina, Brazil. He wrote his doctoral thesis at the Institute of Economics at UNICAMP on rural development in the state of Santa Catarina. He has been a researcher with

RURBANO (in UNICAMP) and has conducted extensive research on the agrarian question in Santa Catarina and Brazil.

Sam Moyo is Executive Director of the African Institute for Agrarian Studies, Harare, Zimbabwe. He has published extensively on land, agrarian and environmental issues in Zimbabwe, Southern Africa and beyond. He served as Associate Professor of Agrarian Studies at the University of Zimbabwe until 2000, and as director on various boards of research networks and institutes in Africa.

Gerardo Otero is Professor of Sociology and Director of the Latin American Studies Program at Simon Fraser University in Vancouver, Canada. He has published over sixty articles and book chapters and is the editor of two books, *Neoliberalism Revisited: Economic Restructuring and Mexico's Political Future* (1996), and *Mexico in Transition: Neoliberal Globalism, the State and Civil Society* (Zed, 2004), and author of *Farewell to the Peasantry? Political Class Formation in Rural Mexico* (1999). His current research is on neoliberal globalism and agricultural biotechnology, and on indigenous struggles for autonomy and control of natural resources.

Minar Pimple has been Senior Associate and Coordinator of Focus on the Global South, India Programme. He is a founder of YUVA, a human rights organization working in India, and presently is executive director of PDHRE, New York. He obtained his Master's degree in social work from Bombay University and has written extensively on social justice issues. He has been engaged with land and anti-eviction/displacement movements for more than two decades.

Manpreet Sethi has been Research Associate and Coordinator of Land Reforms Project, Focus on the Global South, India Programme, Mumbai. She obtained her Ph.D. in International Relations from Jawaharlal Nehru University, where she specialized in Latin American Studies. She has written extensively in national and international journals and has authored *Argentina's Nuclear Policy* (1999) and co-authored *Nuclear Deterrence and Diplomacy* (2004).

Mfaniseni Fana Sihlongonyane is a Lecturer at the School of Architecture and Planning, University of the Witwatersrand, Johannesburg. He has been a community researcher at the Development

Research Institute (DRI) and Commentary editor of the *South African Town Planning Journal* (SAPJ) produced by the South African Town Planning Institution. His research interests are in the political economy of African states, globalization and local economic development, African cities, and the influence of social and cultural issues on development. He is a member of the Gauteng Development Tribunal. He also undertakes consulting for a number of local and provincial governments in South Africa.

Henry Veltmeyer is Professor of Sociology and International Development Studies at St Mary's University, Halifax, Nova Scotia, and Universidad Autónoma de Zacatecas, Mexico. He is the author of numerous studies on the political economy of development, particularly in the Latin American context.

Paris Yeros has been Visiting Professor at the Department of Economics, Federal University of Paraná, Brazil. He wrote his doctoral thesis at the London School of Economics on the agrarian question in Zimbabwe. He is former editor of the London-based journals *Millennium* and *Historical Materialism*.

Index